The Moral Philosophy of W. D. Ross

The Moral Philosophy of W. D. Ross

Metaethics, Normative Ethics, Virtue, and Value

Edited by
ROBERT AUDI AND DAVID PHILLIPS

Great Clarendon Street, Oxford, OX2 6DP,
United Kingdom

Oxford University Press is a department of the University of Oxford.
It furthers the University's objective of excellence in research, scholarship,
and education by publishing worldwide. Oxford is a registered trade mark of
Oxford University Press in the UK and in certain other countries

© Oxford University Press 2025

The moral rights of the authors have been asserted

All rights reserved. No part of this publication may be reproduced, stored in a retrieval system, transmitted, used for text and data mining, or used for training artificial intelligence, in any form or by any means, without the prior permission in writing of Oxford University Press, or as expressly permitted by law, by licence or under terms agreed with the appropriate reprographics rights organization. Enquiries concerning reproduction outside the scope of the above should be sent to the Rights Department, Oxford University Press, at the address above.

You must not circulate this work in any other form
and you must impose this same condition on any acquirer

Published in the United States of America by Oxford University Press
198 Madison Avenue, New York, NY 10016, United States of America

British Library Cataloguing in Publication Data
Data available

Library of Congress Control Number is on file at the Library of Congress

ISBN 9780198914808

DOI: 10.1093/9780198914839.001.0001

Printed and bound by
CPI Group (UK) Ltd, Croydon, CR0 4YY

The manufacturer's authorised representative in the EU for product safety is
Oxford University Press España S.A. of El Parque Empresarial San Fernando de Henares, Avenida
de Castilla, 2 – 28830 Madrid (www.oup.es/en or
product.safety@oup.com). OUP España S.A. also acts as importer into Spain
of products made by the manufacturer.

To the memory of Philip Stratton-Lake

Preface

Robert Audi and David Phillips

For at least the past half century, both the literature and the teaching of ethics in the English-speaking world have been dominated by three kinds of view: consequentialism, Kantian deontology, and Aristotelian virtue ethics. But there has always been a fourth kind of major view, advocated in some form by a number of significant figures and widely recognized as important: ethical intuitionism. W. D. Ross is arguably the leading ethical intuitionist in the history of moral philosophy, and *The Right and the Good* (1930) is increasingly considered the most important general ethics treatise of the twentieth century.

Ross exemplified a major kind of structure that moral theories may take and, within that structure, proposed accounts both of the main kinds of right and wrong acts and of the basic types of good and bad things—prominently including motives and traits of character as central for *moral* value. Ross's lists of our fundamental obligations ("duties," in his terminology) and of the things having basic value are eminently discussable and often addressed in ethical literature. He had a distinctive moral epistemology as well. He said much concerning how we know, or may know, what *is* right or wrong, or good or bad; and his writings, informed by Aristotle and selectively drawing on him, may also contribute to virtue ethics.

This volume comes at a time when Rossian intuitionism has earned progressively wider recognition in applied as well as theoretical ethics. This trend would be more prominent if there were more self-identified intuitionists. Given the diversity of usage of 'intuitionism', it is not surprising that there are not, and the term is clarified in some of the papers in this book. In the broad sense in which intuitionism is paradigmatically illustrated by Ross, we count among de facto intuitionists such authors as Thomas Nagel, Derek Parfit, T. M. Scanlon, and Judith Thomson, but there are many more. This book will make it considerably easier for people doing ethics to recognize both the importance of Rossian intuitionism and, in many cases, some intuitionist strains in their own thinking.

Ross's work also connects with many leading ideas in contemporary ethical thinking. One is pluralism, about both the right and the good: Ross argued that there is no single foundation of right action and no one kind of intrinsic value. Another Rossian contribution that has gained wide acceptance is the idea that obligation is *gradable*—which Ross explained mainly by comparing strengths of prima facie duties, especially where they conflict. This is a historically important insight that liberates ethics from the absolutism of many views and corresponds closely to the idea that some moral reasons for action are stronger than others.

We have divided the papers into four sections. Both the sections and the individual papers overlap with one another in content, but the four parts of the book represent natural clusters of topics. They may suggest to prospective readers where they might begin or, for those teaching ethics, what parts or papers they might want to discuss with students. To facilitate research, we include both a brief introduction and an index. The introduction locates Ross in both his historical context and that of contemporary ethics, where his influence is perceptible and apparently growing.

Acknowledgments

The idea of constructing a volume of critical studies on Ross arose from the editors' years of work focused on or connected with his writings. Some of these studies led to an international ethics conference held at the University of Notre Dame in April 2022, codirected by Robert Audi (University of Notre Dame) and Stephen Finlay (Australian Catholic University) and co-sponsored by Notre Dame and ACU. Earlier versions of the papers by Crisp, Cullity, Hooker, Hurka and Chan, Phillips, and the late Stratton-Lake were presented at the conference. The other papers, many with connections to Ross, were presented by David Copp, Terence Cuneo and Russ Shafer-Landau, Stephen Finlay, Zoe Johnson-King, Renee Jorgenson, Clayton Littlejohn, Caleb Perl, Tamar Schapiro, Sarah Stroud, Mark Timmons and Terry Horgan, and Ralph Wedgwood. Each paper had a commentator and was followed by extensive discussion.

We are grateful to all of these authors and to their commentators for helping us to think through the issues addressed in this volume. Particular thanks should go to Philip Stratton-Lake, who was coediting the volume with us until his untimely death in December 2022. For comments and exchanges of ideas regarding the volume we are also grateful to Selim Berker, Sarah Buss, Roger Crisp, Garrett Cullity, Brad Hooker, Tom Hurka, and Nandi Theunissen. For editorial advice, we thank Peter Momtchiloff, for expert copyediting, Rachel Addison, for further work in the publication process, Aimee Wright, for expert guidance in managing the production process, Gopinath Anbalagan, and, for financial support, we are grateful to Notre Dame, ACU, and the University of Houston.

Contents

List of Contributors   xiii

1. Introduction   1
   Robert Audi and David Phillips

PART I: THE GENERAL STRUCTURE OF ROSS'S ETHICAL THEORY

2. Duty, Moral Knowledge, and Intrinsic Value in Rossian Intuitionism   13
   Robert Audi

3. The Prima Facie/Overall Duty Distinction: What is it? Where did it come from? Why does it matter?   37
   Roger Crisp

4. Ross and the Foundations of Morality   52
   Garrett Cullity

5. The Ethical Theory of W. D. Ross   73
   Brad Hooker

PART II: ROSS'S NORMATIVE ETHICS

6. Can Sidgwick and Ross Converge in Moral Theory?   93
   David Phillips

7. Prima Facie Duties, Real-World Contexts and Moral Emotions   117
   Sabine Roeser

8. Ross's Explanatory Resources   135
   David Kaspar

9. Ross and the Problem of Permissibility   154
   Philip Stratton-Lake

PART III: ROSS ON VIRTUE AND VICE

10. Ross On Virtue and Vice   169
    Thomas Hurka and Bowen Chan

11. Ross and the Ethics of Virtue 189
    Natasza Szutta and Artur Szutta

PART IV: ROSS ON VALUE

12. Ross and Aesthetic Value 209
    Gwen Bradford

13. On the Value of Intellectual and Aesthetic Activity: A Reply to Ross 226
    L. Nandi Theunissen

14. Heterarchy and Hierarchy in Ross's Theories of the Right
    and the Good 250
    Anthony Skelton

Index 269

Contributors

ROBERT AUDI is John A. O'Brien Professor of Philosophy at the University of Notre Dame.

GWEN BRADFORD is Associate Professor and Chancellor Henry N. R. Jackman Professor in Philosophy at the University of Toronto.

BOWEN CHAN is a PhD candidate in Philosophy at the University of Toronto.

ROGER CRISP is Director of the Uehiro Oxford Institute, Uehiro Fellow and Tutor in Philosophy at St Anne's College, Oxford, and Professor of Moral Philosophy at the University of Oxford.

GARRETT CULLITY is Professor of Philosophy at the Australian National University.

BRAD HOOKER is an Emeritus Professor at the University of Reading, a Distinguished Research Fellow at Oxford Uehiro Centre for Practical Ethics, and an Honorary Fellow of St Anne's College, Oxford.

THOMAS HURKA is Chancellor Henry N. R. Jackman Distinguished Professor of Philosophical Studies Emeritus at the University of Toronto.

DAVID KASPAR is Lecturer in Philosophy at Rutgers University.

DAVID PHILLIPS is Professor of Philosophy at the University of Houston.

SABINE ROESER is Professor of Ethics at Delft University of Technology.

ANTHONY SKELTON is Professor of Philosophy at the University of Western Ontario.

PHILIP STRATTON-LAKE (deceased) was Professor of Philosophy at the University of Reading.

ARTUR SZUTTA is Professor of Philosophy at the University of Gdansk.

NATASZA SZUTTA is Professor of Philosophy at the University of Gdansk.

L. NANDI THEUNISSEN is Associate Professor of Philosophy at Rice University.

1
Introduction

Robert Audi and David Phillips

C. D. Broad began his 1940 review of Ross's second book on moral philosophy, *Foundations of Ethics*, by observing that his first, *The Right and the Good*

> was much the most important contribution to ethical theory made in England for a generation. Everyone interested in ethics had to take serious account of it, and it gave rise to a vast amount of critical discussion.[1]

Broad was surely correct. Widening the historical lens a little, Sidgwick's *The Methods of Ethics* (first edition 1874), Moore's *Principia Ethica* (1903), and *The Right and the Good* (1930) were surely the three most important contributions to ethical theory made in England—indeed, perhaps anywhere—between Mill's death and the start of World War II. Widening the lens further, we should add that Ross's work connects importantly to both Kantian ethics—with which he expressed important points of disagreement as well as elements of significant concurrence—and to Aristotelian ethics. Ross has been described as "the leading Anglophone Aristotelian scholar of the 20th Century."[2] We mention that because too few writers in ethics have recognized how well Ross's normative theory reflects an appreciation of Aristotle's insights about human psychology in general and virtue in particular.

I Ross's Moderate Deontology

What made *The Right and the Good* (hereafter "RG") so important was that Ross gave the first full articulation and defense of a moral theory with a distinctive structure: moderate deontology.[3] In its most widely read second Chapter, "What Makes

---

[1] The review appeared in *Mind* n.s., v. 49, April 1940, pp. 228–39. It ends with a characteristic Broad one-liner: "I hope that generations of undergraduates, in the intervals between making the world safer and safer for democracy, will come to know and appreciate this book under the affectionate, and accurate, nickname of *"The Righter and the Better."*

[2] See Terence Irwin (himself a historian of ethics and distinguished Aristotelian scholar entitled to make the judgment), *The Development of Ethics: A Historical and Critical Study*, vol III (Oxford: Oxford University Press 2014), 678.

[3] Ross is clear in the Preface to RG that he drew key inspiration from his friend and colleague H. A. Prichard, in particular from Prichard's 1912 paper "Does Moral Philosophy Rest on a Mistake?"

Robert Audi and David Phillips, *Introduction* In: *The Moral Philosophy of W. D. Ross*. Edited by: Robert Audi and David Phillips, Oxford University Press. © Oxford University Press 2025.
DOI: 10.1093/9780198914839.003.0001

Right Acts Right?", Ross's view emerges by qualifying and combining consequentialism and absolutist deontology. Consequentialists think that the only thing that makes acts right is that they produce more good than any alternative. Ross agrees that this is *one of the things* that makes acts right. But he denies that it is *the only thing*. Absolutist deontologists tend to think that there are true moral principles like "Promises always ought to be kept." Ross thinks that absolutist deontologists are correct in thinking that promising, and other features they emphasize, have a moral significance that consequentialism does not properly capture. But he thinks that they are wrong in their absolutism. The correct moral principle about promising is not "Promises always ought to be kept." It is instead a principle of what Ross called "prima facie duty"— – something like "A promise, as such, is something that prima facie ought to be kept" (that is, roughly, it ought to be kept unless there are sufficiently weighty "oughts" that conflict with it.).

The change from thinking (only) in terms of duty proper to thinking (also) in terms of prima facie duty may seem small. But it is a change with big ramifications. To see these, contrast the picture of moral deliberation absolutist deontologists give with the picture a Rossian moderate deontologist gives. For a paradigmatic absolutist deontologist, if a possible action falls under certain moral principles— – say by being the keeping of a promise— – the action's moral status is thereby settled. It is an action we are required to perform. By contrast, for the Rossian moderate deontologist, moral deliberation is never this simple. Any possible action will have multiple morally significant features, some weighing in favor of it, some against. The right action, then, our duty proper, will be the one of the available options with the greatest balance of prima facie rightness over prima facie wrongness, taking all morally significant features of all options into account.

Ross himself is quite pessimistic, however, about our ability to make the kinds of balancing judgments required to determine our duty proper in practice. He draws a very sharp epistemic contrast between principles of prima facie duty, which he thinks knowable on suitable reflection, from judgments of duty proper, which he thinks we can never know for certain. Whether or not his epistemic pessimism is well-founded, moral deliberation for Rossian moderate deontologists is very different from and much more complex than moral deliberation for absolutists. And it isn't just that deliberation looks different. There are also what philosophers these days sometimes call "residues": even if it is an overall duty to break a particular promise, the moral significance of the promise does not disappear. Overriding

---

Prichard, by all accounts a forceful personality, shared with many of his Oxford colleagues a disinclination to publish. Most of the work collected in his *Moral Writings* went unpublished in his lifetime. His writing can be persnickety. Ross, fortunately, did not share this disinclination to publish. And Ross is a marvelous writer. At this historical distance it is hard to divide credit confidently between Prichard and Ross for the key philosophical innovations that make *The Right and the Good* so important. But Ross presented them in compelling form in a way Prichard never did. For more on the historical antecedents of Ross's concept of prima facie duty, see Roger Crisp's contribution to this volume.

is not retroactive elimination. We still owe some form of later amends to the promisee.

II The Plurality of Rossian Moral Principles

Ross did not merely present the general idea of a moral theory with this new and distinctive structure. He also filled in its specific content, listing seven principles of prima facie duty that many moral philosophers have considered quite commonsensical. For him, the key non-consequentialist principles of prima facie duty are the principles of *fidelity*, *reparation*, and *gratitude*, principles to the effect that we have prima facie duties to keep promises, make it up to those we have wronged, and repay those who have benefitted us. The central failing of Moore's ideal utilitarian theory is that it "seems to simplify unduly our relations to our fellows" (RG 19) and "ignores, or at least does not do full justice to, the highly personal character of duty" (RG 22).

There are also three principles of prima facie duty that can be accommodated by the consequentialist. These come "under the general principle that we should produce as much good as possible" (RG 27). They are the prima facie duties of *beneficence*: the duty to promote the virtue, knowledge, or pleasure of others; of *self-improvement*: the duty to promote our own virtue and knowledge; and of *justice*, conceived as the duty to make the distribution of happiness in the world properly proportional to virtue. Finally, there is a prima facie duty surprisingly little emphasized by Ross given how important it is to other familiar accounts of what is wrong with consequentialism: the duty of *non-maleficence*, a duty of not injuring others that Ross regarded as more stringent than the duty of beneficence.

Ross thus presented a new and distinctive form of pluralism about the right. He was also a pluralist about the good. Pluralism about the good was at the time less novel than was Ross's pluralism about the right. Moore, Ross's principal foil, was also a pluralist about the good, as was Moore's now unfortunately neglected contemporary Hastings Rashdall. But the form of pluralism about the good Ross articulated was significantly different from the form Moore defended. Moore argued that all great goods are highly complex organic unities. Ross granted the principle but thought that Moore exaggerated the significance of organic unities. For Ross, the three basic goods are pleasure, virtue, and knowledge. There is then a fourth, higher-order, good, with which the duty of justice is concerned: the proper proportioning of happiness to virtue.

Ross's views on the good are interesting in a number of further ways. One is that his account of virtue is a version of a recursive account according to which virtue is a matter of appropriate attitudes to, including motives regarding, base goods: it is good to love what is good, bad to hate what is good, good to hate what is bad, bad to love what is bad, etc. A second is that, for better or worse, Ross's anti-hedonist impulse was not satisfied by his demotion of happiness from the place hedonists give it, as the only intrinsic good, to the place pluralists most commonly give it, as one among other intrinsic goods. This anti-hedonist impulse led him in Chapter VI of RG to embrace a lexical priority claim: that any amount of virtue, however small, is more valuable than any amount of happiness, however great. In *Foundations of Ethics* (hereafter FE) he rejected the lexical priority claim, and substituted the idea that virtue and happiness are not good in the same sense: virtue is good in being a fit object of admiration, happiness only in being a fit object of satisfaction.

III Metaethical Elements in Ross

These and other topics in normative theory are not the only topics Ross examined. He also presented and defended views in metaethics. He was a metaethical non-naturalist: he held that the fundamental ethical concepts, rightness and goodness, cannot be defined in ordinary factual (roughly, descriptive) terms. And he drew the standard epistemic consequence that we cannot learn the truth of ethical claims by drawing on ordinary factual evidence of the kind basic in scientific inquiry: instead, fundamental ethical claims, like fundamental mathematical claims, are self-evident.

Here again, his views were not as distinctive as his pluralism about the right. His main metaethical views, indeed, were more widely shared than his pluralism about the good: shared by Sidgwick, as well as by Moore and others. But Ross presented these views in a particularly compelling form. There is a case to be made that the first two lectures of FE are the best classical presentation of non-naturalism.

It might be useful to add here that the metaethical view that Sidgwick, Moore, Ross, and others embraced is sometimes put under the heading 'intuitionism'. But the term 'intuitionism' needs to be treated with caution. It always indicates that moral judgment derives from a kind of insight— - from intuition as opposed to inference. But it can refer to different, more specific, views. It can refer mainly to a metaethical view shared by Sidgwick, Moore, and Ross which we might call *epistemic intuitionism*. It can instead refer mainly to Ross's kind of view in normative theory, the deontological pluralism he advocated in opposition to Moore and Sidgwick. And it can refer to the combination of the metaethical view and the normative view.

IV Ross's Relation to Contemporary Moral Philosophy

As the quotation from Broad's review indicates, Ross's work was much discussed in the 1930s. But World War II was an inflection point. When normal university life resumed after its conclusion, a new generation of moral philosophers emerged. They tended initially to focus more on metaethics and less on normative theory. And they tended to be ethical noncognitivists who thought non-naturalism an indefensible position. The views of Ross and his interlocutors ceased to be center stage. And when philosophical interest in moral theory revived, other alternatives to consequentialism got much more attention than did Ross's moderate deontology.

One such alternative is virtue theory, inspired by Aristotle. (Though Ross was a great Aristotle scholar, he apparently did not entertain the idea that Aristotle supplied a third way, an alternative both to consequentialism and deontology. That idea was developed only in the post- World War II era.) Another alternative is a kind of deontology derived from Kant. (Ross wrote a late book on Kant's ethical theory, and Kant is an important influence and foil both in RG and FE. But recent advocates of Kantian ethics appear to suppose that no one writing about Kant in Ross's era fully and properly appreciated the insights on the basis of which a Kantian ethical theory should be constructed.) The development of these further alternatives to consequentialism, however, provides no good reason to neglect Ross's distinctive moderate deontology.

Recent developments in moral philosophy provide further reason to take Ross's work very seriously. One is the revival of non-naturalism. In the 1950s non-naturalism was widely caricatured, ignored, or dismissed. But in the last thirty to forty years it has had a resurgence. Influential defenders include but are by no means limited to Thomas Nagel, Derek Parfit, and T. M. Scanlon. To whatever extent Ross's embrace of non-naturalism provided general reason to ignore his work in the 1950s, it provides no such reason today. And it is not as if contemporary non-naturalism is a different view from the non-naturalism of Sidgwick, Moore, and Ross. If philosophical views defended in different eras and contexts ever count as nonetheless essentially the same philosophical view, the non-naturalism of Sidgwick, Moore, and Ross counts as essentially the same philosophical view as the non-naturalism of Nagel, Parfit, and Scanlon.

It isn't just the metaethical context that encourages renewed interest in Ross's work. Recent developments in normative theory provide even more encouragement. Arguably the most discussed concept in contemporary moral philosophy is the concept of a normative reason. It is not a concept Ross himself much employed. It certainly never occurred to him, as it has to many contemporary moral philosophers, that it could be the basic normative concept, the normative concept in terms of which all others can be explicated.[4] But, like Ross's concept

---

[4] The question of the relation between Ross's concept of prima facie duty and the contemporary concept of a normative reason is difficult. For discussion, see Phillips, *Rossian Ethics*, Chapter 2, Section 2, and Audi's, Cullity's, and Phillips's contributions to this volume. By contrast, the question of the relation between Ross's concept of prima facie duty and the contemporary concept of pro tanto duty seems much more straightforward. An obvious answer is that the relation is identity. Ross was never satisfied with the name "prima facie duty"(as is evident in the paragraph in which he first discusses the name, RG 19--20). Ross later embraced the alternative name "responsibility" (which never caught on). The

of prima facie duty, the concept of a normative reason is, as Jonathan Dancy puts it, the concept of something "contributory." To the extent that many contemporary moral philosophers are tempted by a reasons-first view in normative theory, Ross becomes a very important historical figure: arguably the first moral philosopher to develop a theory of obligation structured like a reasons-first view.[5]

There are significant signs of renewed and burgeoning interest in Ross's work. It has been the focus of recent books by (among others) Jonathan Dancy, Thomas Hurka, and both editors of this volume.[6] But there has still been much less philosophical exploration of Ross's key works, RG and FE, than of the work of many other important figures in the history of ethics. This volume is an effort to help overcome this unfortunate neglect, and to provide new avenues into these rich and engaging texts.

V The Focus of this Volume

The book is divided into four parts, each consisting of papers focusing on major elements in Ross's work. Collectively, they range over topics of major and enduring importance in ethics, but we make no claim to have included discussions of all of Ross's important contributions to moral philosophy. Each part of the book is essentially self-contained, and even the individual papers should be fully intelligible apart from consulting Ross's writings. It may, however, help readers who might want to begin with or concentrate on a single part to consider the following descriptions of some main ethical problems and some Rossian elements addressed in each part. The formulations we offer do not even nearly cover the full range of topics the papers discuss. We simply hope to help readers identify papers of special interest or, whether in one paper or more, explorations of Ross especially good for discussion or in providing teaching moments.

Latinism "pro tanto," imported into philosophy by Shelly Kagan, seems to many to supply a straightforwardly better name for Ross's key concept than Ross himself ever managed to come up with.

[5] In this connection, see Mark Schroeder, *Reasons First* (Oxford, 2021), pp. 25--34.

[6] Jonathan Dancy, *Moral Reasons* (Oxford: Blackwell, 1993); Jonathan Dancy, *Ethics Without Principles* (Oxford: Clarendon Press, 2004); Thomas Hurka, *British Ethical Theorists from Sidgwick to Ewing* (Oxford: Oxford University Press, 2014); Robert Audi, *The Good in the Right* (Princeton: Princeton University Press, 2004); David Phillips, *Rossian Ethics: W. D. Ross and Contemporary Moral Theory* (New York: Oxford University Press, 2019). It is also important to note Philip Stratton-Lake's contribution, in a number of papers but most influentially in his excellent introduction to the Oxford reissue of *The Right and the Good* (Oxford: Oxford University Press, 2002).

Part I: The General Structure of Ross's Ethical Theory

As we have brought out, Ross rejects the view that some master principle accounts for what makes right acts right. His own view defends a pluralism regarding grounds of "duty"—his term for what is right and morally ought to be done. All the papers in this part bear directly on his view so conceived. But what exactly are grounds of obligation, and do they, in the contexts in which they occur, make actions obligatory *overall* or only prima facie? This famous Rossian technical term—which for Ross does not bear the usual meaning of (roughly) 'apparently'—is considered by all of the papers in Part I (and in detail in Robert Audi's opening paper). It is a challenge to explicate, and its applications are complicated (as Roger Crisp's and Brad Hooker's papers show in relation to several issues). How, for instance, does a pattern of one or more prima facie duties (PFDs) yield an overall duty, especially where two or more conflict with one another? Indeed, if duties are *to do*, how can Ross explain the *moral* status of attitudes and emotions, which are not doings (one problem among others brought out by Garrett Cullity)? Attitudes and emotions are, for instance, supportable by moral reasons, but *if* PFDs are equivalent to moral reasons—which is a plausible if controversial interpretation of Ross also explored in Part I—there remains the question how Ross can incorporate such dispositional elements as attitudes and emotions in his overall moral theory. Regarding all the problems so far raised, there are both epistemological and ontological questions. Was Ross right in thinking that the basic principles of PFD are self-evident and that singular judgments—say that a particular person should break a promise to deal with an emergency—are neither self-evident nor even genuinely known to be true? And was he right in thinking that moral truths represent objective reality in the way pure mathematical truths do and cannot be reduced to empirical truths? These questions of general structure leave open much about the substantive moral content of Ross's principles—ranging from comprehensive general obligations of beneficence to highly specific requirements of fidelity in interpersonal relationships. All of these problems figure in the papers in Part I.

Part II: Ross's Normative Ethics

We've stressed Ross's moral pluralism, and in Part II many aspects of its content and value for day-to-day ethics are critically considered. Ross wrote with a keen sense of the work of his utilitarian predecessors, above all Moore—whose view he called "the rival theory" (RG xxx)—, and Sidgwick. Indeed, given that one PFD is to bring into existence "as much … *as possible*" of what is intrinsically good (RG 24, 25, emphasis added), it is natural to ask how close his normative ethics is to Sidgwick's or Moore's (a question pursued in depth in David Phillips's paper). It is true that Ross finds special obligations such as those grounded on promising irreducible to those of beneficence, but how much difference must that make in everyday moral life? To be sure, Ross refuses to allow, as utilitarianism appears to, that promoting one's own pleasure is, as such, a prima facie obligation. But each of us is vastly outnumbered by others, even others living unhappy lives we might ameliorate, so even for Ross there is still the pressing question of how strong the Rossian PFD of beneficence is. However we answer the question of how close Ross's normative ethics might be to some version of Moore's or Sidgwick's, there is likely agreement on the applicability of Rossian pluralism to everyday ("practical") ethics. Ross's stress on the plurality of *non-derivative* duties provides a framework to guide ordinary decision-making. The question of how to resolve conflicts of obligation remains; but here some of the papers in Part II stress the importance of interpreting Ross so as to overcome a top-down subsumptive approach to resolving such conflicts. Can we, for instance, incorporate into Rossian moral appraisals the *evidential* value of emotion in making concrete moral decisions (a value considered in detail in Sabine Roeser's paper) and the related possibility of extending Ross's categorization of duties in ways that both facilitate and more clearly ground moral judgments (a possibility explored in detail by David Kaspar's paper)? Moral intuition itself may be viewed as having a phenomenology that can make it *felt* as attitudinally positive in a way that invites belief, and here the question arises whether emotions such as compassion on one side and indignation on another may play similar evidential and judgment-supporting roles. Given an intuitive weighting of conflicting PFDs, especially where emotional elements support intuitive inclinations, we may not only hope to make sound judgments, but may also explain their basis by describing the basis of our moral decisions in ways that extend the framework Ross explicitly presents. The concluding paper in Part II (by Philip Stratton-Lake) raises a difficult challenge to Ross. Indeed, Stratton-Lake challenges any normative ethics which posits duties that *constantly* make demands on us, as apparently for Ross, the duties of beneficence and self-improvement do. How can such an ethics provide permissions for innocent pleasures and free-wheeling activities? Whether Kantian ethics has resources to explain moral permissibility and how the notions of valuing and fittingness figure in dealing with the problem are also pursued in that paper.

Part III: Ross on Virtue and Vice

Those knowing Ross's eminence as an interpreter of Aristotle and his tendency to cite Aristotelian views as insightful and important may wonder whether he is closer to being a virtue theorist than is usually thought possible for a deontologist (a question pursued by Natasza and Arthur Szutta). Might PFDs correspond to patterns of action characteristic of agents having Aristotelian virtue? And, if so, does Ross see the correspondence as showing that virtue is either in some way a *basis* of rightness or crucial for ability to make rational moral judgments? Here Ross's view is complex in a way that sharply contrasts with any virtue theory on which the *grounds* of rightness rest on the judgments or actions of agents. Instead, these grounds are such objective circumstances as making promises to others (central in grounding duties of fidelity), receiving benefits from them (central for duties of gratitude), and injuring them (central for duties of reparation). Granted, beneficence is *in part* a tendency to contribute to virtue in others; but for Ross, virtue is essentially tied to appropriate motivation to do what is right. If, in this way, Ross's ethics is primarily action-focused and virtue is understood in relation to the obligatory, Ross's theory of value still places *moral* intrinsic goodness—paradigmatically expressed in acting on the basis of virtuous dispositions and in actions motivated toward right action for its own sake—at the pinnacle of goods (RG 153). An important question here is whether the motivation appropriate to morally good action must embody moral concepts such as that of promissory obligation, or may simply be directed toward such elements as *ground* obligation, say the circumstance of being the only person who can save someone's life. A related question, also clarified by Ross and pursued in Part III, is how the intrinsic goodness of an action motivated virtuously is affected by cooperating non-moral motivation (both are questions addressed—among others—in the paper by Thomas Hurka and Bowen Chan). On this issue as elsewhere, regarding the moral significance of mixed motives Ross contrasts with Kant. He also contrasts with Kant—and is similar to Aristotle—in taking judgments on conflict cases not as derivable by subsuming the cases under principles, but rather as to be determined by "perception," understood in a way that invites the question whether, in Ross as apparently in Aristotle, the term designates a kind of intuition. These and other matters are among those Part III considers.

Part IV: Ross on Value

Ross repeatedly characterized intrinsic value both as such that whatever has it can possess it even if it exists "quite alone" (RG 74) and as "a characteristic belonging primarily only to states of mind" (RG 122). Why "'primarily,'", and how might the intrinsically good make human life good (a question pursued in detail by Nandi's Theunissen's paper)? Here it is puzzling that Ross should have held that "the value of material things seems to be instrumental, not intrinsic" (RG 141), while surely aware that some beautiful artworks are material things that could exist quite alone with undiminished beauty. Did he misconstrue the role of artworks in making life good—a relation they may bear to it—and did he have any way of doing justice to the uniqueness of original works of beauty as against mere copies (questions critically pursued in Gwen Bradford's paper)? And regarding moral value, which he considered the highest kind, did he have no way to attribute it to acts of justice and beneficence simply as such? These questions must not be taken to imply that aesthetic value was Ross's central axiological concern. If any single kind of value was central for him, it was moral value, the kind he considered supreme, thus as even greater than that of knowledge, and of a higher *order* than pleasure. He went as to far as to suggest that no amount of pleasure could have a value equal to or exceeding that of virtue of any degree (RG 150). Here an important question arises: Did Ross thereby jeopardize the non-hierarchical, anti-absolutist character of his theory of obligation (a question pursued by Anthony Skelton)? For Ross, "Goodness, rightness, and beauty depend on nothing less than the whole intrinsic nature of their possessors" (RG 123), just as (overall) obligation is a "toti-resultant" attribute that "belongs to an act in virtue of its whole nature" (RG 28). How, then, can he have absolute priority relations among certain intrinsic values when he rejects them in the case of *p f* obligations? Part IV pursues these and other important matters in Ross's theory of value in ways that are significant for ethics as well as aesthetics.

We hope to have made evident some of the values this volume has for both research in moral philosophy and the teaching of ethics, theoretical or applied. Those seeking a deontology not dependent on Kant will find an excellent model in Ross; any rule-ethicists wanting to take adequate account of virtue—or Aristotle's conceptions of it—will find discussions suggesting ways to do that; and any moral philosopher, whether intuitionistic or not, who seeks better understanding of how conflicts of obligation are to be resolved will find important insights in Ross's work. Ross provides a model of moral reflection, exemplary scholarship, myriad connections with Aristotle, Kant, and the moral philosophers of his time, and an enduring ethical theory.

PART I
THE GENERAL STRUCTURE OF ROSS'S ETHICAL THEORY

2
Duty, Moral Knowledge, and Intrinsic Value in Rossian Intuitionism

Robert Audi

W. D. Ross's *The Right and the Good* is easily among the most important works in ethics in the 20th century. My aim here is both to clarify Ross's ethical intuitionism as developed there and to extend his moral theory in ways that show its strength to be greater than often thought and its scope wider than one might expect from even a careful initial reading of that book.[1] His *Foundations of Ethics* is also a major contribution, but for my purposes—and to dispel misunderstandings that have impeded adequate appraisal of RG— I will focus mainly on the latter. I have selected six elements of his intuitionism for interpretation and brief assessment. The first is the increasingly important notion of prima facie duty. The second is the notion of overall duty—"duty proper," in one phrase Ross uses. Given what will emerge from these explorations, it is important to consider Ross's notion of self-evidence. This dimension of his intuitionism is essential for understanding not only his moral epistemology but also his resources for accommodating rational disagreement in ethics. The fourth dimension explored here is axiological—how Ross conceived value and how value is related to duty. Fifth is a dimension central for Ross's normative ethics—indeed for any comprehensive ethics: the nature of beneficence and the scope and strength of the duties of beneficence. Finally, I consider Ross's metaphysics, particularly its relation to ethical naturalism.

I Introduction: Intuition, Intuitions, and Intuitionism

Although Ross's moral philosophy is a paradigm of ethical intuitionism, he does not generally use the term 'intuition' for the cognitions he apparently takes to *be* intuitions. Instead, he speaks of convictions (e.g. 20–21, 23, 41); of "what we really think" (18, 19, 23); of "'perception" (in an intellectual use derived from Aristotle

---

[1] Published by Oxford University Press (1930 and 2002)—hereinafter RG. Page numbers will refer to it unless otherwise indicated; but in places I note elements in Ross's *Foundations* (1939). Where page numbers are given without dates, they refer to RG, ed. by Philip Stratton-Lake (OUP, 2002). For discussion of both books by Ross, see Phillips (2019). For an excellent short portrait of RG, see Stratton-Lake (2002: ix–lviii); and for a critical appraisal of Ross in a historical context, see Hurka (2014).

Robert Audi, *Duty, Moral Knowledge, and Intrinsic Value in Rossian Intuitionism* In: *The Moral Philosophy of W. D. Ross*. Edited by: Robert Audi and David Phillips, Oxford University Press. © Oxford University Press 2025.
DOI: 10.1093/9780198914839.003.0002

[41]); and of intuition as an ordinary human rational capacity. He does not explicate intuition or limit it to the a priori domain, but he does conceive it as entailing ability to apprehend apparent truths non-inferentially (e.g., 39). He apparently has in mind cognitions that respond to the proposition in question "in its own right" rather than inferentially through premises. Having an intuition, then, entails no thought of premises or proof, or of provability or even evidenceability that falls short of proof. At one point, for instance, Ross claims that the supposed coincidence of the right and the optimific is something "we do not know either by intuition, by deduction, or by induction" (39). These three seem the basic epistemological options for him here, and we may take him to be presupposing that at least what is self-evident is both knowable both by intuition and a priori.

As Ross conceived intuitions, they are not just any kind of apprehension of content—in older terminology, a manifestation of the operation of our "faculty" of intuition. They are also doxastic (belief-entailing), as they more clearly are in Sidgwick (1907). This conception contrasts with the seemings conception of intuition that has become common in recent decades, especially but by no means exclusively among epistemologists.[2] For simplicity, consider an intuition with propositional content, say a Rossian intuition that if one promises to A, one ought to A. This intuition implies *believing* that proposition; but (in a now common usage) its seeming to one that one ought to A, though phenomenally positive—where the seeming is something like a non-inferential sense of credibility—does not entail believing this and, like a sense-perception, is not truth-valued.

Epistemologists find this phenomenal conception valuable as indicating regress-stoppers, elements that *confer* justification though they do not admit of it. Moral philosophers have worried less about dealing with the problem of the regress of justification. But intuitionists can all agree that certain seemings play a justification-conferring role. The two conceptions of intuition—call them the doxastic and phenomenal—may largely coincide in Ross's theory. He did not view intuitions as merely beliefs, and an element of the justificatory—as least as a kind of initial credibility—seems implicit in his appeal to intuitive "convictions" as *data* of ethics (41). In any case, clearly RG treats intuitive acceptance of the self-evident moral propositions on his famous list of duties as amply justified. These propositions he considered unprovable though they certainly "need no proof" (30).

In the light of the points so far made and others to come, I suggest a terminological convention on which intuitionism in ethics admits of two understandings. First, it may be conceived as a view taking intuitions to be basic for moral justification and—by contrast with master principle theories like Kant's and Mill's—committed to an irreducible plurality of moral standards. Call this *generic*

---

[2] Huemer (2005) illustrates the kind of usage common in epistemology, and Tucker (2013) contains many papers bearing on the nature and epistemic status of seemings.

intuitionism. Second, such a view may be conceived as a moral epistemology: a view positing at least one self-evident moral principle that plays an important role in normative moral theory. One could call this *epistemological intuitionism*. Third, we might speak of a specific interpretation of generic intuitionism that each yields *an intuitionism*. Among specific versions of intuitionism, there are both rationalist ethical theories, with Ross's as paradigmatic, and empiricist theories. No particular axiology or set of normative standards is presupposed by every species of intuitionism.[3]

II Prima Facie Duty

The concept of prima facie duty (PFD) has been considered Ross's greatest single contribution to ethics. There are historically significant adumbrations,[4] but to my knowledge no one has shown that the concept Ross presented is adequately characterized by earlier authors. This view will be more plausible if one sees the notion as I propose. I will work with Ross's term 'duty', though I believe that 'obligation' as currently used is approximately equivalent and now probably preferable.

The prima facie and the pro tanto

First, Ross meant prima facie duty to be pro tanto—to admit of gradations, as greater or lesser strengths of duty. But, though favored by some over 'prima facie', 'pro tanto' is not a good substitute for it. Admitting of gradations (thus variability in deontic strength) does not suffice to capture what Ross meant. He apparently took prima facie duties to constitute overall (final) duties *provided* they are not overridden. This proviso is not clearly entailed by being a "pro tanto duty." This interpretation is implicit in Ross's speaking of prima facie duty as "conditional," though his terminology is easily misunderstood. He intended to specify a condition for *being* a final duty, not what is often meant by 'conditional duty'—a property of a person that *becomes* a duty *given* realization of a condition, for instance the property of liability to having a duty to do a service *if* asked to. This liability to "activation" applies to conditional duties that, even when the condition is realized, will *not* be final. If you promise to help me if there are too few chairs, then even if

---

[3] In principle, an intuitionism could be noncognitivist. For discussion of this possibility, see Hurka (2014: 103–7) and Ch. 5 of Phillips (2019). Sidgwick (1907) specified several kinds of intuitionism, but I here concentrate on recent usage. The influence of H. A. Prichard, indicated by, e.g., Hurka (2014) and Phillips (2019), is also important and bears independent discussion not possible here.
[4] Richard Price likely comes closest. The influence of Prichard is also important and bears more discussion than is possible here. For numerous relevant points see, e.g., Hurka (2014: 271–2) and Phillips (2019).

you discover there are to too few, you may have a final duty to attend to an emergency instead.

In standard usage, "conditional duties" (legal as well as moral) have a condition embodied in their *content*. Ross is framing a condition for finality of a duty. Final duties may, to be sure, have only *conditional* content, for instance to do a promised deed by proxy *if* the promisee is no longer living. This is conditional but will also be final if unopposed by any set of conflicting duties having at least equal strength. This power to become final is also a *necessary* condition for Rossian prima facie duty. A duty is final, then, if and only if it is a prima facie one that is not opposed by obligatory force at least as great.[5] But these two concepts are different. It is part of the concept of duty proper that it is not overridden, but this is *not* part of the concept of a prima facie duty. Prima facie duties *need* not be overridden, though they very commonly are. Ross is not best seen, then, as giving a definition in this context, but rather as outlining illuminating necessary and sufficient conditions for prima facie duty.

A second point here is that a pro tanto duty, by contrast with a Rossian prima facie duty, need have no threshold of normative significance. The conception may be weak enough to hold for moral considerations favoring an action yet needing aligned "duties" to yield a Rossian PFD. Such a weak duty could by itself be so minor as not to entail overall duty if unopposed, whereas Rossian prima facie duties must meet a threshold of moral significance: sufficient weight to yield overall duty if normatively unopposed. Consider receiving testimony that an ageing uncle remarked that he would like you to visit him. This could, in some cases, provide a pro tanto moral reason (and pro tanto duty) to visit him, but it need not rise to entailing a PFD. As this suggests, a basis for a pro tanto moral duty might not suffice for final duty even if not *decisively opposed*, i.e., not opposed by one or more conflicting duties of at least equal strength overall, thus either overridden (outweighed by a stronger contrary duty) or "neutralized" (rendered discretionary since one may fulfill either it or the opposing overall duty). Ross need not, however, take such testimony to have *no* weight. Granted, if I am told that my uncle *and* my two aunts he lives with would like me to visit, I might have justification for thinking I have a debt of gratitude. Such a debt *would* entail a prima facie duty to respond in some way.

A third point about PFDs is that, for Ross, at least *basic* prima facie duties correspond to self-evident principles, something not necessary for pro tanto duties. Even calling a pro tanto duty basic would not commit one to any such epistemological element. Foundational status is a role in a system, not, like self-evidence, a kind of justifiability or knowability. Foundations as such may be defective, however much is built on them. By contrast, when Ross refers to the prima facie duties

---

[5] Suppose opposing duties are just equally strong, as where a coalition of three favor breaking a serious promise and one is free to satisfy them or the latter. Then keeping the promise is permissible but not obligatory.

on his initial list (21)—justice and non-injury, veracity and fidelity, beneficence and self-improvement, and reparation and gratitude—he takes the corresponding principles to be self-evident (which he conceives as an a priori status). This is compatible with his apparently considering some of them derivable from others, thus compressing his basic list. He thought, e.g., that veracity implicitly depends on fidelity to one's word. But such dependence does not entail reducibility, though it is consistent both with that and with the principle of veracity and that of promissory fidelity each being a priori.

A fourth point about prima facie duties is important for seeing why a Rossian intuitionism need not be dogmatic. PFDs are not brute but *grounded*: "Each rests on a circumstance that cannot seriously be held to be without moral significance" (20). The circumstance might be making a promise. Illustrating this, he maintained (against ideal utilitarianism) that clearly we should regard keeping a promise as our duty even if an alternative would yield an equal amount of good (18). One might have an intuition that this is so in an actual concrete case in which the proposition is empirical and contingent, as well as in a specially designed hypothetical case (like Ross's) in which it is plausibly considered self-evident.

Prima facie duty, consequential duty, and moral reasons

When Ross speaks of the prima facie duties that centrally concern him, he has in mind self-evidence of the corresponding principles. We should not infer, however, that he made no room for subsidiary principles. I assume that even if he would call a subsidiary principle of duty *provable* by appeal self-evident principles of duty, he might not thereby consider it self-evident. This is not only expectable given how long and complicated proofs can be but perhaps also implicit in his treatment of "consequential" duty. He says, e.g., that "the primary duty not to harm others gives rise to a consequential duty to resist the inclination" (22). Giving rise to something is surely short of self-evidently entailing it. A clearer case might be a duty resulting from promise-breaking: a duty to explain (to the promisee) why one broke the promise or to make amends for it. (We can see how one might deduce this; but here deduction must join "mental maturity" if we are to acquire genuine knowledge that such explanatory responsibility is a [non-basic] prima facie duty.)

However one views the relation of Rossian prima facie duty to pro tanto duty, it appears that, for Ross, even if his list of PFDs is incomplete, it includes foundational prima facie duties that any adequate moral theory should recognize. It is not obvious, at least in RG, that he considered PFDs not only duty-sufficing when not decisively opposed, but also *justification-sufficing*, i.e., such that each, if *not* decisively opposed, provides the agent with rational (moral) justification to act accordingly. It seems clear, however, that although 'prima facie' for Ross is not epistemic (say, definable in terms of an agent's having *justification* for ascribing duty), he did think that insofar as one may properly take a prima facie duty *not* to be decisively opposed, one has reason to believe it to be the agent's overall duty. This idea may be an indication of why he chose 'prima facie' in the first place: its normal use implies the existence of some reason (and some degree of justification) to think that what is prima facie the case *is* so, but a prima facie duty has a property that such a duty cannot merely seem to have. *Given* its ground, it must have what (in contemporary parlance) is the property of being a moral reason for the act in question.

Might we, then, interpret Ross as conceiving prima facie duties as moral reasons? He did not regularly work with the notion of moral reasons, as is now common. But he apparently had the concept (as seems evident on 73–74), and he sought a "separate noun" for PFD (2). It is quite plausible to take PFDs to entail moral reasons. This view seems implicit in both being explainable and (arguably) required by the same essentially normative grounds, say promising or, on the negative side, harming. In virtue of either ground, we have moral reasons to act. The difference between prima facie and final duty is not one of kind but of circumstance—the latter are not outweighed by other normative forces, but both possess their normative weight in virtue of the same kind of relation to the same grounding elements.[6]

If, however, we allow for minor reasons, the converse—that moral reasons entail PFDs—is not obvious. Suppose an acquaintance who is directing a project asks your judgment on an important matter when there was no obligation to do so. Do you not still have a minor reason for appreciative action? Suppose you do. It need not be a case of a duty of gratitude, nor does Ross's view clearly require positing a *moral* reason here. Still, arguably a number of such cases would yield some such duty to the person, as well as a moral reason.

Another consideration supporting the view that PFDs are a kind of moral reason is that it tends to support the Rossian view that the grounds of PFDs necessarily have some "moral significance." It is one thing to deny that, e.g., there is always a kind of duty (or obligation) not to lie (grounded in the relevant circumstances of communication); it is quite implausible, however, to say that there is sometimes no reason whatever to avoid lying, in which case it might have no moral significance. Granted, the point is arguably pragmatic: perhaps it is misleading or at least unnatural to *say* this. But even that point is worth noting. There is always something that speaks against violations of veracity, however quiet its voice.[7]

---

[6] Stratton-Lake has suggested something similar: that "for some feature of an act to be morally wrong is not for us to have some kind of duty not to do it, but it to have some feature that gives us a moral reason not to do it" (2002: xxxiv). On my view, the feature, e.g. lying, does *give* us a moral reason, but the relevant features are not PFDs but the *grounds* of both PFDs and the equivalent moral reasons. Note that Ross calls PFDs properties—and having a moral duty is having a kind of property. Perhaps it is the relational property of being in a kind of circumstance that "cannot seriously be denied to have moral significance." Having a moral reason is a candidate to be the same property, but that strong metaphysical claim is not entailed by the claim that one has a PFD to A if and only if one has a moral reason to A.

[7] This is argued in some detail in my (2006), 285–304.

Prima facie duties, like reasons for action, are cumulative—potentially mutually reinforcing though not (strictly speaking) quantitatively additive. This property is difficult to account for if some PFDs have zero weight. How is mutual (normative) reinforcement even possible if the kinds of facts grounding them, such as undertaking communication or receiving benefits, cannot have zero normative force?[8] Perhaps, wherever Ross would regard a reason to *A* as *moral*, he would think there is a prima facie duty to *A*. If we may assume that a reason's being moral entails meeting a threshold high enough to yield a significant element of justification, then we may take Ross's notion of prima facie duty to be an approximate equivalent—and in some respects an anticipation—of the notion of a moral reason as many contemporary writers in ethics employ that notion.

One further point is needed here. It concerns how Ross conceived conflicts between prima facie duties. His view seems *non-hierarchical* in this sense: there are no two kinds of PFD such that one kind has *deontic precedence* over the other kind; i.e., any single prima facie duty in the former category has priority over any single such duty in the other. He clearly resists saying this for non-injury in relation to beneficence, though calling it 'non-maleficence' in this case (21). He describes the former as having "a more stringent character" (21), yet differs on this point from Kant and others.[9]

As these points suggest, Ross is apparently willing to make guarded pairwise generalizations, as where one must break a promise to meet for lunch in order to save an accident victim. He also makes no commitment to the impossibility of generalizations that combine duties, as where both fidelity and non-injury call for keeping a promise that considerations of beneficence alone might lead many utilitarians to break.

III "Duty Proper"

Ross used not only 'duty proper' but also 'final', 'actual', 'sans phrase', and some other expressions in designating what might be conceived as overall duty—a prima facie duty not decisively opposed by conflicting duties. Logically speaking, a duty proper (a "final" one) still satisfies the conditions for being prima facie, but Ross apparently viewed *calling* it prima facie improper because that misleadingly suggests that it might be decisively opposed. The point is roughly this: it is part of the

---

[8] Zero force might be consistent with prima facie duties' being *tendencies*, on some uses of that term, to yield duty. For discussion of prima facie duty in general, the tendency reading, and their relation to reasons for action, see Phillips (2019: 13–56).

[9] Kant is widely, if controversially, taken to regard perfect duties, such as not to lie, as *invariably* overriding conflicting imperfect ones, for instance beneficence or self-improvement. I have argued in "Methodological Reflections on Kant's Ethical Theory," *Synthese* (2021), that this rigorism is not essential to the overall categorical imperative framework.

concept of duty proper that it is not decisively opposed, but this it is *not* part of the concept of a prima facie duty. That a PFD is unopposed is not a conceptual truth, though our PFDs may in fact always be opposed. Indeed, they are so often *not* finally overridden as to support the pragmatic point that the proper use of 'prima facie duty' requires ascribing such duties only where one does not *take* them to be final.

Some writers use 'all things considered' for 'final' and 'overall'. Doing this can mislead in suggesting that all relevant variables have *been* considered. That is a contingent matter and may often be at best difficult to achieve. For Ross, it is never a priori, or, even knowable, that a duty is final. Moreover, *knowledge* or even justified belief that a duty *is* final is normally comparative, in requiring reason to think there is no competing duty of at least equal weight. But *if* I know I have promised to A, I may thereby know that I have a prima facie duty to A.

One may wonder at Ross's epistemic humility about justification for judgments of duty proper. He said, e.g.,

> we are never certain that any particular possible act has not [some characteristic that makes it overall wrong], and therefore never certain that it is right, nor certain that it is wrong... ...There is therefore much truth in the description of the right act as a fortunate act (31).

He meant, of course, to deny not *psychological* certainty, which is subjective, but *epistemic* certainty, which is not: it is not certain, he thought, that any specific act is right. He surely knew that an agent could *be* certain (absolutely sure) that it is. But even if it is intuitive that one should not, for instance, sign a certain petition, one does not know this "for certain." If a proposition is really certain, it is true, and Ross apparently does not assume that *everything* intuitive is true.

Did Ross, who was surely a common-sense philosopher, cede too much to moral skepticism? We might not think this if we agree with him that

> A statement is certain, i.e. is an expression of knowledge, only in one or other of two cases: when it is either self-evident, or a valid conclusion from self-evident premises (30).

But knowledge does not require this kind of a priori certainty. I doubt that it requires even empirical certainty. But in any case, neither Ross's normative ethics nor his metaethics apart from this (I think uncharacteristically strict) statement requires denying that we can be justifiably confident of some judgments of overall duty.

The points so far made and much else in RG indicate that Ross is taking actual duty "objectively," in the external sense that what we finally ought to do is a matter of fact and independent of the strength of our evidence regarding our duty.

It should be noted that in Chapter 7 of *Foundations* he qualified this view and construed the basis of overall duty as significantly evidential and, in that sense, "subjective" (here influenced by Prichard in contrast with Sidgwick). He is right to maintain (as he implied in RG) that what it is reasonable for us to do—even ethically reasonable—depends on our evidence. This is especially plausible if evidence is objective and so actually supports the propositions it evidences.

It seems fair to say that Ross's overall position, like most plausible moral theories, can be worked out either with an objective (external) notion of obligation combined with a theory of excuses and mitigation based on an account of relevant justified beliefs on the part of the agent, *or* a theory on which obligation itself is constructed from sufficient relevant evidence. This is sometimes called a subjective view of obligation, but it allows for a kind of objectivity about good and bad evidence. Consider a surgeon who, using the best available evidence (which is not definable in terms of what is believed best), performs medically optimal surgery, yet still loses the patient. Is the act wrong but excusable, or is it right and in no need of excuse? On the evidential understanding of obligation, it is right; on the objective understanding portrayed in RG, it is wrong but excusable. In neither case should its basis be called subjective.

Most of the leading moral philosophers, like Ross in RG, prefer an objective (and non-epistemic) conception of actual duty and an epistemic conception of excusability. The crucial thing is to work in the right way with the right concepts: duty, evidence, rightness, justified belief, and other notions are needed both in the theory of obligation and in the theory of excuses. Perhaps Ross in RG found the objective, factive view more in accord with "what we really think" when, in clear cases, we deliberate about what *to do* and, in appraising action, judge the moral character of what we *have* done. This is arguable, but far from clearly true. Sensitive usage might take account of both perspectives. The medical ethics panel might say the surgeon acted rightly but with unfortunate results; the patient's family might say he was wrong to operate but should be excused.

Humility about ascribing duty and rightness or wrongness is compatible with either an "objective" or a "subjective" conception of duty. For objectivity about *justification* is not in question on either conception (or should not be in question if ethics is to avoid a subjectivistic relativism). On either conception, moreover, any intuitionism pluralistic in the way Ross's is (as are all the historically prominent examples) tends to preclude absolutism in the sense in which it implies that some acts are not even *possibly* right, as with, say, bombing purely military targets in a way that will kill an innocent civilian.

For Ross, since it is never a priori or even empirically absolutely certain that an apparently final duty is not decisively opposed, we cannot regard any prospective act—that is non-morally described—as necessarily wrong. Though Ross does not put it this way, he likely believed that we cannot validly infer a final duty from a purely descriptive proposition—an *ought* from an *is*, if you like. This is a version of "Hume's Law." But if, as it seems, Ross would accept that, it must not be inferred that he accepts the empiricist requirement that no valid deductive inferences with a moral conclusion may be drawn from such facts as "cannot seriously be held to be without moral significance." Lying does entail doing something prima facie wrong—given a notion of entailment Hume did not accommodate—but it does not entail what is finally wrong, and Ross would not claim that (as Kant is commonly thought to hold) there is always a final duty not to lie.

If there are no absolute duties, can even overall duties be rationally defeasible? Ross seems committed to granting that no duties are *in principle indefeasible*, but this does not commit him to holding that no duty is *undefeated*. He claims that we cannot *know* that a duty is not defeated by overriding conflicting duties, but he is not even committed to denying that with enough evidence we can be "morally certain"—very strongly justified—in taking a duty to be undefeated. It could, for all he says, be a final duty to sacrifice one's life rather than give terrorists instructions for launching a nuclear bomb against a thriving city.

IV Rossian Self-Evidence

Ross has encountered much criticism and even more skepticism by presenting his main prima facie duty principles as self-evident. He did not define this notion and, in explaining it to the extent that he did, used an unfortunately misleading logico-mathematical analogy: he referred to the principles as "self-evident just as a mathematical axiom, or the validity of a form of inference, is evident" (29). One easily thinks here of such obvious logical truths as those corresponding to elementary rules of inference, e.g. <If (p entails q) and (p is true), then (q is true)>. But these conditionals are not only self-evident but obvious, whereas Ross wisely said a few lines earlier,

> That an act, *qua* fulfilling a promise ... ... is prima facie right, is self-evident; not in the sense that it is evident ... ... *as soon as we attend to the proposition for the first time*, but in the sense that when we have reached sufficient mental maturity *and* have given sufficient attention to the proposition it is evident without any need of proof, or of evidence beyond itself" (29, italics added for the attention clause and for 'and').

Must Ross conceive "moral self-evidence" on the model of mathematical self-evidence? He continues in the same paragraph to say (manifesting a conception of self-evidence I shall argue he is free to revise),

> In our confidence that these [moral] propositions are true there is involved the same trust in our reason that is involved in our confidence in mathematics; and

we should have no justification for trusting it in the latter sphere and distrusting it in the former. In both cases we are dealing with propositions that cannot be proved, but that just as certainly need no proof (30).

Doubtless there *is* a trust in our reason implicit in both cases. But the parity claim (of "the same trust") and the rejection of provability in the last statement—though defensible for a certain notion of self-evidence—again invite the impression that the self-evident is obvious and indeed so close to a kind of axiomatic status as to be unprovable.[10]

In the context of this passage (as elsewhere), Ross misses a chance to overcome what might be seen as Prichard's legacy of dogmatism (in, e.g., "Does Moral Philosophy Rest on a Mistake?" [1912]). Is there any plausible conception of self-evidence strong enough to serve Ross's purposes yet moderate enough to avoid these misleading implications? I propose this:

> Self-evident propositions are truths meeting two conditions: (a) an adequate understanding of them is a ground for justification for believing them (which does not entail that anyone who adequately understands them *does* believe them); and (b) believing them on the basis of adequately understanding them entails knowing them.[11]

This conception accommodates the idea that "mental maturity" and "sufficient attention" may often be required to apprehend a self-evident proposition; and the kind of knowledge it describes would meet Ross's standard of certainty. But the conception does not entail either obviousness or unprovability. It also does not require that, say, an errant skeptic in the grip of a false theory could not have justification for believing a self-evident proposition and still wrongly (but intelligibly) deny it. If self-evident propositions meet the conditions I've proposed—and adequacy of understanding is a reasonably demanding notion—Ross's claim of self-evidence for his principles has a stronger footing and can better accommodate the possibility of rational disagreement on moral principles without dogmatically insisting on the truth of those one accepts.

The proposed notion of self-evidence does not seem inimical to anything major in Ross's ethics (as opposed to certain elements in his epistemology). It is doubtful, moreover, that Ross did justice to his own thinking about self-evidence even apart

---

[10] Steeped as he was in Aristotle, he may have thought of rules of inference as corresponding to Aristotelian *indemonstrables* (*Posterior Analytics*, 72b). This would include the kinds of basic axioms such that, since nothing is "better known," nothing is eligible as premises in a proof. Cf. Sidgwick (1907: 382–3), in which the mathematical analogy is even stronger.

[11] This account derives from my work of the 1980s but was first published in some detail only later in my (1996) and then in my (1998) and (1999). I take a *ground* for justification to be such that, in virtue of having it, one is justified. I assume here that false propositions can at best seem self-evident.

from affirming an unprovability condition. He never said that the self-evident is *unevidenceable*, and for intuitionists, evidence may come in a common-sensical form Ross himself illustrated: through developed examples that produce intuitions favoring the proposition in question.

It is a methodological commitment of intuitionism that proof is not the only route to putting truth in high relief. This is illustrated by Ross's appeal, in opposing the "ideal utilitarianism" of Moore, to the PFD to keep promises. It is characteristic of intuitionism—and some would say of philosophical method generally—to suppose that for every good example that in some way supports a proposition, one can frame a premise in an argument for that proposition. But such evidences are not proofs and—though Ross employed such intuitive examples in supporting his view—he would not call them proofs.[12]

Rossian sources for accommodating moral disagreement

Readers of Ross and indeed most philosophers outside epistemology will tend to wonder how Ross as rationalist can accommodate rational disagreement on his principles. I must be brief here, but it is important to see that the charge of dogmatism is unfair to Ross once we recall his epistemological humility about singular moral judgments and realize that his analogy to forms of inference has only limited applicability to his view of everyday moral judgment. The analogy illustrates a priori truth and a kind of foundational status for certain moral principles; but self-evidence is not necessary for either apriority or foundational status, and his appeal to it is misleading in at least the ways just indicated.

Consider examples: <The mother-in-law of the spouse of your second-youngest sibling is your own mother> and <A person may be both parent and grandparent of the same person>. Some bilingual people can translate these immediately into another language, and so have a kind of understanding of them, but do not quickly see their truth. They need what Ross might have called sufficient attention. That seems akin to what I call the need for adequate understanding, but the latter is in some cases even more than a matter of attention and maturity, and it requires considerable explication. Indeed, some mature intelligent people need help to see the truth of the second proposition, but those who know Sophocles's *Oedipus Rex* might recall that Oedipus, who, after unknowingly marrying his

---

[12] Here we might note a quotation from Ross's "The Basis of Objective Judgements in Ethics" (1927) that Stratton-Lake stresses in (2002: xlviii–xlix): "the fact that something can be inferred does not prove that it cannot be seen intuitively." Ross presumably did not take inferrability to entail provability (he used the latter epistemically), but perhaps he meant to indicate that there can be supporting reasons without proof. This is true and important. In any case Ross did not need the unprovability claim for any major point in his overall moral theory.

mother, made her both mother and grandmother of their children, is the kind of person described.

With these points in mind, consider the controversy between Rossian intuitionism and what might be called a strong version of the particularistic view that even prima facie duty does not follow, as Rossians think, from such grounds as promising or receiving a large benefit, but may be affirmed only in the light of *all* the relevant facts of a given case. Suppose A promises B to deliver a package to C. Imagine that A discovers that the package will explode on being opened, causing thousands of deaths. A strong particularist may argue that the promise carries no prima facie weight.[13] We need not settle this dispute to see that Ross might claim that because a strong particularist may have a *plausible* (mistaken) theory that requires this conclusion, affirming the conclusion is not flatly irrational. We can without dogmatism consider disputants to be influenced by a false theory with the result that, in the grip of it, they deny what they have justification—or, alternatively, *better* justification—for affirming. (The alternative view referred to might derive from taking *any* evidence or normative reason for *p* to entail *some* degree of justification for believing it, even if so little that one would not say the person is justified *in believing p*.) Quite apart from this response, there are departures from rationality that may be resisted without dogmatic flat rejection.

The concept of self-evidence I have proposed makes room for Ross to accommodate rational disagreement regarding the principles he considered self-evident and to allow for arguments that, even if not proofs, support those principles. In my view, certain ways of developing Kant's categorical imperative (in both its universality and humanity formulations) can serve this purpose. Ross's acceptance, with Moore and many others, of the idea that self-evident propositions are unprovable gave him a systematic basis for resisting Kant's view that the categorical imperative is a kind of axiom from which all general principles are derivable. But, as already noted, support may come from non-entailing premises. If Ross accepted that, he could still reject Kant's deducibility claim (a kind of claim probably also implicit in Mill regarding derivation of "secondary rules" from the principle of utility).[14] Another relevant possibility Ross could pursue is using Kantian elements to assist in dealing with conflicts of prima facie duties (as will be illustrated in Section V). If we can discern in virtue of what properties one set of PFDs overrides another set, we may be in a position to formulate a consequential comparative principle of prima facie predominance.

---

[13] This has been argued by Jonathan Dancy (1993), and in my (2006) I have replied in detail and supported the Rossian view.
[14] See the closing paragraphs of Ch. 2 of Mill's *Utilitarianism*.

V Ross's Theory of Value

It is somewhat puzzling that Ross's theory of value has received little attention, or at any rate less philosophical attention than Moore's value theory, though it may be in some respects comparably important. In part, Ross's theory of value has likely been eclipsed by his theory of obligation. But it is significant in its own right. Moreover, value theory, despite occupying a central position in ethics, deserves more philosophical study than recent decades have given it. This is not the place for a full-scale discussion of Ross's axiology, but a few points on his central axiological views will help in understanding his overall ethical theory.

Ross's first chapter on value begins with the distinction between two uses of 'good': "(A) the adjunctive or attributive use …… as when we speak of a good runner or of a good poem, and (B) the predicative use of it, as when it is said that knowledge is good or that pleasure is good" (65). Many philosophers have considered the latter use—despite its major role in the history of ethics—at best misleading.[15] It should be granted that one may intelligibly ask, of at least the important predicative ascriptions, 'Good for whom or for what?' Nonetheless, Ross seems unscathed. The main point here is that everything properly said to be good in itself (good, period) *is* of some kind, and that some kinds, such as experiences, are value-anchoring kinds: we know a great deal about which are good and which bad. Nor can the view that (non-instrumental) value is always value *for* be plausibly worked out without appeal to such ideas as that. Granted, suffering is bad *for* the sufferer; but when Moore and Ross said that what is intrinsically good would be good even if it existed "quite alone," they presumably meant to include what suffering *entails*, and suffering entails the existence of the sufferer.

Assuming with Ross that we may quite intelligibly speak of things good in themselves, we should ask what kinds of things Ross regarded as such? In Chapter 5 of RG he says:

> The first thing for which I would claim that it is intrinsically good is virtuous disposition and action, i.e. action, or disposition to act, from any one of certain motives, of which at all events the most notable are the desire to do one's duty, the desire to bring into being something that is good, and the desire to give pleasure or save pain to others" (134).

The second thing he points to is pleasure itself, though he goes on to introduce certain complexities. At least one passage merits reflection here:

---

[15] Judith Jarvis Thomson (1997), partly following Peter Geach, is an example, and Nandi Theunissen (2020) provides reasons for also rejecting the philosophical value of the predicate use.

An act of promise-keeping has the property, not necessarily of being right but of being ...... right if the act has no other morally significant characteristic .... similarly a state of pleasure has the property, not necessarily of being good, but of being something that is good if the state has no other characteristic that prevents it from being good. The two characteristics that may interfere with its being good are (*a*) that of being contrary to desert, and (*b*) that of being a state which is the realization of a bad disposition. Thus the pleasures of which we can say without doubt that they are good are (i) the pleasures of non-moral beings (animals), (ii) the pleasures of moral beings that are deserved and are either realizations of good moral dispositions or realizations of neutral capacities (such as the pleasures of the senses) (138).

Notably, Ross is treating goodness as significantly like obligatoriness. The former has "prima facie" as well as overall forms, and in both cases the overall property is a "toti-resultant attribute." In this, Ross, like Moore (1903), provides space for intrinsic goodness to be organic: "We have no right to assume that the value of a whole is precisely equal to the sum of the values of its elements taken separately" (RG, 72).

The acknowledgment of axiological organicity leads Ross to speak of the "contributively good" (73), illustrated by the overall goodness of the pleasure of seeing (the contributive good of) someone's enjoyment of fulfilling a duty of gratitude. This good on the part of the person observed has pleasure as a contributive good as appropriate to the fulfillment of duty; and the pleasure in seeing this kind of complex pleasure contributes to the overall good of the observer's (higher-order) complex pleasure taken in the virtue-manifesting pleasure of the observed agent. By contrast, Ross might say, sadists' pleasure in the pains of their victims would be "the wrong kind of pleasure" and contributively bad, even if, considered in isolation, it is also prima facie (and intrinsically) good.

The third category of intrinsic value, then, is always complex—arguably organically so in many cases: "the apportionment of pleasure and pain to the virtuous and the vicious respectively" (138). Consider feeding virtuous and malicious prisoners of war. If some meals leave the kitchen tastier than others, is it not intrinsically better that the tastier meals available be given to the former than to the latter or to the repentant among the latter than to the still unrepentant?

A fourth category of the intrinsically good is broadly intellectual:

... ... knowledge, and in a less degree what we may for the present call 'right opinion', are states of mind good in themselves ... ... supposing two states of the universe equal in respect of virtue and of pleasure and of the allocation of pleasure to the virtuous, but such that the persons in the one had a far greater understanding of the nature and laws of the universe than those in the other. Can any one doubt that the first would be a better state of the universe? (139).

The judgment of betterness here is surely meant to reflect an intuition with the same content. The emphasis on states of mind here is even more important. Ross had earlier said something quite comprehensive and striking: that "good is a characteristic belonging primarily only to states of mind, and belonging to them in virtue of three characteristics—the moral virtue included in them, the intelligence included in them, and the pleasure included in them" (122). Here Ross sees and rejects the objection "that there are or may be intrinsic goods that are not states of mind or relations between states of mind at all … … in this suggestion I can find no plausibility" (122). Is he (despite adding relations between states of mind to his grouping of intrinsic goods) unnecessarily narrow here?

Perhaps Ross conceived being virtuous as a state of mind, though this seems a categorization at best difficult to defend if one is speaking of virtue as a personal characteristic. Can one, if unconscious from a fall, be in a state of mind? One can certainly retain one's virtues after recovery. In any case, when Ross says that "the value of material things appears to be purely instrumental" (142), one may perhaps assume that for material artworks, say sculptures, he is thinking of "constitutive means," in the sense of means essential to the relevant ends in the way visual *consciousness* of a sculpture is essential to taking aesthetic pleasure in viewing it.[16] An importantly comprehensive remark is that "what is good or bad is always something properly expressed by a that-clause, i.e. an objective, or as I should prefer to call it, a *fact*" (137). Ross presumably has in mind actual ("obtaining") states of affairs, such as one's being pedagogically pleased at students' aiming at excellence rather than good grades.

If we take seriously enough Ross's metaphysical characterization of goodness and badness as actual states of affairs, his value theory may be taken to give states of mind a central role in the theory of value without their being the only *bearers* of non-instrumental value. He said, e.g., that "it is in virtue of the motives that they proceed from that actions are morally good" (156). Perhaps he was here thinking of actions as "volitional," a kind of undertaking as opposed to an overt doing based on intention. But even on this narrow view of action, on which actions are mental and presumably conscious events, Ross is (wisely) too pluralistic about bearers of value to make it natural for him to squeeze all of them under the rubric of states of consciousness and their relations to other things. Motives need not be occurrent to underlie action; they are presumably dispositional properties whose possession need not be a state of consciousness.[17]

A further consideration favoring a broader understanding of Ross's axiology is that his overall conception of intrinsic value is based on an account of (intrinsic)

---

[16] This is a more sympathetic reading than proposed by Gwen Bradford in her paper in this volume.
[17] I have sought to rectify these and other difficulties in (2023), esp.Ch. 11, which develops a conception of inherent value as *both* an intrinsic property of its bearers and belonging both to multifarious inanimate phenomena and to certain conscious states.

good-making and bad-making elements that are analogous to the grounds—the duty-making elements—underlying prima facie duty. Moreover, his view that overall duty is a "toti-resultant" attribute is nicely paralleled by his axiological view that intrinsic goodness in certain kinds of complex state of affairs is an organic composition of prima facie elements. These may or may not be "ultimately" good—"" intrinsically good overall *and* containing no parts that are not intrinsically good" (69), roughly, no constituent that is not good in itself "throughout", as with the innocent pleasure of a child by contrast with a sadist's pleasure in paining a victim. Here Ross is arguably not only more pluralistic than Moore but also clearer in the substantial area of their agreement.

VI Beneficence and Its Role in Overall Obligation

No one credibly doubts that some standard of beneficence is central to morality. Ross stresses it and has two quite different ways of characterizing beneficence. One seems at least mainly interpersonal, the other broader. This is evident in a number of places in RG, but to cite just Chapter 2, he says both that "Some [prima facie duties] rest on the mere fact that there are other beings in the world whose condition we can make better in respect of virtue, or of intelligence, or of pleasure. These are the duties of beneficence" (22), and that "The bringing of this [apportionment "of happiness to virtue"] about is a duty which we owe to all men alike ... ... This, therefore, with beneficence and self-improvement, comes under the general principle that we should produce as much good as possible, though the good here involved is different in kind from any other" (27). This second quotation reinforces the view that beneficence is owed to all beings we can make better off (applicable to animals as well as persons). It *also* affirms an apparently more basic principle that we should produce as much good as possible. This PFD encompasses all intrinsic goods, and persons-to-be would be included. It *also* embodies a kind of maximization requirement here that is not implicit in the personal formulation. There is no reason, however, to take 'as much as possible' to mean 'as much as logically possible' or even 'as much as psychologically possible'. Neither yields a plausible interpretation, and the most natural reading draws on the notion of what is feasible within the constellation of Rossian normative forces. This is illustrated by a conscientious parent's saying 'I do all I can for my children' and a physician's saying, to the children of an accident victim, 'We're doing all we can'. Possibility here lies within what is morally permissible beyond merely routine helpfulness.

The wider principle has likely often been often taken to *be* Ross's beneficence principle, but from his overall view and the treatment of this principle as more general, I propose that we distinguish the two principles, conceive what might be called *narrow Rossian beneficence* as at least mainly interpersonal, and take the wider beneficence principle—apart from the apparent maximization clause—as extending more broadly to reasons for action. The narrower principle may not be exactly what he had in mind in speaking of "the highly personal character of duty" (22) but is consonant with his overall view. The wider principle, unlike the narrower one, apparently countenances a duty to produce one's own pleasure, which Ross did not consider a moral duty, as well as duties to promote justice, which he did consider moral: "duties to upset or prevent" a distribution "of pleasure or happiness (or the means thereto) ...... not in accord with the merit of the persons concerned" (21).

Pluralism without hierarchy

If Ross considered beneficence our highest duty or even predominant over certain other deontic categories, especially duties of self-improvement, that would pose a serious problem for him and would make his position less distant from utilitarianism. But he is not hierarchical and presumably understands 'as much good as possible' in terms of what we may reasonably see as our overall duty in contexts of deliberation. Indeed, even if he intended to endorse a kind of maximization, achieving it would be constrained not only by the limits of causal possibility but also by the normative force of all the obligations, other then general beneficence, that one has in the relevant context.

It is true that Ross said that no amount of pleasure has as much intrinsic goodness as *any* amount of moral goodness (150).[18] But this concerns value, which he, unlike Moore, does not take to dictate obligation as determined by what acts maximize intrinsic value. It is also significant that Ross did not make any such unqualified comparisons for any other pairs of intrinsic goods. We must also remember his speaking, in criticizing utilitarianism, of "the highly personal character of duty" (22). It is clearly compatible with his overall view to say that in normal human life, the duties of fidelity, say to family and friends, together with those of self-improvement, severely limit what beneficence requires of us. In speaking of a PFD to bring about "as much good as possible,"" then, Ross is surely speaking of the maximum we are capable of taking account of in determining what is *morally* possible within the nexus of PFDs we have. This contextual interpretation both fits the text and indicates how he might provide for supererogation, say in doing more to eliminate injustice than duty requires.

It is not obvious, to be sure, how Ross would account for supererogation and indeed for the permissible.[19] Here the indefinite strength of the duty of

---

[18] Not surprisingly, Ross qualified this view in (1939: 275). As is evident in Skelton's contribution to this volume, it is surprising that Ross does not reject this absolute axiological predominance as he does any absolute predominance in his theory of obligation.

[19] The difficulties confronting a Rossian account of permissibility are judiciously explored in Stratton-Lake's contribution to this volume.

beneficence—and indeed even of fidelity, self-improvement, and likely all the other duties—makes it possible for a kind of activity, such as fighting oppression, to be required up to a certain point, one beyond which it would be outweighed by conflicting duties. Suppose, then, that there is equally strong PFD to undertake a beneficent activity as to do something else. One's final duty here may be to do one *or* the other. The choice of beneficent activity, however, would allow for making more or less effort and for various actions. Imagine that, by fighting disease in a poor country, I beneficently meet all my obligations, balancing this with my promissory obligations, personal and professional, and my obligations of self-improvement. May I not voluntarily invest *more* energy in the work than required to achieve the obligatory level of beneficence needed to counterbalance my conflicting duties? This is surely both permissible and "beyond the call of duty," at least on the narrow Rossian conception of beneficence that does not require maximization.[20]

Perhaps if I *think* of potentially doing more than I must to exactly counterbalance an equally strong conflicting duty, I *then* may not flip a coin between the options. But in order to *do* something that Ross could call supererogatory, I need only do more than required of me in one of the foreseeable situations that, in my actual (sound) deliberations, allow for morally arbitrary choice. You would be criticizable if you did less, and you could be praiseworthy for doing more.

One element in Ross's theory of value that needs explanation is why in RG he denies that there is a prima facie duty to enhance one's own pleasure. If, as I suggest, we take as primary in Rossian beneficence the personal formulation of the duty and its apparent directedness toward *others*, we can then deny that there is a duty or even a *moral* reason to enhance one's own pleasure. If, however, we take as basic Ross's formulation of a principle underlying beneficence, it is not clear what basis this provides for denying a prima facie duty to enhance one's own pleasure. He could, however, have countenanced *non-moral* reasons to enhance pleasure in one's life, and I have found no justification in his work for denying that. These options (perhaps among others) would have given him at least less reason to give up, as he did in *Foundations* (271ff), . the idea that pleasure is intrinsically good. That major change is at best puzzling given his notion of the target good of beneficence as contributing to virtue, knowledge, *and pleasure* in others.

It is possible that when Ross formulated the principle that we should produce as much good as possible, he was thinking of not only the future of persons existing now, but also of future persons, if only later generations in one's own family. In either case, one can think of duty in terms of what grounds it. If, for instance, a

---

[20] How Ross might account for permissibility is also discussed in Stratton-Lake's paper in this volume.

promise I make to you now can ground a duty to do things expected to occur years ahead—and even actions that involve supporting children you are yet to have—one can see how Ross's framework of firmly grounded duties can lead to principles governing future generations. This is not to say he anticipated population ethics. The point is only to suggest that his overall moral theory has implications for that challenge. One aspect of the challenge, however, concerns conflicts of duties, and here as in other areas of applied ethics, some readers of Ross have missed any procedure for dealing with conflicting duties.

The problem of determining the stringency of duties

The duty of beneficence can cause trouble for Ross's ethics, and indeed for any commonsense ethics, not only if allowed too much weight in overriding other prima facie duties (as it apparently does with act-utilitarianism) but also if it leaves *no* procedure for settling such conflicts. In my view, Ross had resources—as other intuitionists do—for dealing with the conflict problem. He surely understated his resources. He said,

> For the estimation of the comparative stringency of these prima facie obligations no general rules can, so far as I can see, be laid down. We can only say that a great deal of stringency belongs to "the duties of 'perfect obligation'—the duties of keeping our promises, of repairing wrongs we have done, and of returning the equivalent of services we have received. For the rest, 'The decision rests with perception'" (41–42, with the Greek quotation from Aristotle, *Nic. Eth.* 1109 b23, 1126b4, replaced by Ross's own footnote translation).

It is unclear what he takes a "general rule" to require, but even here he is implying that—other things equal—perfect duties tend to override imperfect duties. He could, however, go further given his moral ontology. Let me explain.

It is somewhat puzzling that (in RG, anyway) Ross seems loath to formulate more subsidiary principles of duty (including "consequential" duties) than he did that are usable in making moral judgments and leading a moral life generally. Two have been cited—a self-improvement thumbnail rule calling for self-control (say, of anger) in the service of the duty of non-injury and, when one has broken a promise, a rule calling for explaining to the promisee why one has done so (even if there is no need for reparation). Indeed, he later said,

> [I]n comparing goods, and in comparing prima facie duties ... ... where the one good is *much* the greater or the one obligation *much* the more stringent, we seem to be able to grasp these facts with certainty ... ... that in many individual cases the people whose judgement we have learned most to respect in ethical matters

will pronounce the same judgement on acts is some guarantee that objectivity has been attained.[21]

He appears to have thought that, final duty *supervenes* on natural (roughly "descriptive") facts in the sense that no two things alike in natural properties can differ in moral ones. Add to this that it is clearly Rossian to decide conflicts of duty in the light of the facts of the situation calling for decision. It is common for such situations to have elements that are both discernible and generalizable. Surely, if we can decide what our duty is in the light of a pattern of facts, we can in principle formulate at least a rough rule that incorporates the facts crucial in that pattern. What are the facts we focus on? Which seem primary? What are analogous situations? Practical wisdom is not quantitatively codifiable, but it is also not limited to ad hoc deliverances.

It may help to note that Kant had a very similar problem in trying to indicate how we should formulate rationally universalizable maxims. His discussions of his four illustrations of mxims in the *Groundwork* do not adequately serve, and in that context and elsewhere, he could have greatly benefited from employing Ross's notion of prima facie duty. Here Ross is in a more favorable position for formulating everyday moral rules. He took overall duties to be grounded in ("toti-resultant" from) precisely the kinds of facts he describes in explaining prima facie duties.[22] As he may have seen, we can (as Kantians would stress) use a universalizability test in progressively refining the verdictive judgments we find intuitive in the light of such facts, even if we never reach principles that provide unexceptionable descriptive sufficient conditions for overall duty. In framing such generalizations as we can, moreover, Ross is entitled to use reflective equilibrium as a procedure for both discovery and confirmation. Indeed, he foreshadows that procedure toward the end of Chapter 2 where he draws an important analogy between the relation between theory and data in science and that same relation in ethics (40–41).

VII "Resultancy": Ross's Conception of Grounding

Ross is commonly considered a non-naturalist realist. This is partly because he took duties to rest on facts about the world—in a way that implies the existence of moral properties. If duties are grounded in facts—including robustly natural facts such as human actions and sufferings—then we may speak of the property ("attribute") of being a duty. He says, e.g.,

---

[21] Foundations (1939: 190–91). This seems independent of his shift to a "subjective" view of rightness, though the appeal to concurring respected others may suggest some connection. Further evidence of the prospects for "consequential" principles is provided in my (2012).

[22] I take this to include relations among the PFDs, including such facts as that one is stronger than any set of conflicting PFDs.

> In virtue of being the breaking of a promise, for instance, it [the action] tends to be wrong; in virtue of ...... relieving distress it tends to be right. Tendency to be one's duty may be called a parti-resultant attribute, i.e. one which belongs to an act in virtue of some one component in its nature. *Being* one's duty is a toti-resultant attribute, one which belongs to an act in virtue of its whole nature and of nothing less (28).[23]

There seems little question that he means 'in virtue of' to refer to the basis relation now commonly called *grounding* and often (as for Ross), taken to be a relation in which a thing's having a grounding property, say promise-breaking, *necessarily* determines, and in some way explains, its having another property, say prima-facie wrongness. For Ross the resultancy in question is best conceived as a priori and necessary. He likely thought this obviously implicit in its underlying self-evident principles.

In some passages Ross is quite explicitly realist. One major statement is that "The moral order expressed in these propositions [the prima facie duty principles] is just as much a part of the fundamental nature of the universe ...... as is the spatial and numerical structure expressed in the axioms of geometry or arithmetic" (29–30). This puts Ross's moral realism on a par with mathematical realism, a realism that is, for him, at least, neither empiricist nor physicalist: not empiricist because a priori (including self-evident) propositions (contra Hume) need not be analytic, and not physicalist because some of the properties in question are conceived as abstract entities that exist in merely possible universes. If we seek to preserve moral truth and objectivity without robust realism, we must do so for truths of (pure) mathematics as well; if not, then our moral ontology should at least not be less robust than our ontology of mathematics.[24]

Perhaps because of the philosophical continuity between Moore and Ross in rejecting naturalism, philosophers writing on Ross have not generally left room for the possibility that both his realism and his rationalism are compatible with some kind of moral naturalism. It is noteworthy that Ross devotes a great deal of space in RG to refuting naturalistic accounts of duty and of goodness, and this pattern continues in *Foundations*. But, unlike Moore, he does not present a non-naturalistic position as central in his positive theory.

---

[23] Ross may be qualifying the "whole nature" claim in his footnote on p. 33, since clearly not every intrinsic property is morally relevant, but this is not an important matter for the basic notion of grounding (resultancy) he works with. He seems to have in mind the nature of an action properly considered overall, not every element of its nature. A further problem—for any moral theory—is to explain how we should determine what properties belong to the *nature* of an act (act-token or act-type).

[24] Derek Parfit takes the first option in his celebrated (2011), using the term 'nonmetaphysical realism'). This could be construed as one way to answer Gilbert Harman, who said that if the analogy between the knowability of moral principles and that of basic mathematical principles holds, we need an explanation of why this is not a problem for mathematics.

To be sure, we should take Ross as viewing duty and, correspondingly, moral rightness, as conceptually irreducible to any natural property. Nonetheless, both his intuitionist, rationalist moral epistemology and his normative ethics could survive a moderate moral naturalism that works from the kinds of grounds of duty that Ross himself postulates. Suppose, for instance, that the property of being a prima facie duty—obligatoriness for short—*is* simply the disjunctive property of being promised *or* being a rendering of aid to someone suffering *or* (negatively) an avoidance of killing or failing to respond to services rendered . . . . . . and so forth, for all the basic a priori grounds of duty. The idea, in effect, is that obligatoriness is nothing over and above the complete disjunction of its constitutive grounds. Might this disjunctive "property" be a natural one?

There is at least one problem that would prevent Ross's taking this route toward naturalization of obligatoriness (and we are here not even considering goodness). The problem is especially serious if we do not find a way around taking some grounds of duty to be normative, as with Ross's claims that beneficence is in part a matter of seeking to benefit people in their *virtue*, and that the duty of reparation rests on some previous "wrongful act" (21). For Ross, one obstacle to achieving a successful disjunctive reduction is that he said he did not take his list of prima facie duties to be complete. The more important point, however, is that neither Ross's rationalist moral epistemology nor his intuitionism regarding both singular and general moral propositions entails that there cannot be *some* kind of naturalization of moral properties.[25] Non-naturalism is the natural position for any plausible rationalist ethics, but perhaps we can see in Ross the important possibility that in both normative ethics and moral epistemology a rationalist moral philosophy is compatible with certain forms of naturalism.

This paper has not indicated all of Ross's original and important contributions, even in RG alone, but some points have emerged that deserve reiteration. Negatively, Ross's moral theory does not invite dogmatism or absolutism; he is not without resources for principled reconciliations of conflicts of duty; and he need not be taken to deny that we often have what, in commonsense language, would be considered moral knowledge of the truth of many singular moral judgments. More positively, it should be clear that given some revisions of his epistemology and theory of value that are consonant with his overall intuitionism, his moral theory deserves a major place in ethics. His theory of moral obligation is nuanced and eminently defensible in a multitude of its important points; his conception of sound deliberation portrays the interplay between, on an abstract level, moral generality expressed in principles and, on the particularistic level, intuitional specificity focused on concrete cases; and his pluralism about both value and obligation

---

[25] Ch. 8 of my (2023) considers some prospects for naturalization and raises doubts about whether there could *be* a disjunction adequate for naturalizing obligatoriness.

is a framework for guiding commonsense moral conduct and inspiring future reflection.[26]

References

Audi, Robert (1996). "Intuitionism, Pluralism, and the Foundations of Ethics." In Walter Sinnott-Armstrong and Mark Timmons, eds., *Moral Knowledge?* Oxford: Oxford University Press, 1996, 101–136.
Audi, Robert, (1998). *Epistemology: A Contemporary Introduction to the Theory of Knowledge*. London and New York: Routledge.
Audi, Robert (1999). "Self-Evidence." *Philosophical Perspectives*, 13, 205–228.
Audi, Robert (2006). "Moral Generality and Moral Judgment." In James Dreier, ed., *Contemporary Debates in Moral Theory*. Oxford: Blackwell, 285–304.
Audi, Robert (2012). "Kantian Intuitionism as a Framework for the Justification of Moral Judgments." *Oxford Studies in Normative Ethics*, 2, 128–151.
Audi, Robert (2021). "Methodological Reflections on Kant's Ethical Theory." *Synthese*, Supplement 13, : 3155–3170. (Online publication 2018, doi.org/10.1007/s11229-018-01977-x.)
Audi, Robert (2023). *Of Moral Conduct: A Theory of Obligation, Reasons, and Value*. Cambridge: Cambridge University Press.
Dancy, Jonathan (1993). *Moral Reasons*. Oxford: Blackwell.
Huemer, Michael (2005). *Ethical Intuitionism*. Houndmills, Basingstoke, Hampshire: Palgrave Macmillian..
Hurka, Thomas (2014). *British Ethical Theorists from Sidgwick to Ewing*. Oxford: Oxford University Press.
Kant, Immanuel (1785/1997). *Groundwork of the Metaphysics of Morals*, trans. Mary Gregor. Cambridge: Cambridge University Press.
(1788/1996).
Parfit, Derek (2011). *On What Matters*, vol. 1. Oxford: Oxford University Press.
Phillips, David K. (2019). *Rossian Ethics: W. D. Ross and Contemporary Moral Theory*. Oxford: Oxford University Press.
Price, Richard (1787/1974). *A Review of the Principal Questions in Morals*. London. T. Cadell; and (in modern orthography), in D. D. Raphael (1974).
Prichard, H. A. (1912). "Does Moral Philosophy Rest on a Mistake?" *Mind*, 21, 18, 21–37.
Ross, W. D. (1927). "The Basis of Objective Judgements in Ethics." *International Journal of Ethics*, 37, 113–127.
Ross, W. D. (1930). *The Right and the Good*. Oxford: Oxford University Press.
Ross, W. D. (1939). *Foundations of Ethics*. Oxford: Oxford University Press.
Sidgwick, Henry. (1907). *The Methods of Ethics*, 7th ed. London: Macmillan.
Stratton-Lake (2002). Introduction to Ross (1930), ix–lviii.
Stratton-Lake, Philip (ed.) (2002). *The Right and the Good*. Oxford: Oxford University Press, Introduction, ix–lviii.
Theunissen, L. Nandi (2020). *The Value of Humanity*. Oxford: Oxford University Press.
Thomson, Judith Jarvis (1997). "The Right and the Good." *Journal of Philosophy*, 94, 6, 273–298.
Tucker, Christopher (, ed.) (2013). *Seemings and Justification*. Oxford: , Oxford University Press., 2013.

---

[26] For helpful comments on earlier versions or parts of them I thank Guila Cantamessi, Roger Crisp, Brad Hooker, David Kaspar, Greg Robson, the late Philip Stratton-Lake, Nandi Theunissen, and, especially, David K. Phillips.

3
The Prima Facie/Overall Duty Distinction
What is it? Where did it come from? Why does it matter?

Roger Crisp

This paper attempts to elucidate, and to explain the history and the importance of, the distinction between what Ross called 'prima facie' duties and 'overall' duties. The first section outlines Ross's celebrated discussion, distinguishing a conditional account from a comparative account based on the idea of 'tendencies'. Ross's view is set against those of Prichard and Price, and it is suggested that Price could be said to have offered an earlier and clearer account of prima facie duties. The second section shows how Aristotle's ethical view would have been improved through recognition of the distinction. The final section, with reference to the so-called All or Nothing Problem, shows how failure to recognize the prima facie/overall distinction, and again in particular its capacity to explain good aspects of actions which are bad overall, continues to cause unnecessary complications in moral philosophy.

I Prima facie duties: The conditional account

In the excellent introduction to his edition of W. D. Ross's *The Right and the Good* (2002), Philip Stratton-Lake notes that A. C. Ewing, in his *Second Thoughts in Moral Philosophy* (1959: 126), describes Ross's doctrine of prima facie duties as 'one of the most important discoveries of the [twentieth] century in moral philosophy'.[1]

Stratton-Lake finds the description 'over the top', but accepts that the doctrine does advance our understanding of morality. First, it can allow that we sometimes ought to break a promise in order to prevent a bad outcome 'without conceding everything to the consequentialist'. Second, it shows how deontologists can admit conflicts of duties or obligations without those conflicts constituting 'tragic dilemmas', in which we cannot help but do wrong in failing to act on one or more obligations. This, Stratton-Lake suggests, is because the doctrine 'allows us to think of

---

[1] Ross 2002: xxxvii. See also e.g. McCloskey 1963: 336; Atwell 1978: 240; Dancy 2015: 102; Phillips 2019: 13. It is worth noting that Stratton-Lake wisely retained the original pagination of the 1930 edition.

Roger Crisp, *The Prima Facie/Overall Duty Distinction* In: *The Moral Philosophy of W. D. Ross*. Edited by: Robert Audi and David Phillips, Oxford University Press. © Oxford University Press 2025.
DOI: 10.1093/9780198914839.003.0003

moral conflict not as a conflict of duties, but as a conflict of moral reasons, which is, I believe, how things are'.[2]

I also believe that a grasp of the main idea behind Ross's doctrine helps in understanding morality, and, indeed, in not misunderstanding it.[3] Later in the paper, I shall show how it provides a better, because fuller, account of morality than Aristotle's (which was already a major advance on what came before), and how a grasp of it enables one to avoid problems which continue to arise if it is left unrecognized. I shall suggest also that the main elements of the doctrine can be found in philosophy prior to Ross.

But first let us examine Ross's own account—or perhaps I should say 'accounts'. The first is what we might call the *conditional account*:

> I suggest 'prima facie duty' or 'conditional duty' as a brief way of referring to the characteristic (quite distinct from that of being a duty proper) which an act has, in virtue of being a certain kind (e.g. the keeping of a promise), of being an act which would be a duty proper if it were not at the same time of another kind which is morally significant. (2002: 19)

Ross does not mean to suggest that my prima facie duty to keep my promise is not unconditional. Rather, his thought is that it is prima facie if there is some other duty that overrides it. Immediately after the passage, Ross apologizes for his terminology. First, he says, the phrase 'prima facie duty' is misleading, in that it refers not to a certain kind of duty, but to 'something related in a special way to duty'. And, second, 'prima facie' might be taken to refer to the *appearance* a moral situation might have 'at first sight', whereas in fact he is speaking about 'an objective fact involved in the nature of the situation, or more strictly in an element of its nature'.[4]

As Ross begins to elucidate his view, it becomes clear that his first apology was unnecessary. Prima facie duties are duties.[5] But they are indeed related as well to 'duty *proper*', since it is in light of (though not on the basis of) duty proper that they are explained in the conditional account. Ross might, however, apologize for the condition itself. Taken in its most straightforward sense, his definition seems to apply only to duties which are outweighed by others.[6] The keeping of a particular

---

[2] See also see Baier 1958: 102–3; Ewing 1959: 63, 110; Jack 1966: 521; Urmson 1975: 113; Searle 1978: 84, 87; Audi 2004: 22, 24, 158. Ross himself speaks of the 'grounds' of rightness (2002: 46).

[3] See Snare 1974: 235–6. For helpful recent exegesis of Ross, see Audi 2004: esp. Ch. 2; Hurka 2014: esp. 3.2; Phillips 2019: esp. Chs. 2–3.

[4] In 1939: 84, Ross allows that prima facie obligations (i.e. duties) are obligations. He also justifies his use of 'prima facie': these are the moral aspects of a situation that we notice first.

[5] See e.g. Searle 1978: 83–4.

[6] Hurka (2014: 72) reads the definition as circular, taking the moral significance in the definition to be the property of being a prima facie duty. But there merely being a competing prima facie duty does not prevent a prima facie duty's being one's overall duty: it must be outweighed. Hurka sees the conditional account as a consequence of the tendency account, preferring the latter (as do I).

not especially significant promise, then, might be a prima facie duty in so far as it would be one's duty were it not the case that keeping it would be seriously maleficent.[7] But I presume Ross does not mean to be offering merely an account of what it is to be an outweighed duty. In this case, there are two prima facie duties, of fidelity and non-maleficence, and one's proper or overall duty is non-maleficence; and in a case where there were no countervailing duty, my prima facie duty would also be my overall duty.

Indeed, we might ask Ross to go further and apologize for introducing conditionality at all. Imagine that you and a friend are standing in front of a balance scale, with two pans. Your friend points at one of the weights, and asks you what it is. You answer that it is an object such that, if placed on one scale, it might be countered to some extent by another weight placed on the other side. That is an odd response. You might have offered a much simpler definition by answering that the object has weight, and can be placed on one side of the scale. Your friend might then ask what is meant by the tipping of the scale, and here you could answer that it is the movement of a pan downwards through its containing greater overall weight. The notion of weight, then, is explanatorily prior to that of tipping, as indeed are those of grounds to prima facie duty and of prima facie to overall duty.[8]

Ross is right, then, to suggest that the phrase 'prima facie' may be misleading. But as a piece of philosophical jargon, to assist us in grasping or referring to the simple contrast between 'a duty' and 'duty proper' (or 'duty *sans phrase*' (2002: 19) or 'actual duty' (2002: 20),[9] or, as I prefer, 'overall duty', it seems to me unobjectionable.[10] Seeking a better term, Ross turns to Prichard's suggested alternative: 'claim'. Ross sees some merit in this idea, thinking that 'it seems to cover much of the ground'. For example, he notes approvingly, it seems natural to say that 'a person to whom I have made a promise has a claim on me'. But his first objection to the suggestion, in the light of this example, shows that it should have been rejected outright:

[W]hile 'claim' is appropriate from *their* point of view, we want a word to express the corresponding fact from the agent's point of view—the fact of his being subject to claims that can be made against him; and ordinary language provides us with no such correlative to 'claim'. (2002: 20)

---

[7] If we read the definition in this sense, the common charge (see e.g. Atwell 1978: 242) that Ross's account is circular, in so far as the notion of overriding moral significance is itself equivalent to that of an overriding prima facie duty, can be side-stepped. And, if the common-sense interpretation of Ross I shall next explain is correct, he can offer a simple definition of a prima facie duty without circularity.
[8] I am grateful to Robert Audi for this point.
[9] See Audi 2004: 206n24.
[10] Several authors have suggested using 'pro tanto' rather than 'prima facie'. It would have been a better phrase for Ross to choose, but given the prominence of his view it is probably more straightforward at this point to retain his terminology. I admit, however, that keeping it runs the risk of encouraging a potentially misleading distinction between prima facie duties and pro tanto reasons (the phrase 'prima facie reason' is rarely heard). For discussion, see Audi 000: 000.

But of course it does: 'duty'. Claims, so understood, are not duties, but rights;[11] and, even worse, it is not unnatural to speak of prima facie rights as well as of prima facie duties. (Ross's second objection, that we might have a duty to cultivate our own character, is therefore unnecessary, but does bring out a problem for those who believe that all duties must be directed and correlative with rights.)[12]

It seems, however, that Ross misunderstood Prichard (and that Prichard apparently never pointed this out). In his 'What Is the Basis of Moral Obligation?' (n.d.; first published in 2002), in connection with what we ought to do when obligations conflict, Prichard says:

> We can ... point out (a) that obligations admit of degrees, (b) that in a case of conflict the question is simply 'which obligation is the greater?', (c) that in the end the question can only be answered by our immediate recognition, when all the circumstances have been taken into account, that one is the greater or the greatest, (d) that the problem is often one of extreme difficulty, but (e) that in any case there is no general criterion for solving it. (2002: 6)

Later (probably), Prichard is less happy with the idea that obligations can conflict. In 'A Conflict of Duties' (from lecture notes of 1928), Prichard allows that there are things that can be said in favour of the idea that duties can conflict, such as that someone faced with such a conflict may feel that what they do will be wronging someone, or that it is not absurd to speak of degrees of obligation and wrongness (2002: 78). But he goes on: '[I]f we think that of two acts there is a greater obligation to do one of them, we cannot go on to think that we ought to do that action without implying that there is no obligation to do the other in any degree whatever' (2002: 79). Prichard solves the problem by redescribing what might seem a conflict of duties as a conflict of 'claims', these claims being made on us *by the circumstances*.

What Prichard calls a 'claim' here is indeed what Ross calls a 'prima facie duty'.[13] Further, Ross's distinction enables us to see what is wrong with Prichard's argument against speaking of conflicts of duties or obligations. If I say that you have greater obligation to φ than to ψ, and there is no plausible third option in the offing, then I mean that you have a duty, overall, to fulfil your duty to φ than your

---

[11] As Philip Stratton-Lake pointed out to me, this has the consequence that the account will be inapplicable to prima facie duties where there is no corresponding prima facie right (e.g. perhaps a duty not to damage the environment). This problem is avoided if a claim is made 'by the circumstances': see second paragraph in the text below.

[12] In 1939: 85, Ross repeats his objections against Prichard's suggestion, but accepts Carritt's 'responsibility' instead. On the following page, Ross nevertheless continues to use the language of prima facie obligation, switching to responsibility in the final sentence of the chapter: 'responsibilities [i.e. prima facie duties] have often been overstated as being absolute obligations admitting of no exception, and the unreal problem of conflict of duties has thus been supposed to exist'. In 1939: 315, Ross mentions the term 'suitabilities' as yet another alternative to 'prima facie duties'.

[13] Cf. Hurka 2014: 73.

duty to ψ. You have an overall duty, that is to say, not to ψ, but it does not follow that you have no duty to ψ. Imagine that you could just wander off without doing either action. You have no duty to do that, as well as an overall duty not to, and it would have been morally preferable at least to ψ. This is in effect what Ross meant by his distinction, though of course, as I have just shown, we can often say everything we want using just the indefinite article without the phrase 'prima facie'. Prichard saw the facts here well enough, but—probably because he thought it odd to say that one could have a duty which it was one's overall duty not to act on (though that is exactly the point)[14]—was unable to state the obvious: that we have an overriding, or overall, moral duty, or obligation, when obligations conflict, to fulfil the strongest set of non-overall or prima facie obligations (that is, the weightiest set of duties, and the set may, of course, contain only one duty).[15] (To avoid double-counting, this moral duty is best not understood merely as 'a duty', as if it were one among others. Overall duties have no weight in their own right.)

If we now return to Ewing's assessment of Ross, it seems mistaken at least in so far as Prichard had recognized the distinction, though as we have seen he used the term 'claim' instead of 'prima facie duty'.[16] After the publication of *The Right and the Good*, Prichard wrote to Ross to say that he also saw 'prima facie duty' as equivalent to 'a duty', but that what Ross called 'duty sans phrase' is really 'that of a man's duties which he most ought to do' (2002: 287). Doubtless the latter claim arises from Prichard's mistaken worry (as we have seen, sometimes shared by Ross) about conflicts of obligations; but the issues here all seem largely verbal.[17]

II Prima facie duties: The tendency account

Slightly later in *The Right and the Good*, Ross briefly offers a different and non-conditional account of prima facies duties, using the notion of 'tendency': 'We

---

[14] See Searle 1978: 87–9.

[15] Kant ran into similar difficulties: see Timmermann 2013. As we have seen, Ross was also sometimes queasy about allowing that prima facie duties are really duties (see also 1939: 84–5: 'the phrase "prima facie obligation" ... seems to say that prima facie obligations are one kind of obligation, while they are in fact something different; for we are *not* obliged to do that which is only prima facie obligatory'). But at other times he comes much closer to understanding the implications of his own position: 'right acts can be distinguished from wrong acts only as being those which, of all those possible for the agent in the circumstances, have the greatest balance of prima facie rightness, in those respects in which they are prima facie right, over their prima facie wrongness, in those respects in which they are prima facie wrong' (2002: 41; see also 46: 'The more correct answer ... in which it is prima facie wrong'; 1939: 84: 'And secondly ... totality of its aspects'; 1939: 109: 'No doubt ... that is more stringent'; 1939: 315: 'Now, taking rightness first ... have this characteristic').

[16] See Hurka 2014: 70 (Hurka describes the distinction as a 'major innovation' [see also 71, 78]); Dancy 2015: 108.

[17] According to a suggestion by Stratton-Lake, the point here is not merely verbal, since 'there is no sense in which I am obligated to do the wrong act'. But we might say that there is such a sense: one is 'prima facie obligated'.

have to distinguish from the characteristic of being our duty that of tending to be our duty' (28). 'Tend' has a frequentative sense in English, and some have understood Ross to be speaking here in this way.[18] But it also has a kinetic sense,[19] as when we speak of a ship's 'tending to leeward',[20] and this is almost certainly what Ross had in mind, since he goes on to use an analogy with natural forces:

> Qua subject to the force of gravitation towards some other body, each body tends to move in a particular direction with a particular velocity; but its actual movement depends on *all* the forces to which it is subject. (2002: 28–9)

How might we elucidate this notion of 'tendency'? Should we, for example, understand it in terms of moral reasons? This makes sense in so far as duties are construed as moral reasons; but not in so far as some moral reasons may not be duties, but supererogatory. One might speak of 'non-optional moral reasons', but it is probably simpler to stick with the distinction between 'duty' and 'overall duty', understood in terms of an overall or 'meta-'duty always to act on one's strongest set of obligations. Ross's analogy with gravity is an attempt to elucidate this notion of strength, or weight. But to me the analogy seems unnecessary, and here the reference to reasons is helpful. We all know what it is for one reason to be weightier or stronger than another, perhaps weightier or stronger than any other, and hence our 'overall reason'. Since duties are reasons, then, we all know what it is for one duty to be weightier or stronger than another, perhaps weightier or stronger than any other, and hence our 'overall duty'. The notion of a reason is basic or fundamental,[21] and, though there is much to be said about what makes a reason a *moral* reason in particular, that issue is independent of the distinction between the notion of a duty, and duty overall.

Prichard's focus on conflicts of duties, and Ross's analogy of conflicting forces, may be helpful to some in enabling them to grasp the nature of duties. But it is worth noting that both their points were made at least equally, if not more, clearly a century and a half or so earlier by Richard Price, in the seventh chapter of his *Review of the Principal Questions in Morals*.[22] Price is mainly concerned with the

---

[18] E.g. Strawson 1949: 29; see Hurka 2014: 73.

[19] See OED 2021: I.c; also I.3.a, b(a). See Hurka 2014: 72. Hurka (2014: 73–8) provides strong arguments for preferring this account to Ross's later account (1939: 51–3, 79–82).

[20] The OED provides an independent section for the nautical usage: I.4.a. Note that the scale of a balance may 'tend' in one or other direction, which provides us with a link here to the notion of 'weight' (and indeed 'weightier' and 'weightiest').

[21] See Scanlon: 1998: 3; Crisp 2006: 8; Parfit: 2011: 31. Note that this claim is consistent with the claim that other notions are also basic or fundamental.

[22] Ross himself refers to Price's views on rightness as 'fitness' in 1939: 54n. As pointed out by O'Neill (2013: 259), Kant expresses something like Ross's distinction in *The Metaphysics of Morals*, a decade after the third edition of Price's *Review*. This is one of several anticipations in Price of important views now commonly known as 'Kantian'; see e.g. McNaughton 2019.

implications of moral disagreement, but it is clear that he anticipates Ross's non-conditional, tendency account (which I take to be preferable to the unnecessarily complex, back-to-front conditional account):

> Until men can be raised above defective knowledge, and secured against partial and inadequate views, they must continue liable to believe cases and facts and the *tendencies* of actions, to be otherwise than they are. (1974: 172; my italics)[23]

Chapter 7 is concerned with what Price calls the 'principal heads and divisions', or 'branches', of virtue, that is, the individual virtues as properties of persons or their actions: piety, prudence, beneficence, gratitude, veracity, and justice. Having elucidated these, Price notes (1974: 166–7) that though the heads of virtue can agree in recommending the same action, they can also conflict and 'lead us contrary ways'. He goes on: 'This perhaps has not been enough attended to, and therefore I shall particularly insist upon it'. He does not claim to have 'discovered' the distinction, then, but—rightly, I shall suggest below—does think it deserves greater attention. Having given some examples of conflicts of duty, such as those between friendship or justice on the one hand, and public good on the other, Price continues:

> [I]t is not possible for us to judge always and accurately, what degrees or circumstances of any one of these compared with the others, will or will not cancel its obligation, and justify the violation of it.—It is thus likewise, that the different foundations of property give rise to contrary claims, and that sometimes it becomes very hard to say which of different titles to an object is the best.—If we examine the various intricate and disputed cases in morality, we shall, I believe, find that it is always some interference of this kind that produces the obscurity. Truth and right in all circumstances, require one determinate way of acting; but so variously may different obligations combine with or oppose each other in particular cases, and so imperfect are our discerning faculties, that it cannot but happen, that we should be frequently in the dark, and that different persons should judge differently, according to the different views they have of the several moral principles. Nor is this less unavoidable, or more to be wondered at, than that in matters of mere speculation, we should be at a loss to know what is true, when the arguments for and against a proposition appear nearly equal. (1974: 167–8)

---

[23] Price does sometimes use the frequentative sense of 'tendency'; but he also often employs the non-frequentative sense, speaking for example of a state in which the 'natural tendencies' of good and bad things will be 'no more interrupted *in their operation*' (1974: 269; my italics), and of the 'tendencies and consequences' of a *particular* (benevolent) action, as opposed to a type of action (1974: 169).

Price also anticipates the analogy with forces,[24] claiming that asserting that there are no 'moral distinctions' because it is hard to decide which moral principle is overriding in a conflict:

> is not unlike concluding, that, because in some circumstances we cannot, by their appearance to the eye, judge of the distances and magnitude of bodies, therefore we never can; because undeniable principles may be used in proving and opposing particular doctrines, therefore these principles are not undeniable; or because it may not in some instances be easy to determine what will be the effect of different forces, various compounded and acting contrary to each other; therefore we can have no assurance what any of them acting separately will produce, or so much as know that there is any such thing as force. (1974: 168)

The implication, then, is that:

> [I]n order to discover what is right in a case, we ought to extend our views to all the different *heads* of virtue, to examine how far each is concerned, and compare their influence [i.e. 'force' or 'weight'] and demands. (1974: 170)

If anyone deserved Ewing's praise, then, Price has a stronger claim than Ross. Prichard and Ross appear to have seen Price's point,[25] but if anything, rather than explaining it straightforwardly to their contemporaries, concealed it behind unnecessary complications and worries about how we might have duties it would be wrong to perform.

III Aristotle

I shall now provide a couple of illustrations of how apparent failure to properly recognize the distinction between prima facie duties and overall duty can cause problems in moral philosophy.

The first is Aristotle's account of virtue. His 'doctrine of the mean', outlined in *EN* II. 6, has often been mistaken for a doctrine of moderation (Williams 1986: 36), or misinterpreted as empty (Barnes 1976) or absurdly quantitative (Urmson 1973; Hursthouse 1980). There are certainly some confusions in Aristotle's explanation and application of the doctrine, which suggest to me that he had not fully understood it himself, but its basic idea—that through a focus on some emotion

---

[24] According to Stratton-Lake, Ross may be understood as moving beyond the mere notion that duties can conflict (as in Price and Prichard) to the idea that the *grounds* of duty can conflict. But as I understand both Price and Prichard, they recognize that the conflicts between duties in particular cases arise from certain contingent facts in those cases giving rise to conflicting obligations.
[25] Prichard quotes Price on obligation and fitness in his 'Moral Obligation' (2002: 215–16).

or action, one can create a tripartite taxonomy of a virtue alongside a deficient and an excessive vice—seems to me an important insight which contemporary theorists of virtue have largely failed to recognize (this failure probably being caused by widespread acceptance of the various misinterpretations of the doctrine in the secondary literature).

Although Aristotle's list of relevant emotions and actions is, plausibly enough, open-ended, he himself rightly concentrates on paradigmatic cases, since these will play the greatest role in the virtuous life. Consider, say, anger. The virtuous person is the one who feels anger at the right time, for the right reasons, towards the right people, in the right way (for the right amount of time, for example), and so forth. The bad-tempered person is the one who feels anger at the wrong time, for the wrong reasons, and so on, while the deficient vice—whatever we want to call it—consists in a failure to feel anger at the right time, for the right reasons, and so on. As Aristotle makes clear in his discussion of generosity, one implication of his view is that a person may have both vices. (It might be thought that a person disposed to anger at the right and wrong times, and so on, if imaginable, would have both the virtue and the excessive vice. But this would be a mistake: the person who is angry at the right times is the one who gets it right in the domain of time; by getting angry at the wrong times, one demonstrates the excessive vice.)

The analysis works equally well for actions: the generous person (if we ignore Aristotle's peculiar inclusion within the sphere of that virtue of 'taking from the right sources') is the one who gives away money at the right time, to the right people, and so on, and the two vices can be plotted in the same way as those concerning anger. The doctrine does not cover *all* virtues, in particular of course justice, with which Aristotle struggles in Book V. But—perhaps unlike him—we can see why that is the case. There is no neutral emotion or action underlying the virtue of justice, which can be used to describe an excessive and a deficient vice. Justice, as Bernard Williams (1980) brought out so well, is bivalent: either you are just (and concerned with being just, promoting just outcomes, ensuring just procedures, and so on), or you are not. But given that there are so many neutral actions and emotions, to demonstrate that in principle they can *all* be used to ground triadic accounts of virtue is a huge achievement in the history of ethics.

Unfortunately, however—and this may be another consequence of Aristotle's not having spent sufficient time on the doctrine to understand quite what he had discovered—Aristotle's view as stated not only fails to include explicit recognition of conflicts of duty, but wrongly categorizes what we would call actions done in accordance with a 'defeated' duty as entirely vicious, in the relevant sphere. Consider a conflict between, say, generosity and temperance. You are entertaining an honoured guest from some distant land, and have treated them to a dinner at a fine restaurant. They are keen on alcoholic drinks, as are you, but their capacity for alcohol is clearly significantly greater than yours. You are tempted to have a whisky with your coffee, and know your guest would enjoy one also, but you realize that—given your limited capacity—it would be intemperate of you to order one. You recognize that other things equal it would be generous to offer your guest a whisky; but you know also that, if you will not take one yourself, they will decline, and this will bring the meal to an awkward conclusion. Further, taking it without drinking would also be awkward, as your guest is savvy enough to recognize what you have done and not drinking may anyway seem lacking in collegiality.

This looks very much like what Price would call a conflict between two 'heads of virtue'. Let us assume that, after some reflection, you rightly conclude that you should refrain from mentioning the whisky. Your overall duty, then, is temperance, and in being temperate you are indeed hitting the mean in the sphere of bodily pleasure. But, still, there remains something to be said, morally, for ordering whiskies for both of you. In other words, your action would not be morally perfect, and hence right, but it would not be completely wrong in all respects. Unfortunately Aristotle nowhere explicitly allows for this. As well as being intemperate, through buying the whisky you would be spending money at the wrong time, and perhaps in the wrong way, thus meeting the conditions for your action's being excessively vicious.

The problem arises here for Aristotle because of his focus on the value of hitting the target and consequent failure to consider the possible value in certain misses, that is, in what we might call 'overall vicious' or 'overall wrong' actions:

> [O]ne can miss the mark in many ways (since the bad belongs to the unlimited, as the Pythagoreans portrayed it, and the good to the limited), but one can get things right in only one (for which reason one is easy and the other difficult). (2014: 1106b)

Imagine that instead of spending your money on two whiskies, you buy two brandies, fully aware that both of you have a strong preference for whisky. This is even *worse* than buying the whisky, since it involves spending money on the wrong object, as well as failing to meet the conditions unmet in buying the whisky. Or imagine that, after your not mentioning the whisky, the waiter offers—at a price—a commemorative box of chocolates. It would be perfectly reasonable for you to think: 'Well, other things equal, I should have ordered my guest a whisky, and if I had done that then buying these chocolates as well would be excessive. But I didn't order the whisky, so I'll make up for that by buying the chocolates'. On Aristotle's view, as he states it, there is nothing to make up for; and similarly, to use the standard example from our period, if you break a promise to a friend to meet them for tea, so that you can tend to someone seriously injured, you have nothing to apologize for. Aristotle's view, then, in this respect lacks moral nuance. He does not explicitly recognize that the properties of some action, which would ground its being virtuous were there no conflict with an overriding duty, remain in place and hence enable an action which it is one's overall duty not to do nevertheless to have something positive to be said for it from the moral point of view. (Indeed perhaps Aristotle was troubled by the same pseudo-problem as sometimes troubled Prichard and Ross: how one could have a duty it was one's overall duty not to act on.)

This is not to say that a view which allows for such cases would be in any kind of tension with the main thesis underlying the doctrine of the mean. Take an instance in which you have gravely wronged me, in such a way that anger is called for. If I do get angry with you (the right person), for the right reasons, at the right time, and with the right motive, but I remain angry for too long, then my response is morally defective and I have failed to hit the target and hence my response is vicious. This is a reasonable enough position as far as overall duty is concerned: I have indeed missed the target. But I missed it by only a little, and I got a lot of things right. The target analogy can be extended to cover such cases, if, first, we allow a separate target for each relevant aspect of virtue: time, object, person, reason, motive, and manner. One's overall duty is to hit every target on every occasion. If one misses a single target, as in the case above, one may nevertheless have hit other targets, and therefore deserve some credit for, as well as criticism of, one's performance. And, of course, the importance of hitting any particular target in any particular case will depend on the circumstances. If I had got angry for the right length of time, but with the wrong person, that would have been a much more serious error. A point will come at which it would have been better not to respond at all rather than respond in a defective way.

We might then go on to postulate these individual targets within the sphere of concern of any virtue (anger, giving away money, or whatever). One's prima facie duties, then, are to hit the relevant set of targets in that sphere, and in a conflict of duty, such as that in the dinner case, the person who acts overall wrongly may nevertheless have hit several targets in a certain sphere and for that reason deserve some moral credit, perhaps enough to justify their response as morally preferable to no response. Some actions (and perhaps feelings), that is to say, are morally best, and hence overall right; others are overall wrong, but morally better or worse than one another. Indeed, we might even want to allow that someone who kept missing the moral target within the sphere of individual virtues considered independently, or, in conflicts of duties, always performed the 'defeated' duty in those conflicts, especially if the performances were better than nothing, the errors minor, and the conflicts quite finely balanced, could have a life of *some* virtue, containing *some* degree of nobility, and *some* happiness.

IV The All or Nothing Problem

Let me now mention a more recent example of a case where recognizing the distinction between prima facie duties and overall duty may be helpful. In an ingenious paper, Joe Horton (2017) sets out what he calls the 'All or Nothing Problem'. Imagine that two children are about to be crushed by a collapsing building. You have three options: a) do nothing; b) save one child, which will involve the crushing of your arms; c) save both children, which also will involve the crushing of your arms (to the same degree as in (b), and, we should assume, without any additional harms).

As Horton suggests, the following two claims are highly plausible:

(1) It is morally permissible for you not to save the children.
(2) It is morally wrong for you to save only one child.

The first claim is plausible because the great cost to you of saving them makes the action one of supererogation: you do not violate any overall duty by refraining, and hence are permitted to do so. And the second is plausible because, if you save only one child, you will have left the second to die for no good reason.

But, Horton continues, these two plausible claims appear to imply the following:

(3) You ought to save neither child rather than save only one.

As Horton says, this conclusion seems highly counterintuitive. Imagine that you were outside the building yourself, though for some reason unable to enter it. If some other potential rescuer made it clear that they were prepared to save one child, but not two, and asked you for moral advice, would you advise them to save neither? What we want, as Horton puts it, is a moral view which would 'not discourage you' from saving the two children rather than doing nothing—and indeed, we might add, provide some *encouragement* to save the one rather than do nothing.

Horton's own solution involves replacing (1) with:

(1*) If you were not willing to save either child, it would be permissible for you not to save either, but *because you are willing to save one, you ought to save both*.

And this allows him to replace (3) with:

(3*) Because you are willing to save one child, you ought to save both, but if you are not going to save both,[26] you ought to do the next best thing, which is to save one. That is, you ought to save one child rather than save neither.

---

[26] I.e., I presume, 'it is not the case that you will save both'.

A serious problem with (1*), as Horton recognizes, is that it involves denying (1) in cases in which you are willing to save either one or both children. Whether or not an action is supererogatory is usually thought to depend not on whether or not the agent is willing to perform it, but solely on whether (a) the action is not required by duty and (b) praiseworthy. (3*) is also problematic, in that it makes your duties depend not only on what you are willing to do, but on what you are in fact going to do. Duties are most plausibly, and almost always have been, understood as not conditional on the agent's desires, intentions, or will, or on facts about what they will or will not do: they are unconditional, that is, categorical.

Philip Stratton-Lake drew my attention to the fact that a more straightforward solution here is to add the following wide-scope 'ought' to (1):

(1**) It is morally permissible for you not to save the children. But you ought, if you save the first child, to save the second.

This is consistent with the claim that it is not the case that you ought to save both, and that it is the case that it would be wrong to save one. And it avoids any reference to the agent's will or to what they will do. But of course we still require something to *encourage* saving one rather than neither.

Here the notion of prima facie duties allows a straightforward solution to the All or Nothing Problem. This can be seen especially clearly if we consider a case like Horton's, but with two variations. First, there are one hundred children and, if they are not rescued, they are going to suffer very long and excruciating deaths; and, second, with them in the building is a moderately cheerful but elderly parrot, with only a very short time left to live.[27] When the building collapses, unless it is rescued, the parrot will die immediately. The following claims seem plausible:

(1**) It is morally permissible for you not to save the children and the parrot.
(2**) It is morally wrong for you to save only the children and not the parrot.

Here it becomes even clearer that any reasonable moral view will not imply:

(3**) You ought to save neither the children nor the parrot rather than save only the children.

Now Ross's view is somewhat discouraging in this way, in so far as it implies that saving just the children is overall wrong. But, since this is also Horton's view, his view is at this point equally discouraging. It might be thought that Ross's position cannot be used to address the All or Nothing Problem, since that problem involves

---

[27] Compare the case described in Kagan 1989: 16.

the notion of supererogation, which Ross did not incorporate into his account. But in fact including it in a Rossian account is quite straightforward. We might, for example, claim that the prima facie duty of prudence (or 'self-improvement') allows for a certain degree of discretion on the agent's part on whether or not to sacrifice their own interests to advance those of others (that is, to act on their prima facie duty of beneficence).[28]

At this point, then, a Rossian can refer to prima facie duties, and the degrees of rightness and wrongness, and strength of reason, they imply.[29] It is true that if you save the hundred children you will be doing something overall wrong; but it is not *very* wrong. And your prima facie duty of beneficence, though it speaks *most* strongly and encouragingly in favour of saving both the children and the parrot, also speaks *very* strongly and encouragingly in favour of saving only the children.

In the original case, saving only one child would indeed be a significant wrong. But most people, including Horton, will believe that it is better to commit that wrong than to do nothing. And here a positive appeal to the prima facie duty of beneficence provides a solid basis for moral encouragement, without denying the categoricity of duty, to save one child rather than neither.

V Conclusion

The distinction between the particular duties an agent might have at a particular time and their overall duty at that time is crucial to philosophical ethics. As I have shown, with reference to Aristotle and Horton, one important upshot of failing to recognize it is an inability to provide a straightforward explanation of how actions which are overall wrong can, at least sometimes, have something morally to be said in their favour. Ross is often credited with 'discovering' the distinction. It is true that he provides a good account of it, using the notion of 'tendencies', but also that Prichard appears to have grasped it and that the main elements of the notion are found in the much earlier work of Price.[30]

---

[28] I myself find the notion of supererogation problematic (see Crisp 2013). It is possible that Ross's failure to include it in his theory was a result of the (I would say, benign) influence on him of ancient, especially Aristotelian, ethics.

[29] Horton could also refer to these, of course; but then there would be no need to postulate conditional duties.

[30] An earlier version of this paper was presented at a conference on Ross in April 2022, at the University of Notre Dame. I am most grateful to Robert Audi for inviting me to speak, and to the audience for comments and discussion. For further written comments and discussion, I am indebted to Robert Audi, Brad Hooker, Theron Pummer, John Skorupski, and my deeply missed friend and colleague Philip Stratton-Lake.

References

Atwell, J. 1978. 'Ross and Prima Facie Duties', *Ethics* 88: 240–9.
Aristotle. 2014. *Nicomachean Ethics*, trans. R. Crisp, rev. edn. Cambridge: Cambridge University Press.
Audi, R. 2004. *The Good in the Right*. Princeton: Princeton University Press.
Baier, K. 1958. *The Moral Point of View: A Rational Basis of Ethics*. Ithaca: Cornell University Press.
Barnes, J. 1976. 'Introduction' to Aristotle, *Nicomachean Ethics*, trans. J. Thomson and H. Tredennick. Harmondsworth: Penguin.
Crisp, R. 2013. 'Supererogation and Virtue', *Oxford Studies in Normative Ethics* 3: 13–34.
Ewing, A. C. 1959. *Second Thoughts in Moral Philosophy*. London: Routledge and Kegan Paul.
Dancy, J. 2015. 'More Right than Wrong', in M. Timmons and R. Johnson (eds), *Reason, Value, and Respect: Kantian Themes from the Philosophy of Thomas E. Hill, Jr*. Oxford: Oxford University Press, 101–18.
Horton, J. 2017. 'The All or Nothing Problem', *Journal of Philosophy* 114: 94–104.
Hurka, T. 2014. *British Ethical Theorists from Sidgwick to Ewing*. Oxford: Oxford University Press.
Hursthouse, R. 1980. 'A False Doctrine of the Mean', *Proceedings of the Aristotelian Society* 81: 57–72.
Jack, H. H. 1966. 'More on Prima Facie Duties', *Journal of Philosophy* 63: 521–3.
Kagan, S. 1989. *The Limits of Morality*. Oxford: Clarendon Press.
McCloskey, H. J. 1963. 'Ross and the Concept of a "Prima Facie" Duty', *Australasian Journal of Philosophy* 41: 336–45.
McNaughton, D. 2019. 'Richard Price', in E. Zalta (ed.), *Stanford Encyclopedia of Philosophy* (Winter 2019 Edition), https://plato.stanford.edu/archives/win2019/entries/richard-price/.
OED 2021. 'Tend, v.2', OED Online, December 2021. Oxford: Oxford University Press, https://ezproxy-prd.bodleian.ox.ac.uk:2446/view/Entry/199030?rskey=r9KIKg&result=4 (accessed 4 January 2022).
O'Neill, O. 2013. *Acting on Principle*, 2nd edn. Cambridge: Cambridge University Press.
Parfit, D. 2011. *On What Matters*, vol. 1. Oxford: Oxford University Press.
Phillips, D. 2019. *Rossian Ethics: W. D. Ross and Contemporary Moral Theory*. New York: Oxford University Press.
Prichard, H. A. 2002. *Moral Writings*, ed. J. MacAdam. Oxford: Clarendon Press.
Price, R. 1974. *A Review of the Principal Questions in Morals*, ed. D. D. Raphael. Oxford: Clarendon Press.
Ross, W. D. 1939. *The Foundations of Ethics*. Oxford: Clarendon Press.
Ross, W. D. 2002. *The Right and the Good*, ed. P. Stratton-Lake. Oxford: Clarendon Press.
Scanlon, T. M. 1998. *What We Owe to Each Other*. Cambridge, MA: Belknap Press.
Searle, J. R. 1978. 'Prima Facie Obligations', in J. Raz (ed.), *Practical Reasoning*. Oxford: Oxford University Press, 81–90.
Snare, F. 1974. 'The Definition of Prima Facie Duties', *Philosophical Quarterly* 24: 235–44.
Strawson, P. F. 1949. 'Ethical Intuitionism', *Philosophy* 24: 23–33.
Timmermann, J. 2013. 'Kantian Dilemmas? Moral Conflict in Kant's Ethical Theory', *Archiv für Geschichte der Philosophie* 95: 36–64.
Urmson, J. O. 1973. 'Aristotle's Doctrine of the Mean', *American Philosophical Quarterly* 10: 223–30.
Urmson, J. O. 1975. 'A Defence of Intuitionism', *Proceedings of the Aristotelian Society* 75: 111–19.
Williams, B. 1980. 'Justice as a Virtue', in A. O. Rorty (ed.), *Essays on Aristotle's Ethics*. Berkeley: University of California Press, 189–200.
Williams, B. 1986. *Ethics and the Limits of Philosophy*. London: Fontana.

4
Ross and the Foundations of Morality

Garrett Cullity

Ross's substantive moral theory—his theory of the content of morality—exhibits a distinctive type of pluralism. It is a pluralism about what makes right acts right: a view of the structure of morality according to which there is more than one foundational right-maker.

This is attractive in several ways. Its picture of the structure of morality is faithful to an important part of moral experience—the experience of conflicting priorities that must be balanced against each other. It allows that often such conflicts can be resolved, since one of the conflicting considerations is weightier than the other, but that the consideration outweighed can still count in favor of the action that ought not, all things considered, to be done. It eschews the search for verdictive principles of the form "All acts of type T are morally right"; but it does so without giving up the ambition of providing an explanation of morality's underlying structure. Ross offers us a model for answering the question "What makes right acts right?" that is not subsumptive but instead compositional.[1] We explain what makes right acts right not by subsuming them as instances under general principles of that verdictive form, but rather by identifying the most basic elements of morality and then examining their relative importance in a given context. A moral theory of the kind Ross advocates allows that the determination of right action is nuanced and context-specific; but it does so without trying to write all of the nuance into a set of justificatory principles whose content is so complicated that moral justification becomes esoteric. It allows that the justifications for right action can be as simple as "Because I promised"—and therefore that they are available to be *given* by ordinary responsible moral agents to each other.

Rossian pluralism, as I shall define it in Section I, is a genus of substantive moral theories that share these attractions. Ross's own theory is one specific member of that genus. His own view treats as foundational a set of "general principles of prima facie duty":[2] on the now-standard interpretation, which I follow, these principles specify normative moral reasons (reasons that have some weight, but need not be

---

[1] (Ross 1930, 27, 31, 41).
[2] (Ross 1930, 30).

decisive) that serve both as reasons for or against acts of certain kinds, and reasons for the rightness or wrongness of those acts.[3] Ross has a specific view of the content of these principles, and a specific picture of how they interact to determine overall rightness.

My aims in this paper are both critical and commendatory. In presenting his list of prima facie duties as provisional, Ross implicitly invites us to consider revisions and extensions.[4] In what follows, I take up that invitation. I examine six distinctive features of Ross's own version of Rossian pluralism, and point to some significant limitations they impose on his theory. The six features on which I will focus are these:

> Self-Containment. His foundational prima facie duties are the sole determinants of rightness and wrongness.
>
> Subsumption. There is one way in which the derivative parts of morality derive from its foundations: by being subsumed as instances of them.
>
> The Right and the Good. Ross has a hybrid view of the priority relation between the right and the good.
>
> Reason-Foundations. His view treats normative moral reasons as derivationally foundational.
>
> Balancing. There is one way in which the considerations that derive from the foundations of morality interact to determine the overall rightness of an action: by weighing against each other.
>
> Invariance. A fact that is a normative moral reason for an act of a certain type is a normative moral reason for that type of act in every situation in which the fact obtains.

Working through these features one by one in Sections II–VII, the critical part of the paper will involve pointing out problems that they invite. However, the more constructive aim will be to identify the ways in which his theory can be supplemented or modified to address those problems, without departing from the more general structure of Rossian pluralism.[5] Overall, what I will be trying to show is that the attractions of Rossian pluralism can be retained while conceiving of the foundations of morality in a different way, and that this speaks to the fecundity and interest of the Rossian approach to moral theorizing.

---

[3] "[T]he fact that a promise has been made constitutes in itself a reason why it should be fulfilled": (Ross 1954, 21). See (Urmson 1974–5, 113); (Audi 2004, 24); (Stratton-Lake 2011, 149); (Shaver 2011, 144); (Hurka 2014, 31–2 and 69–70); (Phillips 2019, 26–37). For Ross's distinction between "acts" and "actions," see (Ross 1930, 32).

[4] (Ross 1930, 23).

[5] For some other proposed supplementations, see (Audi 2004, Chs. 3–5); (Hurka 2014, 186–93); (Phillips 2019, Chs. 2–4).

I Rossian Pluralism

Rossian pluralism, as I shall define it, is the conjunction of two claims. The first is that there is more than one derivationally foundational right-maker. The second is that there is no further principle governing the contributions they make to determining the overall rightness of an act.[6] I begin by explaining those two claims.

The relation of right-making, I am (like Ross) going to assume, is a familiar part of ordinary moral thought and discourse.[7] If you are told that it is right to conceal the truth from Lachlan, you can ask what makes that right. An answer might be: it will protect him from distress. Pressing further, you can then ask: why does *that* make it right to conceal the truth from him? The most obvious way to answer that second question is to appeal to some further part of the content of morality from which this derives. We might say: because being protected from distress will be better for Lachlan, overall. Then, if this answer is successful, it also identifies a right-maker. If the protection of Lachlan from distress makes it right to conceal the truth from him because it will be better for him, then it is also correct to say: its being better for Lachlan makes it right to conceal the truth from him. 'Derivation' is the relation that one part of the content of morality bears to another when morality has the first part because it has the second.

You could keep asking the same question. Why does its being better for Lachlan make this action right? Ross thinks that this, too, has a further answer—namely, because it promotes the general good.[8] There are then two overall possibilities. Either this process—the process of deriving one part of the content of morality from another—stops somewhere, or it goes on for ever. Ross thinks that this (promoting the general good) is a stopping-point. The promotion of the general good is a right-making feature of acts which does not derive from some other right-making feature. He also thinks that this is true of four other features of acts—fidelity, reparation, gratitude, and non-maleficence.[9] In his view, there is more than one derivationally foundational right-maker.

That gives us the first component claim of Rossian pluralism. Given the existence of more than one foundational right-maker, the question then arises how rightness is determined in circumstances when they conflict—when, for example, you face a choice between keeping a promise and promoting the general good. Rossian pluralism's second claim is that there is no master principle governing the answers to that question.[10] There are various ways in which you might deny the

---

[6] (Ross 1930, 31, 41–42).

[7] What further analysis can be given of the right-making relation? There are various possible responses to that question; but since they are available whether you are a Rossian pluralist or not, I will not explore them here.

[8] (Ross 1930, 39).

[9] (Ross 1930, 21–27).

[10] (Ross 1930, 31, 41–2).

second claim while accepting the first. You might think that there is a general rule that gives priority to some right-makers over others. Or you might adopt a version of Scanlonian contractualism, holding that right acts are those required by rules that no one could reasonably reject as a basis for informed, unforced, general agreement.[11] Agreeing with Scanlon, you could deny that that master principle describes a right-making property—insisting instead that it is an account of what rightness *is*, and not merely a description of some further property that makes acts right.[12] If so, you could accept that there is a plurality of foundational right-makers, while claiming that their contributions to determining which act is right, overall, are determined by the contractualist master principle. Rossian pluralism's second defining claim is that there is no such master principle.

Any view that makes those two claims I call a version of Rossian pluralism. But if so, Ross's own view is only one possible species of this genus. Among the further claims that distinguish his specific version are the six I began with. By working through these in turn, examining their limitations, and asking what we might add or subtract to avoid those limitations, we will be helped to appreciate the further range of possibilities that is open to a Rossian pluralist.

II Self-Containment

The first feature of Ross's view to consider is:

Self-Containment. His foundational prima facie duties are the sole determinants of rightness and wrongness.

In Ross's own words: "right acts can be distinguished from wrong acts only as being those which, of all those possible for the agent in the circumstances, have the greatest balance of prima facie rightness, in those respects in which they are prima facie right, over their prima facie wrongness, in those respects in which they are prima facie wrong."[13]

This overlooks the following simple point. In a situation in which I could confer a benefit on someone—and thus where Ross's prima facie duty of beneficence applies—whether it is wrong not to confer the benefit depends on how much is at stake for me. So his prima facie duties are not the sole determinants of rightness and wrongness. The cost of an act to the agent also has a bearing on its rightness or wrongness.[14] It is true that Ross's prima facie duty of beneficence is a duty

---

[11] (Scanlon 1998, 153).
[12] (Scanlon 2007, 11, 16).
[13] (Ross 1930, 41).
[14] Compare (Scheffler 1992, Ch. 7); (Hurka 2014, 179–81).

to promote the general good, and my own interests are part of that. But that is not enough to deal with this point convincingly. Suppose I could reunite a long-separated family, but only by letting the chronic pain of one other person go untreated: would this act promote the general good? To answer that question, we do not need to know whether the other person is *me*; but to determine whether it would be wrong not to perform the act, we do.[15]

However, this simple point is not a deep objection to Ross's view: it can be handled by making a simple supplementation.[16] Instead of treating his prima facie duties as the sole determinants of rightness and wrongness, they can be presented as the determinants of our other-regarding reasons.[17] An act is morally wrong, we can then say, when there are serious other-regarding reasons against it, and no adequate countervailing reason in its favor. So understood, the force of complaining that your act is wrong is that you have no adequate justification for having treated others as you did.[18] The wrongness of my act is determined by the bearing upon it of *all* the available reasons; and these include its impact on my own interests.[19] So although Self-Containment looks like an oversight on Ross's part, it can easily be rectified.

III Subsumption

A second respect in which Ross's view requires supplementation is:

Subsumption. There is one way in which the derivative parts of morality derive from its foundations: by being subsumed as instances of them.

'Derivation,' I stipulated, is the relationship that one part of morality's content bears to another when morality has the first part because it has the second. Ross recognizes one such relationship: derivative prima facie duties are those that can

---

[15] Ross himself makes a similar point at (Ross 1930, 22).

[16] Ross's initial explanation of a prima facie duty talks of "an act which would be a duty proper if it were not at the same time of another kind which is morally significant" (19). To handle the point in the text, he could just add that the cost of an act to the agent, although not itself the source of a prima facie duty, is morally significant.

[17] On the connection of moral wrongness to other-regarding reasons, see (Frankena 1970, 158); (Nagel 1986, Ch. 10); (Mill 1991, Ch. 4); (Scheffler 1992, Ch. 7); (Thomson 1997); (Scanlon 1998, 6–7).

[18] This leaves room for a variety of different possible proposals about what it is for a countervailing reason to be "adequate." This might be held to depend simply on the relative strengths of the reasons for and against the action, as Ross maintains, (1930, 28–9); or alternatively on whether the action calls for reactive attitudes such as resentment, indignation, and blame (Watson 2004, Ch. 8); on which reasons must be recognized as prevailing if our interaction is to be governed by the exchange of reasons rather than coercion (Scanlon 1998, Ch. 5); or on whether the action meets the demands of second-person accountability we are entitled to address to each other (Darwall 2006, Ch. 5).

[19] This point is sometimes expressed by saying that not all morally relevant reasons are moral reasons—e.g. (Harman 2016, 368).

be subsumed as instances of one or more of the foundational ones. For example, Ross derives the prima facie duty not to lie from the foundational prima facie duties of fidelity and non-maleficence, the prima facie duty to reward and punish from the foundational prima facie duties of promoting the good and fidelity, and the prima facie duty to obey the law from the foundational prima facie duties of gratitude, fidelity, and promoting the good.[20] These derivations have a subsumptive form: it is because there are always prima facie duties not to harm and not to break one's promises, and because all instances of lying are instances of either harming or promise-breaking, that there is a prima facie duty not to lie. Since all instances of lying are instances of either harming or promise-breaking, the prima facie duty not to lie is contained by, or subsumed under, the prima facie duties not to harm or break one's promises.

But this is not the only way in which one part of morality's content can derive from another. Here is a simple example: suppose I borrow $100 from you and promise to repay it in ten weekly installments. Then, since I have a prima facie duty to keep my promise, I have a derivative prima facie duty to pay you $10 in the first week. This is another way in which one duty (the duty to pay you the first $10 installment) can derive from another (the duty to repay the whole $100). But here the relationship is not one of instantiation. Paying you $10 is not an instance of paying you $100; it is part of paying you $100. We might still think of this as a form of subsumption; but it is not subsumption by instantiation. Instead, the relevant relationship in this kind of derivation is that of mereological composition—the relationship between part and whole.

Having noticed this, we can next observe that not all derivations are subsumptive even in that broader sense. From my prima facie duty to repay the $100 I borrowed, there also derives a prima facie duty not to gamble away the only $100 I have available. Here, however, the derivation relationship is not a kind of subsumption: instead, it is a relationship of enabling. Restraining myself from gambling away my only $100 is neither a specific way nor a part of keeping my promise: it is an enabling condition for doing so—something I need to do in order to be able to perform another action (namely, giving you $100) that constitutes the keeping of my promise. It is then possible to distinguish a wide variety of different enabling relationships between A and B through which, from a prima facie duty to do A, we can derive a prima facie duty to do something else, B, that enables A. B might make A likelier; it might remove an obstacle to A; it might make it easier to perform some other action, C, that causes (or makes likelier, or removes an obstacle to) A; and so on.

However, again, this does not amount to a deep objection to Ross. It draws attention to a range of further derivation relationships, beyond the one he recognizes.

---

[20] See (Ross 1930, 21, 54–5, 56–64, 27–8); and, for secondary discussion, (McNaughton 1996, 436–8).

But nothing prevents us from supplementing his theory by adding them, thereby making it possible to account for a range of further cases.

Having noticed this, we can now turn to a deeper set of questions. These are not going to be resolved by simply taking the structure of Ross's existing theory and adding to it: they point to the need for more significant structural changes.

IV The Right and the Good

Ross presents a substantive theory of the right, whose structure is based as we have seen upon a plurality of foundational right-makers. He also has a substantive theory of the good, structured in a similar manner: intrinsic goods are traced to the four basic classes of "virtue, pleasure, the allocation of pleasure to the virtuous, and knowledge."[21] He also has a discussion of "moral goodness," which attaches to three kinds of thing—persons, feelings, and the motivation of actions.[22] Here, he treats the moral goodness of character as basic, and seeks to explain the moral goodness of actions and feelings through their relationship to good character. His leading example of a morally good feeling is sympathy with someone else's misfortune.[23]

What is the relationship between the right and the good, according to Ross? There are two ways to read that question. It can be read as a question about the structure of Ross's substantive theory of the content of morality. To use a common framing: is he a deontologist, who treats the right as prior to the good, or a consequentialist, who treats the good as prior to the right? Alternatively, it can be read as a metaethical question: what view does he have of the relationship between the property of rightness and the property of goodness? Ross offers answers to both of those questions: both are hybrid answers.

Ross's substantive moral theory is developed in opposition to Moore's consequentialism, but his way of opposing Moore is by annexation rather than outright rejection.[24] Acting to promote good states of affairs is treated by Ross as one source of prima facie duties alongside others. Ross has a hybrid view on which in one part of morality (the part based on the prima facie duty to promote the good) the good is prior to the right, while in the other parts (the parts deriving from the other prima facie duties) it is not. A view with this structure displays one of the problems with the attempt to classify substantive moral theories as either deontological or consequentialist according to whether they make the right prior to the good, or vice versa. When the distinction is made in that way, Ross's theory is both.

---

[21] (Ross 1930, 140).
[22] (Ross 1930, Ch. 7).
[23] (Ross 1930, 155).
[24] (Ross 1930, 16–19); (Hurka 2014, 178–83); (Phillips 2019, 8).

In *Foundations of Ethics*, Ross also offers a metaethical account of the relationship between the properties of goodness and rightness. He begins by connecting goodness to worthiness. Ross uses the noun 'worthiness' to refer to the relation we find in the suffix of evaluative terms such as 'blameworthy,' 'praiseworthy,' 'trustworthy,' and 'choiceworthy'—the relation that the blameworthy bears to blame, the praiseworthy to praise. Thoughts about worthiness are an essential part of attitudes of approval and disapproval, according to Ross. To approve of something, you must think it is worthy of approval; to disapprove of it, you must think it is worthy of disapproval.[25] There are different kinds of approval, and these give rise to two main senses of 'good.'[26] First, there is a sense in which good things are worthy of admiration. The things that are good in this sense are "[c]ertain moral dispositions and actions, and certain activities of the intellect and of the creative imagination."[27] Goodness in this sense is non-relational: it is an intrinsic property of the things that are worthy of admiration, and they are worthy of admiration *because* they have this intrinsic property.[28] Distinct from this is a sense in which "the pleasures of others (except those which are immoral)" are good: these are worthy of satisfaction.[29] Here, goodness is relational and not intrinsic. The goodness of the pleasures of others just *is* their being worthy objects of satisfaction: it is not that they are worthy of satisfaction because they are intrinsically good.[30] To this, Ross then adds a further claim that connects the good to the right. For an object to be worthy of a response is for that response to be right. So goodness in the second sense is analyzed in terms of rightness: "this is a preferable way of putting the matter because, instead of introducing the new and not altogether clear notion of worthiness, it defines the goodness of innocent pleasures by using a notion which has already been recognized as foundational in ethics, the notion of rightness."[31] The result is a metaethical account of the relationship between the properties of goodness and rightness that is also a hybrid view. 'Goodness' refers to two properties. One is an intrinsic and irreducible property of admirable actions, dispositions, and activities; the other is a relational property of others' innocent pleasures—a property that Ross reductively identifies with the rightness of feeling satisfaction directed toward that object.

This combination of views is interesting and suggestive; but it raises two main sets of issues. One concerns the respects in which it is incomplete; the other concerns the respect in which it is incorrect.[32]

---

[25] (Ross 1939, 262, 34).
[26] (Ross 1939, 282–4).
[27] (Ross 1939, 282–3).
[28] (Ross 1939, 278–9); (Hurks 2014, 60).
[29] (Ross 1939, 283). For discussion of Ross on immoral pleasures, see (Hurka 2014, 224).
[30] (Ross 1939, 279).
[31] (Ross 1939, 279).
[32] For further critical discussion, see (Phillips 2019, Ch. 4, Sec. 3).

In his treatment of goodness, Ross is drawing our attention to an important point: morality concerns more than right acts. It also includes our attitudes and feelings—some of these, such as admiration and satisfaction, are invoked in his account of the two senses of 'goodness'; while others, such as sympathy with others' misfortune, are not. Once we notice this, further reflection shows that there is a broader range of responses—spanning responses of action, feeling, perception, thought, and speech—that we make in responding as we ought to the things that are morally important. The morally important responses to others' welfare, for example, extend beyond the actions of promoting or not damaging it that are covered by his prima facie duties of beneficence and non-maleficence, and the feelings of sympathy that are not. They also include being attentive to and perceptive about it, thinking that it is important, and speaking out to express solidarity with those who are badly treated. If so, Ross's theory of morality is incomplete: it needs to be developed further if it is to accommodate the full content of morality. His substantive theory of right acts identifies various foundational normative moral reasons, in the form of his prima facie duties. But the moral responses of thought and feeling, although they are not the kinds of responses we can have *duties* to make, are responses that we can have normative reasons to make. What, then, are the sources of those further reasons, and how are they related to our reasons for action?

Thus, more needs to be added to Ross's theory; but something also needs to be subtracted. His attempt to connect the right to the good by first connecting goodness to worthiness and then identifying worthiness with rightness does not work. To see why not, we can look at an earlier passage in *Foundations of Ethics* where he is explaining why he agrees with Broad that rightness can be identified with "the greatest amount of suitability possible in the circumstances."[33] To explain this, he emphasizes the difference between rightness and goodness:

> It is worth while in this connexion to contrast the meaning of "the right road [or key]" with that of a "good road [or key]". Goodness is an attribute which belongs permanently to the road or key, so long as it remains unchanged in its other characteristics; rightness is an attribute which they have only relatively to a particular situation and a particular need.[34]

The difference he is pointing to here is equally a problem for his attempt to connect the right to the good by identifying worthiness with rightness. There is a dilemma. On one horn, he can conceive of the 'worthiness' relation in the way indicated earlier: as the relation that the praiseworthy bears to praise, and the relation we are thinking of when, in approving of something, we think it is worthy of approval.

---

[33] (Ross 1939, 23). Whereas in (Ross 1930, 12), he had claimed that rightness is a simple, irreducible property, he now maintains that it is a complex property—a kind of suitability: see (Ross 1939, 54).
[34] (Ross 1939, 51).

But *that* relation is not rightness. Whether it is right, all things considered, in the present circumstances to praise a threatening villain is a different question from whether he is praise*worthy*; and the two questions could have different answers. If, given the circumstances, praising the villain is likely to prevent some terrible harm from coming about, that fact could make it right to praise the villain; but it would do nothing to contribute to his goodness and make him praiseworthy.[35] Cases of this kind do not raise a problem for Ross's claimed connection between goodness and being worthy of either admiration or satisfaction; but they suggest that his analysis of worthiness in terms of rightness is a mistake. On the other horn, he could try to avoid this problem by stipulating that the 'worthiness' of an object for a response is to be identified with the response's overall suitability in the circumstances. But if we followed that stipulation, we would lose the connection between worthiness and goodness: we could no longer say that the praiseworthy actions are those that are worthy of praise, or more generally that good things are those that are worthy of positive responses such as admiration and satisfaction. Either way, the good and the right are not connected in the way he maintains. If we want a moral theory that explains the connection between the right and the good, it will need to do so in some other way.

V Reason-Foundations

What resources are there within Rossian pluralism for addressing these issues? To examine this, let us start with a conservative suggestion, and work from there toward a view that makes some more radical departures from Ross.

Ross is working with two main sets of ideas. First, there is the part of morality concerned with rightness, where the determinants of right acts are the normative moral reasons he identifies with prima facie duties. Second, there is the part of morality concerned with goodness, which he connects to the worthiness of the positive responses of admiration and satisfaction. One way of revising Ross's view to deal with the issues raised above is to broaden the range of responses covered in the second part of Ross's theory, and then offer a different account of the connection between the first and second parts.

To broaden the second part of Ross's theory, we can draw on a distinctive tradition of theorizing about value. This is the tradition that recognizes that things can be good or bad in different ways, which correspond to the different kinds of positive and negative responses they call for.[36] These differences are reflected in our

---

[35] See (Rabinowicz and Ronnow-Rasmussen 2004).
[36] See (Ewing 1947, Ch. 5); (Von Wright 1963, 8–13); (Rescher 1969, Ch. 2); (Nozick 1981, 429–30); (Gaus 1990, Secs. 13–14); (Thomson 1992); (Anderson 1993, Ch. 1); (Scanlon 1998, Ch. 2, Sec. 3); (Zimmerman 2001, 85–6); (Rabinowicz and Ronnow-Rasmussen 2004, 393).

fine-grained evaluative language: 'praiseworthy,' 'desirable,' 'shameful,' 'awesome,' 'boring,' 'pleasing,' 'outrageous,' 'repulsive,' and so on. In calling something praiseworthy, desirable, or shameful, we are saying that it stands in the relation that Ross calls 'worthiness'—and others call 'aptness' or 'fittingness'—to praise, desire, or shame, respectively.[37] As we have seen, Ross belongs to that tradition: he distinguishes between the good things that are worthy objects of admiration and those that are worthy objects of satisfaction. A first suggestion for dealing with the issues raised above is to broaden this to cover the full range of responses—responses of action, feeling, perception, thought, and speech—through which a morally good person responds well to the things that are morally important. Applying this thought to others' welfare, we could do so by incorporating into our theory a principle of this form:

($W_{worthiness}$) Others' welfare is worthy of promotion, protection, attentiveness, sensitivity, sympathy, and solidarity.

So that gives us a first kind of revision to Ross's theory. The second revision is to correct the mistake he makes in identifying an object's being worthy of a response with the rightness of that response in the circumstances. An alternative suggestion to consider is this: we could instead identify an object's being worthy of a response with the existence of a normative reason to make that response. This would allow us to replace ($W_{worthiness}$) with a principle formulated in terms of normative reasons instead, as follows:

($W_{reasons}$) Facts about others' welfare give us normative reasons to promote it, to protect it, not to damage it, to be attentive to it, to be sensitive to it in thought, to sympathize with others, and to express our solidarity with them.

If our duties are duties to act, and not to think or feel, then a principle like ($W_{reasons}$) that ranges broadly across responses of thought and feeling as well as action cannot be presented as a principle of prima facie duty. However, it could still play the role within a moral theory that Ross's principles of prima facie duty play—identifying the normative reasons from which duties to act such as the duties to promote and not to damage others' welfare derive. A theory containing ($W_{reasons}$) invites the question whether it should be treated as derivationally foundational or whether it derives from some other, deeper principle (either by subsumption or in some other way). However, if it does have a further derivation, it will not be the one that Ross gives for prima facie duties of welfare-promotion. He derives those from a foundational prima facie duty to promote the general good; but our reasons to

---

[37] For "aptness," see (Gibbard 1990, 6); for "fittingness," see (Ewing 1947, 132–3).

respond to others' welfare with feelings of sympathy do not derive from reasons to make *that* response to the general good. One possibility would be to treat ($W_{reasons}$) itself as derivationally foundational—claiming, as welfarists do, that the reasons we have to make these responses to others' welfare do not derive from another part of the content of morality. But if you also held that there are other derivationally foundational parts of morality, with no master principle governing their contributions to overall rightness, you would still qualify as a Rossian pluralist.

A view with this structure would now abandon both of Ross's hybrid accounts of the relationship between the right and the good. It drops his substantive claim that the rightness of acts sometimes derives (and sometimes does not) from a prima facie duty to promote the good. And it also drops his metaethical claim that there is one property of goodness that is reductively explained in terms of rightness and another that is not. Rather, a theory of this alternative form treats normative reasons as the common foundation of both the part of morality that concerns rightness and the part that concerns goodness. The way in which an object such as others' welfare is good is specified by reference to the range of positive responses that we have normative reasons to make to it; and the rightness of making those responses is determined by all of the reasons that there are for and against making those responses.

A theory based on principles of this form thus has some significant attractions. It gives us a way of developing Rossian pluralism that offers to accommodate the full range of responses for which morality gives us normative reasons. And it does so in a way that neatly connects the right and the good.

However, this attractive idea still faces some formidable objections, from two directions. First, the proposed reduction of worthiness to reasons still faces the same kind of problem that we saw with Ross's proposed reduction of worthiness to rightness. Sometimes, there are normative reasons—indeed, decisive reasons—to make positive responses to objects that are not good. If a villain is going to torture my children unless I praise him for being so menacing, then that could give me a decisive reason to praise him, without making him praiseworthy.[38] So the worthiness relation that good things bear to positive responses, which we earlier saw cannot be identified with rightness, cannot be identified with the normative reason relation either. Moreover, the two relations come apart in the other direction as well. If Anna is a public servant in Lithuania who handles delicate policy discussions with great integrity and tact, that could be enough to make her praiseworthy. But more would be required to give me a reason to praise her. There would need to be some relevant connection between the actions of this distant person and me, and I would need to have the capacity to praise her. If I suffered an impairment

---

[38] Again, see (Rabinowicz and Ronnow-Rasmussen 2004).

that rendered me unable to praise Anna, that would be irrelevant to Anna's praiseworthiness, but it would make it false that I had a reason to praise her.

However, while these are objections to identifying worthiness-relations with normative reasons, they are not objections to thinking that all reasons *derive* from worthiness-relations. On the contrary, they encourage that view. There are two ways in which reasons to praise someone can arise. In the case of Anna, when there is a reason to praise her it derives from her praiseworthiness. (It derives from her praiseworthiness rather than being identical with it: to derive a reason to praise her, additional conditions of capacity and personal relevance must obtain.) In the case of the menacing villain, the reason to praise him derives from the reason I have to prevent my children from being tortured; but the latter reason derives in turn from the prevention-worthiness of torture.

This encourages a simple response to the objections: again, it is a conservative suggestion. We ventured two revisions to Ross's theory: the first recognized a broader range of morally significant responses and offered us ($W_{worthiness}$); the second identified the worthiness- and normative reasons relations, producing ($W_{reasons}$). The conservative suggestion is simply that we drop the second revision and keep the first. This gives a version of Rossian pluralism that treats principles such as ($W_{worthiness}$), not ($W_{reasons}$), as derivationally foundational. ($W_{worthiness}$) is not itself a claim about reasons, but it is a claim about the worthiness-relationships from which reasons to respond to others' welfare derive. It proposes a derivational source for the reasons we have to make a range of responses of action, feeling, perception, thought, and speech to others' welfare; and beyond that a source of further derivative instrumental reasons to do the things that are means to making those responses (up to and including welfare-protecting praise for villains). This retains the idea that there is a common set of principles which are derivationally foundational to both moral rightness and moral goodness. But it now proposes that those foundational principles are principles not of normative reason, but principles of worthiness from which our reasons derive.

It is true that just saying this leaves us without a reductive answer to the question: what is 'worthiness'? We have now rejected two such answers: a reduction in terms of rightness, and a reduction in terms of normative reasons. We do have the earlier non-reductive answer: worthiness is the relation that an object bears to blame when it is blameworthy, to desire when it is desirable, and so on; and it is the relation you think an object bears to approval when you approve of it. But this leaves open two possibilities: that there is some other reductive explanation of worthiness, or that we should treat it as an irreducible normative property.[39] Those possibilities amount to alternative variants of the proposed form of Rossian pluralism we are now considering. But instead of pursuing those alternative variants

---

[39] An alethic reduction is proposed by (Tappolet 2011, 119–20); an evaluative reduction by (Johnston 1989, 158). For a critical discussion of all of these reductive strategies, see (Svavarsdóttir 2014).

here, let us note that they remain open, and focus instead on assessing the merits of the core proposal.

VI Balancing

So far, we have seen two main reasons for formulating the foundational principles of a moral theory in terms of the relation of worthiness rather than normative reasons. Once we distinguish these two relations from each other (as we must), we find that the latter derive from the former: worthiness-relations are more fundamental. And formulating our theory in this way—treating principles like ($W_{worthiness}$) as foundational—produces a unified treatment of the deontic and evaluative parts of morality.

Now we can point out a further advantage of a view with this structure. It allows for a range of apparent exceptions which Ross's own view struggles to recognize. Ross's view treats as foundational a set of prima facie duties that *always* have reason-giving force. As Ross says, the prima facie duties he recognizes as foundational right-makers function in the same way as Newtonian forces.[40] When a prima facie duty is instantiated, it can be outweighed and thereby fail to generate a duty proper, but it retains its force as a reason. On this picture, whenever a consideration that derives from one of the foundations of morality is instantiated, it carries a reason-giving weight, and the only way in which such considerations can interact with each other to determine the rightness of an act is by contributing that weight to the overall balance of reasons for and against.

To see the case for questioning this picture, we can consider the ways in which welfare-promotion can be problematic. Sometimes, it is a mistake to treat considerations of welfare as reasons to be balanced in your deliberation about what to do. If you have a fiduciary responsibility as a trustee, you cannot properly balance the interests of your relatives in benefiting from the fund under your management against the interests of the legal beneficiary. And if you are a surgeon whose patient decides against having an operation, you should not simply treat that as one input into your assessment of the balance of reasons for and against operating, to be weighed against the benefit they will receive if you go ahead with the operation.[41] In these cases, something has gone wrong even if you end up deciding not to embezzle the money or perform the operation. The fiduciary obligation in the first case and the patient's autonomous decision in the second make the consideration of welfare you are wrongly thinking about unavailable to be balanced as a reason by you.

---

[40] (Ross 1930, 28–9); (Ross 1939, 86). For discussion, see (Pietroski 1993).
[41] As Daniel Groll says, the patient's will is "structurally decisive" in this case: see (Groll 2012, 699–706).

We need to be careful with these examples. Perhaps there can be cases in which a consideration *is* a normative reason for an act but nonetheless shouldn't register as such in your deliberation. So that reading of the cases remains open to someone who wants to insist that considerations of welfare always provide normative reasons for the acts that promote it. That reading does raise the question: *why* should we exclude these welfare-considerations from deliberation if they really are reasons? But we would need to consider possible answers to that question before ruling this out.[42]

However, notice that the view on which our normative reasons have deeper derivational sources in worthiness-relationships readily allows for the context-dependence of reasons. If ($W_{worthiness}$) is treated as the foundation from which reasons to promote others' welfare derive, then this allows that such derivations can be blocked, in various ways. Two were mentioned earlier: the derivation of a reason from a worthiness-relationship can be blocked by your incapacity, or by facts about personal irrelevance. But perhaps it can also be blocked, in cases such as those just described, by fiduciary obligations, or by considerations of respect for the autonomous decisions of those whose welfare is at stake.

This allows that a person's welfare can be *worthy* of promotion, although features of the context deprive an agent of a reason to promote it. In the examples just described, your relatives' interests in financial security and your patient's interests in getting the best medical treatment remain promotion-*worthy*: your obligations as a trustee or your patient's decision have no impact on that. Those interests do, after all, provide you with reasons for acts of various other kinds: reasons to give your relatives financial advice, help them out of your own pocket, and direct them towards other benefactors; and reasons to draw your patient's attention to facts they may have overlooked.

Thus, grounding our normative reasons in deeper principles of worthiness from which they derive has several advantages. It explains the different sources of normative reasons, offers a theoretically unified treatment of the value- and normative-reasons-generating parts of morality, and allows that the derivation of reasons from worthiness-relationships can be blocked where, apparently, it is.

VII Invariance

So far, we have seen two supplementations and two modifications that a Rossian pluralist can make to Ross's own theory to improve its account of the content of morality. The supplementations involve recognizing other determinants of rightness (Section II) and other, non-subsumptive forms of derivation (Section III).

---

[42] For further discussion, see (Cullity 2013).

The modifications involve changing the foundational principles of the theory to recognize the full range of responses for which we can have reasons and to reflect the fact that normative reasons have deeper derivational sources in relations of worthiness (Sections V–VI).

A final, more radical, departure from Ross is encouraged by this question: can the foundations of morality be captured by a set of *exceptionless* principles? Aren't there—not just exceptions to the derivation of reasons from worthiness, but— exceptions to principles such as ($W_{worthiness}$) themselves? If your welfare is what it is in your interests to get, and you are a bad person, couldn't your welfare be promoted by harming or exploiting others? But if *that* is what your welfare consists in, then it will not be worthy of promotion, protection, sympathy, or solidarity.

Judgments of those kinds are sometimes resisted—either by denying that the wicked really flourish,[43] or by insisting that we do have reasons to promote their welfare (which are outweighed). If either of those views is right, then ($W_{worthiness}$) could serve in its exceptionless form as a foundation for the part of morality that concerns our responses to others' welfare. However, if that is unconvincing, we must refine our theory further. There are three main strategies to consider.

The first would repeat the strategy that we used to allow for exceptions to our reasons to promote others' welfare: the strategy of maintaining that these reasons have deeper derivational sources in worthiness-relations, and that the derivations are sometimes blocked. One might then search for some yet deeper source from which worthiness-relations derive, giving us the possibility that those derivations too can be blocked.

However, that does not look promising. Talk of 'worthiness,' although not itself a prominent part of ordinary moral thought and discourse, refers to something that *is* a prominent part of ordinary moral thought and discourse—the relation we are talking about whenever we say that something is blameworthy or desirable. If we are looking for something else with good credentials to be a genuine part of morality that can furnish a deeper derivational source of facts about worthiness without being subject to the same exceptions, we seem to be running out of candidates.

A second strategy for revising our theory to accommodate exceptions to ($W_{worthiness}$) would be to identify all the exceptions and write them into a foundational principle of the form:

($W_{specified}$) When others' welfare is of type T, it is worthy of promotion, protection, attentiveness, sensitivity, sympathy, and solidarity
    —with T being replaced by a list of all the exceptions that are ruled out.

---

[43] See e.g. (Foot 2001, Ch. 6); (LeBar 2013, 29); (Badhwar 2014); and (Bloomfield 2014).

However, that also looks unpromising. The only plausible way of covering *all* of the possible exceptions in a version of ($W_{specified}$) would be to replace "of type T" with something equivalent to "not constituted by doing what is, all things considered, morally wrong." But then we would have a principle that could not serve as part of a Rossian pluralist theory identifying the derivational foundations for morality, telling us what makes actions right and wrong. Rather than explaining what determines rightness and wrongness, this principle would instead require prior determinations of wrongness for its application.

This encourages a third, simpler strategy. We could simply qualify our foundational principles with exception-clauses, in this way:

(W_{hedged}) Others' welfare is worthy of promotion, protection, sensitivity, sympathy, and solidarity, unless its being worthy of those responses is undermined.

At first glance, this looks unhelpful. In adding the hedge-clause, it allows that ($W_{worthiness}$) has exceptions, but does not say what they are. It just has the form:

Object O calls for response R, unless it does not.

But claims of that form are never falsifiable, for any object O and response R whatever—so they seem trivial.[44] A principle like (W_{hedged}) could only be part of an informative explanation of the content of morality, it would seem, if accompanied by an account of the conditions under which its exception-clause is triggered; and if we had an account of those conditions, the content of that account would have to be more fundamental than (W_{hedged}). Once we hedge a principle with an exception-clause in this way, it apparently ceases to have the right form to be foundational to morality.

However, I think this third idea should not be dismissed so quickly. It is possible, as others have shown, to give explanations that treat exception-hedged principles as explanatorily basic.[45] In an explanation of this form, some applications of these principles—those in which the exception-clauses are not satisfied—can be invoked in the course of explaining why other applications are subject to undermining.

Here is a sketch of how an explanation of this form could be structured in the case of (W_{hedged}).[46] Suppose undermining occurs just when a welfare-state is a state of "loving the bad" or "hating the good"—a state of positive or negative orientation directed toward an object that is worthy of the opposite response.[47] Then, to explain why some welfare-states are not worthy of the responses specified in

---

[44] (McKeever and Ridge 2006, Ch. 3).
[45] See (Horty 2007); (Lance and Little 2004); (Horty 2012).
[46] For a less sketchy development of this thought, see (Cullity 2019).
[47] For Brentano's dictum that loving the bad is bad, see (Brentano 1969, 23); (Chisholm 1976); and (Chisholm 1986, Ch. 6).

(W_{hedged}), we can proceed as follows. We can start by applying (W_{hedged}) to those constituents of welfare that are never misdirected in that way. The state of suffering from physical pain, for example, is a (negative) constituent of welfare that is never a state of either loving the bad or hating the good. So the exception-clause in (W_{hedged}) is never triggered for this constituent of welfare: it is always worthy of the responses of protection against it, sympathy with those who suffer it, and so on. We can then invoke this in applying (W_{hedged}), next, to welfare-constituents that are states of cruel or malicious enjoyment of others' suffering. These *are* states of loving the bad, since they are states of positive orientation toward an object (others' suffering) that is worthy of the opposite responses of protection and sympathy; so here the exception-clause in (W_{hedged}) *is* triggered and states of cruel or malicious enjoyment are not worthy of promotion. In this way, a theory whose foundational principles contain exception-hedges, like (W_{hedged}), can determine the value of those welfare-constituents that are responses to good or bad objects, at progressively higher levels. This could be done, without circularity, even in a theory with no unhedged base principles.[48] If so, the exceptions allowed for by principles like (W_{hedged}) can be explained without presupposing any further principle of form ($W_{specified}$). Indeed, a theory of this form can be more, not less, explanatory than one that has principles of form ($W_{specified}$) at its foundations, since it can tell us not just that some welfare-states do not call for promotion, but *why* that is so.

Thus, I think a view with this structure—one that proposes exception-hedged principles such as (W_{hedged}) as foundational to morality—deserves to be taken seriously. It remains a version of Rossian pluralism, since it still satisfies the two conditions set out in Section I. However, it now makes a radical departure from Ross's own view. A theory with exception-hedged principles like (W_{hedged}) at its foundations abandons his Newtonian model of moral "laws of tendency" in favor of a picture on which morality's foundational elements do not always contribute to a balance of considerations for and against.[49] However, in favor of this departure, it allows us to say a pair of things that seem correct. Welfare, when it is important, is important foundationally. When Lachlan's welfare makes it right to protect him from distress, the fact that his welfare is worthy of protection does not derive from some further, more fundamental part of the content of morality. So when welfare has moral importance it does so non-derivatively. But it also allows us to say that there are some forms of welfare that lack moral importance. So a theory of this form seems worth trying to develop in detail. The test of its adequacy will be whether this can be done in a way that provides the resources we need to explain the full complexity and nuance of morality.[50]

---

[48] Suppose all the principles in your value theory have the form: If and because X belongs to type T, then X has value V, unless (a) X bears relation U to Y and (b) Y has value W. Then there are two ways to settle the value of an object O, prior to any other value-assignment: (i) if O does not belong to any type T, and (ii) if O does not bear any relation U to another object.

[49] (Ross 1939, 86).

[50] Compare (Ross 1930, 39–41).

VIII Conclusion

I have canvassed six main departures from Ross's own version of Rossian pluralism. Departing from the Self-Containment of his view, we can allow that, alongside the sources of our other-regarding reasons, there are other determinants of rightness and wrongness. We can recognize relations other than Subsumption through which the derivative parts of morality's content derive from its foundations. We can give a more unified account of the relationship between The Right and the Good than his own hybrid view: this can be done by replacing his Reason-Foundations, and treating reasons as deriving from more fundamental worthiness-relations that cover a range of morally relevant responses beyond those of action. This also allows that those derivations can be blocked in various ways, so that the interactions between the considerations that determine the content of morality are not limited to the Balancing of normative reasons. And, finally, it is possible to develop a Rossian pluralism that departs from Invariance by positing foundational principles for morality that are exception-hedged.

I do not claim that these suggestions exhaust the possibilities for Rossian pluralism. Although they involve progressively greater departures from Ross's own view, they retain the generic attractions of Rossian pluralism that we began by noting: the attractions of approaching the explanation of what makes right acts right not by searching for general verdictive principles of rightness, but instead trying to account for the complexity of morality by identifying its basic elements and the principles through which those elements interact.

Of course, further questions can be raised about the ultimate viability of all of these suggested departures from Ross—the last of them especially. I actually think a promising theory of morality can be developed that has all of these features.[51] However, I cannot hope to convince you of that here. Instead, what this discussion has tried to show is that Ross's approach to substantive moral theory broke important new ground. He opened up a theoretical landscape that remains largely unexplored and will reward further investigation.

References

Anderson, Elizabeth. 1993. *Value in Ethics and Economics* (Cambridge, MA: Harvard University Press).
Audi, Robert. 2004. *The Good in the Right: A Theory of Intuition and Intrinsic Value* (Princeton: Princeton University Press).
Badhwar, Neera K. 2014. *Well-Being: Happiness in a Worthwhile Life* (New York: Oxford University Press).

---

[51] (Cullity 2018).

Bloomfield, Paul. 2014. *The Virtues of Happiness: A Theory of the Good Life* (New York: Oxford University Press).
Brentano, Franz. 1969. *The Origin of Our Knowledge of Right and Wrong (1889)* (London: Routledge & Kegan Paul).
Chisholm, Roderick M. 1976. 'Brentano's Theory of Correct and Incorrect Emotion'. In Linda L. McAlister (ed.), *The Philosophy of Brentano* (London: Duckworth).
Chisholm, Roderick M. 1986. *Brentano and Intrinsic Value* (Cambridge: Cambridge University Press).
Cullity, Garrett. 2013. 'The Context-Undermining of Practical Reasons', *Ethics*, 124: 1–27.
Cullity, Garrett. 2018. *Concern, Respect, and Cooperation* (Oxford: Oxford University Press).
Cullity, Garrett. 2019. 'Exceptions in Nonderivative Value', *Philosophy and Phenomenological Research*, 98: 26–49.
Darwall, Stephen. 2006. *The Second-Person Standpoint: Morality, Respect, and Accountability* (Cambridge, MA: Harvard University Press).
Ewing, A. C. 1947. *The Definition of Good* (New York: Macmillan).
Foot, Philippa. 2001. *Natural Goodness* (Oxford: Clarendon Press).
Frankena, William K. 1970. 'The Concept of Morality.' In G. Wallace and A. D. M. Walker (eds.), *The Definition of Morality* (London: Methuen).
Gaus, Gerald. 1990. *Value and Justification: The Foundations of Liberal Theory* (Cambridge: Cambridge University Press).
Gibbard, Allan. 1990. *Wise Choices, Apt Feelings* (Oxford: Clarendon Press).
Groll, Daniel. 2012. 'Paternalism, Respect, and the Will', *Ethics*, 122: 692–720.
Harman, Elizabeth. 2016. 'Morally Permissible Moral Mistakes', *Ethics*, 126: 366–93.
Horty, John F. 2007. 'Reasons as Defaults', *Philosophers' Imprint*, 7.
Horty, John F. 2012. *Reasons as Defaults* (New York: Oxford University Press).
Hurka, Thomas. 2014. *British Ethical Theorists from Sidgwick to Ewing* (Oxford: Oxford University Press).
Johnston, Mark 1989. 'Dispositional Theories of Value', *Proceedings of the Aristotelian Society (Supplementary Vol.)*, 63: 139–74.
Lance, Mark, and Margaret Olivia Little. 2004. 'Defeasibility and the Normative Grasp of Context', *Erkenntnis*, 61: 435–55.
LeBar, Mark T. 2013. *The Value of Living Well* (Oxford: Oxford University Press).
McKeever, Sean, and Michael Ridge. 2006. *Principled Ethics: Generalism as a Regulative Ideal* (Oxford: Clarendon Press).
McNaughton, David. 1996. 'An Unconnected Heap of Duties?', *The Philosophical Quarterly*, 46: 433–47.
Mill, John Stuart. 1991. *On Liberty (1859)* (Oxford: Oxford University Press).
Nagel, Thomas. 1986. *The View from Nowhere* (New York: Oxford University Press).
Nozick, Robert. 1981. *Philosophical Explanations* (Oxford: Clarendon Press).
Phillips, David. 2019. *Rossian Ethics: W. D. Ross and Contemporary Moral Theory* (Oxford: Oxford University Press).
Pietroski, Paul M. 1993. 'Prima Facie Obligations, Ceteris Paribus Laws in Moral Theory', *Ethics*, 103: 489–515.
Rabinowicz, Wlodek, and Toni Ronnow-Rasmussen. 2004. 'Strike of the Demon: On Fitting Pro-Attitudes and Value', *Ethics*, 114: 391–423.
Rescher, Nicholas. 1969. *Introduction to Value Theory* (Englewood Cliffs: Prentice-Hall).
Ross, W. D. 1930. *The Right and the Good* (Oxford: Clarendon Press).
Ross, W. D. 1939. *Foundations of Ethics* (Oxford: Clarendon Press).
Ross, W. D. 1954. *Kant's Ethical Theory: A Commentary on the Grundlegung zur Metaphysik der Sitten* (Oxford).
Scanlon, T. M. 1998. *What We Owe to Each Other* (Cambridge, MA: Harvard University Press).
Scanlon, T. M. 2007. 'Wrongness and Reasons: A Re-examination', *Oxford Studies in Metaethics*, 2: 5–20.
Scheffler, Samuel. 1992. *Human Morality* (New York: Oxford University Press).

Shaver, Robert. 2011. 'The Birth of Deontology'. In Thomas Hurka (ed.), *Underivative Duty: British Moral Philosophers from Sidgwick to Ewing* (Oxford: Oxford University Press).

Stratton-Lake, Philip. 2011. 'Eliminativism About Derivative Prima Facie Duties'. In Thomas Hurka (ed.), *Underivative Duty: British Moral Philosophers from Sidgwick to Ewing* (Oxford: Oxford University Press).

Svavarsdóttir, Sigrún. 2014. 'Having Value and Being Worth Valuing', *The Journal of Philosophy*, 111: 84–109.

Tappolet, Christine. 2011. 'Values and Emotions: Neo-Sentimentalism's Prospects'. In Carla Bagnoli (ed.), *Morality and the Emotions* (Oxford: Oxford University Press).

Thomson, Judith Jarvis. 1992. 'On Some Ways in Which a Thing Can Be Good'. In Ellen Frankel Paul, Fred D. Miller, Jr., and Jeffrey Paul (eds.), *The Good Life and the Human Good* (Cambridge: Cambridge University Press).

Thomson, Judith Jarvis. 1997. 'The Right and the Good', *The Journal of Philosophy*, 94: 273–98.

Urmson, J. O. 1974–5. 'A Defence of Intuitionism', *Proceedings of the Aristotelian Society (Supplementary Volume)*, 75: 111–19.

Von Wright, G. H. 1963. *The Varieties of Goodness* (London: Routledge & Kegan Paul).

Watson, Gary. 2004. *Agency and Answerability* (Oxford: Clarendon Press).

Zimmerman, Michael J. 2001. *The Nature of Intrinsic Value* (Lanham, MD: Rowman & Littlefield).

5
The Ethical Theory of W. D. Ross

Brad Hooker

I Introduction

W. D. Ross seems to me to be one of the most important ethicists yet. In this chapter, I will outline the *structure* of Ross's theory and point out its strengths. Then I will assess the *content* of his theory. I will concentrate on the areas where his theory seems to me to need revision and supplementation, especially concerning justice.

II The Structure of Rossian Deontological Pluralism

There has recently been a revival in intuitionism as a moral epistemology. Thomas Nagel, Judith Thompson, Tim Scanlon, Derek Parfit, Frances Kamm, and very many others obviously *employ* this moral epistemology. And Robert Audi, George Beeler, Jonathan Dancy, Michael DePaul, David McNaughton, Roger Crisp, Robert Shaver, Russ Shafer-Landau, Michael Huemer, David Enoch, and Philip Stratton-Lake, among others, *defend and develop* it. I am not going to defend intuitionism as a moral epistemology here, but I am going to employ it, much in the same way Ross did.

A virtually irresistible intuition is that there is a moral duty, shared by every rational agent, to bestow benefits on and prevent harm to others in general on at least some occasions. (The duty might in fact be much stronger than I have just stated. But the stronger the duty is stated, the less irresistible it seems.) To be plausible, deontological intuitionism must accept that there is a duty to bestow benefits on and prevent harm to others on at least some occasions. Other ethical theories must likewise accept this duty if they are to be plausible. In Ross's version of deontological pluralism, the duty to promote the good is called the duty of beneficence. Ross's duty of beneficence incorporates a duty to promote one's own intelligence and virtue, a matter to which I will return below.

Deontological pluralism adds to the duty of beneficence other fundamental duties. I will go into greater detail about what those duties are later. But in order to explain what is attractive about deontological pluralism's structure, I need one illustrative example. For this purpose, I will use the duty to keep one's *binding promises* (Ross 1930, 17, 21).

There is some controversy about some conditions on a binding promise. My own view is that a promise is not morally binding if it was obtained by fraud or coercion or if the promise is to do something immoral. An alternative view is that promises obtained by fraud or coercion or to do something immoral are binding but the moral duty to keep them is very weak and thus easily overridden. What is not controversial is that a promise is not binding if the promisee releases the promisor from the promise. The promisee might well release the promisor from the promise if the promisee can see that the keeping of the promise will harm the promisee or someone else. Let us focus on a case where the promisee does not release the promisor. In such a case, the duty to keep the promise stands, providing a moral reason for the promisor to keep the promise.

A promise can be binding even if no benefit will come from keeping it (cf. Ross 1930, 36, 40; 1939, 99–101; Phillips 2019, 64–74). The duty to keep promises is not merely an implication of the duty to bestow benefits on and prevent harm to others (Ross 1930, 38, 40). Rather, the duty to keep promises is an independent moral duty, capable of conflicting with the duty to bestow benefits on and prevent harm to others (Ross 1930, 19, 34–5).

Consider a spectrum of possible cases of conflict between these two duties. One end of the spectrum consists of cases in which keeping a very minor promise would conflict with preventing immense harm. The other end of the spectrum consists of cases in which keeping an immensely important promise would conflict with preventing a tiny harm for someone. Along part of this spectrum of cases, the duty to bestow benefits on and prevent harm to others outweighs the duty to keep one's promises. Along the opposite end of the spectrum of cases, the duty to keep one's promises outweighs the duty to bestow benefits on and prevent harm to others. Thus, neither the duty to bestow benefits on and prevent harms to others nor the duty to keep one's promises necessarily trumps the other. Which is the more important duty in the situation depends on such factors as how important the promise was to the promisee, how much benefit or harm is at stake, and perhaps whether there are other special connections between the promisor and promisee (to which I will return).

A good way of expressing such ideas is to employ Ross's distinction between *prima facie* duties and *overall* duty (sometimes called final duty, verdictive duty, duty *simpliciter*, or duty *sans phrase*). We have a prima facie duty not to break our binding promises, but this duty is not always stronger than other prima facie duties when they conflict with it. On the one hand, that an act would involve breaking one or more of our binding promises always has the same negative moral polarity—that an act would involve breaking our binding promise always counts morally against our doing the act. On the other hand, while keeping our binding promise is always a *prima facie* duty, keeping our binding promise is sometimes not our duty *overall*.

One could try to be a deontological pluralist without making a distinction between prima facie and overall duty. In order to construct such a deontological pluralism, one might try to rank duties in an ordering of strict priority. The proposal might be, for example, that the duty to keep one's promises is *always* more important than the general duty to bestow benefits on or prevent harms to others. To be sure, in some cases, one morally ought to keep one's promise rather than bestow benefits on or prevent harms to others. But in other cases, where the importance of the promise is less or the amount of benefit or harm at stake is greater, the right thing to do is bestow benefits on or prevent harms to others even though this involves breaking one's promise. No strict priority ranking obtains between the duty to keep one's promises and the general duty to bestow benefits on or prevent harms to others. That will be true of many other proposed priority rankings among abstractly stated duties (Nagel 1979, 131).

Instead of trying to maintain strict priority orderings, could we restrict or qualify the pluralist elements to eliminate conflict between them entirely? Some narrowing of duties so as to minimize conflict between them might be desirable. For example, the duty not to injure others might be narrowed so that it doesn't apply in situations where injuring attackers is the only way to protect the innocent from the attack. Protecting the innocent from attack falls under both the general duty of doing good for others and the duty to promote justice. In situations where the only way to protect the innocent from attack is to injure the attackers, there is no conflict of duties, since the duty not to injure is narrowed so as not to apply in such cases.

But there are plenty of examples where wider duties do conflict and some of these wider duties are outweighed. This is what happens in the examples I gave where the duty to keep one's promises conflicts with the duty to bestow benefits on or prevent harm to others. Examples where duties conflict and some duties outweigh others exemplify the need for Ross's distinction between prima facie and overall duty, since it is the prima facie duties that conflict and the one that is most important in the circumstances is overall duty.

Furthermore, the phenomenon of 'moral residue' testifies to duty A's being *outweighed by* duty B instead of the duty A's being *restricted in order to avoid conflict* with duty B (Ross 1930, 28). If duty A outweighs duty B rather than eliminates or cancels duty B, then, even if we have done as we ought in complying with duty A, for our noncompliance with duty B we might owe some people explanations and apologies and even more.

The materials that structure Ross's ethical theory are his deontological pluralism and his distinction between prima facie duties and overall duties. The result is a very powerful structure. It is a structure that explains conflict between moral pressures, rather than construing conflict between duties as casting doubt on the duties (Hurka 2014, 150–61). If we are intuitively attracted to a plurality of duties but are unwilling to ascribe *absolute* priority to any of these, then we will find a deontological pluralism that gives these duties only prima facie status very attractive (Audi 2004, 28–9).

Some philosophers complain that Rossian deontological pluralism does not provide us with enough help when we are trying to make moral decisions. I admit to being disappointed by the advice that we can but use good judgement to work out which moral duty is stronger in a particular situation. However, first, deontological pluralism's commitment to weighing plural moral pressures that do not fall into a strict lexical ordering is what enables this theory to have intuitively plausible implications about what is right or wrong in various circumstances. Second, while we may be disappointed that making moral decisions by employing Rossian deontological pluralism must draw heavily on the exercise of good judgement, I concede that good judgement has an ineliminable role since the correct resolutions of conflicts among prima facie duties seems not to be completely codifiable in informative principles. Third, I concede that there may be conflicts among prima facie duties in particular cases where the correct moral resolution is indeterminate. I therefore think that the objection that Rossian deontological pluralism does not provide us with enough help when we are trying to make moral decisions is an unconvincing objection to this theory.

As I have argued elsewhere (1996; 2000), before being content with deontological pluralism, we should look to see if there is a rival (probably multilevel) theory that is equally successful at generating intuitively plausible verdicts and yet does so from a *single* foundational moral principle. This single foundational principle would ideally be an *impartial* one. (For attempts to argue in this way, see Rawls 1971; Hare 1981; Scanlon 1998; Hooker 2000; Audi 2004; and Parfit 2011; 2017, especially 420–2, 432–3, 450). If such a single foundational principle really can match deontological pluralism's ability to generate intuitively plausible verdicts, then the single foundational principle has greater explanatory power, in that it explains just as much but on the basis of more parsimonious assumptions. Ross himself admitted that his classification of prima facie duties 'makes no claim to being ultimate ... If further reflection discovers a perfect logical basis for this or for a better classification, so much the better' (1930, 23).

III The Content of Rossian Deontological Pluralism

Thus far, I have focused on Rossian deontological pluralism's structure, though I have had to make a few assumptions about the content of the plural duties in order to illustrate that structure. Now, the primary focus shifts to the content of the plural duties. Chapter 2 of Ross's 1930 *The Right and the Good* (21) offers the following prima facie duties:

1. Duties of Fidelity—i.e., to keep one's explicit and implicit promises, including the implicit promise to tell the truth, which promise is implied when one enters into conversation.

2. Duties of Reparation
3. Duties of Gratitude
4. Duties of Justice—i.e., duties to upset or prevent mismatches of happiness to merit.
5. Duties of Beneficence—to promote others' virtue, intelligence, or pleasure.
6. Duties to improve our own intelligence or virtue.
7. Duties of Non-maleficence, i.e., duties not to injure others.

This list and what Ross says about the list seem to me commendable in many ways. I have already explained how I think that Ross's postulating a duty to keep one's promises is not to be assimilated to a duty to bestow benefits on or prevent harm to others. Likewise, Ross is right not to assimilate duties of gratitude, reparation, and justice to duties of beneficence and non-maleficence. I think he should have added a duty not to steal or damage others' property, another duty not assimilated to duties of beneficence and non-maleficence.

Ross is also right that the duty of non-maleficence is 'of a more stringent character' than the duty of beneficence without being necessarily overriding (1930, 21, 22; see also 1938, 74–5). Take a case where you could sit still and fail to prevent (and so in a sense 'allow') a harm to innocent person A or you could instead actively prevent this harm to A but only by imposing a slightly smaller harm on innocent person B. On the assumption that there are no other relevant facts (i.e., you didn't make promises concerning A or B, neither of these people have special relations to you, and so on), you should not harm B in order to prevent a somewhat greater harm to A. We might infer from this that there is a morally relevant distinction between *doing* harm and *allowing* harm (for explanation and discussion, see Woollard 2015).

I now turn to criticisms of Ross's list. These criticisms are not hostile. Ross claimed neither completeness nor finality for his list (1930, 20). I think he, or at least many of those sympathetic to his type of theory, could accept each of the criticisms I offer below as merely revisions to his theory rather than a rejection of it.

The most striking thing about Ross's list is that, although Ross complained (1930, 19) against utilitarianism that morally significant relations between people include not only benefactor to beneficiary but also spouse to spouse, child to parent, friend to friend, etc., two pages after making that complaint, Ross did not include agent-relative duties to family and friends in his list of prima facie duties. Nor do agent-relative duties to family and friends appear in his list of special relations on the page after his list. In contrast, deontological pluralists characteristically hold that agents can have morally relevant special relations not only to their benefactors (generating duties of gratitude), victims (generating duties of reparation), and promisees (generating duties to keep the promises given) but also to their family and friends and perhaps others (generating duties of loyalty). In each of these cases, the special relations generate agent-relative duties for the agent to the particular others with whom the agent has these special relations.

Ross later attempted to fold agent-relative duties to friends and parents under duties of gratitude (1938, 76). And Ross tried to fold duties to friends under an implicit promise of loyalty (1938, 273). But siblings' duties towards one another cannot plausibly be *fully* accounted for under the headings of duties of gratitude and promise-keeping. There are special relations between siblings that underpin agent-relative duties of loyalty to one another *even in cases where there are (a) no explicit or implicit promises between them, (b) no wrongs for which reparation is owed, and (c) no unfulfilled duties of gratitude.* Here I am not relying on the bare relation of siblinghood. I admit that to have duties of loyalty to siblings might require a shared history of experiences with them. But such duties of loyalty are not grounded in, conditional upon, or limited to promise-keeping, reparation, and gratitude. Equally, not all parents' duties towards their children can be fully accounted for under gratitude and promise-keeping (Hurka 2014, 192). (I have more to say about agent-relative duties of loyalty later in this chapter.)

A second criticism of Ross's list concerns his inclusion of the prima facie duty to improve one's own virtue and intelligence. Ross accepted that there is a prima facie duty of beneficence (1930, 21; 1938, 252, 271). But then, according to Bernard Williams, Ross needed a 'fraudulent' duty *to oneself* to protect one's other projects from being swamped by duties to other people (Williams, 1985, 181–2). A prima facie duty to do good for others should be either restrained or opposed by some other moral pressure, such as a duty to oneself, or permission to give some priority to one's own good and projects in order to keep the prima facie duty to do good for others from seizing control of virtually all one's attention and action (for ideas about this, see Wolf 2002, 175, 99, 183–4; Hooker 2007).

However, Ross's duty of self-improvement *in terms of virtue* is hardly going to carve out a realm of freedom to pursue one's own self-regarding projects. If the duty of self-improvement in terms of virtue will not do the job needed, will the duty to improve one's own intelligence do it? We all devote a lot of our time and attention to projects other than keeping our promises, complying with duties of gratitude and reparation, promoting justice, benefitting others, and avoiding doing others harm. Is devoting a lot of our time to those other projects morally permissible? The idea that it is morally permissible only if what we are doing is increasing our intelligence seems to me ridiculous.

I agree with Ross that there are duties to develop one's own virtue and intelligence. However, I think these duties concerning oneself are derivative from moral duties to others, not fundamental as Ross held. Denying that there are non-derivative moral duties to develop one's capacities does not preclude accepting that there are *non*-moral *reasons* to develop one's capacities so as to approximate excellence as closely as we can.

In his *Foundations of Ethics*, Ross was resolute that there is no moral duty to promote one's own pleasure (65, 72, 75, 272, 277, 302). Ross thought the duty of beneficence incorporates a duty to promote one's own good, but then he held in *Foundations* that pleasure has no intrinsic value. I agree that there is no moral duty to promote *one's own* pleasure. But my explanation of why there is no moral duty to promote one's own pleasure is the opposite of Ross's. Unlike Ross, I maintain that pleasure is intrinsically valuable. But, again unlike Ross, I construe the duty of beneficence as a duty to do good *for others*. Thus, I hold that the duty of beneficence does not include moral pressure on one to promote one's own pleasure.

A third and more general problem with Ross's theory concerns permissions concerning self-sacrifice. As already forshadowed, Ross should have recognized a moral permission to give one's own good some degree of *extra* weight when no promises or special duties come into play and one is deciding what to do with one's own resources. In such cases, keeping a benefit for oneself when one could have instead bestowed a somewhat greater benefit on someone else is permissible. If, when no promises or special duties come into play and one is deciding what to do with one's own resources, one instead sacrifices a benefit for oneself for the sake of bestowing a slightly greater benefit on someone else, the act is *supererogatory*, not a duty. Furthermore, there is also a moral *permission* to give one's own good some degree *less* weight when no promises or special duties come into play and one is deciding what to do with one's own resources. Hence, sacrificing a benefit for oneself for the sake directing a somewhat smaller benefit to someone else is also permitted and supererogatory (Hooker 2013, 719; 2022, Sec. 2; Hurka 2014, 179–81; Stratton-Lake 2025).

A fourth criticism of Ross's theory is connected to the previous one that Ross pays too little attention to permissions. Arguably, permissions are a certain kind of moral right: if you are morally permitted to do X, then you have a moral right to do X and you do not have a moral duty not to do X. However, permissions are hardly the only kind of right. And my fourth criticism of Ross's theory concerns rights.

Before I turn to that criticism, I want to commend some of the things Ross says about rights. He distinguishes between moral rights and legal rights and suggests that moral rights often predate legal ones. He insists that the existence of moral rights does not depend on their social recognition: 'to make the existence of a *moral* right depend on its being recognised ... would imply that slaves, for instance, acquired the moral right to be free only at the moment when a majority of mankind, or of some particular community, formed the opinion that they ought to be free ...' (1930, 51) More generally, 'everyone will admit that there are certain forms of treatment of others which are wrong and which the sufferer has the right to have removed, whether this right is recognized by society or not' (1930, 51).

Some philosophers hold that propositions about rights can always be reduced to propositions either about duties that others have or about permissions that the right-holder has. For example, the proposition that you have a right to walk in the park during its opening hours can be reduced to propositions about others' duties not to prevent you from doing this plus the permission you have to walk in the park. A simpler example is that your right not to be physically attacked might be reduced to everyone else's duty not to physically attack you. If all propositions about rights could be reduced to propositions about duties and permissions, then our moral ontology would be simpler if we omitted rights.

However, Ross pointed out that duties are not always correlated with rights. He thought humans have a duty not to treat animals inhumanely, a duty owed to animals and based on the badness of animals' pain (1930, 49). But he also held that animals do not have rights against such treatment, because animals are incapable of claiming such rights (1930, 50). If humans have a duty to animals but animals have no corresponding rights, then not all duties can be captured in propositions about rights.

Of course, that line of thought depends on the idea that beings cannot have rights that these beings are incapable of claiming. Whether this idea is correct matters enormously for the debate about what the best understanding of human rights is (see the papers in Crisp [ed.] 2014). The issue also matters for the debate about which moral theory is best (Carruthers 1992; Hooker 2000, 66–70; Hills 2010). In any case, the question of whether beings' rights are contingent on these beings' being able to claim such rights is far too big for me to address here.

Rather than relying on the idea that there are duties to animals without the animals' having corresponding rights, Ross raised the question of whether our prima facie duty to be beneficent correlates with rights others have to our beneficence (Ross 1930, 50, 52). Ross acknowledged that no one has a right to others' doing beneficent acts 'in the spirit of beneficence' (53). This acknowledgement does not, Ross thought, entail that there can be duties of beneficence towards people who lack moral rights to this beneficence. For Ross held that the duty of beneficence, like other duties, is a duty concerning acts, not concerning the motive for such acts nor the spirit in which such acts are done. Thus, he held that we can have a duty of beneficence to do good for others without others' having rights that we do good for them 'in the spirit of beneficence'.

Nevertheless, Ross was moving in the direction of the conclusion that our duties of general beneficence always correlate with rights others have to our beneficence. He conceded that the term 'rights' began by referring to legal rights. But he noted that usage of the term 'rights' now extends 'so as to include certain things that cannot be claimed at law; but its usage has not yet broadened out so much as to become completely correlative to duty. Once we start on the process of broadening it out, however, there seems to be no secure resting-place short of this' (1930, 53). The implication here is that duties of beneficence to others will end up being correlative to rights that others have to this beneficence.

In contrast, I hold to the idea that there is a *general* imperfect moral duty to do good for others that is not correlative to rights others have to be beneficiaries of such do-gooding (cf. Mill 1861, Ch. 5, paragraph 15, in Crisp [ed.] 1998, 94; Audi 2015b, 237, 247). If you are my family member or my friend, then I have a *special*, or agent-relative, moral duty to do good for you and you have a moral right that I do so. The same is true if I have promised to do good for you. But if I haven't made such a promise concerning your good and if you stand in no other special relation to me, then my moral duty to do good for others is not correlated with a moral right you have to my beneficence. Now if we accept this idea that only some duties to others are correlated with rights possessed by others, we need the concept of moral rights to distinguish between duties that are correlated with moral rights possessed by others and duties that are not correlated with moral rights possessed by others.

Something else that cannot be accounted for if our moral ontology consists of only duties and permissions is power rights. Power rights are not duties: people often have no duty to exercise their power rights. That is also true of liberty rights (i.e., freedoms, or permissions). Admittedly, where people have liberty rights or power rights, others will have corresponding duties not to prevent the exercise of these rights. But power rights cannot be completely reduced to some combination of duties and permissions.

People have permissions to make promises, accept or reject others' promises to them, make contracts with people, (if single) get married, consent to various forms of others' treatment of them that would otherwise be wrong, and so on. But what makes these permissions very different from other permissions is that, in exercising these permissions, people exercise *normative powers to change their or other people's duties and permissions.* For example, if you promise you will meet me for lunch tomorrow and I accept the promise, then you have created a duty for yourself to meet me for lunch tomorrow and you have also created a right in me that you meet me for lunch tomorrow. Both the duty you thereby create for yourself and the right you create for me depend on your having exercised your *prior* power right to create them. The power right is the basis of the duty that you create. The power right cannot be explained in terms of prior duties. Nor can the power right be explained merely in terms of the simple concept of permissions, for *most* permissions are not also powers. Hence, deontological pluralism needs to posit power rights as well as duties and permissions (Hurka 2014, 189–90).

I believe that deontological pluralism is more plausible if it posits other rights as well. I have in mind especially rights that serve to protect people's rational capacities to make judgements about what to believe, to value, and to pursue, and people's agency in acting on their judgements. We might try to explain these rights in terms of the protection of agency, autonomy, freedom, or self-expression (Griffin 2008; Hurka 2014, 189-90; Cullity 2018, 47–52). These rights will make vivid the importance of consent (Audi 2015a) and not treating others as mere means (Audi 2004, 90–120; Cullity 2018, 195–216). Such rights will extend, I think, to some set of property rights (Williams 1985, 185; Hurka 2014, 191–2). Admittedly, perhaps all these autonomy and property rights could be reduced to combinations of permissions for the right holders and duties of others towards the right holders. But felicity of expression, if not moral ontology, will be simpler if we include these autonomy and property rights.

My fifth and final proposal about how Ross's theory should be revised concerns justice. Ross wrote,

> Some [duties] rest on the fact or possibility of a distribution of pleasure or happiness (or of the means thereto) which is not in accordance with the merit of the persons concerned; in such cases there arises a duty to upset or prevent such a distribution. These are the duties of justice. (1930, p. 21)

> The duty of justice is particularly complicated, and the word is used to cover things which are really very different—things such as the payment of debts, the reparation of injuries done by oneself to another, and the bringing about of a distribution of happiness between other people in proportion to merit. I use the word to denote only the last of these three... The bringing of this about is a duty which we owe to all men alike, thought it may be reinforced by special responsibilities that we have undertaken to particular men. (1930, 26–7)

In this second passage, Ross acknowledged that the word 'justice' is used to cover payment of debts created by previous acts of the agent. With respect to both paying debts and making reparation, duties are owed to people with particular relations to the agent. The agent has promised to do a service or provide a good, and so the duty is agent-relative, in the sense that the agent's duty is to keep the promises she made. The duty to make reparations is likewise agent-relative, since an agent is to make reparations to the victims of wrongs she perpetrated on them, not to the victims of wrongs that others have perpetrated. These agent-relative components of justice are elements that Ross wants to list under duties that rest on actions the agent has done, such as promises the agent has made or wrongs the agent has perpetrated.

Are the only agent-relative elements of justice the agent-relative ones that Ross identified? Suppose that I could devote my free time to helping a stranger or to helping my sibling, and each of them would benefit about the same amount from my help. As mentioned earlier in this chapter, my sister has a morally relevant special relation to me and thus a special claim on my attention and energy; the stranger has no special relation to me and thus no special claim on my attention and energy. If I help the stranger rather than my sister, my sister might complain that I am treating her unjustly, or perhaps unfairly, because I am ignoring the fact that she has a special relation to me that the stranger does not have.

Earlier, I wrote that siblings' duties towards one another cannot plausibly be fully accounted for under gratitude and promise-keeping. (That is compatible with accepting that special relations between siblings can be strengthened by explicit or implicit promises, by duties of reparation for wrongs done to one another, and by duties of gratitude for services provided to one another.) Since there are such agent-relative duties of loyalty that do not rest on duties of promise keeping, reparation, or gratitude, and these duties of loyalty can be relevant to justice, an account of justice should accommodate them.

Could Ross accommodate duties of loyalty by folding them into his account of *merit*? Couldn't Ross say that my sister *merits* my attention in a way that a stranger doesn't (unless of course the stranger would benefit much more from my help than she would)? Ross could not in consistency say this, for he restricted merit to virtue. The bare fact that she is my sister cannot add or detract from her virtue and thus for Ross cannot add or detract from her merit.

Ross indicated at the end of the second quotation above that bringing about the distribution of happiness in proportion to merit is something *owed to all others*. A second possible view is that bringing about the distribution of happiness in proportion to merit is something *owed to those whom this distribution would benefit but not to anyone else*. A third possible view is that the duty is *not owed to anyone*.

For the sake of teasing out which of these three views is most plausible, suppose that at the moment a lot of vicious people are happy and a lot of virtuous people are unhappy. And suppose that at the click of a finger we could bring about a different distribution with the same amount of virtue, vice, happiness, and unhappiness, but in which the virtuous are happy and the vicious unhappy. Those who believe that punishment is owed to the guilty would probably say that bringing about the distribution in which the virtuous are happy and the vicious unhappy is owed to everyone. In contrast, my view is that, if bringing about the distribution in which the virtuous are happy and the vicious unhappy is owed to anyone, then it is owed to the virtuous, since they are the ones who would benefit.

Be that as it may, I think it is difficult to deny that the good is comprised of, among other things, aggregate well-being and the extent to which benefits go to those who deserve them. Ross gave us a thought experiment with immense appeal:

> If we compare two imaginary states of the universe, alike in total amounts of virtue and vice and of pleasure and pain present in the two, but in one of which the virtuous were all happy and the vicious miserable, while in the other the virtuous were miserable and the vicious happy, very few people would hesitate to say that the first was a much better state of the universe than the second (1930, 138; see also 1938, 73–4).

I would amend the point made in this passage so that it refers to the distribution of *positive well-being* in proportion to virtue, without tying positive well-being to happiness (see Hooker 2015).

IV Virtue, Rights, and Fairness

Even where social practices and institutions are designed to promote and reward virtue, these social practices and institutions might be designed badly and so have the reverse effect. Other social practices and institutions are designed to ignore virtue and achieve other ends. In either case, social practices and institutions might *require*, indirectly *incentivize*, or merely *permit* injustice. How might practices or institutions require, incentivize, or permit injustice? In a Rossian spirit, we might try to answer that these practices or institutions could require, incentivize, or permit divergence between benefit and virtue.

Very many social practices and institutions focus on other things than virtue. To take a simple example, consider a 100-yard dash. Suppose that I have been self-obsessed and devious, and you have been altruistic and honest. We compete in a 100-yard dash, the rules of which are that the winner is the first across the finish line without cheating. Suppose another runner in the race accidentally trips you and so I get to the finish line first. I wasn't the one who tripped you, and I did not cheat in the race. Thus, if the rules of the race are followed, I am declared the winner. This makes me happy but leaves you unhappy. Since you are more virtuous than I am and following the rules of the competition in this case results in happiness for me rather than for you, following these rules results in a divergence between benefit and virtue.

Competitions (not including games of chance) have as their point ranking contestants in terms of their display of skill or talent or some other esteemed property (Feinberg 1970, 64). The skill or talent or some other property spotlighted in the competition will typically not point to virtues, with the exceptions perhaps of wisdom and courage. To take the case we have been discussing, the runner who is most skilled is not the one who crosses the finish line first, since she was accidentally tripped by another runner. In such a case, the rules of the race entitle the one who crosses the finish line first to be the winner, yet the most skilled contestant is someone else, and very possibly the most virtuous contestant in the race is neither the one who crossed the line first nor the one with the greatest skill.

In such a situation, what does justice require? The answer seems to ignore both virtue and happiness. The point of the competition is to assess skill in racing 100 yards, not to assess virtue. And what the competition offered as a prize was not happiness but rather a medal or money or at least being recorded as the winner. Though the winner is typically happy about winning, happiness for the winner is not required by justice.

The person who crossed the finish line first is *entitled* by the rules of the race to be declared winner. Perhaps, the person with the greatest relevant skills *deserved* to win the race, though was thwarted by bad luck. Feinberg suggested that conflicts between entitlement and desert are 'conflicts between one claim of justice and another' (1970, 80). Where the rules of the competition were known to all in advance, justice requires that the rules of the competition be followed, even if doing so does not result in the most skilled contestant's being declared the winner.

Consider the idea that practices are just as long as their operation *in general* and *on the whole* results in a correspondence between happiness and virtue—even if, in many individual cases, their operation yields greater happiness to the less virtuous. There are good reasons to reject this idea. Many practices are configured for the sake of efficiency, being easy to remember, and for other non-moral advantages. For example, if you list names in alphabetical order, you have provided a list in which, no matter how long the list is, someone can very quickly check to see if a name is included, and you have made no suggestion as to which names are more important than others. There is no reason to assume that this practice will in general and on the whole result in greater benefits for the more virtuous. The same seems true of very many other useful and acceptable practices that have purposes other than to recognize and reward virtue.

If social practices were assessed *only* in terms of how much they reward virtue, the spectre of obsessive moralism would loom. The extent to which virtue is rewarded—in Ross's terms, the degree of justice—is hardly the only thing that matters. A way of making this point vivid is to rework Ross's thought experiment:

> Compare two imaginary states of the universe. In one, there is far greater aggregate well-being but a bit less of a match between well-being and virtue. In the other, there is far less aggregate well-being but a bit more match between well-being and virtue.

Why might there be greater aggregate well-being where the match between well-being and virtue is a bit less? If the match is better between well-being and virtue, the *likely cause is that people are relentlessly trying to bring about this match*. But too great a concern for bringing about a match between well-being and virtue would be oppressive, leaving far too little room for the pursuit of other aims, such as efficiency. Moreover, imagine a mindset that left no room for non-judgemental joy taken in undeserved benefits. Such a mindset would be much too puritanical.

So far, I have admitted that justice is *partly* a matter of reward of virtue. I have also contended both that often justice requires following the rules of an established practice or institution whose rules are focused on things other than matters of virtue, and that the consequences of following the rules of the practice or institution can be a divergence between well-being and virtue. I added that, even if social practices can be assessed in terms of how effective they are at rewarding virtue, this is not the only dimension along which they should be assessed. My example suggested that another dimension along which they should be assessed is aggregate well-being.

I now want to suggest that there are remarks in Ross that can support the idea that justice can come into our assessment of social practices in ways that bypass the question of whether the distribution of well-being is proportional to virtue. *The Foundations of Ethics* has a few passages in which Ross seems to place more importance on the observance of rights than he does anywhere in *The Right and the Good*. The most striking of these passages in *The Foundations of Ethics* is this:

> In its typical manifestation, the sense of duty is a particularly keen sensitiveness to the rights and interests of other people, coupled with a determination to do what is fair between them... (304)

Where in Ross's normative theory do rights and fairness sit? Rights to have promises kept are created by promises. Rights against various kinds of harm correspond to the duty of non-maleficence. As I contended earlier, there are other rights that do not fall into those categories. If we have to choose where in Ross's list of prima facie duties to put rights that are not created by promises and rights that are not the flip side of the duty of non-maleficence, I think the most natural answer is under the duty of justice. Equally, if we have to choose where in Ross's list of prima facie duties to put concern for fairness, I think the most natural answer is under the duty of justice.

Suppose we accept that part of assessing the justice of social practices consists in ascertaining whether the practices generate a distribution of benefits in proportion to virtue. Another part of assessing the justice of social practices seems to consist in ascertaining whether the practices respect the rights that people have. If this is correct, then justice involves not only distribution of well-being in proportion to virtue but also (at least) respect for people's rights.

Ross's comment about a determination to do what is fair *between people* suggests he thinks of fairness as essentially involving a comparison of the treatment of, or evaluation of, different individuals or groups. Indeed, in that spirit, consider this account of fairness:

> Fairness requires both that entities who are *not* relevantly different be evaluated and treated as if they're *not* relevantly different and that entities who *are* relevantly different be evaluated and treated *in accordance with their relevant difference*.

With Ross in mind, we might say that one way people are relevantly different is that some are more *virtuous* than others. Another relevant difference might be that some people are ones to whom we have made *promises* and others are not. Yet another relevant difference might be that some people have some other *special relation* with us, such as being our benefactor or victim or sibling, and others do not have any *special relation* with us. There will be many situations in which any or all these differences between people will be relevant to deciding how we should treat them.

As a test case, suppose we are deciding which of two people to give some item, and the two people do not differ in any of the ways just mentioned, and yet one of these people would benefit more than the other from getting the item. Is this difference between them relevant to fairness? Perhaps one of these people is *needier* than the other and that is why one of these people would benefit more from getting the item than the other would. Many people hold that the difference in the extent to which needs would be satisfied is a relevant difference.

Now let us consider a different test case. While holding everything already stipulated in place, suppose that neither of the possible beneficiaries is needy. Each of the two people would benefit from being given the item, but each is already above any reasonable threshold of need, and so the benefit obtained would be beyond need. Does fairness designate as relevant the fact that, though neither person is needy, one person would benefit more than the other would?

A prominent view is that fairness is limited to comparison of people's moral *claims* (Broome 1990). It might be held that there are moral claims based on moral desert, promises, special relations, and need, but none based on purely the availability of an unneeded benefit. As indicated earlier, I accept that people without special relations to us do not have *rights* to unneeded benefits from us. However, I also think that the fact that one person would benefit more than the other would benefit *can* be a difference relevant to fairness even where neither of the two people is needy. To complicate the picture further, differences in utility gains can pull in the opposite direction from the pull of one or more other differences relevant to fairness.

Notice that I wrote '*can* be a difference relevant to fairness' rather than '*must* be a difference relevant to fairness'. Differences in utility—like differences in moral virtue, in what promises have been made, in special relations, and in need—are often *ir*relevant to fairness. They are irrelevant when agents are engaging in a permissible social practice and the practice requires or allows criteria to operate that ignore differences in moral virtue, in what promises have been made, in what special relations exist, in need, and in utility gains. In the example of the 100-yard dash, all these differences were irrelevant to deciding what fairness requires.

V Conclusion

I have argued in this chapter that Ross does not provide a fully satisfactory version of deontological pluralism. But Rossian pluralism can be revised so as to add moral permissions. Once moral permissions are added, self-improvement can be deleted as a basic moral duty. Deontological pluralism also needs much more provision for moral rights than Ross himself provided. And there should be a more multifaceted discussion of justice than we get from Ross. A deontological pluralism that takes much from Ross but makes these revisions will be Rossian in spirit if not in every detail. Such a theory can, I believe, generate verdicts about what to do that seem intuitively correct.

A moral theory must accord with our most confident moral convictions if this theory is to seem well justified to us. No single-principle moral theory will be justified to us unless it does at least nearly as good a job of agreeing with our various moral convictions as deontological pluralism does. Whether there is some single-principle moral theory that manages to do this is as yet unresolved. Until a single-principle moral theory is shown to do this, then, as Timmons writes, some version of a pluralistic moral theory like Ross's 'ought to be a default position in ethics—a position that monist theories must unseat' (Timmons 2013, 265).*

Acknowledgments

This paper benefited from the discussion at the conference at Notre Dame in April 2022. It has also improved because of subsequent comments from Robert Audi, Roger Crisp, and David Phillips, to whom I am very grateful.

References

Audi, Robert (2004) *The Good in the Right: A Theory of Intuition and Intrinsic Value* (Princeton: Princeton University Press).
Audi, Robert (2015a) *Means, Ends, and Persons* (Oxford: Oxford University Press).
Audi, Robert (2015b) 'Wrongs within Rights', in Audi's *Reasons, Rights, and Values* (Cambridge University Press), 229–48.
Broome, John (1990) 'Fairness', *Proceedings of the Aristotelian Society* 91, 87–102.
Carruthers, Peter (1992) *The Animals Issue: Moral Theory in Practice* (Cambridge: Cambridge University Press).
Crisp, Roger (ed.) (2014) *Griffin on Human Rights* (Oxford: Oxford University Press).
Cullity, Garrett (2018) *Concern, Respect, and Cooperation* (Oxford: Oxford University Press).
Feinberg, Joel (1970) 'Justice and Personal Desert', in Feinberg's *Doing and Deserving: Essays in the Theory of Responsibility* (Princeton: Princeton University Press).
Griffin, James (2008) *Human Rights* (Oxford: Oxford University Press).
Hare, R. M. (1981) *Moral Thinking: Its Levels, Method, and Point* (Oxford: Clarendon Press).
Hills, Alison (2010) 'Utilitarianism, Contractualism, and Demandingness', *Philosophical Quarterly* 60, 225–42.
Hooker, Brad (1996) 'Ross-style Pluralism versus Rule-consequentialism', *Mind* 105, 531–52.
Hooker, Brad (2000) *Ideal Code, Real World: A Rule-Consequentialist Theory of Morality* (Oxford: Oxford University Press).
Hooker, Brad (2007) 'Rule-consequentialism and Internal Consistency: A Reply to Card', *Utilitas* 19, 514–19.
Hooker, Brad (2013) 'Egoism, Partiality, Impartiality', in Roger Crisp (ed.) *Oxford Handbook on the History of Ethics* (Oxford: Oxford University Press), 710–28.
Hooker, Brad (2015) 'The Elements of Well-Being', *Journal of Practical Ethics* 3, 15–35.
Hooker, Brad (2022) 'Should Philosophical Reflection on Ethics Do Without Moral Concepts?', *Ethical Theory and Moral Practice*, 1–15.

Hurka, Thomas (2014) *British Ethical Theorists from Sidgwick to Ewing* (Oxford: Oxford University Press).
Mill, John Stuart (1861) '*Utilitarianism*', in Roger Crisp (ed.), *J. S. Mill: Utilitarianism*. (Oxford: Oxford University Press, 1998).
Nagel, Thomas (1979) 'The Fragmentation of Value', in *Mortal Questions* (Cambridge: Cambridge University Press), 128–41.
Parfit, Derek (2011) *On What Matters*, vol. 1 (Oxford: Oxford University Press).
Parfit, Derek (2017) *On What Matters*, vol. 3 (Oxford: Oxford University Press).
Phillips, David (2019) *Rossian Ethics: W. D. Ross and Contemporary Moral Theory* (New York: Oxford University Press).
Ross, W. D. (1930) *The Right and the Good* (London: Clarendon Press).
Ross, W. D. (1938) *The Fundamentals of Ethics* (Oxford: Clarendon Press).
Rawls, John (1971) *A Theory of Justice* (Cambridge MA: Harvard University Press).
Scanlon, T. M. (1998) *What We Owe To Each Other* (Cambridge MA: Harvard University Press).
Stratton-Lake, Philip (2025) 'Ross and the Problem of Permissibility', in this volume.
Timmons, Mark (2013) *Moral Theory: An Introduction*. 2nd edition (Lantham, MD: Rowman & Littlefield).
Williams, Bernard (1985) *Ethics and the Limits of Philosophy* (Cambridge, MA: Harvard University Press).
Wolf, Susan (2002) 'The Role of Rules', in Walter Sinnott-Armstrong and Robert Audi (eds) *Rationality, Rules, and Ideals: Critical Essays on Bernard Gert's Moral Theory* (Lanham, MD: Rowman & Littlefield), 165–79.
Woollard, Fiona. (2015). *Doing and Allowing Harm* (Oxford: Oxford University Press).

PART II
ROSS'S NORMATIVE ETHICS

6

Can Sidgwick and Ross Converge in Moral Theory?

David Phillips

Sidgwick and Ross are, I think, the most important figures in what Thomas Hurka has recently characterized as the Sidgwick to Ewing school.[1] The philosophers in this school largely agreed about metaethics, endorsing non-naturalism. I am sympathetic to their metaethical views, but they won't be my main focus here. My focus will instead be largely on the normative: on the question whether Sidgwick and Ross can converge in moral theory. I will argue that to a surprising extent they can. We can develop an interesting normative synthesis of Sidgwick and Ross.

Now, I should admit up front, convergence can come cheap. It will at least very often be possible to get philosophers' views to converge if you simply split differences between them, or simply allow that one of them is right in one respect and another right in another. Such cheaply acquired convergence may be a route to a plausible philosophical view. But it doesn't reveal anything much about the philosophers whose views you get to converge beyond the fact that, as you see it, each was on to part of the truth. Cheap convergence is not surprising.

I'm going to sketch a route to a synthesis of Sidgwick and Ross that, I will claim, is more interesting and surprising than that. It does involve some of the less interesting things: some difference-splitting and some mixed verdicts to the effect that Sidgwick is partly right and Ross is partly right. But it also derives from some significant commonalities between Sidgwick and Ross which seem to me well worth highlighting and exploring.

I'll focus in turn on three topics in normative theory: the right, the good, and the appropriate conceptual framework for moral theory. I'll argue that, with respect to the theory of the good and especially with respect to the theory of the right, Sidgwick and Ross share a lot more than they may initially appear to. And finally I'll reflect a bit more on the methodological approach Sidgwick and Ross share.

---

[1] For his fullest discussion, see *British Ethical Theorists from Sidgwick to Ewing* (Oxford: Oxford University Press, 2014).

David Phillips, *Can Sidgwick and Ross Converge in Moral Theory?* In: *The Moral Philosophy of W. D. Ross*. Edited by: Robert Audi and David Phillips, Oxford University Press. © Oxford University Press 2025. DOI: 10.1093/9780198914839.003.0006

I Sidgwick, Moore, and Ross

Let me start by saying a little more about the historical connections between Sidgwick and Ross. Those connections are usually mediated by the third central figure in the Sidgwick to Ewing school, Moore. It isn't that Ross never refers directly to Sidgwick. Still, instructively, there is only one reference to Sidgwick in the index to *The Right and the Good*,[2] whereas there are more references there to Moore than there are to any other philosopher. And there are more references to Sidgwick in the index to *Principia Ethica* than there are to any other philosopher.[3]

In philosophical temperament, Sidgwick and Ross have more in common with each other than either has with Moore, at least with the Moore of *Principia Ethica*. Both Sidgwick and Ross are moderates, inclined to find something right in all the various competing views in ethics. At the start of the *Foundations*[4] Ross says

> It would indeed be strange if any of the main theories of ethics were completely in error; it is far more likely that each has grasped something that is both true and important but has, not through blindness to moral values but by some apparently trivial logical error, claimed as the whole truth what is only one of a set of connected truths. (FE 2)

In a similar vein, in the introductory chapter of the *Methods*,[5] Sidgwick observes that

> Most of the practical principles that have been seriously put forward are more or less satisfactory to the common sense of mankind, so long as they have the field to themselves. They all find a response in our nature: their fundamental assumptions are all such as we are disposed to accept, and such as we find to govern to a certain extent our habitual conduct. (ME 14)

In *Principia* Moore, by contrast, is much more apt to be a radical: to think that almost everyone in the prior history of ethics is guilty of committing the naturalistic fallacy, and so that their thinking is largely worthless.

Nonetheless, despite these similarities in philosophical temperament, it is easy to characterize Sidgwick's, Moore's, and Ross's substantive views in a way that puts Sidgwick and Ross at opposite ends of the spectrum with Moore in the middle. On

---

[2] W. D. Ross, *The Right and the Good* (Oxford: Clarendon Press, 1930). I will refer to it as "RG." Page references will be placed in the text.

[3] G. E. Moore, *Principia Ethica* (Cambridge: Cambridge University Press, 1903). I will refer to it as "PE." Page references will be placed in the text.

[4] W. D. Ross, *Foundations of Ethics* (Oxford: Clarendon Press, 1939). I will refer to it as "FE." Page references will be place in the text.

[5] Henry Sidgwick, *The Methods of Ethics*, 7th edition (Indianapolis IN: Hackett, 1981; original publication date 1907). I will refer to it as "ME." Page references will be placed in the text.

this way of seeing things, Sidgwick is a utilitarian, both a consequentialist and a hedonist. Moore is a consequentialist but not a hedonist. And Ross is neither a consequentialist nor a hedonist. This way of seeing things is not completely wrong, of course. But I will argue that it leaves out important aspects of Sidgwick's and Ross's positions which make an interesting normative synthesis possible.

Why care about that possible normative synthesis? Here's one reason: if, like me, you are a fan of the intuitionist tradition, and if you think, as I do, that Sidgwick and Ross are the best moral philosophers in the Sidgwick to Ewing school, it would be disheartening to discover that the methodology they largely shared led in their hands only to fundamental normative disagreement. It would, by contrast, increase your confidence in that methodology if it turned out that, in the hands of its best exponents, it led to some significant normative convergence.

II The Right

The place where there is most room for interesting normative convergence between Sidgwick and Ross is in the theory of the right. You can, or so I'll argue, get to a plausible, moderately pluralistic theory of the right by drawing from them both. Ross, of course, uncontroversially was a moderate pluralist about the right. So it isn't surprising that he can contribute to such a synthesis. That Sidgwick can also contribute is more surprising, as he was not straightforwardly a pluralist about the right. But the dualism of the practical reason means he was not straightforwardly an impartial consequentialist either. And if we read the dualism as a number of charitable interpreters have, what emerges is a position that shares important features with and plausibly complements the moderate pluralism about the right we straightforwardly find in Ross. Or so I will argue.

Begin with the apparent obstacles to such a synthesis. Sidgwick and Ross can seem to disagree fundamentally in the theory of the right. After articulating his self-evident axioms, Sidgwick writes,

> I have tried to show how in the principles of Justice, Prudence, and Rational Benevolence as commonly recognised there is at least a self-evident element, immediately cognisable by abstract intuition; depending in each case on the relation which individuals and their particular ends bear as parts to their wholes, and to other parts of these wholes. I regard the apprehension, with more or less distinctness, of these abstract truths, as the permanent basis of the common conviction that the fundamental precepts of morality are essentially reasonable. No doubt these principles are often placed side by side with other precepts to which custom and general consent have given a merely illusory air of self-evidence: but the distinction between the two kinds of maxims appears to me to become manifest by merely reflecting on them. I know by direct reflection that the propositions, "I

ought to speak the truth," "I ought to keep my promises,"—however true they may be—are not self-evident to me; they present themselves as propositions requiring rational justification of some kind. On the other hand, the propositions, "I ought not to prefer a present lesser good to a future greater good," and "I ought not to prefer my own lesser good to the greater good of another," do present themselves as self-evident; as much (*e.g.*) as the mathematical axiom that "if equals be added to equals the wholes are equal." (ME 382–3)

In a passage whose target (as usual in Ross's work) is Moore, not Sidgwick, Ross writes,

> If we are told, for instance, that we should give up our view that there is a special obligatoriness attaching to the keeping of promises because it is self-evident that the only duty is to produce as much good as possible, we have to ask ourselves whether we really, when we reflect, *are* convinced that this is self-evident, and whether we really *can* get rid of our view that promise-keeping has a bindingness independent of productiveness of maximum good. In my own experience I find that I cannot, in spite of a very genuine attempt to do so; and I venture to think that most people will find the same, and that just because they cannot lose the sense of special obligation, they cannot accept as self-evident, or even as true, the theory that would require them to do so. In fact, it seems, on reflection, self-evident that a promise, simply as such, is something that prima facie ought to be kept, and it does *not*, on reflection, seem self-evident that production of maximum good is the only thing that makes an act obligatory. (RG 39–40)

At first sight Sidgwick and Ross indeed seem here to be in fundamental disagreement. Sidgwick claims consequentialist principles are self-evident and deontological principles are not self-evident. Ross claims consequentialist principles are not self-evident and deontological principles are self-evident.

But this way of putting it overlooks important differences between the principles they consider. Focus first on the consequentialist principles. The consequentialist principle whose self-evidence Ross denies—which he gets from Moore, not from Sidgwick—is "the only duty is to produce as much good as possible."

The key consequentialist principle Sidgwick endorses is instead the "maxim of benevolence." When in III.XIII Sidgwick finds a version of the maxim in Clarke, one way he formulates it is

A rational agent is bound to aim at universal good. (ME 385)

When the maxim is expressed this way, it is clear, as Hurka and I have both in effect argued, that there are two possible interpretations.[6] On the weaker

---

[6] For Hurka's version of the argument, see *British Ethical Theorists from Sidgwick to Ewing*, Ch. 7, and Hurka (2014), 129–52. For my version, see (2011), Chs. 4 and 5.

interpretation, the maxim of benevolence says that there is a prima facie duty to aim at universal good. On the stronger interpretation, the maxim of benevolence says that there is an absolute duty to aim at universal good. Sidgwick does not distinguish these two interpretations. Some of what he writes suggests the one, some suggests the other. But, once you have made the distinction, it is natural to ask which interpretation gives Sidgwick the better view.

I think the weaker interpretation gives Sidgwick the better view. On the weaker interpretation, the maxim is a good candidate to be self-evident. By contrast, on the stronger interpretation, the maxim doesn't look to be self-evident or indeed to be true. There is surely strong reason to aim at universal good. But there may be conflicting reasons. One kind of potentially conflicting reason is a partial reason. It may be that what best promotes universal good will produce much less good *for me* than some other outcome. In such cases, one view is that I ought to aim at what is best for me not at what is universally best. Another kind of potentially conflicting reason is a deontological reason. It may be that aiming at universal good means violating a deontological principle (either an absolute deontological principle or a deontological principle of prima facie duty). In such cases one view is that I ought not to violate the deontological principle. So it is not at all self-evident that there is an absolute duty to aim at universal good: that I have a duty proper to aim at universal good even where doing so is much less good for me or where doing so means violating deontological principles.

But the maxim of benevolence on the weaker interpretation, the maxim of benevolence interpreted as a principle of prima facie duty, is not merely the consequentialist principle whose truth Ross explicitly denies in the passage above. It is a principle Ross himself accepts. As he writes elsewhere in the same chapter,

> It seems self-evident that if there are things that are intrinsically good, it is a prima facie duty to bring them into existence rather than not to do so, and to bring as much of them into existence as possible. (RG 24)

Thus, I suggest, notwithstanding the apparent contrasts in the passages with which I began this section, Sidgwick and Ross agree about the key self-evident consequentialist principle.

One possible response here is: the prima facie duty interpretation of the maxim of benevolence is *too* charitable. Sidgwick doesn't have the concept of prima facie duty. So the prima facie duty interpretation can at most be an account of what Sidgwick ought to have said or thought, not of what he did say or think.

I respect this possible response. But notice that, if our question is whether Sidgwick and Ross can converge in moral theory, it might not matter very much whether we say that the prima facie duty reading tells us what Sidgwick did think or what he ought to have thought. Either way, we have interesting convergence.

Now focus on Sidgwick's and Ross's views about deontological principles. The deontological principles whose self-evidence Sidgwick denies in the passage with which we began this section are not the deontological principles whose self-evidence Ross affirms. Sidgwick does not, unfortunately, have the idea that deontological principles might be understood as principles of prima facie duty. What he rejects are deontological principles of duty proper. But Ross too rejects deontological principles of duty proper. The deontological principles Ross affirms are deontological principles of prima facie duty. The example he gives in the passage of a deontological claim that is self-evident is "a promise, simply as such, is something that prima facie ought to be kept."

Though Sidgwick regrettably does not consider the possibility of framing deontology in Ross's way, he would be likely to want to reject deontological principles of prima facie duty. But, at least if C. D. Broad is right, Sidgwick would need new arguments against such principles. In books both published in 1930, Ross and Broad independently articulated versions of moderate deontology featuring versions of the concept of prima facie duty.[7] Ross did not have Sidgwick particularly in mind in introducing the concept in *The Right and the Good*. But Broad did when he developed his version in *Five Types of Ethical Theory*. Having endorsed Sidgwick's critique of absolutist deontology, he proposed to

> state a form of [deontology] which is not open to Sidgwick's objections and is not flagrantly in conflict with reflective common-sense. (FT 218)

The key to this form of deontology is Broad's version of the concept of prima facie duty:

> The [deontologist] will have to moderate his claims very greatly. He will be confined to statements about *tendencies* to be right and *tendencies* to be wrong. (FT 222; italics in original)

But it isn't merely that Sidgwick and Ross disagree much less than they initially appear to about which consequentialist and deontological principles are self-evident. They also countenance deviations from impartial consequentialism which have significant commonalities and plausibly complement one another.

Here start with Ross. One characteristic way to understand the core of deontology is as a matter of absolute prohibitions. In introducing and deploying the concept of prima facie duty, Ross of course rejects this line. Other ways to understand the core of deontology emphasize something like a distinction between acts and omissions or between intending and foreseeing harm. Such treatments make

---

[7] Ross did so, of course, in *The Right and the Good*. Broad did so in *Five Types of Ethical Theory* (London: Kegan Paul, 1930). I will refer to it as "FT." Page references will be placed in the text.

the difference between right and wrong (or whatever) turn crucially on how an outcome is brought about.

Ross's deontology has something quite different at its core. To see this, consider some of his famous remarks in Chapter II of *The Right and the Good*:

> The essential defect of the "ideal utilitarian" theory is that it ignores, or at least does not do full justice to, the highly personal character of duty. If the only duty is to produce the maximum of good, the question who is to have the good—whether it is myself, or my benefactor, or a person to whom I have made a promise to confer that good on him, or a mere fellow man to whom I stand in no such special relation—should make no difference to my having a duty to produce that good. But we are all in fact sure that it makes a vast difference. (RG 22)

He goes on to use for the duties of fidelity, reparation, and gratitude the term "special obligations," which he contrasts with the consequentialist "general obligation" to do as much good as possible. Ross makes the existence of special obligations central to his rejection of ideal utilitarianism.

I have argued elsewhere that Ross's special obligations should be understood as involving agent-relative intensifiers.[8] That something would be a good for you gives me a reason to provide it for you if I can. But if I have promised to give that thing to you, I have extra reason that other people don't have to provide it to you. This reading of Ross gets textual support from a number of passages. The most important comes from Lecture V of the *Foundations*, where Ross gives his most extended treatment of his go-to example of a non-consequentialist prima facie duty, promissory obligation:

> We may ... if we like to put the matter so, think of the responsibility for conferring a promised benefit as being n times as great as the responsibility for conferring an exactly similar unpromised benefit, where n is always greater than 1, and, when the promise is very explicit, much greater than 1. It will follow that it is always our duty to fulfil a promise, except when the uncovenanted benefit to be conferred is more than n times greater than the covenanted benefit. (FE 101)

I have also argued that it is charitable to interpret Ross's view as *only* involving the combination of the general obligation to do as much good as possible and special obligations understood as agent-relative intensifiers. The challenge for this interpretation is that Ross does include something apparently different in his list of prima facie duties, something which takes us much closer to contemporary deontologies: the duty of non-maleficence. I draw both on textual and on

---

[8] In my (2019), Ch. 3.

philosophical considerations to argue that the charitable thing to do in reading Ross is to downplay the duty of non-maleficence. Textually, it is striking how little emphasis Ross places on it. Not only is it not his go-to example of a non-consequentialist duty; he often forgets about it when summarizing his view. He often presents his view as featuring simply the combination of the general obligation to do as much good as possible and the special obligations. Philosophically, I suggest, the duty of non-maleficence threatens to introduce something new and problematic that a Rossian theory is better off without—it threatens to introduce the paradox of deontology. We are better off deemphasizing the duty of non-maleficence: endorsing it only to the extent that it can be understood in terms of duties to promote goods or in terms of special obligations (or in terms of both).

In the current connection, it may not matter how successful I am in arguing that this is the charitable interpretation of Ross. Even the weaker claim that much—if not all—of what Ross adds to the general obligation is special obligations which involve agent-relative intensifiers is enough to set the stage for interesting convergence with Sidgwick in the theory of the right.

The argument that there is something in Sidgwick similar to Ross's combination of general and special obligations is more involved. Begin with Parfit's characterization of the dualism of practical reason.[9] He writes,

> According to
> *Rational Egoism*: We always have most reason to do whatever would be best for ourselves.
> According to
> *Rational Impartialism*: We always have most reason to do whatever would be impartially best...
> According to what Sidgwick calls
> *the Dualism of Practical Reason*: We always have most reason to do whatever would be impartially best, unless some other act would be best for ourselves. In such cases, we would have sufficient reasons to act either way. (OWM 1, 130–1)

On this reading, the dualism clearly has some broad similarities to Ross's moderate pluralism. Both involve a combination of impartial and partial elements. In Ross, the impartial element is "the general obligation to do as much good as possible." In Parfit it is "rational impartialism." And both involve a partial element too. In Ross's case, the partial element is special obligations. On Parfit's reading of Sidgwick, it is rational egoism.

Parfit doesn't argue for this interpretation of Sidgwick. But argument is needed, because in reading the dualism in this way Parfit discounts Sidgwick's frequent

---

[9] Derek Parfit, *On What Matters*, volume 1 (Oxford: Oxford University Press, 2011). I will refer to it as OWM 1. Page references will be placed in the text.

descriptions of it as a contradiction. I will first discuss how the interpretive argument that Parfit does not give might go, then consider further how far what Parfit finds in Sidgwick resembles what we have found in Ross, and what a view that combined them might look like.

First, the interpretive question: why, despite Sidgwick's clear official descriptions of the dualism as a contradiction, might you be tempted to read the dualism as Parfit does?[10]

The obvious way to argue for such an interpretation will have two complementary facets. One involves one of the four conditions Sidgwick employs in his argument against dogmatic intuitionism (absolutist deontology). The other is that, as we have already partly seen, the utilitarian and egoistic axioms he articulates are open to multiple interpretations. And the interpretations on which the axioms seem the best candidates to be self-evident—indeed, the only interpretations on which the axioms seem to have any chance of being self-evident—make them weak enough not to contradict one another.

Begin with the first facet of the argument. According to the third of the four conditions Sidgwick employs in III.XI in arguing against dogmatic intuitionism,

> The propositions accepted as self-evident must be mutually consistent. Here, again, it is obvious that any collision between two intuitions is a proof that there is error in one or the other, or in both. Still, we frequently find ethical writers treating this point very lightly. They appear to regard a conflict of ultimate rules as a difficulty that may be ignored or put aside for future solution, without any slur being thrown on the scientific character of the conflicting formulae. Whereas such a collision is absolute proof that at least one of the formulae needs qualification. (ME 341)

By Sidgwick's own lights, the existence of apparent utilitarian and egoist intuitions that conflict with one another is "absolute proof that at least one of the formulae needs qualification." And one obvious way to qualify the utilitarian and egoist principles so they do not contradict one another is to make them principles of prima facie duty rather than principles of duty proper. As we already noticed, this is a charitable reconstruction, an account of what Sidgwick ought to have thought, because Sidgwick does not have the concept of prima facie duty. But it may still be the best way to do what the condition directs us to do in the face of "collision between two intuitions."

And this meshes well with the second facet of the argument, which we have already partly explored. As we argued above, even if you are not explicitly focused on the dualism and the problem of potential contradiction with egoism, the most

---

[10] For fuller discussions of the interpretive debate about the dualism, with references to others' work, see my (2011), Ch.5, and (2022), Ch. 11.

charitable way to interpret the maxim of benevolence is (more weakly) as a principle of prima facie duty rather than (more strongly) as a principle of duty proper. Interpret the principle as a principle of prima facie duty and it plausibly is self-evident; Ross agrees that it is. By contrast, interpret it as a principle of duty proper and it is clearly not self-evident.

A largely parallel argument can be made with respect to the egoistic half of the dualism. The argument is trickier textually because of the multiple perplexities in Sidgwick's discussions of egoism.[11] What, in any case, plausibly emerges is a view according to which the egoistic principle too is a principle of prima facie duty.

But now we should notice some important disanalogies between the dualism Parfit finds in Sidgwick and Ross's special obligations. Ross's special obligations, as I read them, involve agent-relative intensifiers of independent reasons. Ross's view is flexible in what seem to me good ways. In the passage preceding the extract I quoted, he explicitly rejects the view that all promissory obligations have the same weight. Instead, on his view, promissory obligations have weights that vary, as the product of two different inputs: the importance of the thing promised (as I am putting it, the strength of the promise-independent reason I have to do the thing promised); and the strength of the promissory obligation itself (which Ross says varies according to, among other things, the explicitness of the promise). All, to my mind, plausibly flexible. Still, in another important way, Ross's view is not flexible. He thinks that each of our specific prima facie duties has a definite weight. It may be hard or indeed impossible for us to know what that weight is in practice. But still, in principle there is always an answer to the question: how much moral weight does a given promise have.[12] Of course there may be ties: cases where two competing obligations have exactly equal weight. But, other than in those cases, the moral metaphysics leave no room for discretion. In one type of case of conflict he famously discusses, either it is my duty to do what promotes the most overall good, because in that given case this duty outweighs the duty to keep a promise, or it is my duty to keep my promise, because in that given case this duty outweighs the duty to promote the most good. In no such cases (other than cases of genuine ties) do the moral metaphysics leave me options.

We could imagine a view very much like this one where the competing principles are an egoistic principle of prima facie duty and an impartial principle of prima facie duty. We could imagine the view being flexible in the ways in which Ross's account of promissory obligation is flexible: we could imagine an analogue of Ross's n, the intensifier that gives extra weight to one's own good. We could imagine that that intensifier might not be constant, but might vary in some way. But if

---

[11] For a discussion, see my (2011), Chs. 7, 9, and 11. For a summary, see 213–15. I say a bit more about the possible interpretations of the maxim of prudence in Section V below.

[12] For a critical discussion of this combination of epistemic indeterminacy and metaphysical determinacy, see my (2019), 189–92.

we are to stick to the Rossian model, we would be committed also to thinking that there was always a right answer to which prima facie duty was weightier, that the normative metaphysics did not give us options except in the case of genuine ties.

But this is not the view Parfit finds in Sidgwick, and it is not the view he finds plausible. What Parfit finds in Sidgwick is a view according to which, as he puts it, partial and impartial reasons are *wholly incomparable*. He thinks this view is too extreme. But he also thinks something that shares its basic features—a view according to which partial and impartial reasons are very imprecisely comparable—is the correct view.

Two kinds of consideration support reading Sidgwick as Parfit does, rather than as having a view more closely parallel to Ross's. One is a matter of textual evidence. While, on the whole, the textual evidence clearly supports readings according to which the dualism involves a contradiction, there are at least a couple of passages where Sidgwick says things that support Parfit's reading. One comes from the first edition of the Methods:[13]

> Again, there are others who will say that though it is undoubtedly reasonable to prefer the general happiness to one's own, when the two are presented as alternatives: still it remains also clearly reasonable to take one's own greatest happiness as one's ultimate and paramount end. (ME1, 461)

Another comes from Sidgwick's important late paper, "Some Fundamental Ethical Controversies":[14]

> I, therefore, do not see any inconsistency in holding that while it *would* be reasonable for the aggregate of sentient beings, if it could act collectively, to aim at its own happiness only as an ultimate end—and *would* be reasonable for an individual to do the same if he were the only being in the universe—it is yet *actually* reasonable for an individual to make an ultimate sacrifice of his happiness for the sake of the greater happiness of others, as well as reasonable for him to take his own happiness as ultimate end.

The other kind of consideration is a matter of philosophical plausibility. The view Parfit suggests, featuring very significant incomparability between partial and impartial reasons, is more philosophically plausible than is the view that competing partial and impartial prima facie duties are wholly comparable. As evidence of this, we can note that other theorists have argued for something very similar to the view Parfit finds in Sidgwick (or, at least, for something very similar to

---

[13] Henry Sidgwick, *The Methods of Ethics*, 1st Edition (London: Macmillan, 1874). I will refer to it as "ME1." Page references will be placed in the text.
[14] Sidgwick (1889), 473–87, 486.

Parfit's toned-down variant), framed using their own different terminology. To put things as Samuel Scheffler does, what the Parfitian reading of the dualism gives us is an agent-centered *permission*. By contrast, Ross's special obligations generate what Scheffler would call agent-centered *restrictions*.[15] To put things as Josh Gert does, Rossian special obligations involve *requiring* reasons; Parfit's reading of the dualism yields instead *justifying* reasons.[16]

If we combine Rossian deontological reasons with a Parfitian version of the dualism, we get a distinctive form of moderate pluralism about the right. It combines a plausible agent-relative deontological element that Ross argues for and that (at least if Broad is right) Sidgwick has no good argument against with a plausible agent-relative egoistic element that can be found in Sidgwick and that, as we will see further in Section IV, Ross has no good argument against. These agent-relative elements have important structural dissimilarities. Still, the synthesis of the two seems appealing and plausible to me. To anyone tempted to complain about its complexity, we might respond by quoting Ross:

> Loyalty to the facts is worth more than a symmetrical architectonic or a hastily reached simplicity (RG 23).

III The Good

Sidgwick's and Ross's commonalities with respect to the theory of the good are, I think, ultimately less interesting than their commonalities with respect to the theory of the right. But they are interesting nonetheless, and well worth noticing and reflecting on.

The thing to begin with, which Ross never to my knowledge notices, is just how similar the most important alternatives to hedonism he and Sidgwick consider are. Ross's alternative is famously, of course, the theory of the good that he accepts. As he frames it (anyway in *The Right and the Good*), four things are intrinsically good: virtue, knowledge, pleasure, and desert: the allocation of pleasure to the virtuous and pain to the vicious rather than vice versa.

When Sidgwick argues for hedonism in III.XIV, the pluralistic theory he argues against in sections 4 and 5 has it that in addition to happiness

---

[15] Scheffler (1982). The synthesis I am arguing for here could be inspired by the long footnote on page 85. There, Scheffler writes: "It is true, however, that I will not directly discuss any specific proposals that might be made for motivating *only* those agent-centered restrictions which prohibit the breaking of ones promises or the neglect of one's special obligations. And, strictly speaking, this leaves it open to a defender of a fully agent-centered outlook to maintain that those restrictions have a rationale... which is independent of any putative rationale for restrictions [on harming]." Of course, the Rossian version of a restriction is a matter of prima facie duty, not of duty proper.

[16] For one articulation of his view, see Gert (2003), 5–36.

cognition of Truth, contemplation of Beauty, Free or Virtuous action [are] in some measure preferable alternatives to Pleasure or Happiness—even though we admit that Happiness must be included as a part of Ultimate Good. (ME 400)

Both lists include Ross's three basic intrinsic goods, virtue, knowledge, and pleasure. Sidgwick includes also contemplation of Beauty (which Ross too may add in the *Foundations*). Sidgwick definitely does not include Ross's higher-order good, desert. But the lists are still strikingly similar.

Neither Sidgwick nor Ross ultimately endorses the theory in this simple and (to my mind) appealing form. They deviate from it in opposite directions. Sidgwick argues in III.XIV against it and in favor of hedonism. He denies that virtue, knowledge, etc. have any independent intrinsic value. I don't find his argument convincing. He argues first that intuitively, when distinguished from the pleasures that accompany them, correct desire and belief have only instrumental, not intrinsic value. One response—Moore quite explicitly offers it against this argument of Sidgwick's (PE 93-94)—is that in so arguing Sidgwick neglects the principle of organic unities. It does not follow from the fact that correct desires or beliefs have no value on their own that all the value of a whole including both them and pleasure comes simply from the pleasure. Sidgwick goes on, second, to claim that our degree of commendation of states like knowledge is proportional to the pleasure they produce. One response here is that this is the kind of claim about agreement between utilitarian and non-utilitarian verdicts that utilitarians are rather apt to make without providing sufficient evidence. Finally, Sidgwick offers various reasons why common sense might not be happy to say that pleasure is the only intrinsic good even if this were common sense's real view. This, again, is a perfectly respectable procedure. But my inclination is instead to take common sense at its word.

Ross, by contrast, has a strong anti-hedonist impulse that leaves him unsatisfied with the simple pluralist view. In *The Right and the Good* this impulse leads him to endorse the view that virtue is lexically prior to pleasure: that any extra amount of virtue however small compensates for any extra amount of pain however great. But the implausibility of this view can be shown by employing Ross's own favorite argumentative resource in these contexts: what we can call "abstract world arguments." Consider two states of the universe including nearly equal amounts of virtue—differing only in that one person on one occasion was less well motivated and acted less well in universe 1 than in universe 2—but such that universe 1 includes also widespread and intense pleasure and universe 2 widespread and intense pain. On Ross's view we should choose universe 2. But surely we should instead choose universe 1.

In a way you get to a synthesis here by splitting the difference. But it's not just a compromise between distant and unrelated theories each of which tracks part of the truth. It's a compromise that starts with a simple and attractive pluralist view that Sidgwick and Ross both moot; and you compromise by rejecting their ill-advised moves in opposite directions away from that simple and attractive pluralist view.

IV The Conceptual Framework

To complete the synthesis you need to think about the conceptual framework—about what the fundamental ethical concepts are. Here, I suggest, both Sidgwick and Ross have something important and distinctive to contribute. I don't claim that you get a synthesis here by focusing on interesting commonalities between Sidgwick and Ross. Rather you get the best conceptual framework by combining what is distinctively right in Sidgwick (and missing in Ross) with what is distinctively right in Ross (and missing in Sidgwick).

What is distinctively right in Ross and missing in Sidgwick is the concept of prima facie duty, the notion, as Jonathan Dancy puts it, of the "contributory."[17] I take it to be pretty uncontroversial that Sidgwick really doesn't have the concept (or at least, doesn't deploy it at crucial points). As what I've already said will have suggested, I think that when you introduce the concept of prima facie duty you have reason to reject Sidgwick's verdicts about both deontology and egoism: to think that he is too optimistic in thinking that he can dismiss deontology, and too pessimistic in thinking of the dualism of practical reason as involving an unresolvable contradiction.

What is distinctively right in Sidgwick is that—unlike most of the Sidgwick to Ewing school—he makes a distinction between the generically normative and the specifically moral. And, when pressed, it is clear that the generically normative is for him more important. I don't suppose that this claim about Sidgwick will be terribly controversial. That he makes such a distinction is part of the explanation why he treats egoism as a method of ethics.

Ross, by contrast, makes no such distinction. His unitary concept of duty blends the generically normative with the distinctively moral. This means that Ross does not possess the contemporary concept of a normative reason. By way of evidence for this claim, consider a striking contrast between Ross's views and Parfit's. At the very start of *On What Matters* Parfit introduces the concept of a normative reason. Since it is indefinable, it cannot be explained by giving a definition. Instead, Parfit says,

> We must explain ... concepts [like "a reason"] in a different way, by getting people to think thoughts that use these concepts. One example is the thought that we always have a reason to avoid being in agony. (OWM 1, 31)

---

[17] For probably his most influential presentation, see Dancy (2004), Part 1, "Catching the Contributory," 13–72.

Parfit's appeal to this thought at this point suggests that he thinks one of the clearest and most compelling examples of a reason is the reason to avoid pain for oneself.

In a starkly contrasting passage, Ross writes

> We are never conscious of a duty to get pleasure or avoid pain for ourselves, as we are conscious of a duty to give pleasure to or prevent pain for others. (FE 277)

That is, I take it, the difference between Parfit and Ross can be captured like this:

> Ross: We never have a prima facie duty to avoid pain for ourselves.
> Parfit: We always have a reason to avoid pain for ourselves.

There are two possible ways to understand this difference. On one interpretation Parfit and Ross here share the same concept—"prima facie duty" and "normative reason" are just different names for this shared concept—and the difference between them is a substantive difference in opinions about what reasons or prima facie duties we have. On the other interpretation Parfit and Ross do not here share the same concept—Ross's term "prima facie duty" refers to a different concept than Parfit's term "normative reason"—so the difference here between Parfit and Ross is conceptual rather than substantive.

The latter diagnosis seems to me clearly right. To see why, notice first how radical Ross's substantive view would be if he were using the same concept as Parfit. Ross would not merely be denying that we have any *special* reason to avoid pain for ourselves; he would be denying that we have *any reason whatever* to avoid pain for ourselves. Other people's pains and pleasures would give us reasons for action; but our own pains and pleasures would give us no reasons for action. It would surely be exceptionally uncharitable to attribute such a view to Ross. Then, second, notice that there is a way to illuminate the difference between Ross's fundamental concept and Parfit's. Parfit's concept of a normative reason is, as Allan Gibbard puts it, "flavorless." It can be alternately expressed by talking about what makes sense. By contrast, Ross's fundamental concept is morally loaded; it is naturally expressed (as Ross himself does) by talking about "duty" and "obligation." Ross denies that we have a *moral duty* to avoid pain for ourselves; Parfit thinks we always have a *normative reason* to avoid pain for ourselves. These claims do not straightforwardly conflict because they employ different fundamental concepts.

We need the concept of the generically normative to understand the appeal of egoism. Sidgwick has that concept; hence his (reluctant) sympathy for egoism. Ross lacks it; hence his failure to understand the appeal of egoism. In this crucial way, Sidgwick does better than Ross.

Thus neither Sidgwick nor Ross straightforwardly possesses the contemporary concept of a normative reason. To have that concept, you need to make two distinctions: between the generically normative and the specifically moral, and between the contributory and the overall. Sidgwick has the concept of the generically normative as opposed to the specifically moral, but, as we saw, he lacks or anyway doesn't deploy at key places the concept of the contributory. Ross has the concept of the contributory; that's his key innovation, the idea of prima facie duty. But he lacks the concept of the generically normative as opposed to the specifically moral.

V Philosophical Intuitionism: Axioms and Method

Turn finally to methodology. Here too Sidgwick and Ross share something significant. At the start of the most important chapter in the *Methods*, III.XIII "Philosophical Intuitionism," Sidgwick characterizes the philosophical intuitionist project. He asks

> Is there ... no possibility of attaining ... real ethical axioms—intuitive propositions of real clearness and certainty? (ME 373)

Later in the chapter, immediately before articulating the propositions he takes to have this status, he says they are

> self-evident moral principles of real significance. (ME 379)

Though Ross does not use Sidgwick's term "philosophical intuitionism," it is natural to think of him as engaged in the same project. His description of the principles of prima facie duty he endorses makes it clear that he regards them as axiomatic, as intuitive propositions of real clearness and certainty:

> That an act, *qua* fulfilling a promise, or *qua* effecting a just distribution of good, or *qua* returning services rendered, or *qua* promoting the good of others, or *qua* promoting the virtue or insight of the agent, is prima facie right is self-evident...It is self-evident just as a mathematical axiom, or the validity of a form of inference, is evident. The moral order expressed in these propositions is just as much part of the fundamental nature of the universe...as is the spatial or numerical structure expressed in the axioms of geometry or arithmetic. (RG 29–30)

And, like Sidgwick, he thinks only a small number of principles have this special, axiomatic status.

The two most important questions to ask about philosophical intuitionism are (a) What is the form of the axioms? and (b) What is the epistemic status of our convictions about axioms? It turns out, I shall argue, that Ross does much better than Sidgwick with respect to the first question, and that Sidgwick does much better than Ross with respect to the second.

(a) The Form of the Axioms

Ross is clear about the form of the axiomatic principles he endorses. They are principles of prima facie duty. As he articulates the principle that is his go-to example,

> A promise, simply as such, is something that prima facie ought to be kept. (RG 40)

As he counts them, there are a total of seven principles of prima facie duty. There are also principles that specify fundamental good-making (rather than right-making) features. At least in *The Right and the Good* there are four fundamental good-making features: virtue, pleasure, knowledge, and the apportioning of pleasure to virtue (or desert).

Sidgwick is regrettably much less clear on this matter. The least interpretively problematic of Sidgwick's axioms is the axiom of justice. It has a clear canonical formulation:

> (J) It cannot be right for A to treat B in a manner in which it would be wrong for B to treat A, merely on the ground that they are two different individuals, and without there being any difference between the natures or circumstances of the two which can be stated as a reasonable ground for difference of treatment. (ME 380)

Sidgwick thinks that the axiom of justice is the self-evident element in Kant's universal law formulation of the categorical imperative, but that Kant mistakenly believes the whole of morality can be derived from it. Instead, on Sidgwick's view, the axiom tells us only that whatever the moral rules are they should be applied impartially.

The maxim of prudence is much less clear. There are three different possible interpretations. On the interpretation that makes it most like the axiom of justice, it merely rules out pure time preference:

> (P1) Hereafter *as such* is to be regarded neither less nor more than now. (ME 381)

On two other interpretations the maxim of prudence involves a further commitment to promoting one's own good on the whole. Utilizing Ross's distinction between prima facie duty and duty proper, we can distinguish these two additional possible interpretations. On the weaker of these interpretations it says:

> (P2) There is a prima facie duty to aim at one's good on the whole.

On the stronger of these interpretations, it says:

(P3) There is a duty proper to aim at one's good on the whole.

And, as we saw in Section II, there is an ambiguity as to the content of the maxim of benevolence, which partly parallels the ambiguities as to the content of the maxim of prudence. To see this, it helps to draw on a later alternative formulation of the maxim of benevolence. As Sidgwick frames it on page 385, the maxim says

A rational agent is bound to aim at universal good (ME 385)

It is then clear that there are two interpretations, parallel to the second and third interpretations of the maxim of prudence. On the weaker interpretation the maxim of benevolence says:

(B2) There is a prima facie duty to aim at universal good.

On the stronger interpretation it says

(B3) There is a duty proper to aim at universal good.

Ross's axioms have a clear form: they are principles of prima facie duty. By contrast, it is quite unclear what form two of Sidgwick's three axioms have. We have distinguished six possible interpretations: three for the maxim of prudence, two for the maxim of benevolence, and one for the principle of justice. These fall into three categories. The weakest principles, (J) and (P1), tell us only what properties *do not have* normative significance. The principles of intermediate strength, (P2) and (B2), tell us what properties have the normative significance of generating prima facie duties. The strongest, (P3) and (B3), tell us what properties have the normative significance of generating duty proper.

No available interpretation of Sidgwick is costless. Since Sidgwick never makes the distinction between prima facie duty and duty proper—and, in particular, since he never makes that distinction in his critique of deontology—it might be tempting to try to read all his axioms in a way that doesn't require the distinction, to try to read them all as weak principles like (J) and (P1). But this interpretive strategy won't work in general, since there seems to be no available interpretation of (B) that makes it a weak axiom of this kind. And, setting this problem aside, it is instructive to remember Sidgwick's remarks about Kant. Sidgwick thinks that (J) is what is correct in Kant's universal law formulation of the categorical imperative. And he argues that Kant is mistaken in thinking that the whole content of morality can be derived from (J). It would be surprising if all his own preferred axioms shared the problematic feature he finds in Kant's formula of the universal law.

On balance, it seems most charitable to interpret both the maxim of prudence and the maxim of benevolence as principles of prima facie duty.

So interpreted, as (P2) and (B2), they are weak enough to appear self-evident; but they are still strong enough to play a key role in an axiomatic argument for utilitarianism. (P3) and (B3) by contrast are too strong to appear self-evident. It is not plausible, on initial reflection, that we always have to do what promotes either our own good or what promotes universal good. For one thing, these duties may conflict with one another. For another, they may conflict with other independent duties.

But, as we noted above, this reading of Sidgwick whereby the maxim of prudence and the maxim of benevolence are to be understood as (P2) and (B2) is charitable enough to be a significant interpretive stretch; it may be better to see it as a specification of what Sidgwick should have said rather than as a specification of what he did say. If that is right, Ross does much better on this matter than Sidgwick does: the form Sidgwick's key axioms can quite charitably be seen as having is the form Ross's axioms straightforwardly do have.

(b) The Epistemic Status of our Philosophical Intuitions

With respect to the epistemic status of our convictions about putative axioms, important passages in Ross suggest an unfortunate dogmatism. In a footnote to Chapter II of *The Right and the Good*, he writes,

> I should make it plain at this stage that I am *assuming* the correctness of some of our main convictions as to prima facie duties, or, more strictly, am claiming that we *know* them to be true. To me it seems as self-evident as anything could be, that to make a promise, for instance, is to create a moral claim on us in someone else. Many readers will perhaps say that they do *not* know this to be true. If so, I certainly cannot prove it to them; I can only ask them to reflect again, in the hope that they will ultimately agree that they also know it to be true. The main moral convictions of the plain man seem to me to be, not opinions which it is for philosophy to prove or disprove, but knowledge from the start; and in my own case I seem to find little difficulty in distinguishing these essential convictions from others moral convictions I have which are merely fallible opinions. (RG 20–1, note)

Later in the same chapter he says,

> I would maintain, in fact, that what we are apt to describe as "what we think" about moral questions contains a considerable amount that we do not think but know, and that this forms the standard by reference to which the truth of any moral theory has to be tested, instead of having itself to be tested by a theory. (RG 40)

These passages invite a charge of dogmatism by suggesting that mere initial reflection on these propositions is enough to establish their correctness and axiomatic status.

Other passages in Ross are less apt to invite this charge of dogmatism. Some, both in *The Right and the Good* and *Foundations of Ethics*, seem to anticipate what later philosophers would call "reflective equilibrium":

> I propose to take as my starting point the existence of what is commonly called the moral consciousness; and by this I mean the existence of a large body of beliefs and convictions to the effect that there are certain kinds of acts that ought to be done and certain kinds of things that ought to be brought into existence, so far as we *can* bring them into existence. It would be a mistake to assume that all of these convictions are true, or even that they are all consistent; still more, to assume that they are all clear. Our object must be to compare them with each other, and to study them in themselves, with a view to seeing which best survive such examination, and which must be rejected either because in themselves they are ill-grounded, or because they contradict other convictions that are better grounded; and to clear up, so far as we can, ambiguities that lurk in them. (FE 1)

Still, as Sidgwick is regrettably unclear about the form of the axioms, Ross is regrettably unclear about the epistemic status of our convictions about them.

Sidgwick is much less vulnerable to any similar charge of dogmatism. In III. XI he asks whether the putative axioms of the dogmatic intuitionist "possess the characteristics by which self-evident truths are distinguished from mere opinions" (ME 338). To answer this question he articulates four conditions putative axioms have to meet:

I. The terms of the proposition must be clear and precise.
II. The self-evidence of the proposition must be ascertained by careful reflection.
III. The propositions accepted as self-evident must be mutually consistent.
IV. Propositions accepted as self-evident must not be denied by epistemic peers. (ME 338–42; the wording of IV is not exactly Sidgwick's—he gives no economical and non-misleading short version of this fourth condition.)

He then argues that in general the putative axioms of the common-sense moralist do not meet these four conditions. To be made clear and precise they must be made definite enough to give a verdict about every possible case; and when this is done they either no longer seem self-evident (thus failing to meet condition II) or they no longer are acceptable to all epistemic peers (thus failing to meet condition IV).

The brief formulation of the second condition does not bring out its full significance. Sidgwick's idea is, first, that we may be inclined unreflectively to assent to propositions for reasons other than their apparent self-evidence: we may have heard them frequently repeated, or they may be endorsed by those whose authority we respect. Neither of these reasons for unreflective assent will make the proposition satisfy condition II. A proposition satisfies condition II for someone only if it has the same appearance of self-evidence that simple arithmetical judgments have for normal adults. Second, that this is not the end of the list of conditions makes it very clear that Sidgwick thinks that a proposition can seem self-evident to us and turn out to be false. The mere appearance of self-evidence is not sufficient to generate what he calls "the highest degree of certainty." Hence the roles for the further tests specified in III and IV, the intrapersonal and interpersonal consistency tests.

This is not the only way in which Sidgwick makes it clear that a proposition can seem self-evident to sophisticated thinkers and yet turn out not be a genuine axiom. The early part of III.XIII is largely devoted to consideration of the putative axioms offered by ancient philosophers. Sidgwick thinks these putative axioms fail in a different way than the putative axioms of dogmatic intuitionists. The dogmatic intuitionists' axioms are not tautologous—they are genuinely significant—but they turn out not to satisfy the four conditions. By contrast, he thinks that the supposed axioms proffered by the Greeks all turn out to be hidden tautologies or the outcome of exercises in uninformative circular reasoning.

Further reflection on Sidgwick and on Ross suggests other apparently independent conditions putative axioms need to meet. Consider first Sidgwick. Katarzyna de Lazari-Radek and Peter Singer introduce an additional condition to Sidgwick's list: a non-debunking condition.[18] As they frame it, that condition should rule out the possibility that a supposed philosophical intuition is plausibly explained by a non-truth-tracking psychological process. As they argue, the line of thought leading to the condition is not foreign to Sidgwick, though he does not himself articulate a non-debunking condition.

And a further crucial additional condition is suggested by reflection on Ross: a non-derivativeness condition. To see the need for this further condition, we should attend to something that is part of Ross's picture but which he unfortunately tends to forget when characterizing principles of prima facie duty as knowledge from the start: that there can be serious and extended controversy as to whether a normatively significant feature has underivative or only derivative normative significance. Ross of course explicitly introduces the distinction between derivative and underivative duties, for instance treating the duty to obey the laws of one's country as complex and derivative on pages 27–28 of RG. But he does not, I think, fully take on board the epistemic consequences.

To do so, it helps to have examples of theoretical disagreement in mind. It is particularly instructive to consider disagreements about Ross's go-to example of a non-consequentialist principle of prima facie duty, the principle that "a promise

---

[18] Singer and Lazari-Radek (2014), Ch. 7.

as such is something that prima facie ought to be kept." Consider first consequentialists who reject this principle. They do not deny that it appears to us initially that there is a self-evident axiom of promissory obligation. Sidgwick is quite clear that it does so appear. As he says when he turns to promissory obligation in III.XI,

> [This principle] certainly seems to surpass in simplicity, certainty, and definiteness the moral rules we have hitherto discussed. Here, then, if anywhere, we seem likely to find one of those ethical axioms of which we are in search. (ME 353)

But Sidgwick and other consequentialists go on to try in various ways to explain this appearance away. Ross spends a lot of time, both in RG (particularly in Chapter II) and in FE (particularly in Lecture V), arguing that the consequentialist view is mistaken. I think he makes a convincing case. But surely the fact that such extended argumentation is required shows that his principle of promissory obligation is not "knowledge from the start." We can only know that it is an (underivative) principle of prima facie duty after coming to a judgment as to the failure of consequentialist attempts to portray it as merely derivative. The fact that it initially appears to us to be of underivative normative significance does not settle the matter.

And it isn't only consequentialists who deny that Ross's principle about promising is a principle of prima facie duty. Other moderate deontologists also deny it. The philosopher (other than and before Prichard) who most fully anticipated the idea of prima facie duty was Richard Price. But Price and Ross held diametrically opposed positions on promissory obligation (the obligation to keep promises) and veracity (the obligation to tell the truth). Price held that there was an underivative prima facie duty of veracity, and that promissory obligation derived from it.[19] Ross, by contrast, held that there was an underivative prima facie duty to keep promises, and that the duty of veracity derived from it. Again, it takes extended reflection to decide which of Price or Ross is right on this matter (or, indeed, whether the best view for a moderate deontologist to take is that neither is correct on this issue). We start with the convictions that both keeping promises and telling the truth are features with normative significance; but it is only after comprehensive theoretical reflection that we are in a position to claim to know either that keeping promises or that telling the truth is a prima facie duty.

What all this suggests is that we need to be much more cautious than Ross often is about the epistemic status of our initial convictions about principles of prima facie duty. We certainly do start with strong convictions that certain features of possible acts are underivatively normatively significant; and these strong convictions are important and have serious dialectical weight. But multiple further tests need to be passed before we can be properly confident that these

---

[19] See Price (1758). For discussion, see David McNaughton's Stanford Encyclopedia of Philosophy entry on Price.

features are indeed underivatively normatively significant. As Sidgwick's four conditions suggest, the starting convictions need to survive intrapersonal and interpersonal consistency tests. As his reflections in the early part of III.XIII suggest, we need to rule out the possibility that the supposedly substantive axioms are mere covert tautologies. As de Lazari-Radek and Singer suggest, we need to rule out the possibility that our convictions can be given a debunking explanation. And, as reflection on Ross suggests, we need to rule out the possibility that the features the axioms pick out have derivative rather than underivative normative significance.

VI Conclusions

It is possible to present Sidgwick and Ross's normative views as quite starkly opposed: Sidgwick is both a consequentialist and a hedonist; Ross is neither. But this initial way of presenting things obscures multiple interesting commonalities. They largely agree about methodology.[20] And, despite the initial appearances, we can develop an interesting normative synthesis of their views. This normative synthesis is both conceptual and substantive. Conceptually, we should think both in terms of the contributory and the generically normative; that is, we should think in terms of normative reasons. And when we do that, we are primed to see the appeal of a view that draws substantively both from Sidgwick and from Ross. Sidgwick and Ross are both committed to consequentialist reasons, to the reason to promote the good as one crucial element of normative theory. And they both think that there is another crucial element of normative theory, something agent-relative. They disagree about what this agent-relative element is. Sidgwick thinks there is nothing right about deontology but something right about egoism. Ross thinks there is something right about deontology but nothing right about egoism. Once we get the conceptual scheme right and see the similarities between Sidgwickian egoistic reasons and Rossian deontological reasons, we can admit reasons of both kinds: we can agree with Sidgwick about egoism and with Ross about deontology. And we can embrace the plausible pluralist view about the good that both Sidgwick and Ross articulated but unfortunately deviated from in opposite directions.[21]

---

[20] For a sophisticated contemporary account of some key elements of this methodology, see Audi (2018).
[21] Many thanks to Robert Audi, Tom Hurka, Pol Pardini Gispert, Anthony Skelton, Marta Soniewicka, Joel Van Fossen, and audiences at LSU, Notre Dame, and the Rocky Mountain Ethics Congress for most helpful comments on earlier versions of this material.

References

Audi, Robert (2018). "Understanding, Self-Evidence, and Justification," *Philosophy and Phenomenological Research*.
Broad, C. D. (1930). *Five Types of Ethical Theory*. London: Kegan Paul.
Dancy, Jonathan (2004). *Ethics Without Principles*. Oxford: Clarendon Press.
Gert, Joshua (2003). "Requiring and Justifying: Two Dimensions of Normative Strength," *Erkenntnis* 59: 5–36.
Hurka, Thomas (2014a). *British Ethical Theorists from Sidgwick to Ewing*. Oxford: Oxford University Press.
Hurka, Thomas (2014b). "Sidgwick on Consequentialism and Deontology," *Utilitas* 26.2.
Lazari-Radek, Katrzyna and Singer, Peter (2014). *The Point of View of the Universe: Sidgwick & Contemporary Ethics*. Oxford: Oxford University Press.
Moore, G. E. (2003). *Principia Ethica*. Cambridge: Cambridge University Press.
Parfit, Derek. (2011). *On What Matters*, Volume 1. Oxford: Oxford University Press.
Phillips, David. (2011). *Sidgwickian Ethics*. New York: Oxford University Press.
Phillips, David. (2019). *Rossian Ethics: W. D. Ross and Contemporary Moral Theory*. New York: Oxford University Press.
Phillips, David. (2022). *Sidgwick's* The Methods of Ethics: *A Guide*. New York: Oxford University Press.
Price, Richard. (1758). *A Review of the Principal Questions in Morals*.
Ross, W. D. (1930). *The Right and the Good*. Oxford: Oxford Clarendon Press.
Ross, W. D. (1939). *Foundations of Ethics*. Oxford: Oxford Clarendon Press.
Scheffler, Samuel. (1982). *The Rejection of Consequentialism*. Oxford: Clarendon Press.
Sidgwick, Henry. (1874). *The Methods of Ethics*, 1st Edition. London: MacMillan.
Sidgwick, Henry. (1889). "Some Fundamental Ethical Controversies," *Mind* 14, 473–87.
Sidgwick, Henry. (1907). *The Methods of Ethics*, 7th Edition. London: MacMillan.

7
Prima Facie Duties, Real-World Contexts and Moral Emotions

Sabine Roeser

I Introduction

This chapter discusses Ross's ideas about normative ethics and moral epistemology (Section II) and shows its relevance for practical moral decision making (Section III). In addition, this chapter proposes to broaden Ross's moral epistemology by also acknowledging the importance of emotions for the formation of particular moral judgments. This can help to make Ross's theory even more highly relevant for public decision making about complex ethical challenges (Section IV).

W. D. Ross's theory of prima facie duties has been very influential in many areas of moral philosophy: in metaethics, normative ethics, as well as applied ethics. Indeed, the standard approach in bioethics is inspired by Ross's work (Beauchamp and Childress 2019). Ross, and after him various other intuitionists, emphasized that in concrete situations, different morally relevant considerations have to be balanced. This has to happen on a case-by-case basis, bottom-up, in order to take into account the salient moral aspects that are specific to a concrete situation (Ross 1930; also see e.g. Stratton-Lake 2002; Phillips 2019). This approach can be very helpful in practical moral decision making. I will argue that this also holds in domains that have not been widely discussed in the context of Ross's moral philosophy, namely concerning ethics of technology.

I will also discuss an area of improvement of Ross's theory. Ross and other intuitionists believe that ethical intuitions are beliefs or judgments, which they take to be cognitive, rational states.[1] Rationalists who are generalists, such as Kantians, aim to provide for an account of general moral principles as constituted or understood by reason. They argue that particular judgments are derived from such principles, top down. However, it is much less clear how a rationalistic approach to particular moral judgments on a bottom-up approach such as the one defended by Ross and most other intuitionists works. I will propose an alternative to the rationalist paradigm endorsed by Ross and other intuitionists. Proceeding from

---

[1] In other words, for Ross and the other intuitionists, intuitions are doxastic states. This is in contrast with contemporary non-doxastic 'seemings' interpretations of intuitions (for more discussion of this, cf. Roeser 2018, Ch. 5, and Audi (pp. 14–15, this volume)).

Sabine Roeser, *Prima Facie Duties, Real-World Contexts and Moral Emotions* In: *The Moral Philosophy of W. D. Ross*. Edited by: Robert Audi and David Phillips, Oxford University Press. © Oxford University Press 2025.
DOI: 10.1093/9780198914839.003.0007

a cognitive theory of emotions we can understand intuitions paradigmatically *as* emotions, without equating them with non-doxastic states or irrational gut reactions. In this way, Ross's account of prima facie duties can be made even more relevant for ethical decision making in real-world contexts. Complex societal challenges, such as those related to technological developments, often give rise to emotional debates. I will argue that this is not a problem, rather, emotions can highlight potentially conflicting values and prima facie duties that need to be carefully assessed. Emotional deliberation can help us to assess on a case-by-case basis what our prima facie duties and our duty proper are.

II Ross's contextualist ethics: prima facie duties

W. D. Ross developed his moral philosophy in two important books on which I will draw in what follows: *The Right and the Good* (Ross 1930 or RG) and *The Foundations of Ethics* (Ross 1939 or FE).[2] Ross, and after him various other intuitionists, emphasized that in concrete situations, different morally relevant considerations have to be balanced on a case-by-case basis, in order to take into account the salient moral aspects that are specific to a concrete situation.

Ross argues that there are two different ways in which an act can be related to a duty: as 'prima facie duty'[3] and as 'duty proper' (or 'actual duty'). Whether an act is a duty proper or an actual duty depends on *all* morally relevant sorts of acts of which it is an instance (RG 19, 20). An act that is of a certain kind, such as a keeping of a promise, is a conditional duty or prima facie duty (RG 19). If it does not have other morally relevant properties it also qualifies as a duty proper. Ross says that a duty proper is a 'toti-resultant attribute' of an action (RG 28). In contrast, Ross calls a prima facie duty a 'parti-resultant attribute'; it has the *tendency* to be our duty, and is grounded in *some* attributes of an act (RG 28). According to Ross, in a concrete situation, one prima facie duty can be overridden by another. However, according to Ross that does not mean that the first duty does not continue to exist. Rather, we then have a residual duty, for example to apologize or to make amends. Robert Audi formulates this as follows: prima facie duties, given their grounds, are "ineradicable but overridable" (Audi 1997, 34, 35). Ross also argues that we should have an appropriate feeling of remorse or compunction for not acting according to the first prima facie-duty (RG 28). This is relevant for my argument in Section IV, where I propose to complement Ross's account with an important role for emotions.

---

[2] This section draws on Roeser (2011).
[3] In contemporary literature the notion 'pro tanto reason' is sometimes used instead of prima facie duty.

Ross argues that at least some different prima facie duties cannot be reduced to any other one:

> Why should two sets of circumstances, or one set of circumstances, *not* possess different characteristics, any one of which makes a certain act our prima facie duty? When I ask what it is that makes me in a certain case sure that I have a prima facie duty to do so and so, I find that it lies in the fact that I have made a promise; when I ask the same question in another case, I find the answer lies in the fact that I have done a wrong. And if on reflection I find (as I think I do) that neither of these reasons is reducible to the other, I must not on any *a priori* ground assume that such a reduction is possible. (RG 24)

Hence, Ross's account is intrinsically pluralistic. Ross proposes the following list of prima facie duties:

1. Duties that rest on acts that I have done, such as:
   a. promises that I have made ('duties of fidelity'); or
   b. wrong things that I have done ('duties of reparation').
2. Duties that rest on acts that others have done, for example if somebody has done me a favor ('duties of gratitude').
3. Duties that rest on the prevention of an undeserved distribution of pleasure or happiness ('duties of justice').
4. Duties that rest on the fact that we can improve the condition of other beings in the world concerning virtue, intelligence, or pleasure ('duties of beneficence').
5. Duties that rest on the fact that we can improve ourselves concerning virtue or intelligence ('duties of self-improvement').
6. Duties of non-maleficence ('not injuring duties'). (RG 21)

It is important to note that Ross does not claim that he has provided a complete or systematic list (RG 23). This means that the list can also be updated and adjusted.[4] Nevertheless, Ross provides for some further categorization, by distinguishing prima facie duties that are special obligations and those which fall under the general obligation to do as much good as possible.[5]

Ross thinks that we cannot avoid reflecting on what we really think in order to get to knowledge of moral principles (RG 23). Ross thinks that we learn general moral principles on the basis of particular moral judgments. He calls this *intuitive induction* (FE 170; cf. also Dancy 1993, 94, 95 and 107, n. 4). According to Ross

---

[4] I will come back to this in Section III when I will discuss how Ross's account can be highly relevant for contemporary ethical challenges.
[5] Thanks to David Phillips for this point.

human beings are practical beings well before they are theoretical beings: they can perform social and helpful behavior before they are able to engage in abstract reflections about what is right. The more we develop, the better we understand that an action is demanded by a situation (FE 169, 170). In setting out his arguments, Ross draws on the phenomenology of moral experience. According to Ross, we only deduce particular judgments from general principles in two cases: when we accept a moral principle in a stage of our development before we have judged ourselves that it is true, and when we forgot a complex proof for a moral principle. This is not necessary in the case of a basic, or self-evident, moral principle where we can see the rightness of particular instances directly, without reference to the principle (FE 172, 173).

Ross argues that we cannot rank prima facie duties a priori. Rather, we need to attend to the concrete circumstances to determine which of potentially conflicting prima facie duties is the most important one or duty proper (FE 168). For example, one prima facie duty tells us that we should be honest, another that we should be kind. Particular moral judgments are needed to make a case-by-case assessment as to which prima facie duty prevails in a concrete situation. This involves deontological as well as consequentialist considerations, i.e., concerning the intrinsic character of a possible act, but also the consequences that result from it (FE 54).

Ross thinks that an absolutist theory such as Kant's deontology does not do justice to moral complexity:

> It ignores the fact that in many situations there is more than one claim upon our action, that these claims often conflict, and that while we can see with certainty that the claims exist, it becomes a matter of individual and fallible judgment to say which claim is in the circumstances the overriding one. (FE 189)

Ross also argues that:

> Loyalty to the facts is worth more than a symmetrical architectonic or a hastily reached simplicity. If further reflection discovers a perfect logical basis for this or a better classification, so much the better. (RG 23)

According to Ross such a logical basis or classification has not yet been convincingly established. Ross argues that utilitarianism also cannot avoid balancing of options. G. E. Moore's pluralistic 'ideal utilitarianism' has to account for the selection between different good and possibly incommensurable options, for example whether to maximize knowledge or pleasure. Hedonistic utilitarian theories in turn need to admit that there are different forms of pleasure that can be hard to compare and rank. In addition, the possible outcomes of our actions can be hard to predict. Hence, utilitarianism cannot always provide clearcut recommendations on what to do and also needs to rely on an opinion, just as Ross argues concerning assessing what is our actual duty in a specific situation (RG 23, 24).

Ross emphasizes that it is a challenge to predict the results of an action (FE 173–5). While we can have secure knowledge of prima facie duties, particular judgments about complex situations, *all things considered*, are not a form of secure knowledge. Concrete moral judgments are more problematic since contextual information is needed, which can be hard to obtain.[6] But people are able to acquire moral knowledge:

> … it seems as self-evident as anything could be, that to make a promise, for instance, is to create a moral claim on us in someone else. Many readers will perhaps say that they do *not* know this to be true. If so, I certainly cannot prove it to them; I can only ask them to reflect again, in the hope that they will ultimately agree that they also know it to be true. The main moral convictions of the plain man seem to me to be, not opinions which it is for philosophy to prove or disprove, but knowledge from the start; and in my own case I seem to find little difficulty in distinguishing these essential convictions from other moral convictions which I also have, which are merely fallible opinions based on an imperfect study of the working for good or evil of certain institutions or types of action. (RG 20, 21, n. 1)

Nevertheless, Ross thinks that we have to do with this. However, there are ways in which we can check our moral judgments, namely by consulting others whose opinion we find trustworthy:

> The fact that in many individual cases the people whose judgement we have learned most to respect in ethical matters will pronounce the same judgement on acts is some guarantee that objectivity has been attained. (FE 191)

Hence, Ross thinks that in making moral judgments we are not left to our own devices with our subjective opinions or locked in traditional views. Instead, we can engage with the points of view of other people, thereby being able to revise our moral judgments. However, this is not an ultimate guarantee:

> In many such situations, equally good men would form different judgements as to what their duty is. They cannot all be right, but it is often impossible to say

---

[6] This connects with a currently emerging discussion on 'normative uncertainties', cf. Taebi et al. 2020.

> which is right; each person must judge according to his own individual sense of the comparative strength of various claims. (FE 189)

So forming a moral judgment essentially involves a personal assessment. This involves information about the facts and the duties they give rise to. This is what Ross calls the objective elements of a situation. Furthermore, there is a subjective element consisting of the beliefs an agent has concerning the situation. I take Ross to mean here that the objective part comprises the descriptive as well as normative aspects of the situation, and the subjective part the beliefs a person has regarding the descriptive and normative aspects. In this sense Ross's account differs significantly from, e.g., subjectivists in ethics, who would argue that while the descriptive aspects of the situations are objective, the normative aspects are subjective. It is important to keep in mind that Ross is a non-reductive moral realist. He thinks that normative aspects of situations are objective, without being reducible to descriptive aspects. Rather, normative aspects are resultant properties of the complex interplay of descriptive aspects of a situation. But that there is a truth to the matter is no guarantee that we succeed in grasping it, rather, we should strive for it and need to keep critically checking our beliefs.

According to Ross, an action is *morally suitable* if (1) the agent can indeed perform it, and (2) the agent believes that she should do it to fulfill her duties. However, in order for an action to be *completely right*, it has to fit the agent's subjective thoughts as much as it has to fit the situation's objective facts (FE 146). For example, Mary may believe that John stole the bike and therefore she judges that she should scold him and call the police. Given her beliefs, the action is morally suitable. However, if the bike is actually John's own property, then her action is not completely right. Ross argues that we should try to find out what is the best thing to do, even if it turns out in the end that we had it wrong (FE 160). As Ross puts it:

> To find a difference of opinion between ourselves and others, or between our own ages and previous ages, should weaken perhaps our confidence in our own opinions, but not weaken our confidence that there is some opinion that would be true. (FE 19)

In other words, while it can be hard to make the right moral judgments, it is always worth striving to find the right answers, and not to give up and become a skeptic or relativist. Instead, we should always try to refine our moral judgments.

Hopefully this short introduction to Ross's moral theory has helped to show that he provides a sophisticated account for a contextualist approach to ethics, while still being strongly committed to non-reductive moral realism. This means that his framework is well suited for ethical decision making in complex, real-life situations, without giving up the strong normative commitments that any ethics approach worth its name should have.

III The importance of contextualist ethics for real-world decision making

While Ross's own work is very theoretical, it can be inspiring for practical ethical decision making. What makes Ross's approach especially attractive for ethics in practical societal contexts is its combination of being explicitly attuned to real-world decision making in complex situations with not always definitive factual information, potentially conflicting ethical demands, attention for people's ethical intuitions, and the importance of calibrating one's own views with those of others, without giving up on strong normative commitments. I will elaborate on this in more detail in what follows.

IIIa Contextualism

Generalists in ethics argue that ethical decision making should be grounded in general, exceptionless moral principles. A general moral principle would have the form 'All Fs are Gs', e.g. 'promise-breaking is always wrong', 'killing a person is always wrong'. In contrast with such general principles, prima facie duties allow for exceptions, depending on specific circumstances. Ross thinks that there is an objective truth to the matter of what the right thing to do is, but that this depends on the features of a specific context. Ross's theory of prima facie duties shows how the balance of instances of general duties can shift depending on the empirical aspects of a specific situation, which also explains why it can be hard to find out what the right thing to do is.

Ross's account is one of the most elaborate ones in contextualist ethics. In recent years, Jonathan Dancy (e.g. Dancy 2004) has developed this further in his theory of particularism. Dancy argues that Ross's account is 'atomistic', in that the valence of duties or reasons is fixed, only their relative weight depends on the specific context. Instead, Dancy argues for what he calls 'holism' of moral reasons: moral reasons can not only change their weight, but also their valence depending on the context. For example, helping is *by default* a positive thing, but if we intentionally help someone to do something evil, it is a bad thing. It is important to note that while the weight (Ross) and valence (Dancy) of reasons are context-dependent, they are not relative in the sense of cultural relativism or subjectivism. There is an objective truth to the matter that helping someone to do something evil is morally wrong, while helping someone in doing a morally right action is right. There is a debate in the literature whether Dancy's interpretation of Ross is correct (e.g. Audi xx), as well as whether Dancy's substantive position is convincing (e.g. Hooker and Little 2000). Audi argues that Ross is a particularist about overall (actual) duty and a generalist about prima facie duty (Audi, p. 25, this volume). Dancy's point remains here that we also have to consider the possibly changing valence in the case of a prima facie duty. I have argued elsewhere that I find Dancy's arguments convincing, but that he is unduly critical of the notion of 'intuition'. In addition, I have argued that Dancy as well as Ross do not sufficiently acknowledge the role emotions can play in the formation of ethical intuitions (Roeser 2006). I will come back to this later, in Section IV.

IIIb The complexity of real-world decision making

Given Ross's emphasis on attention to concrete circumstances, it is not surprising that his framework can be helpful for real-world decision making. Indeed, Ross's approach has provided the theoretical foundation for the most widely used approach in biomedical ethics, Beachaump and Childress's *Principles of Biomedical Ethics* (2019). In what follows I will argue that Ross's theory can also be very informative in the context of ethics of technology—a quickly growing subfield of ethics that is engaging with urgent and complex societal challenges.

Decision-making about technologies often involves disagreement concerning safety and desirability. Ethical aspects are important but often ignored in such debates, or considered to be at the center of deep disagreement and in that sense not helpful. However, closer inspection shows that abstract moral principles and values underlying these debates are often not controversial, but how they are instantiated, evaluated, and ranked in specific situations is. We can observe this in the context of ethical discussions of energy technologies. For example, in discussions about nuclear energy, there is agreement by opponents and proponents on general values, such as sustainability, justice, fairness, accessibility, and energy security (cf. RLI 2022). However, opponents and proponents of nuclear energy disagree on the operationalization of these values as well as on the assessment of empirical facts. In such a context, we can make headway in deeply rooted public stalemates by starting an ethical deliberation with the agreed upon values and then branching out into where the disagreement lies. This is a constructive alternative to conventional approaches, which start from the disagreement, often in the form of combative debates on the basis of strongly opposed positions. Such combative approaches leave little room for new insights, typically enforcing the opposition. Instead, a contextualist approach such as Ross's can highlight the consensus on general principles and values, but also how difficult it is to balance these values in concrete circumstances.

This is due to often ambiguous and uncertain information, as in the case of risky technologies and complex socio-technical systems such as the energy mix. We saw before that Ross thinks that unlike knowledge of general moral principles that hold prima facie, moral knowledge in concrete circumstances, concerning our duty proper, is difficult because we need to get the facts right, as well as predictions of uncertain future outcomes, which in turn makes it hard to be sure what the moral implications are. One could even say that Ross sees a main challenge in getting the right descriptive and predictive knowledge, and the lesser reliability of our concrete moral judgments might be primarily due to the uncertain resultance base, rather than the normative nature of moral judgments. This turns the common view upside down, where descriptive knowledge is seen as more reliable than normative knowledge.

Furthermore, Ross's approach can help to understand the difficulty of how to rank different options in light of different views on the relative importance of generally agreed upon values that may need to be traded off against each other. Ross's approach can also help to see the importance of checking one's own views with those of others. Hence, Ross's ideas discussed in Section II can provide for insights into the sources of disagreement as well as concerning ways of how to deal with such disagreement. This can lead to more respectful discussions and more fruitful new insights.

Hence, Rossian ethics can highlight the difference between uncontroversial general principles and values versus the messiness and complexity of their instances in real-world contexts. This does not only apply in thinking about one option for action in isolation, such as whether or not to employ nuclear energy, but also in the context of complex multifaceted decision-making, e.g. by considering nuclear energy and other energy technologies in the context of the energy transition. If we just look at one energy technology in isolation, we may be tempted to reject it due to risks and concomitant ethical concerns. However, if we see energy technologies in a societal context of a responsible and sustainable energy mix, we may realize that we have to make certain trade-offs and accept certain risks and disadvantages, as a purely beneficial energy technology may not be feasible. In other words, while the prima facie duty of non-maleficence may suggest not to employ a certain energy technology, we may need to make concessions and strive for those energy technologies which have the best balance of benefits and risks, which is a consequentialist consideration, as well as taking into account deontological ethical issues such as how risks and benefits are distributed. This can mean redirecting investments from traditional fossil energy sources into renewable energy sources such as solar and wind energy. Indeed, these have become much more efficient than previously predicted, due to investments, tax benefits etc. (IEA 2023).[7] In other words, Ross's contextualist ethics can pave the way for a pro-active, anticipatory ethical assessment of complex technological developments, instead of categorical judgments that may stifle solutions to urgent societal challenges.

---

[7] Also, recent studies show that there are still huge governmental subsidies supporting fossil fuels. This also challenges previous arguments which claimed that fossil fuels are much more affordable (i.e., updated descriptive knowledge). In the light of the urgency of the climate crisis, such funds should be redirected into sustainable energy sources (i.e., a normative statement reinforced by the updated descriptive resultance base).

Moral philosophers have often shied away from discussing socio-technical challenges like the ones mentioned, mainly focusing on interpersonal relations and thought experiments and at most discussing ethical challenges in medical contexts. However, in the face of climate change and other technologically related societal challenges such as those raised by digital technologies, e.g. AI, we need ethicists more than ever.[8] Most decision-makers such as policy-makers and engineers have no training in ethics, and they tend to reason on the basis of instrumentalist and reductivist views. Ethicists can have huge impact if they are willing to engage with such challenges. As I have tried to illustrate with the examples above, Ross's approach can inform discussions on such socio-technical challenges in crucial ways. Ross's theory of prima facie duties can help us make sense of such complex situations, structuring disagreements and providing clarity in often messy debates. But it is not just a matter of applying Ross's theory top down, which would also go against the spirit of his theory. Rather, we need to attune to the specific challenges provided by the context, which also means expanding Ross's initial list of duties, by adding values that are, e.g., specific to decision-making in the context of the energy transition, such as sustainability. That is also why the notion 'applied ethics' is a misnomer. Ethics of technology is a—novel—philosophical subfield in its own right, requiring new ethical theories, drawing on the unique challenges posed by the context while also drawing on existing philosophical work. Ross's theory can help to make sense of this on a metatheoretical level: ethics requires a continuous reflection between concrete context and general principles, rules, and values. In addition, Ross's framework provides us with a toolset to disentangle arguments without succumbing to relativism, cynicism, and despair. It can provide for the grounds of a more nuanced deliberation, something that is dearly needed in a lot of discussions on controversial topics.

However, there is one crucial element of such debates that does not feature prominently in Ross's ethical theory, and that is the role of emotions. In the next section I will argue that Ross's framework can be fruitfully expanded by combining it with a theory that sees emotions as source of ethical insight.

IV Expanding Ross's approach with a role for emotions

Ross and other intuitionists believe that ethical intuitions are cognitive, rational states (cf. Roeser 2011; Stratton-Lake 2013). Rationalists who are generalists, such as Kantians, aim to provide for an account of general moral principles as constituted or understood by reason. They argue that particular judgments are derived

---

[8] Indeed, a lot of philosophy departments are currently hiring AI ethicists, but given the urgency of climate change, arguably even more priority should be given to creating positions for ethicists working on climate ethics, energy ethics, and sustainability.

from such principles, top down. However, it is much less clear how a rationalistic approach to particular moral judgments on a bottom-up approach such as the one defended by Ross and most other intuitionists works. I propose an alternative to the rationalist paradigm endorsed by Ross and other intuitionists, on the basis of a cognitive theory of emotions. So while I think that many of Ross's ideas are convincing, I think his moral epistemology should be expanded with an account of emotions.

Cognitive theories of emotions have been developed in psychology and philosophy. They emphasize that emotions can have cognitive aspects (Scheler 1948, Frijda 1986; Solomon 1993, Nussbaum 2001). There is a broad range of affective states (cf. Griffith 1997; Ben-Ze'ev 2000). Some of these states may be unreflective, irrational states such as gut reactions, but this is not the case with all emotions. There are also higher-order, cognitive emotions that have cognitive or reflective aspects (Frijda 1986; Roberts 2003; Zagzebski 2003). According to some of these theories, emotions are cognitive value judgments (e.g. Nussbaum 2001). Several of these theories argue that emotions are paradigmatically affective and cognitive at the same time (e.g. Zagzebski 2003; Roeser 2011). These theories argue that emotions are crucial in order to be sensitive to ethical aspects (cf. Roberts 2003; Roeser and Todd 2015), and that they can play an epistemological role. Feminist ethicists have emphasized the importance of care for our moral experience (e.g. Tronto 1994; Held 2006). Emotions are intentional states (Goldie 2000) that help us to draw our attention to what morally matters (Blum 1994; Little 1995).

Grounded in these insights, I have previously developed the theory of 'affectual intuitionism'. Affectual intuitionism combines ethical intuitionism as developed by Ross with a cognitive theory of emotions. According to affectual intuitionism, paradigmatically, moral intuitions are emotions (Roeser 2011). Intuitionists such as Ross saw intuitions as cognitive, doxastic states that they understood as rational states. Proceeding from a cognitive theory of emotions we can understand intuitions paradigmatically *as* emotions, without equating them with non-doxastic states or irrational gut reactions; rather, emotions can also be cognitive and doxastic (Roeser 2018, Ch. 5). Affectual intuitionism insists on the importance of emotions in moral experience as emphasized by Humeans and other sentimentalists, while at the same time maintaining that ethics is objective, as emphasized by intuitionists and Kantians. In doing so, it does more justice to the phenomenology of moral experience than its subjectivist or rationalist alternatives. This possible combination of emotions and objectivity has largely escaped moral philosophers in the past, since most of them saw emotions as subjective feelings.

Affectual intuitionism understands moral emotions as felt value-judgments (Roeser 2011). They can play the role that intuitions play for intuitionists such as Ross: moral emotions are not deductive, inferential, or strictly argumentative.

Instead, typically moral emotions help us to assess the moral value of a situation in a direct, experiential way, analogous to perception. They can ground our further moral reasoning, in a similar way as intuitionists have argued concerning intuitions. However, the idea that moral intuitions are paradigmatically emotions can give us a richer understanding of moral intuitions. Most intuitionists emphasize the importance of particular, context-sensitive ethical judgments. Emotions are better suited to such judgments than reason, since emotions are especially well suited to be sensitive and attuned to morally relevant aspects of concrete circumstances.

We saw that Ross, like most intuitionists, emphasizes a bottom-up approach to moral knowledge. We initially make particular moral judgments on which we then base our general moral judgments. Ross does not mention the role of emotions in this process. However, moral emotions can play an important epistemological role here. Care, sympathy, and feelings of responsibility can help us to understand other people's perspective, to be sensitive to what other people's needs might be and that we, e.g., should help them. Hence, attention to emotions can complement Ross's contextualist account very well.

Zagzebski (2003) argues that moral knowledge is grounded in emotional experiences in concrete circumstances. These experiences are the bases on which we form more general, less intensely, or not at all felt moral judgments by what she calls 'thinning' out the initial, emotional judgment. These ideas can form an important addition to Ross's moral epistemology. Emotions allow us to have a deeper *understanding* of the evaluative and normative aspects of a concrete situation. For example, if we read in the newspaper that a tragedy has happened somewhere in the world, we can directly judge that this is terrible without needing to have a strong feeling. However, if we start to see live footage from the scene or when even being a direct spectator let alone a victim, we have more intense emotions, leading to more thorough understanding of the complex aspects as well as lived-through moral judgments.

Hence, the affective phenomenology of emotions is not a contingent addition to a purely rational belief. Rather, the affective phenomenology of emotions provides for a unique *richness of experience*. Compare this to sense perception. In sense perception, we unconsciously experience countless details and their interrelations. A phenomenological account of sense perception is richer than and cannot be reduced to a list of propositions. Someone else's meticulous report on the beautiful aspects of a mountain range cannot replace the direct experience. Analogously, purely cognitive moral beliefs without any related affective states cannot fully capture moral knowledge (cf. McNaughton 1988 and Little 1995 who draw the analogy with a colorblind person). In order to illustrate the conceptual relationship between the affective and cognitive (doxastic, judgmental) aspects of emotions we can compare the components of color perception and moral perception, as follows:

Color Vision
1. Our *capacity* to see colors *enables* us to have [capacity, enabling]
2. color *vision*, that is we see a color, which [perception]
3. paradigmatically (unless refuted) comprises a color *belief* [contains belief]
4. and *if* that color belief is *justified and true* (plus possible additional conditions) [if JTB+],⁹
5. then we have (visual) color *knowledge* [then knowledge].

Moral Emotions
1. Our *capacity* to feel moral emotions *enables* us to have [capacity, enabling]
2. a *'felt value judgment'*, that is, we feel a moral emotion, which [perception]
3. paradigmatically (unless refuted) also comprises a moral *belief* [contains belief]
4. and *if* that moral belief is *justified and true* (plus possible additional conditions) [if JTB+],
5. then we have emotional moral *knowledge* [then knowledge].¹⁰

These schematic representations of color perception and moral perception illustrate how we can understand both in analogous ways. Similar to the way in which color perceptions (and other forms of visual perception) are unitary states that comprise sensations and beliefs with truth values that track visual features, paradigmatically, moral perceptions can be conceptualized as emotions that are unitary states with affective and cognitive aspects with truth values that if successful track moral features.

Affectual intuitionism's emphasis on doxastic aspects of emotions does not mean that emotions are fixed and cannot be developed and trained. Indeed, developing our emotions requires education and care. Furthermore, works of art and documentaries can help us to train our emotions, imagination, and moral judgments (cf. Nussbaum 1992). Related to this, Zagzebski has developed a moral theory that emphasizes the importance of narratives of moral exemplars that we want to imitate, grounded in the emotion of admiration and in attuning to the emotional responses of others:

> Since narratives are a form of detailed observations of persons, exemplarism gives narrative a crucial place within the theory analogous to scientific investigation in the theory of natural kinds. (Zagzebski 2013, 200)

---

⁹ JTB refers to the notion 'justified true belief' in epistemology. There is a huge debate in epistemology concerning the role of justified true belief in the analysis of knowledge. There is broad consensus that JTB is not sufficient for knowledge as it can lead to counter examples, so-called Gettier-cases. To avoid entering into this complex discussion, I have here included the formulation JTB+.
¹⁰ These schemas have initially been published in Roeser 2018, 90–1.

In addition, I would like to propose a corollary of this point by Zagzebski: namely, the important role of narratives of morally negative exemplars (imaginary and historical). With this I mean the morally repulsive villain whose actions, mindset, etc. we want to avoid, grounded in the emotion of abhorrence, and also supported by the emotions of others. The exemplars and the abhorrent villains form as it were the boundary conditions of the moral spectrum in which we want to strive to be as much like the exemplar and as little like the villain. This makes historical narratives, also of atrocities, intriguing, as they perform on the borderlines of morality and help instruct us in fundamental values. In a Rossian spirit, we can argue that these narratives instruct us, bottom up. It is not that we already have a full grasp of the concept of moral evil on the basis of which we reject the doings of the villain. Rather, engaging with the narrative of the evils of the villain provides us with a more thorough understanding of the evil that was imposed on the victims of the villain, and proceeding from this understanding, we further refine and develop our more general moral concepts and principles. Of course this is not an infallible approach, as we and our surroundings may be mistaken concerning the empirical facts as well as the normative evaluation and in our admiration or abhorrence of a person. Like all epistemological routes, this one needs continuous examination and critical reflection.

Ross might still think that an unemotional form of practical rationality is more reliable. However, this is ultimately an empirical claim, which requires to be investigated empirically. This is frequently not acknowledged by rationalists; they typically take the superiority of rationality for granted. Empirical research by social psychologists and neuropsychologists such as Haidt, Greene, and others seems to support the superiority of rationality as it shows that moral emotions can mislead us. However, I would argue that it is not surprising that moral emotions, just as all other sources of knowledge, are fallible, but that does not mean that they should be discarded in moral epistemology. Rationality is also fallible: it can lead to narrow self-interest, with suboptimal and morally problematic decisions and behavior, for example so-called prisoners' dilemmas (cf. rational choice theory). While fallible emotions may need to be corrected by rationality, in cases such as prisoner dilemmas, lobsided rationality can be corrected by moral, other-regarding emotions (cf. Frank 1988). In other words, emotions are not special: like other sources of knowledge, they require attention, critical reflection, and correction, and emotions can fulfill such a role for fallible rational states.

Still Ross (and other rationalists) might argue that emotions are more susceptible to error than rationality, and in case of doubt, one should prefer purely rational judgments to ones that involve emotions. However, this again is an empirical claim, and empirical research shows that emotions play a crucial role for moral knowledge. Studies of sociopaths show that these people may be cognitively highly functioning but lack emotions as well as the capacity to form concrete moral judgments (cf. Nichols 2004 for an overview of these studies). The neuroscientist

Antonio Damasio (1994) famously studied patients with damage to their amygdala. He showed that while their rationality may still be intact, and they can still grasp general moral principles, they lose their capacity to have emotions as well as to make *particular* moral judgments. In other words, specifically the kinds of moral judgments that are so crucial to Ross's moral philosophy apparently require emotions. They provide us with the necessary 'Fingerspitzengefuehl'. Moral emotions allow us to attune to the evaluative and normative aspects of specific circumstances and contextual features.

Why then do we associate emotions with irrationality in metaethics, public debates, approaches to decision theory, etc.? Here we often see a certain form of circular reasoning and problematic assumption of equivalence of emotions and irrationality: as soon as there is an epistemic mistake, it is taken to be due to emotions, but without providing evidence that this is actually the case, while the mistake could also be due to failed sense perception or failed rational, logical, or mathematical reasoning skills, etc. Furthermore, emotions tend to get to the fore when there is a clash of emotions, or when emotions get extreme, in other words, in cases where emotions tend to be problematic. However, emotions frequently are unnoticed when they work well, for example in providing us with compassion and direct understanding, and when they provide the 'social glue' that lets people interact smoothly. This is similar to a popular view concerning ethics: ethics is taken to be what people disagree about, but this may be because we typically discuss ethics explicitly in those cases. However, we make ethical decisions all the time, and often these are unproblematic and uncontested, but for those reasons also tend to get unnoticed.

Indeed, a lot of ethical decisions are embedded in our routines through habituation and experience. Still, a lot of ethical decisions are also challenging. Ethical aspects of real life can be messy and complex, especially in the context of grand societal challenges such as pandemics, climate change, the energy transition, ethically responsible use of AI, etc. These are unprecedented challenges for which most of us do not have well-developed emotional and ethical responses and which involve many different perspectives that can challenge and contribute to our own, requiring deliberation with others, also involving our emotions (Roeser 2018). But also in terms of interactions at work and in our personal lives, we need to frequently reflect and deliberate, also involving our emotions. In other words, we need emotional deliberation (Roeser and Pesch 2016). Interestingly, centuries ago this was also argued for by the Confucian philosopher Mencius, who saw emotions as sprouts of virtue that we need to cultivate and develop through deliberation (cf. Ryan 2017, Ch. 4).

This again connects nicely with a theme from Ross discussed earlier in this chapter: there we saw that Ross thought that moral judgments about concrete circumstances are difficult but not impossible. We need to engage in exchanges of viewpoints with others. What I propose is to expand this form of collective reflection and deliberation by also including emotions. This is supported by empirical evidence, as well as the phenomenology of moral experience, something that is also crucial in Ross's philosophy. In other words, expanding Ross's moral epistemology with an important role for emotions, as in affectual intuitionism, actually can strengthen Ross's theory and is in continuity with it, and can help to make it even more relevant for contemporary ethical challenges.

In addition, Zagzebski (2003) has argued that more emotional moral judgments do not only play an epistemological role, but also a motivational role. In other words, by being cognitive and affective at the same time, they provide us with ethical insights as well as with motivational strength to act accordingly. This can help overcome a challenge for cognitivist ethical theories such as ethical intuitionism, what Michael Smith (1994) has called the 'moral problem'. Smith argued that our moral verdicts are either cognitive beliefs, but then they cannot motivate, or they are sentiments or desires, in which case they can motivate but are not truth-apt. I have argued previously (Roeser 2011, 169–79) that on the basis of a cognitive theory of emotions this is a false dilemma, and that affectual intuitionism can overcome Smith's moral problem. According to affectual intuitionism, ethical intuitions paradigmatically understood *as* emotions are cognitive and doxastic while also being affective, emotional, and motivational. Hence, emotions are epistemologically as well as motivationally crucial, and in that sense they are extra important for decision-making on urgent societal challenges such as climate change (Roeser 2012).

V Conclusion

In this chapter I have discussed metaethical and normative ethical ideas developed by W. D. Ross and how they are still highly relevant for moral philosophy and ethical decision-making about contemporary challenges such as the energy transition and other urgent and multifaceted socio-technical developments. I have argued that Ross provides us with a sophisticated framework that can help us in dealing with complex societal debates in which context-sensitive features and different perspectives need to be taken into account. Ross also helps us to see why this does not surmount to skepticism or relativism but is compatible with the idea that there are better and worse moral answers, as hard as it may be to attain these. I have argued that Ross's theoretical framework can be complemented with a cognitive theory of emotions, which I call affectual intuitionism. Affectual intuitionism understands ethical intuitions paradigmatically as cognitive emotions. This can help to provide further insights into how to refine and educate one's ethical intuitions, and how to deal with heated societal debates. What I call 'emotional deliberation' can help to assess different perspectives on prima facie duties and competing values, and how to deliberate on how to weigh and balance these and come to better grounded insights into what is our duty proper in such cases.

Acknowledgments

I would like to thank Robert Audi and David Phillips for their very helpful comments on various drafts of this chapter, and Rachel Addison for the thorough copyediting of the chapter. The funds to conduct the reseach for this chapter were provided by the 'Ethics of Socially Disruptive Technologies' research project (ESDiT), which is funded through the Gravitation programme of the Dutch Ministry of Education, Culture and Science and the Dutch Research Council (NWO grant number 024.004.031).

References

Audi, Robert (1997). *Moral Knowledge and Ethical Character*. Oxford: OUP.
Audi "Duty, Moral Knowledge, and Intrinsic Value in Rossian Intuitionism," this volume pp. 13–36
Beauchamp, Tom, and James Childress (2019). *Principles of Biomedical Ethics*, Oxford: OUP.
Ben-Ze'ev, A. (2000). *The Subtlety of Emotions*. Cambridge, MA: MIT Press.
Blum, L. A. (1994). *Moral Perception and Particularity*. Cambridge England; New York, NY, USA: Cambridge University Press
Damasio, A. R. (1994). *Descartes' Error: Emotion, Reason and the Human Brain*. New York: G. P. Putnam.
Dancy, J. (1993). *Moral Reasons*. Oxford: Blackwell.
Dancy, J. (2004). *Ethics without Principles*. Oxford New York: Clarendon Press/Oxford University Press.
Frank, Robert (1988). *Passions within Reason: The Strategic Role of the Emotions*. New York: W. W. Norton.
Frijda, N. (1986). *The Emotions*. Cambridge: Cambridge University Press.
Goldie, P. (2000). *The Emotions: A Philosophical Exploration*. Oxford, New York: Clarendon Press.
Griffith, Paul E. (1997). *What Emotions Really Are: The Problem of Psychological Categories*. Chicago: University of Chicago Press.
Held, Virginia (2006). *The Ethics of Care*. New York, NY: Oxford University Press
IAE (2023). "Renewable power on course to shatter more records as countries around the world speed up deployment," https://www.iea.org/news/renewable-power-on-course-to-shatter-more-records-as-countries-around-the-world-speed-up-deployment (accessed December 6, 2023).
Little, M. O. (1995). "Seeing and Caring: The Role of Affect in Feminist Moral Epistemology," *Hypatia: A Journal of Feminist Philosophy*, 10(3), 117–37.
Hooker, Brad, and Margaret Little (eds.) (2000). *Moral Particularism*. Oxford: Oxford University Press.
McNaughton, D. (1988). *Moral Vision*. Oxford: Basil Blackwell.
Nichols, Shaun (2004). *Sentimental Rules*. Oxford: Oxford University Press.
Nussbaum, M. C. (2001). *Upheavals of Thought: The Intelligence of Emotions*. Cambridge etc.: Cambridge University Press.
Nussbaum (1992).
RLI (2022). *Splitting the Atom, Splitting Opinion?* Advisory report by the Dutch Council for the Environment and Infrastructure, https://en.rli.nl/news/2022/rli-publishes-advisory-report-splitting-the-atom-splitting-opinion-decision-making-on-nuclear-energy (accessed December 6, 2023)
Ryan, James (2017). *Chinese Philosophy: A Reader*. CreateSpace Independent Publishing Platform

Phillips, David (2019). *Rossian Ethics: W. D. Ross and Contemporary Moral Theory*. Oxford: OUP.
Roeser, Sabine (2005). "Intuitionism, Moral Truth, and Tolerance," *Journal of Value Inquiry* 39, 75–87.
Roeser, S. (2006). "A Particularist Epistemology: 'Affectual Intuitionism,'" *Acta Analytica* 21, 33–44.
Roeser, Sabine (2011). *Moral Emotions and Intuitions*. Basingstoke: Palgrave Macmillan.
Roeser, Sabine (2012). "Risk Communication, Public Engagement, and Climate Change: A Role for Emotions," *Risk Analysis* 32, 1033–40.
Roeser, Sabine (2018). *Risk, Technology, and Moral Emotions*. London: Routledge.
Roeser, Sabine, and Cain Todd (eds.) (2014). *Emotion and Value*. Oxford University Press.
Ross, W. D. (2002) [1930]. *The Right and the Good*. Oxford: Clarendon Press, with a new introduction by Philip Stratton-Lake.
Ross, W. D. (1968) (1939). *Foundations of Ethics*. Oxford: The Gifford Lectures, Clarendon Press.
Scheler, M. (1948). *Wesen und Formen der Sympathie*. Frankfurt/Main: Schulte-Bulenke.
Smith (1994).
Solomon, R. C. (1993). The Passions: Emotions and the Meaning of Life. Indianapolis: Hackett Publishing Company.
Stratton-Lake, Philip (ed.) (2002). *Ethical Intuitionism: Re-evaluations*. Oxford: OUP.
Stratton-Lake, Philip (2013). "Rational Intuitionism," in Roger Crisp (ed.), *The Oxford Handbook of the History of Ethics*. Oxford: OUP, 337–57.
Taebi, B., Kwakkel, J. H., and Kermisch, C. (2020). "Governing Climate Risks in the Face of Normative Uncertainties," *WIREs Clim Change* 11, e666.
Tronto, Joan (1994). *Moral Boundaries: A Political Argument for an Ethic of Care*. New York, NY: Routledge
Zagzebski, L. (2003). "Emotion and Moral Judgment," *Philosophy and Phenomenological Research* 66, 104–24.
Zagzebski, L. (2013). "Moral Exemplars in Theory and Practice," *Theory and Research in Education* 11, 193.

8
Ross's Explanatory Resources

David Kaspar

I Introduction

What attracts most to Ross's theory is its moral content. In whatever form we express the following thoughts, we all really think that lying is wrong, keeping promises is right, and stealing is wrong. The intuitive persistence of these propositions indicates their extremely high epistemic credibility among all the moral propositions ethicists study. In fact, we rely on these propositions and others like them when we argue for, examine, or criticize supreme principles of morality, such as the principle of utility and the categorical imperative. We simply can't get away from these highly intuitive moral truths.

It is Ross's metaphysics, as commonly understood, that makes many wary of his moral theory, if it doesn't persuade them to reject it outright. The accompanying epistemology has been responsible for additional abandonments. Starting in the late 1990s, and continuing this century, several theorists have defended intuitionism. Some expressly defend Rossian ethics. Others don't. Several contemporary authors provided more defensible accounts of intuitionist epistemology, including Robert Audi (1996; 2004), Russ Shafer-Landau (2003), and Michael Huemer (2005).[1] Intuitionist metaphysics and the grounds of duty it contains has received some attention, especially in my 2012 and 2019 and in Christopher Kulp's 2016 and 2019. But not as much as its epistemology.

In this chapter I focus mainly on Ross's moral metaphysics. By examining his moral ontological commitments we can find out what his grounds of duty actually are. Currently, the most popular view of Ross's moral grounds is that they are *moral reasons*, and that such reasons are prima facie duties. About prima facie duties, Shelly Kagan states that "it is actually pro tanto reasons that Ross has in mind" (Kagan 1989, 17). Philip Stratton-Lake holds that Ross has given "us enough clues" so that we can determine what "Ross was trying to articulate": a theory of basic normative reasons (2000, 82). Here, rather than considering what I think Ross had in mind, or assessing clues Ross left us, I will investigate what Ross *says* about grounds of duty. I proceed with one question foremost in mind: Does Ross's theory have the resources to explain—in his phrase—what makes right acts right?

---

[1] This has been accompanied by a new interest in the history of 19th- and 20th-century British ethics. See Hurka 2018.

David Kaspar, *Ross's Explanatory Resources* In: *The Moral Philosophy of W. D. Ross*. Edited by: Robert Audi and David Phillips, Oxford University Press. © Oxford University Press 2025.
DOI: 10.1093/9780198914839.003.0008

One development coming out of the recent intuitionist revival is that a general framework of Rossian intuitionism has formed, which works within Rossian lines without necessarily adhering to his theory's details. Most Rossian intuitionists skirt Ross's metaphysics.[2] This, I think, is a mistake. For Ross's metaphysics can help us to explain morality, both in normative and in metaethical matters.

Here I will outline Ross's moral metaphysics, which includes his grounds of duty. He claims that certain properties contribute to making certain kinds of acts right, and other properties contribute to making other kinds of acts wrong. So contrary to what some critics charge, Ross does provide partial explanations of what makes acts right. After establishing that, I'll show how by analyzing and extending Ross's grounds of duty, we can systematically establish *core deontic grounds* of duty, which promise to provide what may reasonably be considered complete explanations of what is right. By drawing out an internal order of moral grounds that is implicit in Ross's theory, we can give Rossian intuitionism greater explanatory depth and range.

II The State of Play

Ross has a distinctive way of speaking of moral matters. It is often quite different from ours. A new way of understanding Ross's moral theory has emerged, so that we can identify a rough consensus in terminology. We speak of Ross as having a system of principles, which crucially involve moral reasons. Prima facie duties "are principles of normative moral reasons specifying which considerations provide moral reasons" (Stratton-Lake 2000, 89). We cognize these principles and reasons through concepts we have. What all these terminological shifts seem to have in common is that it is thought that they provide a better entranceway to Ross's moral theory. By modernizing Ross's moral theory, this line of thinking goes, we can keep what is vital to it, discard what serves it ill, and work toward a more viable moral theory.

Ross's prima facie duties are best understood as principles, according to the prevailing view. This is not a new claim, and it may be found in numerous introductory treatments of Ross's theory. What is new is that Rossian principles give reasons a prominent and foundational place. As Russ Shafer Landau states, "a prima facie 'duty' is not really a duty, but rather a permanent, very strong reason to do something" (Shafer-Landau 2012, 235). Shafer-Landau provides examples of such reasons: "to keep one's word, be grateful for kindnesses, avoid hurting others" (Shafer-Landau 2012, 232).

---

[2] Although it's rare for Rossian intuitionists to embrace Ross's metaphysics, there has been a new interest in non-naturalist moral theories that reduce the traditional claims of Moore's non-naturalism. See Parfit 2011 and Scanlon 2016.

For many years, theorists had difficulty defining prima facie duty in a direct way.³ Most formulations of prima facie duty were in a subjunctive mood, like this: "Something is a prima facie duty if it is a duty other things being equal, that is, if it would be an actual duty if other moral considerations did not intervene" (Frankena 1973, 26). So it's understandable that many would regard the reasons view of prima facie duty as a welcome approach. We can simply say, in a direct way, that "something is a prima facie duty if it is a moral reason for an act."

When intuitionism was experiencing a rebirth at the turn of the century, the reasons first view came into prominence. It says that reasons are normatively basic, and that other normative features, such as the right and the good, are based on reasons. One attractive feature of this approach is that we all accept that there are reasons for action, and so, it is thought, there is no requirement to explain what reasons are. By connecting prima facie duty to this approach, the theory seems simpler and loses some of its unattractive baggage. Stratton-Lake claims that what Ross says, "and the context in which he says it, give us enough clues to propose an account which expresses the idea Ross was trying to articulate in his various formulations; which is that his theory of prima facie duties is a theory of basic normative reasons" (Stratton-Lake 2000, 82).

The way we access moral truths is through our understanding of concepts, according to several Rossian intuitionists, such as Robert Cowan 2017 and Terence Cuneo and Shafer-Landau 2014. Such a view is thought to enable us to intelligibly speak of people knowing what their prima facie duties are, in a way that Ross's approach would not. Cowan holds that, "the implicit conception which individuates the concept MORAL REASON encodes the Rossian Principles. Individuals who possess that concept are in possession of informational content such that their judgmental and inferential dispositions reflect a tacit commitment to the Principles" (2017, 829). Cuneo and Shafer-Landau, who claim there are non-natural moral truths, take the strategy of focusing on moral concepts, but do "not take a stand on whether there are any nonnatural properties or facts" (2014, 403).

Principles, reasons, and concepts can all certainly play a role in a completed Rossian intuitionism. Being familiar with the current state of play enables us to better understand an outline of Ross's moral metaphysics including the elements he takes to be moral grounds. Why the current stances just outlined are considered improvements makes sense only when we consider some of the stronger criticisms of Ross's theory. The critical question for principles, reasons, and concepts is: should they be fundamental and central to Rossian intuitionism?

---

³ I will use Ross's terminology of "prima facie duty" here. Examining Ross's metaphysics, as we'll see, casts doubt on the hypothesis that the foundation of Ross's theory is a set of "pro tanto" reasons.

III The Explanatory Criticism

Ross's ethics has long been considered explanatory barren. Recent critics have said: "Ross's claim that we know moral truth simply by consulting our intuitions explains nothing about what *makes* things right or wrong. Those who find this unappealing would say that Ross's theory lacks *explanatory power*" (Burnor and Raley 2011, 155). Another critic goes further and states that intuitionism "is characterized more by its resistance to the answers to explanatory questions in ethical theory, than by any positive answers of its own" (Schroeder 2009, 203). But what, at bottom, is considered the explanatory lack? Ross's theory is thought not to explain what makes right acts right, even though his most famous writing is Chapter 2 of *The Right and The Good*, titled "What Makes Right Acts Right?" (Ross 1930).

Ross introduces the theory of prima facie duty with a particular moral case. Suppose, he tells us, one promises to meet a friend for a trivial purpose, which seems to obligate one to keep the appointment. He says, "I should certainly think myself justified in breaking my engagement if by doing so I could prevent a serious accident or bring relief to the victims of one" (Ross 1930, 18). The case is so well known, and is so often used by others to explain the theory of prima facie duty, that we might call it "Ross's Case." His theory is that the agent in this situation has both a prima facie duty to keep his promise to his friend and a prima facie duty to relieve others in distress. His *actual duty* is to relieve others in distress. One way this is put is that, in this case, the prima facie duty to relieve others in distress *overrides* the prima facie duty to keep a promise. Most agree with Ross's assessment of the case. However, Ross doesn't explain how this overriding works.

The explanatory lack present here concerns the metaphysics of Ross's moral grounds. I thus leave aside the common criticism that, without a supreme principle, Ross's theory can't explain what makes acts right. That topic deserves its own treatment, which I've previously provided.[4] One reason Ross's theory seems explanatorily deficient is due to the way he lays it out in Chapter 2. Nonetheless, as I'll show, there is much in that chapter that provides the materials for adequate moral explanation.

In *Foundations of Ethics* Ross is quite clear that he is seeking to determine the grounds of acts being right. He expresses interest in the question of "what is the other characteristic, or what are the other characteristics, in virtue of which we describe conduct as having the characteristic of being right or obligatory" (Ross 1939, 12). At several points in Chapter 2 Ross speaks of grounds of duty, with different, specific moral characteristics playing the role of grounds—a point I will expand upon at different points in this chapter. Moreover, he devotes an entire chapter of *Foundations* to criticizing other theories because of their explanatory

---

[4] See Kaspar 2012, Ch. 7.

inadequacies: "IV. Theories About the Ground of Rightness" (Ross 1939). Of Taking these points together puts into question the basis on which Ross's recent critics claim that his theory is explanatorily deficient.

G. J. Warnock 1967 and W. D. Hudson 1983, critics from a previous generation, are well aware that Ross provides grounds of prima facie duty, and that among such grounds are *kinds* of acts. Consider a situation like Ross's Case in which it is prima facie right for an agent to meet her friend because it is the keeping of a promise. Hudson expresses the explanatory problem in the following way. Ross "does not offer any explanation of how, for instance, being the fulfillment of a promise constitutes rightness, or why rightness is a consequence of it" (Hudson 1983, 93).[5] Hudson's criticism raises perhaps the most important, and the most puzzling, question in moral explanation. If an act is the fulfillment of a promise, and is thereby right, it is unclear *exactly how* that provides an explanation of its being right. At the very least, something should be said to explain how such an explanation works.

Nonetheless, it seems clear that if an act is the keeping of a promise, that provides *some* explanatory relation to it being right. But recognizing that an act is the keeping of a promise provides more than that. Suppose that Johnson performs act A, which is of the kind *promise-keeping* (K), and suppose there is no other prima facie duty in the situation. That act A is of the kind K provides an *initial explanation* of why it was right. How so? If someone asked *why* A was right, the clear and correct answer would be, "Johnson kept his promise." What else in the world, aside from A's being the keeping of a promise, would better explain why it was right to do? Also, what other single normative factor, aside from A's being the keeping of a promise, has greater epistemic credibility for explaining A's being right than A's being a *promise-keeping*? The reason Ross's approach can seem unilluminating is that we accept that keeping promises is right and we wish to find a further explanation why it is so. The puzzle we face is that, although an act A's being of a right-making kind K seems to give us the most convincing initial explanation of A's being prima facie right, we tend to look away from K and think that the explanation must come from somewhere else, or be nowhere at all.

Ross pairs kinds of acts, such as *promise-keeping*, with normative properties, such as *rightness*. In doing so, he provides a *partial explanation* of an act being right, one that fits his focus on prima facie duty. Such an explanation is partial in two ways: one, it seems to explain prima facie duty, without appearing capable of explaining actual duty, and two, as just stated, further explanation seems required to convince us that a property such as *promise-keeping* does indeed explain

---

[5] G. J. Warnock states, in a similar vein, that Ross, "asserted that these characters 'depended upon' other characters, that there were features of things that somehow *made* them right, or good. But he did not do more than assert that this was so: he did not explain what this puzzling kind of dependence of some 'characters' on others might be. Though he recognized the point, he cast no light upon it" (1967, 14).

rightness. Ross makes no statement of how keeping a promise makes an act right, apparently relying on the self-evidence of the proposition that "Keeping promises is prima facie right." He makes no attempt to go beyond identifying the right-making property involved to further illuminate what it is about promise-keeping that can make an instance of it right. And he makes no claim of how combinations of such grounds can explain actual duties, and not just prima facie ones. For these reasons, we can say that he certainly does not provide a *complete explanation* of an act being right.

IV The Action-guiding Criticism

Stating precisely and directly what constitutes a prima facie duty remains somewhat elusive. What everyone understands about prima facie duties is that we often understand the content of each one in a given situation, and that when they are in conflict, we will often see that one prima facie duty overrides another. But how do we see this? Why exactly in Ross's Case does bringing relief to the victims of an accident override keeping a promise? Because it has greater moral weight, we are told; because it is more of a duty (Ross 1930, 18).

When we are given scenarios in which one prima facie duty clearly overrides another, we can agree that it does. What Ross's theory does not do is give us guidelines, or principles, for determining on what basis such overriding occurs. Since the theory provides no effective basis for determining which option is our actual duty, we must rely on our intuitive judgment that it is so. The result is that Ross's theory is not action-guiding, except for simple and obvious cases. Hudson makes this point thus: "The difficulty which immediately arises about this view is as follows: upon what *scales*, so to speak, is this 'weighing' to be done? We must weigh certain features of an act against one another, but how? Ross's answer is: by intuition" (Hudson 1983, 95).

Hudson's criticism raises two questions. First, *are there* moral scales for weighing prima facie duties? Second, what procedure might we use to determine what one's actual duty is? That is, what procedure can show us which prima facie duty has greater moral weight? Given that my focus is on the grounds of duty, I will focus on the first question. If we can establish that there are moral scales for weighing moral grounds, then we will be in a better position to explore procedures for deciding what to do.

The explanatory criticism and the action-guiding criticism are related. The lack of illuminating explanations for particular prima facie duties is compounded when we consider actual duties. Since there seem to be no scales for weighing prima facie duties, we apparently have no way to explain what constitutes overriding. That means that Ross's moral theory cannot explain what makes a set of normative factors an actual duty. Even supporters of Ross's theory agree that he "ultimately fails to offer a satisfactory account" of the relation between prima facie duty and actual duty (Stratton-Lake 2000, 82). That actual duties can't be adequately explained seems to me to be the biggest problem for Ross's moral theory.

V Ross's Metaphysics

Ross doesn't set the metaethical table and declare his stances, as we often do. He does not say, for example, "I believe right and wrong are mind-independent properties of acts." So we have to read what he says closely to figure out what his moral metaphysics is. Much of Chapter 2 of *The Right and the Good* has the purpose of clarifying what prima facie duties are. His focus is on how they operate in moral situations to form actual duties. So we could say that Ross tells us what his moral metaphysics is by his use of the object language of his system.

Here I am providing an outline of Ross's moral metaphysics. Most people who come to Ross's *The Right and the Good* have heard about prima facie duties, and have heard that they are principles. Open the book, and you'll find some of what you expected. Here we're doing something different. If you open the book seeking to learn what Ross's moral metaphysics is, you will see that much of Ross's metaphysics is right there. In fact, your perspective of Ross's theory is likely to change given how much of what he says has plain metaphysical import. In Chapter 2, for instance, there is much more moral reality talk than moral principle talk.

Ross provides a metaphysical definition of prima facie duty in *The Right and the Good*. A prima facie duty is a *property* of an action. "Characteristic" is his term, though he uses "attribute" too. When we use the term "prima facie duty" we are referring to such a property. He states, "I suggest 'prima facie duty' or 'conditional duty' as a brief way of referring to the characteristic (quite distinct from that of being a duty proper) which an act has, in virtue of being of a certain kind (e.g. the keeping of a promise), of being an act which would be a duty proper if it were not at the same time of another kind which is morally significant" (Ross 1930, 19). Where certain kinds of acts, such as keeping a promise or helping someone in distress, are concerned, these two kinds are also considered characteristics by Ross. He states, "When a possible act is seen to have two characteristics, in virtue of which it is prima facie right, and in virtue of the other prima facie wrong, we are (I think) well aware that we are not certain whether we ought or ought not to do it" (Ross 1930, 30).

His understanding of the grounds of rightness as characteristics applies to all moral theories. He states that utilitarianism and egoism are "attempts to state a single characteristic of all right actions which is the foundation of their rightness" (Ross 1930, 16). Understanding this about Ross's approach is significant, especially for the explanation problem. All objectivist theories offer characteristics that ground the rightness of acts, and they can be compared and evaluated on that basis. If, as Hudson claims, an act *A*'s *being the fulfillment of a promise* doesn't explain what makes it right, then how well does *A*'s *being the act that maximizes good* compare to it in explaining *A*'s being right? I would say not well at all. Act *A*'s being the keeping of a promise is more closely related morally to *A* being right than *A*'s maximizing good is.

In *Foundations* Ross claims that quite familiar ethical terms are to be understood as referring to characteristics. He states, "the two main ethical characteristics or groups of characteristics are those which are designated by such terms as 'right,' 'obligatory,' 'my duty,' on the one hand, and by 'good,' 'noble,' 'valuable,' on the other" (Ross 1939, 10). In Chapter 2 of *The Right and the Good*, Ross uses the property-expressions "character," "characteristic," "kind," "attribute," "respect," "aspect," and "relation" much more than he uses "principle," "principles," and "rule," and certainly a great deal more than he uses "reason." Taking all these points into consideration, we should consider whether Ross's moral theory is better characterized at the fundamental level as a theory of moral properties rather than as a theory of principles or of reasons.

Facts also play a critical role in Ross's moral theory. At many points when Ross speaks of the details of prima facie duties, their nature and structure, we are to understand him as referring to *moral facts* of a certain sort. As he states, "'Prima facie' suggests that one is speaking only of an appearance which a moral situation presents at first sight, and which may turn out to be illusory; whereas what I am speaking of is an objective fact involved in the nature of the situation, or more strictly in an element of its nature, though not, as duty proper does, arising from its *whole* nature" (Ross 1930, 20).

A prima facie duty that an agent has in a moral situation is an objective fact in that situation, which has one property, a ground, and a normative property, such as *rightness*, which is based on the ground. This gives us greater clarity on the metaphysics of prima facie duties. In a given moral situation, one in which two prima facie duties are in conflict—say, keeping a promise and helping another in distress—there are two distinct moral facts each of which is constituted by properties, and the actual duty is the whole moral fact that comprises the elements.

Moral facts are also important in Ross's theory where he distinguishes categories of duty. "Each rests on a definite circumstance" (Ross 1930, 20). Some duties of fidelity arise because of "previous acts of my own" (Ross 1930, 21). "Those resting on a previous wrongful act" (21)—they are duties of reparation. "Some rest on the fact or possibility of a distribution of pleasure or happiness" (21) "Some rest on the mere fact that there are other beings in the world whose condition we can make better in respect of virtue, or of intelligence, or of pleasure" (21). In short, every prima facie duty rests on a definite fact of one sort or another, which determines the category of duty to which it belongs.

Moral relations are another kind of moral reality that is fundamental to intuitionism. Moral relations give rise to prima facie duties. Take note of the facts in which people have moral relations to others in the following well-known passage. Ross criticizes utilitarianism as seeming "to simplify unduly our relations to our fellows. It says, in effect, that the only morally significant relation in which my neighbours stand to me is that of being possible beneficiaries by my action. They do stand in this relation to me, and this relation is morally significant. But they may also stand to me in the relation of promisee to promiser, of creditor to debtor, of wife to husband, of child to parent, of friend to friend, of fellow countryman to fellow countryman, and the like; and each of these relations is the foundation of a prima facie duty" (Ross 1930, 19). What is easily overlooked is that, here, Ross's system is ontologically committed to a wide variety of moral relations. Ross does not attempt to make a complete list of different moral relations here. That suggests that there are many more that we can identify.

VI Moral Realities

That is the outline of the elements of Ross's moral metaphysics. Since we are given only an outline by him, we don't have a clear picture of how it all fits together. Here is one question that is bound to be raised: if a prima facie duty is a principle *and* is an objective fact involved in the nature of the situation, how are these two related? It will depend on the view of principles one holds. Nevertheless, we have covered enough of Ross's moral metaphysics to establish that his theory is a theory of *moral realities*, if it is nothing else. Many ethicists, including many intuitionists, would think these realities are better left behind, or at least bracketed until we know more about moral concepts. But our aims here are to establish what is Ross's actual view, what in it makes it a target for criticisms, and what in it might overcome such criticisms.

Ross's moral theory has two fundamental problems that are our focus. It doesn't have a very illuminating explanatory account, and it has no "scales," to use Hudson's term, for weighing prima facie duties. Ross himself agrees with the second claim: "For the estimation of the comparative stringency of these prima facie obligations no general rules can, so far as I can see, be laid down" (Ross 1930, 41). As to the explanatory problem, as I've pointed out, we cannot claim that Ross provides no explanations of moral rightness. He does. But we can claim that his grounds only provide partial explanations requiring further illumination, and that while they can explain prima facie duties, they don't explain actual duties.

VII Three Explanatory Opportunities

Ross's theory has the materials out of which an adequate explanatory theory can be constructed. I believe it also contains the capacity to provide the elusive scales which, when made part of an explanatory theory, will enable us to explain actual duty. Looking at his theory from this perspective, we can say that Ross made insufficient use of the explanatory resources of his system. We should not be too hard on him for this, for most ethicists after Ross have overlooked the explanatory resources his theory contains.

Call the three explanatory opportunities that Ross did not exploit the Analysis Opportunity, the Separation Opportunity, and the Scales Opportunity. All of them, as you will see, are interconnected. Ross provides no basis for analysis of the grounds of rightness. Call this the *Analysis Opportunity*. Ross doesn't expressly identify the different kinds of grounds that deserve study. This may be why we haven't studied them. The first order of business would be to determine what the different grounds of duty are. The main grounds Ross discusses are different kinds of acts, some of which we've already mentioned. They are properties such as *promise-keeping* and *helping-another-in-distress*, *lying* and *stealing*, and many others. To distinguish these grounds from others, call them *moral kinds*. They are act-kinds or act-types. Another category of moral ground, which we've discussed, is *moral relations*.

Second, Ross made insufficient use of the *Separation Opportunity*. He doesn't clearly distinguish and separate *categories of duty* from moral kinds, and because of this doesn't sufficiently single out relevant species of grounds. What is the difference? Leave aside for now the claim that Ross argues for seven fundamental prima facie principles. Let's see what he says: "Of prima facie duties I suggest, without claiming completeness or finality for it, the following division" (Ross 1930, 20). The division is of *categories* of duty. There are "duties of fidelity," "duties of reparation," "duties of gratitude," "duties of justice, "duties of beneficence," "duties of self-improvement," and "duties" of "non-maleficence" (Ross 1930, 21).

What do all of these have in common? They are stated in *the plural* and associated with different types of grounds. There is not just one kind of duty of fidelity. There are several. Ross himself recognizes several kinds of duty that fall under non-maleficence: a duty not to kill, a duty not to commit adultery, a duty not to steal, a duty not to bear false witness (Ross 1930, 22). Surely there are many more. In laying out his division of duties, he is separating them into different generic categories, each with its own distinctive origin. But under each category there are several kinds of duty viewed in terms of act-kinds. Moral kinds are properties with greater specificity than generic categories of duty. They are more fine-grained. When Ross speaks of particular cases he most often makes use of moral kinds rather than generic categories of duty. It may be objected that Ross's clearly separates what I am calling categories of duty from moral kinds. I would agree that at some points he does. But he blends categories and kinds enough in the discussion in Chapter 2 of *The Right and the Good* so that it is unclear which roles each plays in the theory. The importance of separating these two levels of moral property classification will soon become apparent.[6]

Ross suggests that there are no objective moral scales. This takes us to the third explanatory opportunity Ross passed up that only becomes obvious once we recognize the import of the first two. We've covered his claim that, apparently, no general rules can determine the comparative stringency of prima facie obligations. He also states, while acknowledging that duties of "perfect obligation" have "a great deal of stringency" (Ross 1930, 41), that we must accept that "the decision rests with perception" (Ross 1930, 42). His final note on this point: "This sense of our particular duty in particular circumstances, preceded and informed by the fullest reflection we can bestow on the act in all its bearings is highly fallible, but it is the only guide we have to our duty" (Ross 1930, 42). Our sense of our particular duty—is it really our *only* guide?

Ross's critics on this point are content with only repeating what he stated.[7] Such critics and perhaps Ross himself did not suspect that his system *does have* the resources for providing scales of comparative stringency. There are, I will argue, three distinct kinds of objective scales of moral weight within his system, each of which contributes to determining what one's duty is in a different way. And the reason he didn't suspect their existence is because he provided no basis for analyzing the grounds of duty and did not clearly separate moral kinds from moral categories. The third explanatory opportunity that Ross did not seize, the *Scales Opportunity*, is that Ross's system has distinct categories of objective moral scales.

VIII Ross's Explanatory Resources

Ross's moral theory has the resources for moral explanation. Taking the three explanatory opportunities into account and seeking to construct illuminating moral explanations enables us to arrive at the *core deontic grounds* of duty for Rossian intuitionism. Intuitionists have long claimed that what makes an act right or wrong is the *nature* of the act. Ross uses the term "nature" to cover all of the morally significant properties that make an act an actual duty (Ross 1930, 20, 28, 44).

With these grounds of duty we can provide ways of analyzing and explaining the natures of moral acts.[8] The critical ground of duty is a *moral kind*. In a situation with no moral kind, there is no duty. In a situation with a moral kind, moral kinds are what integrate the other grounds to determine what is right in the situation. *Moral relations* are present in every moral situation as well.

---

[6] None of this is to suggest that Ross doesn't give prima facie duties some order and structure. For example, he distinguishes special obligations from general obligations (Ross 1930, 27–8).
[7] See Rawls 1971, 34 and Hudson 1983, 95.
[8] For an alternative approach to Ross's theory of grounds, see Phillips 2019.

The remaining core deontic ground of duty that must be included is *value*. The values of *good*, *bad*, and *indifferent* are critical for explaining what makes acts right, and for determining what prima facie duty is more of a duty. The inclusion of value as a core deontic ground, we should note, puts my approach at odds with one point in Ross's moral theory. Ross expressly denied that there are intrinsically morally good acts, that is, acts that are good independently of motive (Ross 1930, 4).[9] Also, since he holds that only four things are intrinsically good—"virtue, pleasure, the allocation of pleasure to the virtuous, and knowledge" (Ross 1930, 140)—acts, on his view, cannot be good without the presence of a good motive.

We can now show how Rossian intuitionism can provide more than merely initial moral explanations. Here is an initial explanation. Consider a case in which Jones says (*s*) "I was sick" to Smith to explain why she missed her appointment with her. Jones was not sick. So was it wrong of her to say she was? Assume that there is no other prima facie ground in the situation. Assume Jones's saying *s* to Smith constitutes a lie. The fact that it is a lie explains why it is wrong. Holding all other situational conditions constant, if Jones's utterance of *s* were not a lie, it would not be wrong. We tend to miss this because we really think that lying is wrong. So Jones's utterance of *s* to Smith being a lie provides a partial, initial explanation of why it was wrong to do.

To move beyond this level of explanation toward a more illuminating moral explanation, however, we must better understand one thing about how Ross sees duty. In *Foundations of Ethics*, he states,

> Any possible act has many sides to it which are relevant to its rightness or wrongness; it will bring pleasure to some people, pain to others; it will be the keeping of a promise to one person, at the cost of being a breach of confidence to another, and so on. We are quite incapable of pronouncing straight off on its rightness or wrongness in the totality of these aspects; it is only by recognizing these different features one by one that we can approach the forming of a judgement on the totality of its nature; our first look reveals these features in isolation, one by one; they are what appears prima facie. (Ross 1939, 84)

All of this is correct. In a given moral situation we cannot see the whole normative structure of the situation. We are positioned only to see our prima facie duties in a situation. What Ross didn't seem to recognize is that the thinking in this passage also provides a methodology to determine which grounds of his moral theory might provide more adequate explanations. Here we are examining different properties in isolation in order to determine the fundamental grounds of morality. We are examining properties *in abstracto* here, not with the immediate

---

[9] I address this matter in Kaspar 2012, Ch. 6, and show that, were Ross consistent, he would embrace intrinsically morally good acts.

purpose of understanding how prima facie duties operate in moral situations. So you could say that our inquiry is of a subject that is *prior* to Ross's inquiry. We are focused on which properties are grounds of morality, which properties have greater moral weight than certain others, and on the possible conditions which can account for one prima facie duty overriding another, independently of evaluations of particular moral situations. Think of this parallel: we're doing basic arithmetic rather than showing a clerk-in-training how to give customers correct change at a store. We must know that 7 is greater than 5 before we can give people exact change. In order to correctly evaluate a situation involving murder and lying, we must have some intuition of the comparative weight *murder* has to *lying*. By examining grounds one by one, then considering how they might form combinations of grounds, we might have the resources to explain a whole moral act.

Let's look into the moral kind *lie* instantiated by Jones. For Jones to lie to Smith a number of conditions must be met. Suppose the necessary instantiation conditions for the moral kind *lie* are as follows: (1) Person A says *p*; (2) A believes *p* to be false; (3) A says *p* to another person B; and (4) A intends that B believes *p* to be true.[10] That Jones's speech act *s* is a lie is the partial, first level of explanation for why it is wrong, given the nature of lying.

To provide a second level of explanation for why a particular lie is wrong involves taking account of the necessary components of the complex property *lie*. Determining whether each is good, bad, or indifferent, our bases of explanation expand. To give an idea of how this works, continue to bracket the matter of prima facie duty, so that we can focus on lying. Imagine that the only moral ground in play is the kind *lie*. In isolation, giving another person incorrect information instead of knowledge seems bad, even if it was unintentional. This is in line with Ross's view that knowledge is intrinsically good. Also in isolation, knowing that a person will walk away with bad information, without correcting what that other person believes, seems bad. For example, if you witness someone being misinformed by another person about the directions they should take to get to the Capitol, it would be good to give them the correct information. In isolation, merely intending to give another person false information seems in itself bad. Yet, none of the components of a lie in itself are wrong. It is only when they come together in an act, the whole of which is a lie, that that act is wrong. So by bringing these distinct components together, and considering whether the act as a whole is good, bad, or indifferent enables us to provide an explanation of why Jones's lying to Smith is wrong. Such an explanation, based on the whole kind, constitutes a third level of explanation. Starting with thinking of a moral kind like *lie*, moving to considering each of the values of its necessary components in isolation, then arriving at the

---

[10] J. E. Mahon calls this "the most common definition of lying" (2015). I use this definition without claiming it is the correct one.

value of the whole kind provides a progression of greater explanatory illumination at each stage.

IX Moral Scales

Ross thought that intuition is our only guide for deciding tough moral cases. He also stated that, so far has he could see, no general rules for determining the comparative stringencies of prima facie duties could be established. But that can't be the final word on the matter—can it? The fact that some prima facie duties override other prima facie duties must have *some basis* in the moral grounds themselves. And if our intuitions of cases are ever correct, that too must be based on the natures of distinct moral grounds. Which raises the question: what prevents our establishing general rules of comparative stringency? It seems that it is the number and variety of grounds that can come into play in a moral situation. So let us proceed step by step. To arrive at a promising account of comparative stringency, we should take the different moral grounds which we've identified, distinguished, and categorized to sketch how grounds of different moral weights can influence overriding.

Let us explore this possibility. Ross's theory allows moral grounds to function in a different capacity than in just making acts right. Such grounds might also function as objective moral scales with which we can explain actual duty. Based on our examination of Ross's moral grounds, we can state that there are three categories of moral scales. Simply put, the moral grounds *are* the moral scales. They are moral kinds, moral relations, and the values good, bad, and indifferent. Distinguishing these three categories of moral scales facilitates stringency comparisons. We must weigh grounds against grounds of the same category. Moral kinds are weighed against moral kinds; moral relations against moral relations; values against values. So for example, the moral kind *promise-keeping* is weighed against *helping-another-in-distress*. The relation *being-a-parent-of* is weighed against *being-a-fellow-human*. The values weighed against one another are numerous: being worth $100 is weighed against being worth $5. Being conducive to health is weighed against causing illness. Having a good reputation is weighed against having a bad reputation.

Before we consider such scales further, three preliminary points are in order. First, as I've stated, my focus will be on identifying objective moral scales. Determining whether there are such scales is the explanatory inquiry which we must undertake before we consider how agents might best determine what is their duty in particular moral situations. Second, the items that make up the scales that we are considering will all be *properties*, in the broad sense that includes monadic, dyadic, triadic properties. Different theorists have made different demands on what an intuitionist moral scale must be like.[11] Here I simply introduce pairs of

---

[11] See Mill 2002, 235 and Rawls 1971, 34.

properties that are relata of the *worse-than relation*. For example, the moral kind *murder* is morally worse than *promise-breaking*. That implies that the prima facie duty not to murder is more stringent than the prima facie duty not to break a promise. Lastly, in introducing these moral scales, I am dealing only with pairwise comparisons. I make no claim of what their comprehensive and ultimate compositions will be like.

X Moral Weighing

Here I explain and illustrate the application of the scales just sketched.[12] A friend comes to you and tells you, "I've got a problem. I harmed Jim and my conscience is killing me. I can't take it!" You are wracking your mind to figure out what he did. You wonder, "Betrayal? Theft? Murder?!" You ask him. "I made fun of his Hawaiian shirt in front of the guys the other day, and he got upset," he replies. There is a series of harms from the very slight to the monstrous. Duties of non-maleficence cover all the harms it is morally wrong to do. Ross recognizes that duties of non-maleficence are more stringent than those of beneficence (Ross 1930, 21). We can endorse the generalization while recognizing it matters a great deal what kind of harm is being done.

The moral kinds Ross uses to illustrate this point occupy different points on a series. And incidentally, Ross puts them in an order from worst to least-wrong: *killing, adultery, theft, lie* (if we understand "thou shalt not bear false witness" in a general sense) (Ross 1930, 22). To solidify his point that duties of non-maleficence are "prima facie more binding" than duties of beneficence Ross himself descends to moral kinds to do so: "We should not in general consider it justifiable to kill one person in order to keep another alive, or to steal from one in order to give alms to another" (22). Killing and saving, stealing and giving alms—these are kinds of acts, not categories of duty. That's one important reason to separate moral kinds from moral categories. For moral kinds have greater epistemic weight and credibility, as well as greater detail, than do categories of duty.

Each moral kind in an initial analysis must be evaluated on its own terms, and independently of other normative factors. Consider the following pairs of moral kinds in isolation from everything else:

murder and *promise-breaking*
torture and *theft*
rape and *lying*.

[12] I simply introduce these scales here. I don't consider how the scales cover the finer intricacies involved in complex and subtle moral situations. I do cover more of the application of such scales in Kaspar 2019.

In each pair, the first kind is much worse than the second kind, and so much so that self-evident comparative stringency claims can be made about them. Moving to moral kinds that are closer to one another: an act *in so far as* it is a theft is worse than an act *in so far as* it is a lie. Or briefly, the nature of stealing is worse than the nature of lying. That means that, considered alone and alongside each other in the abstract, the prima facie duty not to steal is more stringent than the prima facie duty not to lie. But can't a particular lie be worse than a particular theft? Certainly. But only *other grounds* of duty can make it so, i.e., render it morally better to prefer the theft to the lie. Identifying the core deontic grounds of duty allows us to do more than just rely on our intuition that one moral kind is more stringent than another. The second level of moral explanation, which identifies and evaluates the components of moral kinds, enables us to analyze why stealing, by its very nature, is worse than lying. It can also enable us to explain why some instance of lying can be worse than an instance of stealing. A vicious lie (a kind) that can damage a person's reputation (a value) can be worse than pilfering (a kind) a dozen paperclips (a value) from the office for home use. The great disvalue in the first action makes it a greater harm, in part, due to the low value of what is stolen in the second. In this case values play the key role in explaining why this particular comparative stringency was reversed. Moral kinds make up the first category of moral scales.

Moral relations provide us with the second category of moral scales. Jane committed a theft. She stole a necklace from Mary. It's wrong to steal, but it's better that she stole from Mary than murdered her. Jane and Mary are both human. As Prichard claims, there is a moral relation we bear to everyone else, simply in so far as they are human (Prichard 1912, 29).[13] Call this the *human-human relation*. But Jane didn't break into Mary's place in order to steal the necklace. She was welcomed into Mary's house. Mary invited her. She did so because Jane and Mary are sisters. For as long as they've both been alive they've borne the *sibling relation* to one another, which is a distinct moral relation. It's bad that Jane stole a necklace from anyone. But that she stole one from her sister makes it much worse.

The third category of moral scales is based on values. The day after Jane's visit with Mary ended, Mary notices something awry with her jewelry box. She has a tennis match coming up, and wishes to wear her rhinestone tennis necklace. It cost her $11.19. Thankfully she finds it. But then her heart drops. She screams "No!" She digs deeper and finds that it is gone. Her sister made off with "A Heritage in Bloom," which has an estimated worth of $200,000,000. Stealing that necklace is a much worse theft than stealing the tennis necklace. The value involved, the value at stake, in a given moral act plays an important role in determining just how bad it is, and, as a consequence, just how wrong it is. This is something we all recognize, and this insight is embedded in our legal system. In New York state, for example, Jane's

---

[13] Ross has such a relation in his theory 1930, 30.

theft is a first-degree larceny, because the possession purloined is worth more than $1,000,000. If she had stolen the tennis necklace, it would have been a petty larceny, a misdemeanor, and it's likely that no police officer would have visited Mary to make record of the theft.[14]

Given the core deontic grounds of duty covered here, we can specify the moral nature of Jane's act. She stole (moral kind) an extraordinarily expensive necklace (value) from her sister (moral relation). Had any of these properties been different, the moral nature of the act would have been different. Thinking of alternative scenarios enables us to see that moral kinds have a moral importance that the other kinds of grounds lack. If Jane had not stolen anything, the moral relation and the value involved in the nature of the act would not have had the moral significance that they do have.

XI Conclusion

Ross's moral theory is fundamentally a theory of moral realities. This chapter has concentrated on Ross's metaphysics. His metaphysics provides the materials for adequate moral explanations, covering both prima facie and actual duties. The kind of explanations his metaphysics provides equips us to explain with some degree of detail what the *natures* of moral acts are. Previously, ethicists, including many from Price to Ross, spoke of the moral natures of acts. The core deontic grounds of duty covered here give us a way to analyze and specify what these particular natures are.

The greatest strength of Rossian intuitionism is found in its moral content. That intuitionism captures what we really think morally is what draws us to Ross's moral theory. The reason most people dismiss Ross's moral metaphysics is that they misunderstand it. Ross's grounds of duty neatly fit the moral propositions we really think to be true. They consist of properties such as moral kinds and moral relations. As we reflect on them and compare them to the explanatory properties of other theories, it's difficult to think of what other properties can better explain rightness, actual as well as prima facie.

Out of the moral metaphysical materials Ross provides, I have outlined an account of Rossian intuitionism that enables us to appreciate its explanatory power. The core deontic grounds of duty are moral kinds, moral relations, and values. By developing the opportunities Ross did not pursue, we have the resources for providing illuminating moral explanations beyond the partial explanations that Ross gives. Moral kinds are at the center of intuitionist explanation. Identifying the

---

[14] I have provided a case that makes use of monetary values to give a clear illustration of the value of one thing outweighing another. A fuller treatment of value scales would involve weighing apparent goods against those of the same class and against those in other classes. These would include life, health, pleasure, beauty, and so on.

components of different moral kinds enables us to determine what values within a kind are instantiated when it is. These in turn provide a basis for determining the value of the whole moral kind in its relation to rightness. By isolating and identifying moral kinds, moral relations, and values, we can establish three distinct yet related categories of moral scales by which to weigh prima facie duties in conflict situations, which enables us to explain actual duties.

How well this kind of explanatory approach fits with other concepts in a completed Rossian intuitionism remains to be determined. Although Ross speaks about moral realities a great deal, he also speaks about moral principles. How properties relate to principles is something that will need to be carefully worked out. Moral kinds, moral relations, and values which are present in moral situations undoubtedly give us reasons to act. Are they reasons? Or do they instead give us reasons? That will also have to be determined. Lastly, concepts are not expressly a part of Ross's ontology in Chapter 2. When he speaks about "our apprehension of the prima facie rightness of certain types of act" (Ross 1930, 29), it indicates that, with no mental intermediary between mind and property, we apprehend rightness and some specific moral kind. As different versions of Rossian intuitionism are worked out, it will be interesting to see what elements of Ross's theory are retained and what improvements might be made upon them.

Acknowledgments

I would like to thank Frances Kamm, Carolina Sartorio, Michael Otsuka, and Frederick Choo for their helpful comments on an early draft of this chapter. Thanks also to David Phillips for his several recommendations for improving it. And many thanks to Robert Audi for his numerous comments, criticisms, and suggestions for taking this chapter to a higher level.

References

Audi, R. 1996. "Intuitionism, Pluralism, and the Foundations of Ethics," in W. Sinnott-Armstrong and M. Timmons (eds), *Moral Knowledge? New Readings in Moral Epistemology*. Oxford: Oxford University Press, 101–36.
Audi, R. 2004. *The Good in the Right: A Theory of Intuition and Intrinsic Value*. Princeton: Princeton University Press.
Burnor, R., and Raley, Y. 2011. *Ethical Choices: An Introduction to Moral Philosophy with Cases*. New York: Oxford University Press.
Cowan, R. 2017. "Rossian Conceptual Intuitionism," *Ethics* 127, 821–51.
Cuneo, T., and Shafer-Landau, R. 2014. "The Moral Fixed Points: New Directions for Moral Nonnaturalism," *Philosophical Studies* 171, 399–443.
Frankena, W. K. 1973. *Ethics*, 2nd ed. Englewood Cliffs, NJ: Prentice-Hall.
Huemer, M. 2005. *Ethical Intuitionism*. New York: Palgrave Macmillan.
Hudson, W. D. 1983. *Modern Moral Philosophy*, 2nd ed. New York: St. Martin's Press.

Hurka, T. 2018. *British Ethical Theorists from Sidgwick to Ewing.* Oxford: Oxford University Press.
Kagan, S. 1989. *The Limits of Morality.* Oxford: Oxford University Press.
Kaspar, D. 2012. *Intuitionism.* London: Bloomsbury Press.
Kaspar, D. 2019. "The Natures of Moral Acts," *Journal of the American Philosophical Association* 55(1), 117–35.
Kulp, C. B. 2017. *Knowing Moral Truth.* Lanham, MD: Lexington.
Kulp, C. B. 2019. *Metaphysics of Morality.* New York: Palgrave Macmillan
Mahon, J. E. 2015. The Definition of Lying and Deception, in *Stanford Encyclopedia of Philosophy.*
Mill, J. S. 2002. "Utilitarianism," in Dale E. Miller (ed.), *The Basic Writings of John Stuart Mill.* New York: Modern Library, 233–301.
Parfit, D. 2011. *On What Matters: Volume One.* Oxford: Oxford University Press.
Phillips, D. 2019. *Rossian Ethics: W.D. Ross and Contemporary Moral Theory.* Oxford: Oxford University Press.
Prichard, H. A. 1912. "Does Moral Philosophy Rest on a Mistake?" *Mind* 21, 21–37.
Rawls, J. 1971. *A Theory of Justice.* Cambridge, MA: Harvard University Press.
Ross, W. D. 1930. *The Right and the Good.* Oxford: Clarendon Press.
Ross, W. D. 1939. *Foundations of Ethics.* Oxford: Clarendon Press.
Scanlon, T. M. 2016. *Being Realistic About Reasons.* Oxford: Oxford University Press.
Schroeder, M. 2009. "Huemer's Clarkeanism," *Philosophy and Phenomenological Research* 78(1), 197–204.
Shafer-Landau, R. 2003. *Moral Realism: A Defence.* Oxford: Clarendon Press.
Shafer-Landau, R. 2012. *The Fundamentals of Ethics,* 2nd ed. Oxford: Oxford University Press.
Stratton-Lake, P. 2000. *Kant, Duty, and Moral Worth.* London: Routledge.
Warnock, G. J. 1967. *Contemporary Moral Philosophy.* London: Macmillan.

9
Ross and the Problem of Permissibility

Philip Stratton-Lake

Ross's ethic of prima facie duty is generally thought to capture well common-sense morality. It may be that we need to add more basic prima facie duties to Ross's list of five, and perhaps add to his list of intrinsic goods as Audi (2004) and Hurka (2014) argue. But the basic scaffolding and much of the content fits well with our considered moral judgements. There is, however, one way in which it does not fit well with ordinary moral thought. It fails to leave room for merely permissible acts—that is, for acts that are neither obligatory nor wrong. This is because of the ever-present prima facie duty to promote the good, which in the absence of other prima facie duties generates an obligation (Ross, 2002, 39; 1939, 252).

The absence of the merely permissible results in three implausible consequences. First, this maximizing duty is very demanding, requiring us (absent other prima facie duties) to put aside our own good whenever doing so would promote the greater good, impartially considered. This will entail that nearly all of us act wrongly almost much of the time, as we so often give priority to our own good when we could be acting to promote the greater good.

The second implausible implication follows from the first. Many other people will often be engaged in activities that are important to them, but do not maximize goodness. If we help them engage in such activities, we would be helping them to do wrong acts. Cullity (2004, 136) gives an example of a gifted music student for whom some small effort of yours would determine whether she is able to pursue a musical career. It seems that it would be wrong not to help in this situation. But if pursuing this career is not doing what will maximize the good of others impartially considered, which it almost certainly isn't, then she is acting wrongly in pursuing it. But then I am acting wrongly in helping her, as it is wrong to help other people to do wrong acts. So our apparently kind acts will in fact be wrong.

The third implausible implication is that this view makes supererogatory acts impossible. This is because if the act would be instrumentally better, then, ceteris paribus, we would be required to do it. But if we are required to do it, it would not be supererogatory. Part of the worry here is covered by the demandingness problem, already mentioned. But this implausible implication is not exhausted by demandingness. If it turns out that supererogatory acts are what we are required to do, then it is not clear that we can retain the admirable aspect of such acts. This is because part of what makes such acts admirable is that we are going beyond what is required of us, beyond a minimum, or even medium level of decency, as Thomson would put it (1971, 62).

All of these problems stem from Ross's maximizing prima facie duty, and the fact that it leaves no space for merely permissible acts. Let's call this 'the permissibility problem'. There have been various attempts to deal with the permissibility problem in Ross (see particularly Audi 2004; Hurka 2014; and Hurka and Shubert 2012), but I have not found these attempts wholly satisfactory. In this paper I tentatively offer an alternative approach to the problem. This alternative rejects Ross's subsumption of the prima facie duty of beneficence under the duty to promote the good. Taking my lead from Kant's notion of an imperfect duty, I suggest that the relation between beneficence and value is primarily a requirement on our attitudes. What the duty of beneficence requires is not that we produce as much value as we can by benefitting others, but that we value the good of others appropriately. By moving away from a focus on the intrinsic value of some state of affairs to appropriate valuing, I think we can introduce some latitude into Ross's ethic of prima facie duties. This latitude carries with it space for the merely permissible, and thus avoids the implausible implications mentioned above. It does this as what it is fitting to value is context-relative in a way that good-promotion is not. I make no pretence to have solved this incredibly tricky and large problem here. My aim here is simply to outline a framework for thinking through it.

I Imperfect duties

Kant thinks of beneficence as an imperfect duty, and its being imperfect he thinks introduces latitude (1991, 194 [6: 390]), and therefore mere permissibility. Ross was very disparaging of this claim (1954, 45), but he interpreted it from a footnote in the *Groundwork*, where Kant says that an imperfect duty is one that allows of exceptions in the interest of inclination (1964 [4: 421n]). Ross rightly objected that a duty we can free ourselves from if we feel so inclined is no duty at all. But the footnote Ross refers to in the *Groundwork* does not, I think, express Kant's considered view. This is developed later in his *Metaphysics of Morals*.

In the *Metaphysics of Morals* Kant says that imperfect duties require us to adopt certain ends. The imperfect duty of beneficence requires us to make other people's ends our own. Adopting an end, for Kant, means adopting the relevant maxim of ends. A maxim is a subjective principle of action (1964, 69n [4: 400n])—subjective in the sense that it is the principle on which the agent acts. To adopt a maxim of ends is, then, to make it our principle that we will make other people's ends our own. But to adopt such a principle does not involve taking every opportunity to pursue it. I could have the goal of keeping fit, or adopt a maxim of keeping fit, without taking every opportunity to exercise. I would still have this end if, for instance, on a rainy afternoon, I have the time to go for a run but don't, because I don't fancy getting wet. If I never did anything in pursuit of this end that would clearly indicate that I do not really have this end, and if I sincerely claim that I do, then I would probably be self-deceived. But there is plenty of space between this extreme and the other extreme of taking every opportunity to exercise. This space allows for different degrees of commitment to this end. If I take very few opportunities to exercise, then I might be said to have this end, or, as Kant would have said, to have adopted it, but I would have only a weak commitment to it. If, on the other hand, I take every opportunity to pursue it, I will have a maximally strong commitment to this end, which in the case of exercising will almost certainly be a sort of fanaticism rather than a virtue.

It is this feature of possessing an end as Kant understands it—degrees of commitment—that allows for latitude. If I am required to make others' ends my own, then I have done this whether or not I am what Thomson called a minimally decent Samaritan or a good (saintly) Samaritan (1971, 62).

The important move for Kant is to understand the duty of beneficence as a duty not to do certain actions, but a duty to adopt certain maxims. It is this point about the content of imperfect duties that introduces latitude.

> ... if the law can prescribe only the maxim of actions, not actions themselves, this is a sign that it leaves a latitude... for free choice in following (complying with) the law, that is, that the law cannot specify precisely in what way one is to act and how much one is to do by the action for an end that is also a duty (1991, 194 [6: 390]).

In the *Groundwork* it looked like Kant thought that imperfect duties are not as binding as perfect ones, in the sense that you can permissibly fail to comply if you feel so inclined. This is what Ross thought could not be correct. But we can see from what Kant says in the *Metaphysics of Morals* that imperfect duties are distinctive not relation to their stringency, but with regard to their content. Perfect duties prohibit and imperfect duties require quite different things. Perfect duties forbid the performance of certain actions whereas imperfect duties require the adoption of certain principles (maxims of ends). This distinction does not commit Kant to the view that these different duties have a different deontic force. Imperfect duties, as I understand Kant, require us to adopt certain maxims with the same categorical force that perfect duties prohibit certain actions.

I think this approach to the problem of permissibility is a promising one. I do not suggest that we buy into the whole Kantian story here, but that we take our clue from the idea that the duty of beneficence does not directly require that we do certain acts, but rather that we adopt a certain principle or attitude. My suggestion is that we should understand the duty of beneficence as a requirement to value the good of others appropriately.

II Value and appropriate valuing

By subsuming the prima facie duty of beneficence under the prima facie duty to promote the good Ross wanted to link a person's happiness, the intrinsic value of happiness, and how we should respond to that value. The way Ross does this is by moving from the intrinsic value of happiness to the claim that this value requires us to promote this good, where promoting means 'maximize'. This way of thinking of things caused a number of problems for Ross, apart from the problem of permissibility. It also caused a problem for him about the moral relevance of our own happiness. In *The Right and the Good* he thought this committed him to the idea that we have a prima face moral obligation to produce happiness for ourselves, which he reluctantly accepted (though in the *Foundations* he tried to avoid this commitment by arguing that happiness is good in an agent-relative sense.) But this is not the only way in which we can understand the relation between happiness, its intrinsic value, and what we are prima facie required to do.

Another way to connect these things is through appropriate valuing. To get clear on this we need to start with the distinction between appropriately valuing something and believing that it is of value.[1] I could value something non-instrumentally that has no intrinsic value. I might, for instance, value some worthless goal, such as counting the blades of grass in my garden, and even orientate my life around that goal. But if my valuing is appropriate or fitting[2] to its intentional object then that object must either have final value or be suitably connected to final value. I could value grass counting but that valuing could never be appropriate, since what is valued is worthless.[3] So if nothing in the world is of value, then it could never be appropriate to value anything. But happiness has final value, so is something that is appropriately valued.

But although appropriate valuing is necessarily linked to value, appropriate valuing and value (being *of* value) can come apart. It is fitting for me to give my own children's happiness a certain priority and in general to value them more than other people's children. This valuing is, I think, appropriate, but it does not imply that my children have greater value, or are more valuable than other people's children. I can coherently believe that the happiness of all children has equal intrinsic value *and* that it is appropriate for me to value my children's happiness more than that of other children.

---

[1] Scanlon discusses this briefly (1998, 95), though he tends to talk merely of valuing rather than appropriate valuing.
[2] I treat these terms as synonyms.
[3] One might think the same is true of valuing something personal, such as an old photograph of a loved one. It may be claimed the photograph is as intrinsically worthless as grass counting. But such valuing sometimes at least seems to be appropriate. In response I would say that that is because it is suitably linked to something that does have intrinsic value—namely a valuable personal relationship.

There are of course limits to this. It would not be inappropriate to give priority to my own child in a situation where I could confer a tiny benefit on them or confer a huge benefit on many other children. But within certain limits, which are bound to be vague, it is appropriate to value my own children and their happiness more. This is because of the special relationship I have to them, which I do not have to other children. The key point is that this relationship affects how to value them appropriately but does not affect their value.

The same is true of my friends and loved ones. It is fitting to value the happiness of my friends and loved ones over the interests of strangers. This is also because of the special relationship in which I stand to them. Once again, this relationship affects how to value their happiness appropriately, but does not affect the value of their happiness. Neither my friends' happiness nor my friends are more valuable than other people, or at least need not be for it to be appropriate for me to value them more.

As Ross believed in *The Right and The Good*, my happiness is also of intrinsic value, and so I would claim is something that is appropriately valued. Within certain limits it is fitting to value my own happiness over the greater happiness of a stranger, even though I am not more valuable than other people, and my happiness isn't more valuable than theirs. Again, this is because of the intimate relation in which I stand to myself. The idea here is that, just as a certain special relation to my children, friends, and loved ones can make it appropriate to value their happiness more than that of strangers, so the special relation in which I stand to myself, my projects, and my interests can, within certain limits, make it appropriate to value my happiness more than the interests or happiness of others.

This is not to say that I need to stand in a special relation to someone for it to be fitting to value them. The happiness of strangers is of value just as my friends' and loved ones' happiness is, and this is sufficient to make it appropriate to value their happiness. And to value their happiness appropriately is how I am suggesting we link up their happiness, its value, and how I ought, prima facie, to respond. Where I depart from Ross is that I reject the idea that the link between the intrinsic goodness of happiness and how I should respond to this value is that I should produce as much of it as possible. To do that would make it impossible to value the happiness of my children, friends, and loved ones more than others' happiness. So I think we should regard the relevant prima facie duty not as a prima facie duty to produce as much goodness as possible, but as a prima facie duty to value the good (in the case we are interested in, the good of happiness) appropriately. But if we are to understand our relation to value as primarily appropriate valuing, rather than promotion, how are we to understand appropriate valuing?

Appropriate valuing is not merely a matter of having certain pro-attitudes, but also involves doing certain actions. I could not be said to value the happiness of other people appropriately if I do nothing to help them when I could easily do so. It wouldn't be enough merely to *want* to help, to feel inclined to help, or to feel a bit guilty about not helping. Such guilt might show that I value their happiness, but not that I value it appropriately. On the other hand, appropriate valuing does not require us to produce as much good for others as we can, as Ross's maximizing principle specifies. Rather the prima facie duty to value happiness appropriately involves a range of responses. As J. J. Thomson noted, one might help someone in need by doing what a minimally decent person would do or by doing what a good (saintly) Samaritan would do. Failing to act for the benefit of others does reveal that we don't value them appropriately. Like the Kantian notion of adopting a maxim of ends, appropriate valuing allows for different degrees of commitment, and it is this range that introduces latitude.

III Prima facie duties

Our own happiness is intrinsically good just as the happiness of other people is, and so our own happiness, as well as that of others, needs to be valued appropriately. If it is fitting to value our own happiness, then each of us has reason to value our own happiness. But this reason does not look distinctively moral, as the reasons involved in Ross's other principles do. I understand his prima facie duties as facts that provide us with moral reasons. So, as I understand it, the prima facie duty to keep our promises states that the fact that I have promised someone that I would Φ is a moral reason to Φ, and the prima facie duty of gratitude states that the fact that someone has benefitted me in the past is a moral reason to confer a benefit on them, and so on.

If prima facie duties are understood as picking out reasons in a more generic sense, we would not be able to make any sense of Ross's worry that we have a prima facie duty to promote our own happiness. Clearly the fact that some act would make me happier is some reason to do it, but it is not a moral reason. In fact Ross does not seem to have a more generic notion of a reason.[4] It seems that he thinks that one either has a moral reason (a prima facie duty) or no reason at all. Outside of morality it seems that he thinks that it is just a matter of what we want and how to get it. That seems to me to be a clear mistake. So I do think that we have reason to promote our own good. It is just that this is not moral reason.

If I am right that the reasons involved in valuing our own good appropriately are not moral, then this principle of self-interest would not be a moral principle. So there would not be a prima facie duty to promote our own good. There may be, as Ross thinks, a moral reason to make ourselves better in terms of knowledge and virtue. That could be a moral reason. I take no stand on that here. But the reason we have to promote our own interests is not. But because our own interests (as well

---

[4] For a related discussion, see Phillips (2019), Ch. 2, Sec. 2.

as the interests of other people) have final value, we do have reason to value our own good appropriately. These reasons of self-interest can conflict with the moral reasons to make other people happy, and these need to be weighed up. It is not just other people's happiness that is good, as Ross thought in the *Foundations* (1939, 276). My own happiness has value as well. So both need to be valued appropriately. Sometimes valuing happiness appropriately will involve valuing our own happiness over that of others. Sometimes it will involve valuing the happiness of others over my own. But because the relation to value is indirect—through appropriate valuing—rather than directly (from value to promotion), it may sometimes be fitting to value my own lesser happiness more than the greater happiness of others, just as sometimes it may be fitting to value the lesser good of my loved ones over the greater good of strangers. This makes no sense if we omit the link to appropriate valuing as an intermediary between intrinsic value and how to act, but is quite coherent once we include that link.

On this account then, it does not follow that I have a prima facie duty to sacrifice my own good when and because I can produce more happiness for others. That would follow if the relevant prima facie duty is to produce value, but not if it is to value the good appropriately. As we have seen, sometimes it is fitting to value my own lesser good, and sometimes not. Which is the right response cannot be read simply from the value of the relevant outcomes, any more than a decision about whether to benefit my friends or a stranger can be decided by an assessment of the relevant outcomes. This aspect of the right is to be decided not by a calculation of the amount of goodness to be produced, but by a judgement about whether it is fitting to value my own happiness or that of my friends over the happiness of strangers.

It may well be that it is appropriate to value my own happiness more *and* appropriate to value the happiness of others more. It may be appropriate to prioritize my own lesser happiness, because although this is lower than the happiness of others, it would nonetheless be a significant sacrifice not to do this. It may, at the same time, be fitting to value the greater happiness of others more. To do so at significant cost to oneself would be admirable, and it seems to me that it could not be unfitting to value something that is admirable.

IV Permissions not to pursue one's own good

But it may be objected that this approach goes too far and makes it wrong *not* to prioritize my own happiness over the greater happiness of others. Failing to prioritize my own happiness would be wrong, one might claim, in cases where it is fitting to value my own happiness more. This would be a problem because we are here trying to make space for valuing our own happiness or welfare more than others, and to make it permissible to sacrifice the benefit of a greater happiness for ourselves for a lesser benefit to others—what Hurka calls agent-favouring and agent-sacrificing permissions. The objection is that we have made space for the favouring kind, but not the non-favouring kind.

I do not, however, think this problem is real. It would be a real problem if the following implication were true:

> If (and when) it is fitting to value my own happiness more than the greater happiness of others, I *ought* to value my own happiness more than the greater happiness of others.

If this implication were true, it would follow that it would be wrong if I don't prioritize my own happiness when it is fitting to value it more.

But although there is a type of fittingness that seems peremptory, and thus ought-implying, there are other determinate forms[5] that are not. Suppose we analyse the loveable as a fitting object of love and the shameful as a fitting object of shame. I think different fittingness relations are involved in these two analyses. The fittingness that figures in the analysis of shamefulness seems peremptory, and thus ought-implying. A shameful act is one *I ought* to be ashamed of. But the fittingness involved in the analysis of the loveable does not have this peremptory character. If some puppy is loveable it is fitting to love it, but it doesn't follow that if I do not love it I have failed to have the attitude I ought to have. If I don't love the loveable puppy I have done nothing wrong, or even prima facie wrong. It is just that if I do, my attitude fits its loveable-making features (see Berker 2023).

It is this non-peremptory form of fittingness that I have in mind when I say it is sometimes fitting to value my own happiness over the greater happiness of others. Since this form of fittingness is not ought-implying, it does not follow that if I do not value my own happiness over others I have acted wrongly. So this claim is compatible with my sacrificing my own happiness for the sake of others, and is thus compatible with agent-sacrificing permissions, so long as it is fitting to do this as well. And in cases where this would be admirable, at least, it would have to be fitting.[6]

This is not like a case in which there is a plurality of conflicting duties (one to promote one's own good and one to promote the good of others), but more like a case in which there is a plurality of worthwhile goals I could pursue, where I can't pursue them all. There are many worthwhile goals I could pursue at some point in time. I can't pursue them all, but if I choose to pursue any one of them, then my

---

[5] I am inclined to think of fittingness as a determinable and of the various types of fittingness as determinate forms of that determinable. In correspondence Berker argued that this cannot be so, because determinate forms of determinables that are at the same level of specificity cannot both be present in the same object.

[6] Although he is not a friend of fittingness, this permissive, non-peremptory form of fittingness may be a way of capturing Hurka's permissions.

choice is fitting to its object and its value. My failure to pursue any of the other goals it would also be fitting to choose is not in any way prima facie wrong, even if the goal I have chosen to pursue is not the best. To use our loveable puppy example, the spaniel may be more loveable than the Labrador, but I do not have the wrong attitude if I love the Labrador but not the spaniel.

Valuing other people's happiness appropriately does not always involve the idea that, absent other considerations, I should do something to promote their happiness. Think about valuing your friends. It would be a mistake to conclude that I do not value my friends, or friendship, appropriately if I fail to promote their happiness absent other competing prima facie duties. Similarly valuing the happiness of others appropriately does not mean that I must maximize happiness, absent competing moral considerations. This is the sort of thing that Kant tried to capture with the requirement to adopt a maxim of ends. If this is correct, then it looks as though this approach holds out the prospect of dealing with the demandingness problem. We can make progress with this problem if we think of the duty of beneficence as primarily a duty to value the happiness of others appropriately.

V Is this approach too permissive?

I have said that it does not follow from the fact that when it is fitting to value my own happiness over the good of others I ought in those circumstances to favour my own happiness, and I act wrongly if I do not. This does not follow, I have claimed, because the relevant type of fittingness here is not peremptory. But if that is so, it looks as though we have the opposite problem. Often valuing the good of others appropriately seems to *require* certain actions rather than merely permit them. This is the case in easy rescue cases—that is, cases in which I could easily confer a large benefit on someone else at little or no cost to myself. Surely valuing the good of others appropriately will require, rather than merely permit, me to help in such cases. But if the notion of fittingness involved in appropriate valuing is non-peremptory, we would only have a permission to help and not a requirement.

It may seem that the simplest way to deal with this problem is to maintain that in easy rescue situations, there is only one way to value the good of others appropriately—and that is to help them. If there were a range of acts which would constitute appropriate valuing, any one of them would be permitted, and none would be required. But if there is only one way to value the happiness or well-being of another person, that would be the only permissible option, and so would be required. What makes it permissible to favour one's own happiness in situations where it is fitting to value one's own good over the good of others is the fact that it is also fitting to favour their good over one's own, so both options are permitted. But in situations like easy rescue cases, there is only one acceptable option, and so that one is required.

Now although this may seem the simplest solution to this problem, I do not think it is viable. To think that it is is to underestimate the non-peremptory sort of fittingness I have been using. Remember, we started with the idea of the loveable as a fitting object of love, and have been using the notion of fittingness that figures in the loveable. Failing to love the most loveable puppy does not involve anything wrong; nor does loving the less loveable puppy. The analogy with an easy rescue case would be one in which there is only one loveable puppy, just as there is only one fitting way to value the good of others. The suggestion was that in such cases, since there is only one fitting option, that option becomes required. But we can see that that is not the case in the puppy example. Even if there were only one loveable puppy, it would not turn out that we would be required to love it. Similarly, even if there is only one way to value the good of another person, it would not turn out that valuing them in that way is required if we are using the same sense of fittingness. So as simple as this solution appears, I do not think it works.

What we need is a more peremptory notion of fittingness. But we have already come across such a determinate form of fittingness—namely, the form of fittingness that figures in the analysis of the shameful. This form of fittingness seems peremptory, and thus ought-implying. A shameful act is one of which *I ought* to be ashamed. So to accommodate easy rescue cases in our account of appropriate valuing, I think we have to include this peremptory form of fittingness into our account as well as the non-peremptory form we have been using so far.

Which form of fittingness is relevant to which circumstances is a matter of judgement, as is the form of valuing that is fitting. One not only has to decide on what would be the fitting way to value the good, but also what form of fittingness is relevant. This certainly complicates matters. But if this helps us get things right then this complication would all be in the Rossian spirit—a spirit that disparaged simplicity over faithfulness to the facts (2002, 23).

VI Euthyphro problem

I have been attempting to explain the permissibility of prioritizing my own lesser good in terms of appropriate valuing. But, it may be objected, this gets things back to front.[7] It is not the case that certain acts are permissible because they are appropriately valued; rather they are appropriately valued because they are permissible. If this were correct, then appropriate valuing will not have explained anything.

---

[7] My worry here is based on an objection made to an earlier version of this paper by Dale Dorsey at the Notre Dame-Australian Catholic University International Ethics conference at Notre Dame in April 2022.

This is a Euthyphro-style objection. In response, I would start by saying that I think all Euthyphro-style questions tend to set up false dichotomies. Take a classic version:

Does God forbid Φing because Φing is wrong, or is Φing wrong because God forbids Φing.

My answer is that both options are false. Φing is wrong because of certain other facts, such as the fact that Φing would break a promise, or would harm an innocent person, and God would forbid Φing not because it is wrong, but because it has those wrong-making features. It is the wrong-making features that plausibly play the dual role of grounding God's prohibitions and grounding the wrongness of the prohibited acts.

Does this approach work with the above-mentioned Euthyphro question to my account of permissibility in Ross? Suppose I am considering sacrificing my life to save four other people. Both their lives and my life matter, and I value both. But I want to know whether it is permissible to favour our own lesser good over the greater good of the four others. To ask this question is to ask whether it is fitting to value their good over my own, or whether it is fitting to sacrifice myself. As we have seen, if the concept of fittingness involved in this question is non-peremptory, we do not need to choose. It can be fitting to value their good over my own, and to value my own good over their greater good. If this is right, what would make each option fitting?

One naïve answer would be to say that it would be fitting to prioritize my own good because of the significant cost to me of not doing so.[8] What would make it fitting to prioritize the good of others is simply the significant benefit I could confer. The answers to both these questions explain why it is permissible both to prioritize my own welfare and to help the others (at great cost to myself). Whether this naïve answer is correct is a matter for substantive judgement. So my point is not to defend this naïve answer. The point is to show that one does not have to answer questions about why it is fitting to prioritize one's own welfare or that of others by saying that it is permissible to do either. Whatever explains why each act is fitting will also explain why it is permissible to do it. In that respect my answer to the Euthyphro question is similar in structure to my answer to the traditional version. Permissibility does not explain why these acts are instances of appropriate valuing: different things do in each case. And whatever explains why each option counts as appropriate valuing will also explain why each option is permissible. If that is correct, then this Euthyphro-style objection to my account does not succeed.

---

[8] Hurka suggests such a reply when he writes that 'the demand always to maximize is excessive' (2014, 180).

But, it may be objected, although permissibility does not explain appropriate valuing, appropriate valuing does not explain permissibility either. So it may be said that we still have a problem. The problem is that appropriate valuing is not doing the explanatory work. But I don't think that is correct either. Appropriate valuing is not, I am conceding, a permissibility-*maker*. But being a permissibility-maker is not the only explanatory role it could have. It could have a unifying role, picking out what the very different facts that make very different acts permissible have in common—they are all the sort of thing that make it appropriate to value those acts.

I take this idea to be structurally similar to the way in which Scanlon's contractualism works. According to Scanlon's contractualism, the morality of what we owe to each other is grounded in the idea of acting on principles which those affected could not reasonably reject. A principle of mine that allows me to exploit you could be reasonably rejected by you, and so acts that fall under this principle are wrong. But they are not wrong because they fall under principles that could be reasonably rejected. Reasonable rejectability is not the wrong-making feature. What makes such acts wrong is the ground of reasonable rejectability, not reasonable rejectability as such. And the exploitation principle could be reasonably rejected just because it is exploitative, or because it fails to respect your personhood, or autonomy, or something like that. As I read Scanlon, there is a diverse range of wrong-making features, and reasonable rejectability does not figure on the list. Reasonable rejectability is not a fundamental wrong-making feature, but picks out what all the different wrong-making features have in common.[9] This is what I am suggesting for appropriate valuing. It does not pick out what makes certain options permissible. But it picks out what all the diverse permissibility-making features have in common—they are all features that are fitting to value.

VII Conclusion

Although the details would have to be worked out, it looks as though we might be able to deal with the problem of permissions better by thinking of our relation to the good as mediated by appropriate valuing, rather than linked directly to what we ought prima facie to do by requiring us to maximize the good. Doing this separates how we may permissibly act from which acts would maximize the good, and in doing so provides a way of solving the permissibility problem. It is also a way that fits well with other aspects of Ross's ethic of prima facie duty. For instance, it sits well with the guiding idea that personal relationships have inherent moral significance. This personal aspect of morality gets lost completely with Ross's prima facie

---

[9] See Stratton-Lake 2003a and 2003b.

duty to maximize goodness, and causes various significant problems for him. But once we think of the link between the good and what we prima facie ought to do as mediated by appropriate valuing, we can allow special relations to others and to ourselves to determine what sort of valuing is fitting. And that gives us moral space both to favour ourselves and to sacrifice ourselves, within certain limits.

References

Audi, R., (2004) *The Good in the Right*. Princeton: Princeton University Press.
Berker, S., (2023) 'The Deontic, the Evaluative, and the Fitting'. In *Fittingness* (Howard and Rowland, eds). Oxford: Oxford University Press.
Cullity, G., (2004) *The Moral Demands of Affluence*. Oxford: Oxford University Press.
Hare, R. M., (1972) 'Nothing Matters', *Applications of Moral Philosophy*. Macmillan.
Hurka, T., (2014) *British Ethical Theorists from Sidgwick to Ewing*. Oxford: Oxford University Press.
Hurka, T., Shubert, E., (2012) 'Permissions to Do Less Than the Best: A Moving Band'. *Oxford Studies in Normative Ethics*, 2, 1–27.
Kahane, G., (2014) 'Our Cosmic Insignificance'. *Nous*, 48:4, 745–72.
Kant, I., (1964) *Groundwork of the Metaphysic of Morals*, trans. by H. J. Paton. New York: Harper and Row.
Kant, I., (1991) *Metaphysics of Morals*, trans. by M. Gregor. Cambridge: Cambridge University Press.
McHugh, C., (2017) 'Attitudinal Control'. *Synthese*, 194: 8, 2745–62.
Munoz, D., (2021) 'From Rights to Prerogatives'. *Philosophy and Phenomenological Research*, 102:3, 608–23.
O'Neill, O., (1989) 'Universal Laws and Ends in Themselves', in her *Constructions of Reason*, 126–44.
Phillips, David, (2019) *Rossian Ethics: W. D. Ross and Contemporary Moral Theory*. New York: Oxford University Press.
Ross, David, (1939) *The Foundations of Ethics*. Oxford: Oxford University Press.
Ross, David, (1954) *Kant's Ethical Theory: A Commentary on the Grundlegung zur Metaphysik der Sitten*. Oxford: Oxford University Press.
Ross, David, (2002) *The Right and the Good*. Oxford: Oxford University Press.
Stratton-Lake, P., (2003a) 'Scanlon's Contractualism and the Redundancy Objection'. *Analysis*, 63:1, 70–6.
Stratton-Lake, P., (2003b) 'Scanlon, Permissions and Redundancy: Response to McNaughton and Rawling'. *Analysis*, 332–7.
Thomson, J. J., (1971) 'A Defense of Abortion'. *Philosophy & Public Affairs*, Autumn, 47–66.

PART III
ROSS ON VIRTUE AND VICE

10
Ross On Virtue and Vice

Thomas Hurka and Bowen Chan

Alongside his pluralist theory of the right, with its multiple prima facie duties, W. D. Ross had a pluralist theory of the good, recognizing the distinct intrinsic goods of pleasure, knowledge, virtue, and the rewarding of desert. This chapter examines his account of the good of virtue and evil of vice and argues that it's in several ways superior to the better-known ones of Aristotle and Kant.

I Virtue and Vice as Higher-Level Moral Properties

Ross thought virtue is, distinctively, morally good, as other goods such as pleasure and knowledge are not, and vice is morally evil. This wasn't, however, a substantive distinction. For him to be morally good is just to be intrinsically good by having a certain type of property, the one that makes for the goodness of virtue (1930, 155). Moral goodness therefore isn't a distinct normative property but the same property of goodness when had by a specific kind of item, primarily an attitude, and on a specific basis.

This basis involves a certain relation between an attitude and its intentional object. In *The Right and the Good* Ross said an act is virtuous if it's done from a virtuous motive and that there are three basic such motives: (1) the desire to do one's duty, or to do what is right, (2) the desire to bring into being something good, and (3) the desire to produce some pleasure or prevent some pain for another being, where that being's pleasure is good (1930, 160). Relatedly, an act is vicious if it's done from any of three vicious motives: (1) the desire to do something wrong because it's wrong (though he thought this desire rare), (2) the desire to bring about something evil, and (3) the desire to produce some pain for another (163). Since in all these cases a desire's being virtuous or vicious depends on a moral quality in its object, on its object's being right, good, wrong, or evil, his account makes virtue and vice derivative moral properties, ones defined by their relation to other more fundamental moral properties or to items that have them. It can't be virtuous to desire something right or good unless, prior to your desiring, it's right or good, nor can it be vicious to desire something evil unless it's independently evil. His view therefore contrasts with those radical versions of virtue ethics that make virtue the fundamental moral property in terms of which others are understood,

Thomas Hurka and Bowen Chan, *Ross On Virtue and Vice* In: *The Moral Philosophy of W. D. Ross*.
Edited by: Robert Audi and David Phillips, Oxford University Press. © Oxford University Press 2025.
DOI: 10.1093/9780198914839.003.0010

so, for example, right acts are those done from a virtuous motive (Slote 2001) or those a virtuous person would do (Hursthouse 1999). It also contrasts with neo-Aristotelian definitions of the virtues as those traits needed for a good or flourishing life (Anscombe 1958). Given an independent account of flourishing they too make virtue derivative, but Ross's account does so in a different way. It characterizes virtue by its relation not to some property of the life it figures in, but to a moral property such as rightness or goodness of the object it's intentionally directed at.

More abstractly, his account takes virtue to involve a matching relation between the orientation, either positive or negative, of an attitude and the moral quality, again positive or negative, of its object. Thus a positive attitude such as desire for something with the positive quality of rightness or goodness is virtuous and good, as is a negative attitude to something wrong or evil. In his examples the positive-positive relation is present in the desires to do what is right, to produce some good, and to produce some pleasure; the negative-negative one appears only in the desire to prevent pain, but he would surely also count desires not to act wrongly and not to produce some evil as virtuous. Conversely, the unmatching relation in a positive attitude to something wrong or evil, as in his three examples of vice, or what his discussion again omits, a negative attitude such as aversion to acting rightly or a desire to destroy some good, is vicious. (He counted the desire to corrupt another's character as an instance of the desire to produce something evil [1930, 163], but if the goal is only that the other become somewhat less virtuous it's better described as a desire to destroy a good.) Whereas positive-positive and negative-negative intentional relations are virtuous and good, positive-negative and negative-positive ones are vicious and evil. Virtue and vice are then higher-level moral properties found in certain matching or unmatching attitudes to other previously given moral properties or to items that have them.

Broadly similar accounts of virtue had been given by others before Ross. Hastings Rashdall identified virtue with "the settled bent of the will towards that which is truly or essentially good" (1885, 224; 1907 I, 59, 65, II 41–2), while G. E. Moore, though not using the word "virtue," affirmed the intrinsic goodness of loving the good and hating the evil and the evil of loving evil and hating good (1903, 203–4, 217, 208–9, 211). Ross's second and third forms of virtue likewise involve attitudes to values, but his first, the desire to do one's duty, adds a desire directed at the right. Rashdall and the Moore of *Principia Ethica* identified the property of rightness with that of most promoting the good, so the desire to act rightly just is, in someone who understands this, a desire for value (Moore 1903, 218–19). Ross rejected that identification, and in its absence the desire to act rightly is distinct from any desire about value, both when the right act doesn't maximize the good, as his deontic theory allows, and when it does. Even then wanting to do an act because it's right differs from wanting to do it because it promotes value.

Present-day discussions of moral motivation often distinguish between its de dicto and de re forms. You desire something right or good de dicto if you desire it *as* right or good; you desire it de re if you desire it for the properties that make it right or good without, in that desire, thinking of it as right or good or of those properties as making it so. (You can therefore simultaneously desire something both de dicto and de re.) Ross recognized this distinction when he added his third form of virtue, the desire to give pleasure to another. To the question why, if another's pleasure is good, the desire to produce it isn't included in the desire to bring about something good, he replied that you can think of something as pleasant, and therefore want to produce it, without thinking of it as good (1930, 161–2). His third form therefore involves a de re desire for another's pleasure, which means his second form must include only de dicto desires, ones for good things thought of as good. But this points to a puzzling omission in his account. Why didn't he also count de re desires for knowledge, virtue, and the rewarding of desert as virtuous? He didn't add or ever acknowledge separate forms of virtue for these, yet if someone wants to know just as such, or wants to desire others' pleasure without thinking of that desire as good, her wanting those things seems virtuous in the same way as wanting another's pleasure de re. Ross did think the goods of knowledge and virtue call for admiration, which involves the thought of its object as good and so necessarily is de dicto (1939, 278–9). But that admiration is one virtuous response to a good doesn't mean there can't be others, such as a de re desire to know or to be benevolent. Nor did he see any virtue in de re versions of the motive of duty, as in strong desires not to lie or cause harm independently of thinking of those acts as wrong. Yet that all these de re attitudes are virtuous seems to follow from his underlying picture of virtue as matching orientation to moral quality, since if one positive quality of an object is its being good or right, another is its having the properties that make it so. In giving a list of basic virtues where all but one, the third, are de dicto, he may have been excessively influenced by Kant, but his granting the one exception was still important. Present-day discussions are dominated by Kantians who think the only morally good motive is de dicto and opponents who think only de re ones have worth. Like many in his era, though less extensively than one might like, Ross recognized that both forms can be virtuous, and that the best motivation combines both. Imagining that the motive of duty has 10 units of value and that of love, presumably read de re, has 8, he said an act done from both duty and love has 18 units of value, whereas one done only from duty has 10 and one done only from love has 8 (1930, 171–2). For him each of the de dicto and de re forms has some worth, and each makes action from it to some degree good.

At a related point Ross resisted Kant's influence. Whereas Kant thought the motive of duty differs in kind from any inclination, Ross took it to involve a desire to do what is right that is of the same psychological type as other desires; it just has a distinctive object (1930, 156–8; 1939, 205–6). And he thought this desire is needed for action from duty to result. Whereas internalists about moral motivation think judging that an act is right itself involves an impulse to do it, he took the externalist view that even moral beliefs are motivationally inert and need to be supplemented by the desire to do what is right if they're to influence conduct (1930, 156–8; 1939, 205–6, 226–8). He thought most of us have a general desire to act rightly, as we have a general desire for pleasure, so in us the belief that an act is right does prompt a motive to do it. But that is only because we have this specific instance of the general category of desire.

Theories of virtue can differ about which states of us virtue is primarily located in. Aristotle and those influenced by him take these to be dispositions or lasting states of character, so occurrent desires and acts are virtuous only derivatively. Thus Aristotle said an act is virtuously done only if it not only has a certain motive but also proceeds "from a firm and unchangeable character" (1984, 1105a34). A contrary view ascribes virtue primarily to occurrent desires or attitudes and understands virtuous character traits derivatively, as dispositions to have these attitudes. The two views differ about whether an out-of-character act can be virtuous, or have the full value of virtuous action, the Aristotelian view saying no and the rival one saying yes. To us the non-Aristotelian view is far more attractive. Imagine that we're a military committee deciding whether to give a medal for bravery to a soldier who knowingly sacrificed his life to save several comrades from love of and loyalty to them. If an Aristotelian says, "This is a medal for acting bravely, and we can't know if he did that unless we know whether he would have acted similarly a month earlier or a month later," we'll throw him out of the room. What matters is only the soldier's motivation at the time he acted (Hurka 2006).

Ross's view on this issue wasn't entirely consistent. He first identified virtue with "action, or disposition to act, from any one of certain motives" (1930, 134); this suggests the non-Aristotelian view since it treats virtuous desire as a separate good, independent of disposition. But he later said "morally good" means "good either by being a certain sort of character or by being related in one of certain definite ways to a certain sort of character," so "an action or feeling is morally good by virtue of proceeding from a character of a certain kind" (1930, 155). This, in contrast, suggests an Aristotelian priority for dispositions. But his final discussion reverted to the earlier, to us more attractive view. It first identified morally good acts simply as those "proceeding from certain motives" (1939, 290) and then extended its account to include desires that aren't acted on and emotions more generally before finally adding that dispositions to have these attitudes are also good (291–2). Here the goodness of the dispositions was an addition to that of occurrent attitudes rather than a condition for it, allowing out-of-character acts to be virtuous. He did say a character is "a larger and grander bearer of moral goodness than any single manifestation of character" (293), but he may have been thinking here of a character as involving many dispositions and present at many times. And he stressed that we can understand a virtuous character only as a disposition to have independently virtuous attitudes (293), so conceptually the occurrent forms of virtue come first.

If virtue is a higher-level good, a natural further claim says the degree of value of an attitude depends on the degree of value or importance of its intentional object. Other things equal, it's better and more virtuous to desire a greater good, for example a greater pleasure for another, than to desire a lesser one. Ross assumed this when he said the desire to produce knowledge or virtue is better than the desire to give pleasure (1930, 165–6; 1939, 302); this follows if, as he held, virtue and knowledge are greater goods than pleasure (1930, 149-52). In *Foundations of Ethics* he called the desire to produce pleasure or knowledge in everyone better than desires for particular instances of these goods, as it must be if a good for all is better than that good in one person, and a desire for knowledge or virtue in everyone better than a similarly general desire for pleasure (298, 302). He seems to have intended the superiority of desires for knowledge or virtue to hold across the board, so any desire for knowledge or virtue is better than any desire for pleasure. This follows about desires for virtue if, as he notoriously held (1930, 150–1), virtue is infinitely better than pleasure. But he seems to have allowed that knowledge, when separated from a virtuous desire for knowledge, isn't to that extreme degree better than pleasure (151–2). If it isn't, there should be cases where an intense pleasure is better than some trivial item of knowledge, so desiring it is better than desiring the knowledge. A similar conclusion follows if, as a second claim says, the degree of value of a virtuous attitude also depends on its intensity, so a stronger desire for a good is better than a weaker one. Then even if a pleasure and an instance of knowledge are equally good, a stronger desire for the pleasure can be better than a weaker one for the knowledge. Ross implicitly accepted this second claim when he said an ideal agent has desires whose strengths are proportioned to their objects' degrees of value, with as much more for a greater good as its value exceeds that of a lesser (1939, 293, 309). He took a similar view of vice, saying a desire for intellectual or moral evil, for example to corrupt another's character, is worse than a desire to inflict pain (1930, 166; 1939, 301) and generalized versions of all these desires worse than particular ones.

He also thought it better to want to fulfil a stronger than a weaker prima facie duty, and better to want to fulfil any such duty more intensely, so an ideal agent's desires are proportioned to his various duties' strengths (1939, 309). It's less clear what view he took of desires to do one's duty proper, or all things considered. Imagine that in one situation the act that is your duty proper is supported by strong prima facie duties with no serious duties on the other side, while in another the act that is right fulfils a weak duty and is only slightly preferable to some alternative. One view says the desire to do your duty proper in the first situation is better and more virtuous, since the duty there is more strongly supported, whereas a contrary view says the two desires are equally good because their objects share a property, that of being simply right, that doesn't admit of degrees. Ross didn't address the choice between these views, but his overall position may go best with the first, on which the value of the desire to do your duty proper can vary.

In both books he held that the motive of duty is the intrinsically best motive, better than any directed at a good or against an evil (1930, 164; 1939, 303–5). But he probably didn't intend this claim to hold across the board, which would make any desire to act rightly, in any situation, better than any instance of another form of virtue. Recall his suggestion that in an act done both from duty and from a de re desire to give pleasure the motive of duty may have 10 units of value and the de re one 8. If an attitude's degree of value depends on the degree of value of its object, the de re desire in a different act that gives twice as much pleasure is better than the de re desire in the first act and may be better than the desire to act rightly in the first act. Even if the de re desire in the second act isn't twice as good as in the first, it can surely have more than the 10 units of value of the motive of duty in the first.

Ross's arguments for the superiority of the motive of duty didn't exclude this possibility, since they compared this motive only with other possible motives in the same situation. But if the desire to do your duty proper always had the same value, as on the second view above, this desire would have the same 10 units of value in the second act as in the first and could therefore be less good than the de re motive in the second. So to hold that the desire to do your duty proper is always better than any other motive in the same situation, he would have to say this desire's value varies and in particular is greater when the duty proper is more strongly supported. But is this always plausible? It's overwhelmingly your duty proper not to kill a hundred innocent people in order to get a minor pleasure for yourself, but your desire not to do this because it's wrong doesn't seem of enormous intrinsic worth. To maintain even his limited claim that the desire to do your duty, including your duty proper, is always better than any other motive in the same situation, Ross would have to say the value of a desire to do your duty proper is greater the more strongly supported the duty is. And that is at least questionable when the prima facie duty grounding your duty proper is a strong negative one like the duty not to kill.

Ross didn't argue at length for the superiority of the motive of duty. He just thought it obvious that if you think act A is right but are drawn to a different act B by love of some particular person, you'll act better if you do what you think is right (1930, 164). But this case doesn't fully establish his conclusion. If you think A is right, you must think there are other properties that make it right and that outweigh the properties that favour B. And that it's better to act from duty than from a de re desire for the less weighty properties favouring B doesn't imply that it's also better to act from duty than from a de re desire for the weightier ones favouring A; that desire could in principle be better than the desire to do A because it's right. More generally, Ross's claim that the motive of duty is best would be contested not only by those who think only de re motives have worth but also by some who value both forms; they can think that sometimes a de re desire is better. In some cases cited for these contrary views the motive of duty involves a false belief about what is right, as when Huck Finn thinks it's his duty to return an escaped slave to the slave's owner (Arpaly 2002). These cases wouldn't impress Ross given his sharp distinction, discussed below, between the right and the morally good. But in some other such cases the belief about what is right can be true. Thus some hold that it's less admirable to visit a friend in hospital from duty than from love even if you have a duty as a friend to visit (Stocker 1976), or less good to save your spouse rather than some strangers with the explicit thought that you're required or permitted to do so (Williams 1981), even though that thought may be true. In both cases, it's argued, action from a de re motive is preferable.

Our own view is that the relative values of de dicto and de re motives are different in different situations. When an act will affect a friend, spouse, or someone you're close to, as in the hospital and saving cases, the motive of love does seem more admirable. It's not that when visiting a friend in hospital you must have no thoughts of duty, even of your duty as a friend; that is too extreme. But visiting only from duty is less good than visiting only from love, and an ideal visitor will be motivated mostly by love with duty a less prominent accompaniment. But in other cases the motive of duty seems better. Imagine a judge who takes care to give similar sentences to criminals who have committed similar offences. Surely it's better if he does so because he thinks this required by duty or justice than if he has just a de re attraction to patterns where punishments are proportioned to crimes; here the de dicto motive should predominate. And there may be cases where the two types of motive are roughly equally good. Ross was right, we think, to hold that both de dicto and de re motives can be virtuous and good but wrong to think the former are always better, as it's equally wrong to always prefer the latter; their relative values can vary between contexts.

The moral evil of vice overlaps with the non-moral good of pleasure in cases of cruel or malicious pleasure, such as pleasure in another's pain. Ross held that, like undeserved pleasure, or the perhaps otherwise innocent pleasure of a morally bad person, malicious pleasure is not good but bad. A state of pleasure "has the property, not necessarily of being good, but of being something that is good if the state has no other characteristic that prevents it from being good" (1930, 137–8). But this claim allows two readings that he didn't explicitly distinguish. On a "summative" view, even a malicious pleasure is to some degree good as a pleasure, though it's also bad as malicious and, since the badness outweighs the goodness, bad on balance. On an "undermining" view, the pleasure's being malicious undermines any goodness it may have as a pleasure so it's purely and entirely bad. Philip Stratton-Lake (2002, 126) and David Phillips (2019, 125) have taken Ross to intend the undermining view, but three facts tell against this interpretation.

Shortly after saying malicious pleasure is bad, Ross cited it in an argument for the infinitely greater value of virtue compared to pleasure: "If the goodness of pleasure were commensurable with the goodness or badness of moral disposition," he wrote, "it would be possible that such a pleasure [a malicious one] if sufficiently intense should be good on the whole. But in fact its intensity is a measure of its badness" (1930, 151). But he couldn't give this argument if he had the undermining view. Since a malicious pleasure's goodness as pleasure can't outweigh its badness if there's no such goodness, the argument assumes summation. And he repeated the argument in *Foundations of Ethics*. After introducing the view that "immoral pleasures are good *qua* pleasures but bad *qua* immoral," he said an objection to it can be given a "sound reply" and concluded that "the goodness which springs from pleasantness is never so great as to outweigh the badness that springs from (or consists in) immorality" (274). Moreover, he later gave the desire to get a bad pleasure "as being a pleasure" the same value as a desire for an innocent pleasure, as if the two types of pleasure had, *qua* pleasures, the same value (302).

The undermining view is also in tension with his sharing Moore's view that a state's intrinsic value can depend only on its intrinsic and not on its relational properties (1930, 74, 75, 114–15). This tension is clearest in the companion case of undeserved pleasure. Here what is bad is a vicious person's enjoying even an innocent pleasure, but if that involved the undermining of the pleasure's goodness it would mean the pleasure's value depended on the relational property of occurring in the same life as the vice. In fact Ross endorsed Moore's treatment of desert as an organic unity (1930, 72), and in it undeserved pleasure retains its goodness as pleasure. The case of malicious pleasure is more complex, since here there are not two distinct states but a single state with two properties, that of being a pleasure and that of being malicious. But an extension of Moore's view says the value a property gives a state can depend only on its intrinsic character and not on any relations it has to other properties of that state; this too excludes undermining. Whether or not one accepts this extension, an undermining reading of Ross's view of undeserved pleasure is plainly inconsistent with his Moorean understanding of intrinsic value.

Finally, the summative view is strongly suggested by the way he elaborated his claim that a pleasure is good only if it has no other property that prevents it from being so. He compared the merely conditional value this gives pleasure with the conditional obliging force of a prima facie duty and even called pleasure "prima facie good" (1930, 138). But his view wasn't at all that an outweighed prima facie duty is undermined in the sense of cancelled; it remains "an objective fact involved in the nature of the situation" and can still have normative implications, such as requiring compensation to the person to whom the duty was owed (1930, 20, 28). By analogy, the goodness *qua* pleasure of a malicious pleasure should remain an "objective fact" even when it's outweighed by the badness *qua* malicious, so the pleasure is bad only on balance. Though the undermining view is one some philosophers may want Ross to have held, at multiple points it doesn't fit what he said.

II Virtue the Greatest Good and Vice the Greatest Evil

Ross's treatment of malicious pleasure reflected his view that virtue is the greatest intrinsic good and vice the greatest evil, but *The Right and the Good* stated this view in two ways, one stronger and one weaker. The stronger statement says that while pleasure and knowledge are comparable in value with virtue, they're not "commensurable with it, as a finite duration is not commensurable with infinite duration," so virtue is "infinitely better" (150, 152). The weaker one says virtue "belongs to a higher order of value, beginning at a point higher on the scale of value than that which pleasure ever reaches" (150). Though consistent with virtue's being infinitely better, the second claim is also consistent with its being just finitely so, as it will be if the gap between the best pleasure and least good virtue is some finite amount. On one version of this last view only the value of a single pleasure at a single time can't exceed a maximum; given many pleasures or ones that last a long time there can be more value than in some instance of virtue. This seems to be how Ross read the second claim in *Foundations of Ethics*, since he there raised the possibility of enough pleasures outweighing some virtue as an objection to the claim (275). His preferred view seems therefore to have been the strong one that virtue is infinitely better than all other goods, so no amount of them can outweigh any instance of it.

This strong view wasn't at all shared by his philosophical predecessors. In *Principia Ethica* Moore held that what Ross called virtue is a lesser good, in the sense that a virtuous attitude always has less value than its intentional object. Thus compassion for another's pain is not as good as the pain is evil, and a world with pain and compassion for it is less good than one with no pain and no compassion (1903, 220). Rashdall, in contrast, thought a virtuous attitude has more value than its object (1907, I 94, II 106) but held that it has only finitely more and gave several examples where it can be right to do what you know will worsen your own or another's character if that does enough to promote other goods (II 43–4. 47). To adapt one of these, you may know that if you become a nurse or a surgeon that may harden your character, making you less prone to feeling strong compassion for others' pain. But if you'll also effectively relieve their pain, the good that involves can make this career choice on balance best.

Ross's arguments for the infinite superiority of virtue were, frankly, feeble. In *The Right and the Good* he first said your own pleasure is a "cheap and ignoble object in comparison with virtue," one there's rarely if ever a duty to pursue whereas there's always a duty to pursue virtue (151). But though he often denied that there's a duty to pursue your own pleasure (1930, 21; 1939, 272), he affirmed a duty to promote other people's pleasure that can sometimes outweigh competing duties such as promise-keeping (1930, 18). And it's hard to see how the lack of a duty concerning your own pleasure shows anything about how the value of others' pleasure compares with that of your or their virtue, let alone that it's infinitely less. He did say that, since "that which is good owes its goodness not to being possessed by one person rather than by another, but to its nature" (1930, 151), what is true of your own pleasure's value compared to virtue must be true of all pleasures' value. But the central assumption of his whole argument here is that we can deduce an object's degree of value from the strength of the duty to promote it, and on his view your and others' pleasure relate completely differently to duty. Moreover, in *Foundations of Ethics* he would allow the relativity of value the last quote denies, saying that, relative to you, your own pleasure isn't good whereas others' pleasure is (271–84); this clearly makes a claim about your pleasure irrelevant to the comparative value of theirs. And far from being an ignoble object, others' pleasure is an admirable one that is arguably sometimes, as in Rashdall's examples, worth pursuing at the cost of some virtue in yourself or them.

The Right and the Good's other argument was the one about malicious pleasure: that unless virtue is infinitely better, a sufficiently intense such pleasure can be on balance good (151). But this argument is simply fallacious. Any increase in intensity that makes the pleasure better *qua* pleasure can also make it worse *qua* malicious, and so long as the badness increases at a rate at least as fast as the goodness the pleasure will always be on balance bad. (If a mild malicious pleasure has 1 unit of goodness *qua* pleasure and 2 units of badness *qua* malicious, one that is ten times as intense can have 10 units of goodness and 20 of badness.) Ross seems to have recognized this in *Foundations of Ethics*. The objection he there imagined to the summative view of malicious pleasure was precisely that it allows such pleasure to be on balance good, and his "sound reply" was that the pleasure "can be intensely pleasant only when it is intensely immoral; a man can enjoy cruelty intensely only if he intensely wishes to hurt another" (274). This seems to acknowledge that if the badness of the immorality increases as quickly as the goodness of the pleasure, a summative view can find malicious pleasure always on balance bad even if virtue isn't infinitely better.

Yet in *Foundations of Ethics* he continued to hold the infinite-superiority view, though in a different form. He now rejected the idea that virtue starts at a higher point on the scale of goodness than where pleasure leaves off, arguing instead that pleasure, when good, is good in a different sense than that in which virtue is. Whereas virtue and also knowledge have an unanalysable property of intrinsic goodness, pleasures are at best good in a secondary and analysable sense, that of being "*worthy objects of satisfaction*" (275–6), and items that are good in different senses don't fall on the same scale and can't be compared in goodness (283). But this new view of Ross's is multiply problematic. He gave as one reason for recognizing the different senses of goodness that, since we never have a duty to produce an immoral pleasure, the goodness due to pleasantness can never outweigh the badness due to vice (274). But hadn't the "sound reply" he'd just given shown that this can also be true if virtue has just finitely more of the same goodness? Nor is it clear why a claim of infinite superiority requires separate senses of "good." Can't virtue just have infinitely more of the same value? In *The Right and the Good* (152), though perhaps not in *Foundations of Ethics* (284), he thought virtue is infinitely better than knowledge even though both are good in the same unanalysable way. Moreover, if there are two entirely separate kinds of goodness, why think an item with one of them, virtue, is preferable to an item with the other, pleasure, rather than vice versa? In fact, shouldn't the two be entirely incomparable, so neither can be said to be better? Ross seems to have held that the first or unanalysable sense of "good" is primary, since anything that is good in that sense is also good in the second, analysable one (1939, 283). But then it's *not* true that virtue and pleasure don't fall on the same scale of goodness; they're both worthy objects of satisfaction and can be compared for their position on a scale of worthiness.

Ross did have a reason to think pleasure is good in a different sense than virtue, but it had nothing to do with comparative values. In *The Right and the Good* his strong feeling that there's no duty to pursue your own pleasure was in tension with the belief he then had that pleasure is intrinsically good (24–6, 135), but in *Foundations of Ethics* he resolved this difficulty by distinguishing the two senses of "good." Whereas anything unanalysably good is good agent-neutrally, so everyone has equal reason to promote it, the secondary sense allows agent-relativities, since what is a worthy object of satisfaction for one person needn't be a worthy object for another. And he now held that, relative to you, what is good in this sense is only others' pleasure and not your own, so your only duty is to promote theirs (271–84). The secondary sense is needed for this relativity, but the relativity is unconnected to pleasure's comparative worth.

It's hard to find anything persuasive in Ross's arguments for the immense superiority of virtue to other goods, especially given the contrary arguments of Moore and Rashdall. His view here may reflect his Scots Presbyterianism or the influence, which he elsewhere resisted and which is almost always pernicious, of Kant. But not much in his overall theory would change if he gave virtuous and vicious attitudes only finitely more, or even finitely less, value than their intentional objects. He could still give the same general account of what virtue is and why it's intrinsically good, with the same general philosophical merits. He would just have abandoned an exaggerated claim about its comparative worth.

III Individual Virtuous and Vicious Acts

While recognizing, especially in *Foundations of Ethics*, that virtue can be found in many mental states, including desires, pleasures, and other emotions, Ross gave special attention to virtuous or morally good action. Here his view had several distinctive features.

Unlike some philosophers, he didn't think a morally good act must be right, or your duty proper. Aristotle held that, to be done virtuously, an act must not only have a virtuous motive and issue from a stable disposition but be "in accordance with the virtues," or in present-day language right (1984, 1105a29). Some Kantians likewise say a morally worthy act must be right (Johnson King 2020a) and even known by the agent to be right (Sliwa 2016). But Ross thought the right and the morally good are entirely independent (1930, 4–7; 1939, 122–3). Whether an act is right depends only on whether it fulfils the strongest prima facie duties that bear on it, regardless of its motive, and whether it's morally good depends only on its motive, regardless of its relation to duty. He even proposed marking this distinction by using "act" for the thing done just as a thing done and "action" for the doing of it from a certain motive. It would then follow "that the doing of a right act may be a morally bad action, and that the doing of a morally wrong act may be a morally good action" (1930, 7). We think his view here correctly honours a distinction between deontic and morally evaluative judgements that Aristotle and the Kantian views mistakenly blur.

That a right act can be done from a bad motive is, we assume, uncontroversial, and it's at least sometimes straightforward that a wrong act can be virtuous if wrongness is understood objectively, so it depends on the true moral principles and actual empirical facts, which is the one way Ross in *The Right and the Good* thought it should be understood (31–2, 43–6). If a doctor gives a patient a treatment that all her evidence says is safe but that unforeseeably kills the patient, she's acted objectively wrongly. But if her motive was a desire to do her duty as she reasonably took it to be or a de re desire for her patient's welfare, her act was surely virtuous and good. One can also do, from the motive of duty, an act that is objectively wrong because of a false belief about moral principles or their comparative weights. Though Ross didn't discuss this possibility, his sharp separation between the right and the morally good suggests he would count such action too as virtuous. This is a more controversial claim, since it implies that someone who believes it his duty to exterminate a religious minority and does so because he thinks it his duty can be acting morally well. He won't be doing so, at least on balance, if the formation of his false moral belief involved moral vice; if he was merely rationalizing a pre-existing hatred of the minority in order to make action from it seem permissible, the hatred is his main motive. But if he acquired his belief innocently, say as a child from otherwise loving parents, action on it apparently counts on Ross's view as morally good. We don't ourselves find this implication unacceptable and would add that, even when there is rationalization, the fact that a person needed to engage in it shows an at least minimal concern for duty that makes the resulting act somewhat less bad than if he could act from hatred without having to persuade himself that doing so is allowed (Milo 1984, 54–5, 244–8, 251–3; Johnson King 2020b, 419–23).

If a morally good act can be objectively wrong, most simply because of a false empirical belief, those who require such acts to be right may instead understand rightness subjectively, so it depends not on the actual facts but on the agent's beliefs or perhaps reasonable beliefs about them. And in *Foundations of Ethics* Ross, influenced by arguments of H. A. Prichard's (2002), reversed his view and now held that the one correct understanding of rightness is subjective (64, 159–68). On Prichard's and many present-day subjective views, an act's rightness depends on the agent's beliefs only about the empirical facts and not about moral principles; the true principles are still what matter. But this is enough to make the doctor's virtuous act of giving a treatment she reasonably believes will be safe subjectively right, so moral goodness and rightness in this sense go together. These subjective views still allow the more controversial possibility that a wrong act can be virtuous if it's done from a false belief about principles, but Ross's own view was more radical, making subjective rightness depend on the agent's "complete state of opinion," both empirical and moral, or on her final belief about what in her situation is her duty (161–2). On this view it's impossible for an act done from the motive of duty to be subjectively wrong—whatever the agent thinks is her duty is her duty—though an act that is wrong in this sense can be virtuous if it's done from a de re concern for goods that are greater than those the agent thinks determine her duty; Huck Finn illustrates this possibility. But Ross's more radical subjectivism is in several ways problematic, and in particular is incompatible with his later view that subjective rightness is the only rightness. The belief that an act is right, which on this view makes it subjectively right, can't be the belief that it's an act you believe is right, on pain of an infinite regress. It must be the belief that the act is right in some other, plausibly objective, sense, so there must be that other sense. To us the most credible view recognizes several morally relevant senses of "right," one objective and one or more subjective. But as long as there's one objective sense there can be acts that, as Ross allowed, are wrong but virtuous and morally good, because they involve a false belief either about the empirical facts or, more controversially, about principles.

An act's moral value depends on the attitudes and especially desires of the person who does it, but not all her desires are relevant. If the Aristotelian view that prioritizes dispositions is false, it doesn't matter how she was or would be motivated at other times. Nor are all her present desires relevant. While treating her patient our doctor may want to comfort her son that evening and hope a current war will end. These desires bear on the moral value of her total state of mind at the time but not on the goodness of her particular act of giving treatment, most obviously because they don't concern that act. Its value has a more restricted base, and in *The Right and the Good* Ross identified this base causally, saying an act's moral value depends only on the motives from which it's done, or that cause it to be done. This is a quite restrictive base, however, which excludes several desires that do concern the act.

Ross thought it's possible to have several motives for an act but do it only from one of them: "when both sense of duty and ambition would incline a man to do an act, he may, though he is sensible of both motives, do the act wholly from the one or wholly from the other" (1930, 170). If our doctor wants to treat her patient both from duty and from a de re desire but is caused to act only by the former, Ross would say, and not unreasonably, that the moral value of her act depends only on that one motive and not on the other. It may be hard for her to know that this has been the case, but even then there's a fact of the matter as to which motive she acted from and it alone determines her act's worth.

More controversially, Ross's view excludes desires that concern an act by disfavouring it, or motivating an alternative; they too are irrelevant. (Though he didn't state this exclusion explicitly, it follows given that a motive not to do an act can't cause it.) Alongside her virtuous desires to treat her patient our doctor may have various weaker opposed desires. The patient may be her enemy, whom she has a malicious and therefore evil desire to let die. She may wish she could be enjoying the pleasure of a cocktail now rather than working; for Ross such desires have neutral value. Or she may want to be giving a smaller benefit to a less ill patient; that desire is good but less so than her desire to treat this patient. The presence of any of these desires would affect the value of her total state of mind, but if she gives the treatment the fact that she has one is, given its lack of causal role, for Ross irrelevant to her act's degree of worth. His view here can be contrasted with two others, one Aristotelian and one sometimes attributed to Kant.

On an Aristotelian view the presence of opposed desires, or at least of strong ones, makes an act less virtuous and less good. Aristotle thought an ideally virtuous person's psychology is unified, so her appetites, or de re desires for particular objects, harmonize with her judgements about how best to act and so always favour the same acts. If she has strong contrary desires that need subduing she may display continence or self-control, and while that is better than weakness of will or vice it's less good than virtue, as in consequence a self-controlled act is less good than a similar one with no strong opposing motive. That motive must, however, be a strong one. If the doctor has desires for pleasure or to benefit another patient that are proportioned to their objects' degrees of value, they'll be too weak to generate serious inner conflict or require active control by a better desire. On a plausible Aristotelian view only disproportionately strong opposed desires can turn virtue into the lesser state of self-control. When they do, however, they affect the value of an act they don't cause in a way Ross in *The Right and the Good* didn't allow.

The other contrasting view says the presence of a strong contrary desire can make an act better. It holds that effortless virtue, when a virtuous desire faces no serious internal opposition, isn't fully or maximally good. For that, acting on the good desire must be an achievement, or reflect victory in a struggle against impulses that are evil or significantly less good. Richard Henson (1979) has called this the "battle-citation" view of moral worth and attributed it to Kant; whether or not it was Kant's, the view has some appeal and was suggested in remarks by some of Ross's contemporaries (Ewing 1938, 54–5; Carritt 1947, 27, 85; contrast Broad 1930, 199–200). Since it finds the greatest value in virtuous action despite strong temptation, it says the presence of an opposed desire that isn't causally effective can make the resulting act better.

These three views can be contrasted more formally given some assumptions Ross at least implicitly made. They are that desires can differ in their strength or motivating power; that a stronger virtuous desire is morally better and a stronger vicious one worse; and that when one desire outweighs another it can have more strength than the outweighing requires, so there's a surplus of effective motivation, or "some to spare" (1930, 171). Imagine then an act done from a virtuous desire of strength 10 and against a contrary desire of strength 5, and assume, for simplicity, that a desire's degree of moral value is equal to its degree of strength. On Ross's view this act's degree of worth is 10, so the presence of the opposed desire makes no difference. It would be better if the virtuous desire had strength 15 or 20, since then the act would have a more virtuous cause. In Philip Pettit's (2015) terminology, action on the desire would then be more "counterfactually robust," since it would result given a contrary desire of strength not only up to 9 but also up to 14 or 19. But what matters is only the strength of the one virtuous desire, and all its strength, the surplus as well as that needed for the outweighing, matters.

In contrast, the Aristotelian view can be read as making this act's value equal 10 minus 5 = 5, so it depends only on the surplus of virtuous over contrary motivation, or on the amount that isn't needed. The act is then less good than if, given the same virtuous desire, there were no opposed one, in which case its value would be 10. It would again be better if, given the same contrary desire, the virtuous one had strength 15 or 20, since then the surplus would be larger. But the resulting value would still be less than on Ross's view, since it would be 15 or 20 minus 5 = 10 or 15. This reading may not be entirely true to Aristotle, since it allows that a self-controlled act in one situation can be better than a purely virtuous one in another, for example if in the first a virtuous desire of strength 15 outweighs a contrary one of strength 5 whereas in the second there's just a virtuous desire of strength 5; Aristotle might not allow this. But the reading captures the general idea that the presence of a strong contrary desire makes action from a given virtuous one less good.

Finally, the battle citation-view can be read as equating the moral value when a virtuous desire of strength 10 outweighs a contrary one of strength 5 with 6, or with the minimal strength needed for the outweighing; here the surplus doesn't matter. This self-controlled act is better, the view says, than if the same virtuous desire had either no opposing desire, in which case the value would be just 1, or a weaker one of, say, strength 3. But the act wouldn't be better if, given the same contrary desire, the virtuous one had strength 10 or 15; here any excess is irrelevant. It could be argued that this view merely extends Ross's claim that only desires that cause an act are relevant to its worth: if only 6 units of virtuous desire are needed to outweigh a contrary desire, any strength beyond that is unnecessary and so not part of the cause. But Ross could reply that if what exists is only a desire of strength 10—there's no separate desire of strength 6—then what caused the act is just the existing desire with all its 10 units of strength. Whichever of these causal claims is correct, the battle-citation view can be read as making the moral worth of an act depend only on the virtuous motivation needed to produce it, which will be more the stronger any contrary desire and, in consequence, the greater the victory over it.

Whereas Ross's view counts all a virtuous motive's strength, both what is needed and any surplus, the Aristotelian view as we're reading it counts only the surplus and the battle-citation view only what is needed. Our point isn't that one of these views is clearly preferable to the others; we think each has some appeal. But they are different views.

Ross was especially interested in cases, which surely are common, where an act is done from two or more motives, so both are causally effective. In some such cases each motive is sufficient on its own to cause the act. With an opposing desire of strength 5, our doctor may have a desire of strength 10 to do her duty and a de re desire of strength 10 for her patient's welfare, and the two together can cause her act. In that case, Ross held, the overall moral value of her act is the sum of her two motives' values; since he thought de re ones are somewhat less good, that might, as in his example of duty and love, be 10 + 8 = 18. The overall value is also a sum if just one of the motives is sufficient, for example if her motive of duty has strength 10 and her de re one, though still causally relevant, strength 4; then that value might be 10 + (4 x .8) = 13.2. But he also considered cases where neither motive alone is sufficient and they cause the act only in combination, as when, given a contrary motive of strength 5, there's a motive of duty of strength 4 and a de re one of strength 2. Here again he seems to have taken the resulting value to be a sum. He said that when the motive of duty and a morally neutral desire are together just enough to cause an act and each is equally effective, so each supplies half of what is needed, the resulting value is half what it would be if the motive of duty alone sufficed (1930, 172). That equals the sum of the value of a dutiful desire of half the needed strength, which is what is present, and the zero value of the neutral desire. And of a case where the motive of duty and a lesser good one just suffice, he said only that the value is "reduced," as it would be if the value were 4 for the motive of duty and, say, (2 x .8) for the de re, which is less than the 6 or more if the act was done just from duty. In all these cases he seems in his first book to have held that the moral goodness of a virtuous act is a sum of the values, weighted by their strengths and the values of their objects, of the desires that caused it.

This was his early view of virtuous action, and a parallel one of vicious action would make its badness depend just on the motive or motives from which it's done. This fits acts with a positively vicious motive such as a malicious desire for another's pain, but Ross thought such motives are rare and most morally bad action is done from a selfish desire for one's own pleasure (1930, 167). But if a desire for one's pleasure has neutral value, as he repeatedly said (1930, 162, 168; 1939, 302), how can action from it be positively bad? Shouldn't it too have neutral worth?

In *The Right and the Good* he said acting from a selfish desire is morally bad only when it "excludes and makes impossible the doing of one's duty or the bringing into being of something that is good, or some pleasure for another" (167). But that a desire prevents an act that is right or has good consequences only makes it bad instrumentally, and Ross's topic was supposed to be the intrinsic moral values of acts, to which nothing about a desire's effects is relevant. He seems to have been led to this unsatisfactory position by his rejection of an alternative view that rests the badness of selfish action on the combination of desires it involves and, more specifically, on the degree to which this combination departs from the ideally proportioned desiring he himself would later value (1939, 293, 309). It's not, on this alternative view, that any departure from perfect proportionality is on balance bad; small ones can make for just a loss of goodness, or what we can call a shortfall in virtue. But caring much more about something with little or no worth than about some significantly greater good is vicious and evil, as is any act it causes (Hurka 2001, 83–91). Against this Ross gave the example of a soldier with a duty to rest before battle the next day but whose desire for the pleasure of resting is now stronger than his desire to do his duty; surely, Ross said, there's nothing morally bad in his motivation (1930, 167). But the sense of "strength" relevant to degrees of moral worth doesn't involve the intensity with which a desire is felt or present to consciousness; it concerns its tendency to outweigh other desires and issue in action. And in that sense the soldier can indeed have a strong desire now to do his duty if he's firmly committed to fighting tomorrow, and its strength will be shown if, should his orders change so the battle is tonight, he'll forgo his rest and fight now. His desires then are, contra Ross, properly proportioned.

This alternative view can explain the moral badness of vices like selfishness, cowardice, and pride (Hurka 2001, 96–100), but it rejects *The Right and the Good*'s view that the moral value of an act depends only on the motives that cause it, since it considers combinations of those motives with others or their relation to those others. But Ross himself abandoned that view in *Foundations of Ethics*. He there imagined a case where A gives pleasure to B from a virtuous desire for B's pleasure but with comparative indifference to the greater pains this will cause C and D, so the resulting act is wrong. He said that, while this act's motive is "purely good," the act itself isn't purely good and may even, given A's indifference, be "bad on the whole" (307). That indifference to goods and evils, as in apathy and callousness, is bad rather than neutral in value is an attractive extension of the view that virtue and vice are higher-level values (Hurka 2001, 62–5). But to say an act with a good prompting motive is less good or even bad because of an accompanying indifference isn't to rest its moral worth only on the motive that causes it; as Ross saw (306–7), it's to consider something else.

This last case doesn't differ essentially from the one of selfishness he handled differently in *The Right and the Good*. In the earlier case there was action from a morally neutral desire for pleasure rather than from some better desire; here there's action from a good desire for B's pleasure rather than from a better desire to avoid the pain for C and D. And in *Foundations of Ethics* he said we can judge this act by comparing A's motivation with the "attractions an ideally good man would have towards the act in virtue of certain of its characteristics, and aversions he would have in virtue of others" (307), where an ideal person would be more deterred by the thought of hurting C and D than moved by that of pleasing B; we can likewise compare selfish motivation with that of someone who properly balances self- and other-concern. In both cases an act comes out less good because a desire that should have been present and effective wasn't. This new view of Ross's, which counts absent as well as effective motives, concerns only intrinsic values and so is more promising than his earlier one. But he never explained how it can result in the judgement that an act is positively bad rather than just less than ideally good. Why should the absence of a better desire make not just for less moral goodness but also for action that is "definitely bad" (307), especially when the effective desire is either neutral in value or good? It's true that in the *Foundations of Ethics* case this desire is accompanied by an indifference that is morally bad, but in the selfishness case the worst motive present has just neutral value. The strong claim that this act is morally evil can result if disproportionate combinations of desires have negative value as combinations; then the evil in a combination can outweigh even goodness in its component parts (Hurka 2001, 83–91). But in *Foundations of Ethics* Ross didn't consider that possibility. Why exactly the comparison he proposed in that book should sometimes yield a judgement of moral badness, rather than just of reduced goodness, he never explained.

Though his new view no longer made an act's moral value depend only on the motives that caused it, this needn't dissolve the distinction between evaluating a specific act and evaluating the agent's total state of mind at the time. Some elements in that state, such as pleasures and emotions not directed at action, remain irrelevant, as can some desires. If the mandated comparison is only with ideal attractions and aversions "towards the act" (307), only desires that concern the act are relevant. But questions remain about exactly which these are.

One question is whether they may not now include the outweighed contrary desires *The Right and the Good* ignored. If our doctor has, alongside her virtuous desires to treat her patient, a weaker malicious one to let him die, the latter desire concerns the act—it tells against it—and is one an ideal person wouldn't have. Does its presence then affect her act's value and make it at least less good? On a straightforward reading Ross's later proposal seems to push him towards an Aristotelian view of virtuous action on which opposed desires can detract from an act's worth. Moreover, the result would be an attractive version of this view, since it would count only opposed desires that are disproportionately strong or weak. If the doctor has a proportionate desire for her own pleasure or to treat a less ill patient, an ideal person would also have that desire, so a comparison with that person's motives won't change her act's worth. Only disproportionate opposed desires can have that effect.

Ross could resist this Aristotelian view by placing a further condition on relevant ideal desires, such as a causal one saying they must be ones whose presence would change the act that is done. This condition is satisfied in his selfishness and indifference cases, which therefore do involve a loss of value. If in the latter case A had the virtuous concern for C and D he doesn't have, he wouldn't do what hurts them, so that concern is relevant and his motivation is worse for lacking it. But the condition isn't satisfied in cases involving an outweighed contrary desire, since in its absence the same act would be done. Our doctor would still treat her patient if she lacked her weaker malicious desire, so its presence wouldn't make her act less good. Given this causal condition Ross could still, as before, ignore outweighed contrary desires.

The condition may, however, exclude too much. Imagine that, in a variant of the indifference case, A cares equally about B, C, and D and so doesn't please B at the cost of the pains for C and D. But he cares more for all of B, C, and D compared to other people than he should. Perhaps B, C, and D are his children, and though it would be ideally virtuous to give their interests ten times more weight than strangers', he, while weighing them equally against each other, gives them twenty times more weight. I assume the ideal person whose desires we're to compare A's with doesn't have a greater total capacity for virtuous concern, in which case his desires for all goods would be stronger; he has the same capacity but divides it better. But then this person would care less for all of B, C, and D than A does and would have a weaker desire to avoid pain for C and D. This may bear on the value of A's act. Though he isn't acting from disproportionate concern for one child over the others, he is acting from disproportionate concern for his children as a group and that may make his action less good. Yet, considered on its own, his stronger desire to avoid hurting C and D is better than the ideal person's weaker desire, and the weaker ideal desires wouldn't change the act he does, since he still wouldn't hurt C and D. So the causal condition excludes the judgement, which some may want to make, that his acting from excessive concern for his children as a group makes even an act that treats them equally less than ideally good. This judgement can, however, follow from the view that values proportional combinations as combinations. It can say there's a disproportion between A's desire to avoid the pains for C and D and his desires about strangers, and the evil in that disproportion, even if not great, detracts from the goodness of his act. This view, however, departs from the atomism that characterizes, even if just implicitly, all Ross's proposals on this issue, in which desires and attitudes more generally are always valued individually rather than in combinations or in light of their mutual relations.

We're not sure which kind of view here, Ross's with or without a causal condition, a proportionality one, or some alternative, is best. But his discussion highlights an important issue. Though the moral value of a particular act depends on the agent's desires, it doesn't depend on all of them; some, while affecting the value of his total state of mind at the time, aren't relevant to this act's worth. Exactly which desires are relevant, however, isn't easy to determine. The simple view that they're just the desires that cause the act gives the wrong result in cases of selfishness and indifference, so it has to matter that some desires that should have been present and effective weren't. But identifying these desires and how they relate to the ones that were effective is a difficult and to date neglected task.

References

Anscombe, G. E. M. 1958. "Modern Moral Philosophy." *Philosophy* 33: 1–19.
Aristotle. 1984 *Nicomachean Ethics*, trans. W. D. Ross and J. O. Urmson. In *The Complete Works of Aristotle*, vol. 2, 1729–1867. Edited by J. Barnes. Princeton, NJ: Princeton University Press.
Arpaly, Nomy. 2002. "Moral Worth." *Journal of Philosophy* 99: 223–45.
Broad, C. D. 1930. *Five Types of Ethical Theory*. London: Routledge & Kegan Paul.
Carritt, E. F. 1947. *Ethical and Political Thinking*. Oxford: Clarendon Press.
Ewing, A. C. 1938. "The Paradoxes of Kant's Ethics." *Philosophy* 13: 40–56.
Henson, Richard G. 1979. "What Kant Might Have Said: Moral Worth and the Overdetermination of Dutiful Action." *Philosophical Review* 88: 304–28.
Hurka, Thomas. 2001. *Virtue, Vice, and Value*. New York: Oxford University Press.
Hurka, Thomas. 2006. "Virtuous Acts, Virtuous Dispositions." *Analysis* 66: 69–76,
Hursthouse, Rosalind. 1999. *On Virtue Ethics*. Oxford: Clarendon Press.
Johnson King, Zoë A. 2020a. "Accidentally Doing the Right Thing." *Philosophy and Phenomenological Research* 100: 186–206.
Johnson King, Zoë A. 2020b. "Praiseworthy Motivations." *Nous* 54: 408–30.
Milo, Ronald D. 1984. *Immorality*. Princeton, NJ: Princeton University Press.
Moore, G. E. 1903. *Principia Ethica*. Cambridge: Cambridge University Press.
Pettit, Philip. 2015. *The Robust Demands of the Good: Ethics with Attachment, Virtue, and Respect*. Oxford: Oxford University Press.
Phillips, David. 2019. *Rossian Ethics: W. D. Ross and Contemporary Moral Theory*. New York: Oxford University Press.
Prichard, H. A. 2002. "Duty and Ignorance of Fact." In *Moral Writings*, 84–101. Edited by J. MacAdam. Oxford: Clarendon Press. [First published 1932]
Rashdall, Hastings. 1885. "Professor Sidgwick's Utilitarianism." *Mind* o.s. 10: 200–226.
Rashdall, Hastings. 1907. *The Theory of Good and Evil*, 2 vols. London: Oxford University Press.
Ross, W. D. 1930. *The Right and the Good*. Oxford: Clarendon Press.
Ross, W. D. 1939. *Foundations of Ethics*. Oxford: Clarendon Press.
Sliwa, Paulina. 2016. "Moral Worth and Moral Knowledge." *Philosophy and Phenomenological Research* 93: 393–418.
Slote, Michael. 2001. *Morals from Motives*. New York: Oxford University Press.
Stocker, Michael. 1976. "The Schizophrenia of Modern Ethical Theories." *Journal of Philosophy* 73: 453–66.
Stratton-Lake, Philip. 2002. "Pleasure and Reflection in Ross's Intuitionism." In *Ethical Intuitionism*, 111–36. Edited by P. Stratton-Lake. Oxford: Clarendon Press.
Williams, Bernard. 1981. "Persons, Character, and Morality." In *Moral Luck*, 1–19. Cambridge: Cambridge University Press.

11
Ross and the Ethics of Virtue

Natasza Szutta and Artur Szutta

I Introduction

William David Ross is widely perceived as a deontological ethicist, although of a special, pluralistic kind, who largely focused on the nature of moral duties.[1] Given a widely held opinion that virtue ethics is in opposition to deontology[2] and, as noticed by Thomas Hurka, the fact that Ross's theory of virtue has long been ignored,[3] a suggestion that, to some extent, Ross may be viewed as a virtue ethicist strikes as unjustified. It is not controversial, however, to notice that Ross's deontology is much more moderate than that of Kant and those who, following the latter, adopt the possibility of building deductive structures of absolute principles from which one could deduce what one ought to do in particular circumstances. This moderateness may mean a shift from an extreme deontological position towards ethics resembling virtue ethics.

Some authors notice significant similarities between Ross's ethics and virtue ethics. Lisa Sklar, for example, wonders whether Ross's ethics might not be a bridge between virtue ethics and deontology.[4] She draws attention to a few characteristics of Ross's ethical theory that make it different from Kantian ethics. She points to Ross's rejection of the claim that duties are absolute and his acceptance of the possibility of conflicts between duties that the reference to some master principle, such as the principle of utility, cannot solve. Among the similarities between Ross's theory and virtue ethics, she mentions Ross's recognition of the role of circumstances in determining the right (Sklar uses the term *virtuous*) action and his 'acknowledgement that one can never be sure of the correct action to take in a

---

[1] Anthony Skelton, in his paper on Ross in Stanford Encyclopedia of Philosophy, sees the novelty in the pluralistic character of Ross's deontology as well as its critical approach to both Kantian and Utilitarian ethics.

[2] See Anscombe (1958); Statman (1997), 3–41; Hursthouse (2022).

[3] See Hurka (2013), 24. Hurka has in mind not only Ross's theory of virtue but generally ethical works of Ross, Moore, Rashdall, Sidgwick, and other British ethicists active at the end of the 19th and the beginning of the 20th centuries. Of course, there are a few exceptions among contemporary authors who have thoroughly analysed Ross's concept of virtue. For example, Hurka, basing heavily on Ross but also on other abovementioned British ethicists, has developed a concept of recursive virtue which he opposes to that of Aristotelian virtue ethics (Hurka 2001, Ch. 1; 2014, Ch. 10). Also, David Phillips gives a very good, critical presentation of Ross's concept of virtue (2019, Ch. 4).

[4] See Sklar (2009) 52.

Natasza Szutta and Artur Szutta, *Ross and the Ethics of Virtue* In: *The Moral Philosophy of W. D. Ross*. Edited by: Robert Audi and David Phillips, Oxford University Press. © Oxford University Press 2025.
DOI: 10.1093/9780198914839.003.0011

situation.'5 Sklar does not develop her points into longer arguments but notices that the question of Ross's ethics being the bridge between Kantian deontology and virtue ethics deserves further study.

We think Sklar is right in claiming an affinity between Ross and virtue ethics. Therefore it would be desirable to take a closer look at Ross's ethics, aiming to answer the question to what extent Ross's ethical theory is close to contemporary virtue ethics. Such is the goal of this paper. We are going to realize it in the following steps. Firstly, we will expand on the previous sketch of essential features that characterize virtue ethics. We are aware that it is hard to speak of one virtue ethics and that there are more and more various approaches under this label. However, following the authors such as Rosalind Hurtshouse, Julia Annas, Dan Russel, Daniel Statman, and Gregory Trianosky, we believe we can outline a few central claims that make one a virtue ethicist. Having done that, we will explore whether Rossian ethics fits these characteristics of virtue ethics.

It is possible that despite matching the pattern of virtue ethics, at least in some points, Ross's ethics will still contain elements that place it outside virtue ethics. Nevertheless, even with this being the case, we might still speak of Ross bridging deontology with virtue ethics. Before we reach our conclusion, our final step is to find out whether Rossian ethics has anything to offer the advocates of virtue ethics. More precisely, we argue that his concept of prima facie duties may be seen as an opportunity to develop virtue ethics.

II A Characterization of Virtue Ethics

Although contemporary virtue ethics has been developing dynamically into various branches or kinds, some even leaving their Aristotelian, Platonic, or Stoic roots,[6] it still seems to make sense to characterize virtue ethics by reference to a few of its essential claims.[7] Firstly, the notion of virtue plays a central role in this tradition.[8] Virtue is usually understood as a stable disposition, rooted in or expressing one's character, to recognize, choose, and do the right thing. Virtue or virtues (as there could be various fields in which distinct dispositions to right action could be distinguished)[9] are considered central goods, constitutive elements of a good life. The focus on virtue goes along with the emphasis on the category of (intrinsic or

---

[5] Sklar (2009), 52-3.
[6] Rosalind Hurtshouse, in her very informative entry for the Stanford Encyclopedia of Philosophy (2022), points at such historical figures who inspire some new directions within the tradition of virtue ethics as Hutcheson, Hume, Nietzsche, Martineau, or Heidegger. Moreover, as she notices, contemporary virtue ethicists look for inspiration also in Asia.
[7] See Annas (2007); Crisp and Slote (1997) Introduction; Hurtshouse (2022); Trianosky (1990, 335-6); and Szutta (2007).
[8] Crisp and Slote (1997), 3; Statman (1997), 8-9; Trianosky (1990), 335-6.
[9] Of course, there are many controversies concerning the notion of virtue. Virtue ethicists debate issues such as: Do virtues come in degrees? Is there one virtue, or at least a strong unity of virtues, or

autotelic) good, as opposed to the category of right, which seems to be of primary focus in deontology.

Secondly, virtues are not some mechanical modes of reacting to morally salient situations, for example, by blindly following some procedures or authorities; they are based on the ability to understand and reason or reflect on ethical issues. This understanding may also encompass a form of moral perception in which one may just be aware of the appropriate thing to do or what is worthy of one's pursuit. Such perception or understanding is not, however, something that would develop without practice or training. It is closer to the immediate understanding of an expert in a given field than physically seeing simple objects with one's eyes.[10]

Thirdly, virtue ethics is opposed to rule-centred ethics, which focuses more on defining principles and evaluating actions rather than moral agents. Instead of asking *what I should do and what principles I should follow*, virtue ethicists ask *what kind of person I should be or become*. Instead of focusing on dos and don'ts and determining whether actions agree with a duty or principle, they focus on the agent, moral condition, motivations, emotions, etc. Act-centred ethics is also more focused on the notion of right and wrong or the notion of duty. In contrast, virtue ethics focuses on the category of the morally good, which relates not so much to actions as to agents (their intentions, character, or virtues).[11]

Fourthly, virtue ethicists reject the possibility of building a moral theory that would ground morality on absolute, abstract moral principles or offer an algorithm to solve particular moral issues or form moral decisions. If any rules are formulated within virtue tradition, where they are called v-rules, these are (and thus, we return to the third point) related somehow to the moral agent. Instead of saying *do not steal!* or *do not cheat!*, v-rules say: *Be honest! Be just!* Such rules, however, do not tell us what exactly we should do in given circumstances.[12] We need the virtue of practical wisdom to judge what the right thing to do is in the given circumstances.[13]

---

can they be reached independently of instantiating other virtues? etc. We will ignore such differences among the advocates of virtue ethics, focusing on what could count as central to this tradition.

[10] Russell (2015), 99–100; (2009), 20–5; Snow (2008), 52–62.

[11] See Louden (1990), 101–2; Crisp and Slote (1997), 3.

[12] It might be tempting to say that virtue ethics is particularistic because its advocates maintain that making a decision cannot be reduced to just applying a moral rule and requires a form of moral perception of reasons relevant in given circumstances (see McDowell, 1997). If this were the case, it would speak against counting Ross as a virtue ethicist because his view is not fully particularist but much more generalist (see Dancy 2004, 6–7). However, as has been pointed out by Roger Crisp, virtue ethics does not totally reject moral principles or undermine their value in the process of acquiring moral knowledge (see Crisp 2001); thus, it cannot be characterized as particularistic (at least in Dancy's meaning of the word).

[13] See Louden (1990). Although we also use the term 'anti-theoretical' to refer to this fourth feature of virtue ethics, we do not mean that virtue ethicists are against any theory in ethics. Robert B. Louden, whom we follow here, points out twelve features of theories that anti-theorists oppose: (1) complete determining particular decisions, (2) testing moral beliefs, (3) formalism, (4) precision and clarity of

Of course, this short enumeration of virtue ethics' essential features will not fully characterize this tradition. Such characterization, however, is not our purpose here. It should suffice to set certain criteria that would allow us to establish how far Rossian ethics resembles virtue ethics and whether it could be called a bridge between deontology and virtue ethics. Thus, in the sections to come, our next step will be checking to what extent Rossian ethics fits the above four-point characteristic of virtue ethics.

III The Importance of Virtue in Rossian Ethics

As the title of his main work suggests, for Ross, there are two main or ethically salient categories: the right and the good. He characterizes the right in terms of what one ought to do or what is morally obligatory. He makes a sharp distinction between the right and (morally) good. The former relates merely to (external) things done, for example, to saving the life of a person drowning. Thus, in the context of this example, our duty would be to do something that would ensure another person's surviving the danger. The act's rightness does not encompass our motivation, i.e., whether we help the other person out of duty, compassion, care, or hope of getting something in return for our help is not determined by the duty.[14]

The category of the good relates primarily to non-instrumental values or, as Ross puts it, to intrinsic goods. There are only four kinds of intrinsic goods, among which virtue is the most valuable. The other three are knowledge, justice (or apportionment), and pleasure (of another).[15] Such a remark already suggests that virtue is one of the central themes in Ross's ethics. Before making such a conclusion, however, we need to do two things. Firstly, we must shed more light on what Ross meant by virtue. Secondly, we must look more closely at the relationship between the notions of the right and the good in his ethics. It might be the case that Ross understands virtue in a way incompatible with virtue ethics; for example, it plays a secondary role, subordinated to the category of the right (or duty).

---

rules, (5) allowing for decision procedures, (6) universalism, (7) objectivity, (8) abstraction, (9) systematic hierarchy, (10) the ability to solve any moral dilemma, (11) proposing a vision of the best way of life, (12) allowing for expertise based on the knowledge of the theory. Lauden does not say that virtue ethics rejects all the twelve features of an ethical theory or is anti-theoretical strictly speaking; however, in his view, there is some proximity between the anti-theoretical stance as described above and virtue ethics.

[14] Compare Ross (2002 [1930]), 4–12.
[15] See Ross (2002), esp. 134–41.

III.i *The Rossian Notion of Virtue*

Let us then take a closer look at the Rossian notion of virtue. According to Ross, virtue is a feature of character constituted by dispositions to act from motives (or desires), such as to do one's duty, to bring something good into being, or to give pleasure (or save pain) to others.[16] These three motivations are the most notable examples.[17] Among the three, the noblest (or most virtuous) is the action from the desire to do one's duty or (in other words) from the sense of duty. The sense of duty means 'the sense that we ought to do certain acts whether or not on other grounds we desire to do them and no matter with what intensity we may desire to do them.'[18]

Let us first focus on Ross's other two virtuous motivations: the desire to do something good or give pleasure to another person. We sometimes do certain acts, for example, give money to people in need or jump into deep water to save somebody's life, because we are motivated by compassion or other emotions, without thinking whether it is our duty. We may sacrifice our time and effort for the sake of another person, not because it is our duty but because we like her, are in love with her, or want her to be happy. Ross notices that for many people acting from love, the impulse of the heart or the desire for the well-being of another person is better than, as he puts it, actions 'dictated by the *cold*, *hard*, and *rigid* sense of duty.'[19] However, from Ross's perspective, as long as these motivations come only from desires other than the sense of duty, they *have less value*, and it is so for two reasons.

First, acting from a sense of duty should not be understood as obeying a traditional conventional code, as opposed to following one's 'impulse of the heart.'[20] When one acts out of a sense of duty, one does it 'because one thinks one ought to act in a certain way.'[21] This 'thinking' encompasses understanding or awareness of

---

[16] Ross (2002), 134.
[17] It does not mean only these three virtuous kinds of motivation exist.
[18] Ross (2002), 158. One comment is necessary here. Some, following Hurka's interpretation of 'higher-level virtue,' ascribed by Hurka (2013) to Hastings Rashdall, G. E. Moore, and Ross, may object to the claim about the centrality of virtue in Ross's ethics. According to Hurka, virtue, as understood by the three abovementioned- ethicists, derives its value from fitting to other goods (e.g. a saved life, adding pleasure or reducing pain in another person). The value of so-understood virtue is somewhat derivative of the other goods. In Hurka's view, if we were to choose between eliminating either another person's pain or virtue, it would be more reasonable to sacrifice the latter. This suggests that virtue cannot be the primary or highest good, and thus it is not a central notion in ethics. Such an interpretation, however, seems to deny Ross's own words, as he explicitly says virtue is the highest intrinsic good. Additionally, Ross suggests that virtue is infinitely superior to pleasure (see Ross 2002, 151). Using the idea of Ross's thought experiments with two worlds, we may say that the world with a lot of pleasure, no pain, and no virtue would contain less value than the world deprived of pleasure but filled with virtue. We do not suggest that Hurka is not right in his criticism of Aristotle's concept of virtue or that Ross is right in his claim that virtue is infinitely better than pleasure. We do claim, however, that the elements in Hurka's concept of higher-level virtue that deny the centrality of virtue in ethics do not come from Ross.
[19] See Ross (2002), 164.
[20] Ross (2002), 164.
[21] Ross (2002), 164.

some objective reasons for action that make the action a duty. It is not a blind habit or tendency to follow given rules that result from upbringing or indoctrination. Secondly, the moral superiority of acting from the sense of duty becomes more obvious in a conflict between a genuine duty and any other motive. In such a situation, says Ross, we must recognize the precedence of duty. As he argues, if we seriously think that we ought to do something, we are bound to think that we will be morally worse in doing another thing (and it seems that Ross has in mind the thing we desire on other grounds than the sense of duty) instead.[22]

The emphasis on the sense of duty as the noblest motivation of a virtuous person does not mean that virtuous motivation is present only when one acts against one's natural inclinations. Although the sense of duty is easier to identify when 'it has to fight against opposing inclinations,' in such circumstances, it would only be a case of what Ross calls an imperfect character, not one of a virtue developed to the fullest. We may conclude from this that a person of a better (moral) character would be motivated not only by her sense of justice but also by her emotions and other desires.[23]

It might seem that Ross uses two terms, 'virtue' and 'good character,' meaning two different things. 'Virtue' would mean the deep-seated disposition to act from a sense of duty, while 'good character' would signify persons whose emotions and desires (other than the desire to do one's duty) motivate them to do what is good. We could compare a good character to Aristotelian natural virtue. It is good but not as good as being motivated by the sense of duty because such natural motivation is more incidental, depending on external circumstances that could change without the agent's control. However, we may imagine the combination of the two dispositions where a person is motivated by the sense of duty and harmonizes her natural inclinations with the sense of duty. Such a combination, it seems, would exemplify virtue in its most proper sense.

Moreover, Ross seems here to follow Aristotle's distinction between natural virtues, encrateia, and virtue proper. Ross seems to be recognizing three levels of the positive moral quality of an agent: (a) having natural inclinations that happen to motivate in accordance with duty, but one has not yet any awareness or understanding of what is the right thing to do (Aristotelian natural virtues); (b) having such understanding and being motivated by it but at the same time having to overcome one's natural inclinations that direct one in the opposite direction than the right judgement or sense of duty (Aristotelian encratic person); and (c) being motivated in a harmonized way by both the understanding of what is right (or sense of duty) and natural inclinations.[24]

---

[22] Ross (2002), 164.

[23] It is easy to notice here some affinities to Aristotle's example of an encratic person who acts on the recognition of what is right but needs to overcome his or her opposing emotions and desires.

[24] Compare Ross (2002), 164.

If we consider this parallel, it becomes reasonable to interpret Ross as viewing the third kind of person as an example of moral virtue in its fullest or proper sense. Ross himself admits that a person who acts from both sense of duty, which means that such a state (or disposition), is of a higher intrinsic value than just being motivated by a sense of duty.[25]

III.ii Combining Aretaic and Deontological Language

Wondering whether the notion of virtue plays a central role in Ross's ethics, one might still be bothered that Ross uses the term 'sense of duty' and combines his aretaic language with deontological language. To see why Ross does so, we must look closely at where Ross's use of 'a sense of duty' might come from. In his book on Aristotle, two passages (from the chapter on Aristotle's ethics) may shed some light on Ross's understanding of virtue. In the first one, Ross notices that it is essential in Aristotle's doctrine of virtue that feelings 'should be subjugated to the *right rule*, or as we might say, to the sense of duty.'[26] In the second passage, we read that the right rule 'is the rule reached by the deliberative analysis of the practically wise man, and telling him that the end of human life is to be best attained by certain actions which are intermediate between extremes. Obedience to such a rule is moral virtue.'[27]

The Rossian conception of being motivated by the 'sense of duty' is, at least in his view, equivalent to obedience to the 'right rule,' which was an English translation by Ross of Aristotle's *orthos logos*. Various authors claim that Ross has a general rule in mind here.[28] However, there are good reasons to think that by 'the right rule,' Ross means the right judgement about the right thing to do in given circumstances. Two premises support such a conclusion. First, as we find in one of the cited passages above, moral virtue is obedience to the rule reached by a practically wise person through reflection. The rule tells her by which actions the end of human life is to be best attained. Such actions, although they could be described on a general level, for example, *do not lie* or *act courageously*, occur in particular circumstances. Practically wise persons need to grasp what is the right thing to do in given circumstances, not just general formulas.

Secondly, in his ethics Ross does not accept the view that one can determine what one ought 'finally' to do just by inferring it from general rules. General prima facie duties do not tell us what we ought to do; they only point at certain tendencies

---

[25] See Ross (2002), 164.
[26] Ross (2005), 205.
[27] Ross (2005), 229.
[28] E.g. Monica Moss (2014) or Jie Tian (2013).

of certain types of actions to give moral reasons to act in a certain way. If one is to find out what one ought to do in given circumstances, one needs to follow one's actual or proper duty, which is expressed in a particular moral judgement about what one ought to do in the circumstances in which one finds him or herself.[29] Assuming that Ross is consistent in his ethical claims, we need to interpret the formulation 'obedience to the right rule' (as well as the 'following sense of duty') as obedience to the right judgement about what one ought to do in given particular circumstances.

Now, why would Ross speak of a 'sense of duty' (or duty) rather than Aristotelian 'right rule' (or 'the right judgement,' which would be least controversial when it comes to classifying Ross's views as a version of, or at least profoundly akin to, virtue ethics)? It seems that (at least from Ross's perspective) the *orthos logos* is authoritative, meaning that it shows (or discovers) what ought to be done, and, as such, it could be read as a judgement of duty. To have the *orthos logos* (understood either as the right rule or the right judgement) means to be able to 'read' one's moral situation (including what one ought to do). And such moral 'reading' may be regarded (as Aristotle and Ross regarded it) as a kind of moral perception or understanding. If so, it seems reasonable to say that having the *right logos* results from a kind of sensing duty or a sense of duty.

The advocate of virtue ethics might object to such an introduction of deontic language into a theory of virtue; however, it seems reasonable to follow Ross here. To substantiate this claim, let us put ourselves in the shoes of the virtuous person facing the following moral decision. We either stay in the country and defend it against the invasion of a barbarian enemy or run away, leaving many innocent people to a brutal and painful fate. As virtuous people, we should see that a cowardly flight would be unacceptable and deserve our contempt. Therefore, our right judgement is that we should or ought to defend our motherland.[30] We do not mean that something limits our freedom or that some external necessity presses us. The judgement is ours; we make it freely, but simultaneously, it expresses what we sense or grasp as objectively the right thing to do, *the right* meaning the one we should or ought to do. Here, the deontic language seems natural and capable of coinciding with aretaic language in moral judgements regarding what to do in a given situation.[31]

---

[29] On prima facie duties and proper duties, see Ross (2002), Ch. 2.

[30] We are giving here an oversimplified description of the situation of choice, with too little description for the reader to agree that the situation does call for the decision we say it does. We therefore ask the readers to 'fill the gaps' in such a way that the circumstances of choice would be such that the judgement to stay and defend one's country would really be the right judgement.

[31] Such a conclusion seems to be in line with the stance of Julia Annas (2014).

III.iii Virtue as Infinitely the Highest Good

The claim that virtue plays a central role in Ross's ethics is also supported by the fact that he not only regards virtue as the highest intrinsic good but also as infinitely higher than pleasure or even knowledge (at least if we understand knowledge as a 'mere opinion'[32]).[33] Would you take, he asks, any increase in knowledge (as worth having) at the cost of a willful failure to do your duty or deterioration of character? The answer, says Ross, can only be negative.[34] Similarly, no gain in pleasure could make up for a loss in virtue.[35]

Moreover, other intrinsic goods seem to depend on virtue. Justice is understood as the right proportionment of happiness (pleasure) to virtue and misery (unhappiness) to vices.[36] This characteristic means justice depends on a specific relationship between pleasure and virtue. Regarding knowledge, Ross understands it as resembling virtue or expressing moral goodness.[37] In turn, pleasure's status as intrinsic good is dubious in Ross's writings, especially in light of the *Foundations of Ethics*, where, as noticed by Phillip Stratton-Lake, Ross points at the difficulties with the claim that pleasure has intrinsic value.[38] However, even if we agreed that pleasure could be a non-instrumental good, not all pleasure would deserve such description but merely the good pleasure. And by 'good pleasure' Ross means the one which springs from the satisfaction of a good (i.e., virtuous) desire or is

---

[32] Ross is not clear in his comparison here (see 2002, 151–2). A few paragraphs before his saying that he is 'inclined to think that moral goodness is infinitely better than knowledge,' he compares knowledge to pleasure, weighing the former as infinitely better than the latter. There, however, he adds that by 'knowledge', he means not just a 'condition of the intellect' (having a true belief) but an expression of the desire or disposition for the truth. Such a disposition to Ross has moral worth. Thus, his claim about the infinite betterness of moral goodness to knowledge will probably refer to knowledge understood as a 'condition of the intellect'. In any case, virtue in Ross's ethics is viewed as the highest good.

[33] The claim that virtue is infinitely better than, for example, pleasure is found controversial by many authors, e.g. Thomas Hurka and David Phillips. As our aim here is merely to point at the affinities between Ross and virtue ethics, we will refrain from evaluating the abovementioned and some other controversial claims made by Ross. For a critical evaluation of his comparisons of virtue and pleasure, see esp. Phillips (2019), Ch. 4.

[34] See Ross (2002), 153.

[35] Ross (2002), 151. In *The Foundations of Ethics* (1939), Ross modifies his view on comparing virtue and pleasure. He claims these intrinsic goods (virtue and pleasure) belong to different scales, and what distinguishes virtue from pleasure is the fact that virtue can be admired while pleasure cannot. Such a criterion may complicate the comparison of virtue and knowledge if we think that Ross compares virtue with knowledge as the disposition of the mind to successfully find out the truth, as Ross also admits knowledge so understood also deserves admiration. However, Ross seems to uphold his claim of the infinite betterness of virtue over pleasure and knowledge as a mere opinion (see Ross 1939, 266–7).

[36] Compare Ross (2002), 138.

[37] Ross seems to give two premises for treating knowledge as resembling virtue (or having something of virtue). In *The Right and the Good*, when weighing the value of knowledge, he refers to states of mind which are 'to some extent the actualization of a desire for knowledge.' The desire (or disposition) manifested in such states 'has moral worth, is of a nature of virtue' (Ross 2002, 151–2). In *The Foundations of Ethics*, he refers to knowledge as worthy of our admiration (Ross 1939, 267). In one passage of *The Right and the Good*, Ross also speaks of knowledge as consisting of intelligent understanding or insight, which may be associated with viewing knowledge as an epistemic virtue (see Ross 2002, 139).

[38] See Ross (1939), 271 ff; Stratton-Lake (2003), 129.

at least not contrary to the desert or not resulting from the realization of a bad disposition.[39]

We can formulate one more argument for virtue's importance (a central role) in Ross's ethics. From the fact that virtue is infinitely higher than any other good, it follows for Ross that virtue ought to be pursued, i.e., we have a duty to become virtuous. This duty is contained within the prima facie duty of self-improvement. The above claim allows arguing that, to some extent, the good is sometimes prior to the right because the latter (in some cases) is somehow based on the former.[40] The fact that something is intrinsically good gives rise to a prima facie duty to it.[41]

The advocates of virtue ethics could raise one more objection regarding the centrality of virtue in Ross's ethics. They could say that Ross does not focus on defending virtue or aretaic language as contemporary virtue ethicists would; neither does he focus on analysing various types of virtue, such as practical wisdom, justice, or temperance. Ross also does not engage in debates strongly related to the notion of virtue, such as the unity of virtues, their constituting eudaimonia, etc. In response, we would say that the fact that Ross does not engage in many issues that draw the attention of contemporary virtue ethicists does not mean that the virtue category is not central to his ethics.

In Ross's times, there might not have been a need to prove that the language of virtue is a legitimate means of explaining ethical issues. Or at least Ross might not have perceived such a need despite highly valuing Aristotelian ethics and the notion of virtue. Also, particular issues such as the unity of virtues may be somehow related to the time and place when they seem more pressing. Had Ross lived after Elisabeth Anscombe publicized 'Modern Moral Philosophy' in 1958, he might have focused more on defending the language of virtue and its importance. Living now, he could have engaged in the discussions that are currently taking place within virtue ethics.

To wrap up this section: to Ross, virtue is the highest intrinsic good; the other intrinsic goods depend on virtue, and we have a prima facie duty to be virtuous. From this, we can draw one conclusion: virtue plays a central role in Ross's ethics, even if it has to share this centrality with the category of right (or duty), and some issues related to virtue were not drawing Ross's attention.

---

[39] See Ross (2002), 166.
[40] The exception would be the duty to keep one's promises. One has it regardless of the fact that there are any intrinsic goods. Although, keeping one's promises (if done from a sense of duty) is morally good.
[41] Although it might also be argued that because something is our duty it would be good to be motivated by it. So it might be safe to limit ourselves to claiming that both categories, of the right and of the good, are equally central to Ross.

IV The Role of Reasoning in the Fulfilment of Rossian Duties

We have already mentioned in the previous section that action from a sense of duty, i.e., virtuous action, means to Ross action based on understanding or awareness that something ought to be done. Such a claim suggests that Rossian ethics fits another point in our brief characteristic of virtue ethics, namely, that virtue, in his view, does not consist of a merely automatic reaction to one's situation or a blind following of moral rules, but it requires some cognitive grasp of what is right as well as a flexible response to ever-changing circumstances.

Ross believes that our ascertaining of prima facie duties and actual duties requires reflection and intellectual maturity. He is an intuitionist, thinking prima facie duties are self-evident and that we can apprehend their truth. However, grasping the truth of a self-evident duty is not automatic. First of all, it requires experience. According to Ross, our cognition of moral truths begins in particular circumstances when, for example, we promise to do something. We first discover the prima facie rightness of fulfilling this particular promise as a promise. From this, 'we come by reflection to apprehend the self-evident general principle of prima facie duty.'[42] Experience, reflection, and comprehension of relevant notions are needed in this process. We may assume that intellectual maturity[43] consists of these three.

Grasping a prima facie duty does not automatically lead to learning one's actual duty in given circumstances. Again, reflection on the whole situation is needed to weigh all possible prima facie duties that may apply to it. In some cases, i.e., of perfect duties (such as the duty to fulfil one's promise, repair wrongs one has done, or return the equivalent of services one has received), it might be easy to conclude our actual duty. However, even in such cases, there might be conflicts of prima facie obligations that require reflection. The epistemic status of our moral judgements about our actual duties is not as high as that of prima facie duties. The former can never be viewed as self-evident but merely as considered opinions, assuming the reflection condition is met. A lot in grasping our actual duty is also left to perception in Aristotle's meaning of the word.[44]

A careful reader might have noticed that Ross is not explicitly writing about the moral cognition of virtuous agents. Instead, he merely refers to intellectually mature agents. Nevertheless, it seems justified to claim that he has in mind people whom we would consider either virtuous or relatively closer to virtue than most real people. The moral convictions of these thoughtful and well-educated people,

---

[42] Ross (2002), 33.
[43] It is puzzling why Ross speaks of intellectual maturity and does not speak directly of practical wisdom. Nevertheless, we may interpret his view here as compatible with approaches that refer to practical wisdom in the context of recognizing what one ought to do in given circumstances.
[44] See Ross (2002), 41. He refers here to the phrase 'the decision rests in perception' that Aristotle uses in his *Nichomachean Ethics* (1109 b 23, 1126 b 4).

Ross claims, are the foundation or data of ethics.[45] At this point, we can notice another affinity to (at least some versions of) virtue ethics. Ross's treatment of the opinion and example of the virtuous as a point of reference in establishing what is morally good or right resembles Aristotelian views defended by such contemporary virtue ethicists as Linda Zagzebski.[46]

To sum up this section, we can justifiedly say that Ross's ethics, requiring the ability to understand and reflect on ethical issues, meets the second criterion of virtue ethics set at the beginning of this paper.

V Rule-centred or Agent-centred?

Ethical theories such as deontology and utilitarianism are characterized as act-centred or rule-centred. They put a lot of effort into determining moral principles and how we should apply them to particular situations. Their main goal is to formulate answers to the question: *what ought to be done?* The questions of *who we should become* and *what skills or virtues we should develop* (if ever asked) are usually subordinated to determining and doing what is right.[47] Is it the case with Rossian ethics?

Much of Ross's writing is devoted to determining our duties and what we ought to do. This fact, however, does not mean that agency is not important in his ethics. We have already devoted a large part to the category of the good, showing that virtue is central to Ross's ethics; this already suggests that the agent (not just acts) is also (at least to some extent) at the centre of his attention. Both virtue and knowledge are features of agents. Making claims that we should develop such features in us and focusing a lot on their nature shifts Rossian ethics towards the agent-centred approach. Counting the morally good as fundamental for ethics moves his position even further towards agent-centred ethics. The whole category of the morally good comes down to agents' having good motives for action. Motives are not things we decide to do; they manifest our dispositions, which are agents' features.

Still, one might counterargue that Ross does not answer *who I should become* or *what life's goal is*, that he says little or even nothing of eudaimonia. Indeed, while reading Ross, apart from the fragments on the intrinsic good, one can hardly find the effort to relate every topic or notion to virtue or a morally good character. Answering this objection, we need to admit that Ross does not focus on the notion

---

[45] See Ross (2002), 15, 41; (1939), 1–5.
[46] Compare Aristotle (NE 1106b 35—1107a 3) or Zagzebski (2017, 60–98). Of course, Ross does not go as far as Zagzebski does in emphasizing the role of admiration in identifying virtue. However, he does refer to admiration at least in one place in *The Foundations of Ethics*, where he wants to justify his high estimation of virtue (see Ross 1939, 267).
[47] Hursthouse (1999); Louden (1990); Statman (1997).

of eudaimonia. Also, his focus on virtue or knowledge may not be as developed as in many cases of contemporary literature within the virtue ethics tradition. Nevertheless, he indirectly answers the questions of life goals and who one should become. His prima facie duties of beneficence, non-maleficence, and especially self-development concern the agents and their telos. Ross claims that virtue 'is always the thing best worth aiming at'.[48] Moreover, according to him, we should cultivate not only a sense of duty but also intellectual integrity and other elements of a good moral character.[49]

Of course, to Ross, both categories (of the right action and a morally good character) are essential. Such a stance might make him importantly different from paradigmatic deontologists and most virtue ethicists. Combining the two approaches, however, in the most visible way, allows us to see the reason why Shklar labels him as bridging deontology with virtue ethics. And such a position is neither deterioration of deontology nor spoiling virtue ethics. On the contrary, it opens the possibility of enrichment for both perspectives.[50]

VI 'Antitheorietical' Approach

Thus, we pass on to the last point of our short characteristic of virtue ethics.[51] Virtue ethicists adopt the view that one cannot formulate an ethical system with some fundamental absolute general or abstract moral principles from which one could deduce any other moral judgements. In their proper sense, moral judgements refer to particular circumstances; they are not a matter of deducing but grasping either in the act of understanding or some form of moral perception by virtuous moral agents.

Here, Ross seems to fit virtue ethics characteristics very well. Although his prima facie duties may resemble general moral principles, they do not express actual duties. Knowing them will not suffice to make correct overall moral judgements (or decisions). One cannot simply deduce from prima facie duties what one should do here and now. As Ross claims, in particular circumstances one needs to reflect on the whole nature of the situation. Only then, on the condition that one is a mature, well-educated person, can one formulate a considered opinion about one's actual duty.[52] Such a grasp is made intuitively, either through an act of understanding or some form of perception. Its epistemic status depends on the quality

---

[48] Ross (2002), 153.
[49] Compare ibid. Unfortunately, we must admit such claims that Ross makes accidentally when discussing other issues.
[50] We will say more on this issue in Section VII.
[51] We put the word *anti-theoretical* in commas to remind the reader that we do not mean that virtue ethics is literarily anti-theoretical. See Note 13 above.
[52] Compare Ross (2002), 31–2, esp. 123.

of the agent who makes the judgement; however (and here, Ross may differ from most virtue ethicists), such judgement is never self-evident and is always based on partial knowledge.[53]

Of course, Ross does not formulate v-rules; his prima facie duties are deontic. This, however, does not automatically make one lie outside the scope of virtue ethics. Moreover, it may be considered a sign of some development of the virtue approach, as we will argue in the next section.

VII Ross's Concept of Prima Facie Duties as an Opportunity for Virtue Ethics

One issue in virtue ethics seems especially demanding of some development. When asking why one should act in a certain way or why a given act is morally good, a standard answer within this tradition is that a virtuous person would choose such action. This solution does not seem satisfactory since it is open to a vicious circle objection. Most virtue ethicists, following Aristotle, define virtue as a stable disposition to act and feel in the way one should, at the right times, about the right things, to the right persons, and for the right reasons.[54] The definition of virtue already contains terms like 'right' or 'should' (which we could treat as synonymous with expressions containing terms like 'morally good' or 'ought to'). If this is so, then answering the question of why a given action is morally good or right by pointing at virtue cannot be satisfactory. How do we know a given person is virtuous? Because she acts in the right/morally good way, doing the right thing for the right kind of reason. And what does it mean for a person to act in the right or a morally good way? How do we know the choice this person makes is morally good? Because it is the way a virtuous person would choose?[55]

There is another way of justifying moral choices available in the tradition of virtue ethics. Namely, a certain action is morally good because it helps agents realize their eudaimonia or happiness. Such an answer faces another problem: the problem of egoism. If the justification of our choices were our happiness, it would mean that by acting for the sake of another, we primarily act (and intend to act) for our own sake. The other is just an opportunity to cultivate our virtue (or otherwise realize our happiness).[56]

---

[53] This difference might come from the fact that Ross probably has in mind people who are not perfectly virtuous (in the Aristotelian meaning of the term). One may have a sense of duty, i.e., be motivated to do what is right, but still may wrongly read one's situation by missing some of its aspects, and thus wrongly weighing all prima facie duties that apply to the circumstances.

[54] See Aristotle (2014), 1106b18–24.

[55] The vicious circle objection against Aristotle was raised, for example, by Elisabeth Anscombe (1981).

[56] The objection of egoism has been raised, for example, by Thomas Hurka. In his 'Aristotle on Virtue' (2013), Hurka claims that Aristotelian ethics is egoistic, and in his *Virtue, Vice, and Value* (2001),

Both answers pointed out above seem unsatisfactory. The difficulty will become clearer once we ask ourselves how virtuous people would justify their choices to other virtuous people. One might oppose saying that the virtuous do not need justification; they see whether the given action is morally justified, provided they know all the relevant circumstances. There cannot be disagreement among such agents, and thus no argument or justification is necessary. However, let us assume that, at least sometimes, virtuous people may differ in their moral opinions. Or, to be more realistic, let us rather think of people who are very close to virtue but are not yet perfectly virtuous, and therefore some differences of opinion between them are possible. If such people differed in moral judgements or decisions, how could they argue or justify their choices to others? How could they convince other almost perfectly virtuous people that this and not another way of acting would be right? Saying that their choice or judgement is one of a virtuous person does not sound convincing.

A natural way out for a virtue ethicist would be referring to the Aristotelian notion of the *orthos logos*. The virtuous are the ones who willingly follow the *orthos logos*. Whether we translate it as the right rule or the right judgement is not important here. What matters is that the *orthos logos* assumes the existence of an objective criterion of rightness. And this criterion is something the virtuous would refer to when justifying their choices before other virtuous people. We can assume that such justification would consist of referring to moral reasons. However, to avoid the objection of egoism, we cannot point at our own flourishing. *Orthos logos*, then, cannot be limited to identifying the goal of our own eudaimonia and the means leading to it. Now, what, then, would these reasons be?

Here comes help from Ross. In his view, moral reasons are self-evident prima facie duties. He defines them as tendencies of certain types of actions to be morally right, which are plausibly considered tendencies that give us reason to act in a certain way. Thus, we also find the answer to why to introduce the deontic language (however, deontic in the way Ross understood it) into aretaic discourse. It allows us to fill the gap that virtue ethics, restricting justification to the reference to virtue, cannot fill. Thus, although deontic, the concept of prima facie duties is a promising element that could help virtue ethics overcome one of its challenging issues.[57]

---

he devotes a large part of his last chapter ('Against Virtue Ethics') to the claim that virtue ethics, especially in the versions presented by Anscombe and Hurtshouse, assume an egoistic theory of normative reasons.

[57] It is tempting to ask what justifies our prima facie duties. Ross claims that they are self-evident; however, this answer does not exclude further explanations. And such explanations might point to persons and their intrinsic value or dignity. A promising direction of this sort, while elaborating on Ross, is taken by Robert Audi in (2004, Ch. 3). See also his (2015). Due to the lack of space, we cannot develop this issue here.

VIII Conclusion

We started this paper with the question of how far Rossian ethics matches the contemporary ethics of virtue as widely understood. We set four criteria for belonging to the virtue ethics tradition: (1) giving a central, important role to the notion of virtue; (2) treating virtuous action as based on recognition and reflection; (3) having a primary focus on the agent; and finally, (4) taking an anti-theoretical approach to moral matters. Our analysis of Rossian ethics strongly suggests the affinity of his position to virtue ethics. His ethics meets (at least to some extent) all the four abovementioned defining criteria. Of course, one could point at some differences, for example, that Ross did not focus so much on many issues common among virtue ethicists. He did not develop a theory of practical wisdom, did not focus on various kinds of moral virtues, nor did he ask the question of the unity of virtues. He did not think that, at least in his times, such questions were more pressing than the ones that drew his attention. And, of course, a large part of his ethical considerations (reflection, discussion, theorizing) is deontological. However, even this being so, we could say that his deontological approach is at least compatible with providing a major role for virtue both in understanding morality and in guiding action. What is more, he has something to offer to virtue ethics. His concept of prima facie duties is an interesting way of developing the virtue ethics tradition by filling certain gaps in it, thus making his ethics a true bridge between deontology and virtue tradition.

References

Anscombe, Elisabeth. 1958. "Modern Moral Philosophy," *Philosophy*, 33, 1–19.
Anscombe, Elisabeth. 1981, "Knowledge and Reverence for Human Life." In *Human Life, Action and Ethics. Essays by GEM Anscombe*, edited by M. Geach and L. Gormally, 59–66. St. Andrews: Imprint Academic.
Annas, Julia. 2014. "Why Virtue Ethics Does Not Have a Problem with Right Action," *Oxford Studies in Normative Ethics*, 4, 13–33.
Aristotle. 2014 [ca. 300 B.C.E.] *Nichomahean Ethics*. Translated by Roger Crisp. Cambridge: Cambridge University Press.
Audi, Robert. 2004. *The Good in the Right. A Theory of Intuition and Intrinsic Value*. Princeton, NJ: Princeton University Press.
Audi, Robert. 2016. *Means, Ends, and Persons: The Meaning and Psychological Dimensions of Kant's Humanity Formula*. Oxford: Oxford University Press.
Crisp, Roger, Michael Slote, eds. 1997. *Virtue Ethics*. Oxford: Oxford University Press.
Hurka, Thomas. 2001. *Virtue, Vice, and Value*. Oxford: Oxford University Press.
Hurka, Thomas. 2013. "Aristotle on Virtue: Wrong, Wrong, and Wrong." In *Aristotelian Ethics in Contemporary Perspective*, edited by Julia Peters. 9–26. Routledge.
Hurka, T. 2014. *British Ethical Theorists from Sidgwick to Ewing*. Oxford University Press.
Hurtshouse, Rosalind. 2022. "Virtue Ethics," *Stanford Encyclopedia of Philosophy*.
Louden, Robert, B. 1990. "Virtue Ethics and Anti-Theory," *Philosophia*, 20, no. 1–2, 93–114.

McDowell, John. 1997. "Virtue and Reason." In *Virtue Ethics*, edited by Roger Crisp and Michael Slote, 141–62. Oxford: Oxford University Press.
Phillips, David. 2019. *Rossian Ethics: W. D. Ross and Contemporary Moral Theory*. Oxford University Press.
Ross, William, David. 1939. *The Foundations of Ethics*. Oxford: Oxford University Press.
Ross, William, David. 2002 [1930]. *The Right and the Good*. Oxford: Clarendon Press.
Ross, William, David. 2005 [1925]. *Aristotle*, 6th ed. New York: Routledge.
Russell, Dan. 2009. *Practical Intelligence and the Virtues*. Oxford University Press.
Russell, Dan. 2015. "From Personality to Virtue." In *Current Controversies in Virtue Theory*, edited by Mark Alfano, 92–105. Routledge.
Skelton, Anthony. 2010. 'Ross,' *Stanford Encyclopedia of Philosophy*.
Sklar, Lisa. 2009. "Plato's Crito: A Deontological Reading." Electronic Thesis and Dissertations 2004–2019.4088. Available at: https://stars.library.edu/etd/4088
Snow, Nancy. 2008. *Virtues as Social Intelligence*. Routledge.
Statman, Daniel. 1997. "Introduction to Virtue Ethics." In *Virtue Ethics*, edited by Daniel Statman, 3–41. Washington, DC: Georgetown University Press.
Stratton-Lake, Philip. 2003. "Pleasure and Reflection in Ross's Intuitionism." In *Ethical Intuitionism*, edited by Philip Stratton-Lake, 113–36. Oxford University Press.
Szutta, Natasza. 2007. *Współczesna etyka cnót [Contemporary Virtue Ethics]*. Gdańsk: Wydawnictwo Univesrytetu Gdańskiego.
Tian, Jie. 2013. *The Orthos Logos in Aristotle's Ethics*. Berlin. Available at: https://edoc.hu-berlin.de/bitstream/handle/18452/18364/tian.pdf?sequence=1.
Trianosky, Gregory. 1990. "What Is Virtue Ethics All About?" *American Philosophical Quarterly*, 27, no. 4, 335–44.
Zagzebski, Linda. 2017. *Exemplarist Moral Theory*. Oxford University Press.

PART IV
ROSS ON VALUE

12
Ross and Aesthetic Value

Gwen Bradford

While Ross did not, so far as it seems, write directly or extensively on aesthetic value in any work dedicated exclusively to that topic, he nevertheless articulates and defends a view of aesthetic value in *The Right and the Good* that indicates a fair amount of careful reflection. He returns to consider additional dimensions in *Foundations of Ethics*, which further supplement his view of aesthetic value and expand his axiology.

Ross has a *dispositionalist* account of the definition of aesthetic value, meaning that he holds the view that aesthetic value, specifically beauty, is a disposition to induce aesthetic experience. Ross is further an *instrumentalist* about the value of beauty. Beauty is instrumentally, not intrinsically, valuable. Rather, it is aesthetic experience that is intrinsically valuable. However, according to Ross, even though aesthetic experience is intrinsically valuable, its value is *derivative*. Its value is composed of the value of pleasure and the value of knowledge, two underivative goods. Ross's view runs contrary to important views of his time, especially Moore's, and finds company in contemporary views in aesthetics (and, as a result, is subject to similar objections). But Ross enriches his aesthetic axiology in *Foundations of Ethics*, adding that artistic creation may have intrinsic value which he does by, perhaps surprisingly, drawing on a perfectionist rationale. Ross's views on these points have both their strengths and their weaknesses.

This paper presents an overview and critical discussion of Ross's views on aesthetic value. As Ross's views develop, they become somewhat closer to Moore's (at least in some respects and the better for it, or so I will argue) and, further, improve upon them.

I Ross on Aesthetic Value

According to Ross, beauty is "the power in an object of evoking something that has value, the aesthetic experience" (Ross 1930, 70, cf. 127–30). Beautiful objects have only one "common attribute," namely, this power. Further, and perhaps counterintuitively, beauty, and therefore beautiful objects, are not intrinsically valuable. Rather, beauty is the power to produce something else that is of intrinsic value, namely aesthetic experience. Aesthetic experience is intrinsically valuable, yet its

Gwen Bradford, *Ross and Aesthetic Value* In: *The Moral Philosophy of W. D. Ross*. Edited by: Robert Audi and David Phillips, Oxford University Press. © Oxford University Press 2025.
DOI: 10.1093/9780198914839.003.0012

value is *derivative*. That is, aesthetic experience is good for its own sake, but its value is derived from other basic goods that comprise it. The value of aesthetic experience is a matter of the value of pleasure and the value of knowledge, two underivative intrinsic goods.

At the close of the chapter "What Things are Good?" in *The Right and the Good*, Ross presents his position that the value of aesthetic experience, or, specifically, aesthetic enjoyment is derivative:

> Of the three elements virtue, knowledge, and pleasure are compounded all the complex states of mind that we think good in themselves. Aesthetic enjoyment, for example, seems to be a blend of pleasure with insight into the nature of the object that inspires it (Ross 1930, 141).

So the value of aesthetic enjoyment is intrinsic, but derivative because it is composed of the value of pleasure and the value of knowledge.

Given Ross's time, his view is to some degree innovative. Among the main views of Ross's contemporaries is the view that beauty is an intrinsically good property of objects and aesthetic enjoyment is *sui generis* and its value intrinsic and non-derivative.[1] This is G. E. Moore's view (Moore 1993 [1903]) to which Ross is explicitly reacting (Ross 1930, 118–31).

Moore holds not only that aesthetic enjoyment is intrinsically good, but that it is one of the "greatest goods we can imagine" (Moore 1993 [1903], 238). Aesthetic enjoyment is, according to Moore, an organic unity comprised of several parts, which include the "cognition of what is beautiful in the object" as well as "some kind of feeling or emotion" which is "appropriate to differences in the kind of beauty perceived" (Moore 1993 [1903], 238–9). Importantly, it is the whole comprised of the beautiful object, its appreciation, and attendant emotions that has intrinsic value. The component parts on their own may not have much or any intrinsic value. The value of the whole that is aesthetic experience is non-derivative insofar as, while it depends on features of its parts, its value is not reducible to their value.

In certain respects, Moore's view can be compared to that of Clive Bell, according to whom artworks are characterized by "significant form" which is recognized when it gives rise to the specific and particular feeling of aesthetic experience (Bell 1914).

---

[1] Ross is not entirely distinctive in his time as holding an instrumentalist view of aesthetic value. Dewey is another instrumentalist, and he was writing roughly contemporaneously (*The Right and the Good* was published in 1930 and Dewey's *Art as Experience* was published in 1934). Dewey's account goes in quite a different direction, however, insofar as art is instrumentally valuable when it serves the natural needs of human beings. Other important theories around Ross's time include the expressivism of Benedetto Croce and R. G. Collingwood, according to which, very roughly, art is the expression of the artist's emotion, and these thinkers do not, it seems, dwell much on the value of aesthetic experience.

Ross thus makes an interesting contribution by pushing against some perhaps dominant views at the time to break down the value of aesthetic experience, rather than insist that it is *sui generis* and non-derivative. Moreover, Ross's view that beauty is a power has a distinct advantage over accounts such as Bell's, as Ross himself points out: "the chaotic condition of aesthetic theory seems to show that it is extremely difficult, if not impossible, to specify the characteristic or characteristics of beautiful things (apart from the way in which they can affect minds) on which beauty depends" (Ross 1930, 132).

Concerning aesthetic value, although Ross's account initially appears limited in one respect, this turns out to be a strength. Typical of the time, Ross considers *beauty* as identical to aesthetic value. Contemporary philosophers now have more attractively expansive views, acknowledging a much wider range of aesthetic values, both positive and negative, such as charming, humorous, graceful, horrific, ugly, clunky, and so on. In contrast with the contemporary expansive approach to aesthetic values, Ross's view appears narrow and old-fashioned.

However, once we see aesthetic values more expansively, it perhaps becomes less attractive to hold that just one of them, namely beauty, is intrinsically good while the others are not. Looking beyond beauty, not all aesthetic values are good candidates for having intrinsic positive value, most obviously negative aesthetic values, such as the ugly or the clunky, but also some positive ones, such as the cute or the charming. Objects with these aesthetic values are less obvious candidates for also having intrinsic goodness in the sense that's of interest to Ross. This makes Ross's view that beauty is of mere instrumental value more appealing. One can further plausibly extend this analysis of beauty as a power to produce aesthetic experience to the other aesthetic values: the charming, say, is a property of an object that is a power to produce a certain experience, to wit, of being charmed.[2] Whether or not any particular aesthetic value is of instrumental value depends on whether the experience it has the power to elicit is intrinsically valuable. Being charmed perhaps is valuable to the extent that it can be pleasant, but other experiences, such as being repulsed or intrigued, may have less, perhaps zero, intrinsic value. So as far as aesthetic values go, beauty among them, it is not in the end unappealing to hold the position that they are not themselves intrinsically valuable.

Another appealing feature of Ross' account of beauty is its ability to straddle the objective and subjective. The account is objective insofar as the power to induce aesthetic enjoyment is a property that is possessed by the object (Ross 1930, 128) and resides there regardless of whether or not any particular person in fact has that response.[3] Yet beauty is also rooted in subjective experience, making the account neither purely objective nor subjective, at least construed in these ways.

---

[2] Ross in fact compares the beautiful to the charming, holding that both are best understood dispositionally (Ross 1930, 89).

[3] Although: "even if it be held that beauty might exist in a mindless universe, there is no reason for regarding the beautiful things in such a universe as having any value in themselves. Their value would

We thus can distinguish between Ross's *descriptive definition* of aesthetic value—i.e., the account of what the feature of central aesthetic significance *is*—and Ross's account of the *value* of aesthetic value—i.e., the account of how this property is *valuable*. Ross is a *dispositionalist* about the descriptive definition of aesthetic value, specifically beauty: it is a power to produce a certain kind of experience. And Ross is an *instrumentalist* about the value of aesthetic value: beauty is instrumentally valuable because it produces aesthetic experience, which is of intrinsic value.

A similar combination of a dispositionalist definition of aesthetic value and instrumentalist account of the value of aesthetic value can be found elsewhere in analytic aesthetics. Monroe Beardsley is perhaps the most obvious example. He holds that aesthetic value is the capacity to produce aesthetic experience, and he further agrees with Ross that aesthetic value is instrumental value. Beardsley gives the following instrumentalist definition of aesthetic value:

> If it be granted that aesthetic experience has value, then "aesthetic value" may be defined as the capacity to produce an aesthetic experience of some magnitude (Beardsley 1958, 533).

Thus, like Ross, Beardsley is a dispositionalist about the definition of aesthetic value (i.e., it is a power) as well as an instrumentalist about the value of aesthetic value (i.e., it is instrumentally valuable because it is the power to produce intrinsic value in the form of aesthetic experience).

Ross's view also can be compared to that of Robert Stecker, who articulates a similar instrumentalist account of the value of aesthetic value. Stecker shares with Ross that it is aesthetic experience that is intrinsically valuable, and that aesthetic values such as beauty, as well as objects with aesthetic value, are instrumentally valuable insofar as they produce this intrinsically valuable experience (Stecker 2019; 2023).[4]

An instrumentalist position is also sometimes associated with Malcom Budd, but his view is less clearly instrumentalist than Stecker's. In fact, Budd insists that his view is *not* instrumentalist. Budd holds that the value of a work is in some important sense a matter of the intrinsic value of the aesthetic experience it offers. Yet because this experience is an experience *of the work*, it is the work that has the value. That is, the properties of the aesthetic experience are, in fact, properties of

---

be solely instrumental to the production of aesthetic enjoyment in such minds as might later come into being" (Ross 1930, 130).

[4] Stecker further holds that aesthetic experience has aesthetic value (something Ross does not consider), and, unlike Ross, Stecker rejects that aesthetic experience and its value must involve pleasure (Stecker 2023, 104). Stecker also holds that the aesthetic value of objects can also enhance other kinds of value, such as cognitive and ethical value, in various ways (Stecker 2019).

the work, presumably in the same sense that the properties of your experience of, say, redness, is, one might say, really the property of the red apple. In Budd's words:

> [T]he value of a work of art is intrinsic to the work in the sense that it is (determined by) the intrinsic value of the experience the work offers... [T]he experience a work of art offers is an experience *of the work itself* and the valuable qualities of a work are qualities *of the work*, not of the experience it offers. It is the nature of the work that endows the work with whatever artist value it possesses; this nature is what is experienced in undergoing the experience the work offers; and the work's artistic value is the intrinsic value of this experience. (Budd 1995, 4–5)

Why "determined by" is in parentheses is unclear, but presumably the thought is to clarify that the value of the work is indeed located in the work, and is a function of the value of the aesthetic experience afforded by it. Budd's view, looked at one way, is that because artworks have instrumental value in producing valuable experiences, they therefore have intrinsic value. Looked at another way, Budd's view is that works can be *constituents* of valuable experiences, rather than causes of them, and therefore are intrinsically valuable themselves.

We can, therefore, make a distinction between a dispositionalist account of the descriptive definition of aesthetic value and a dispositionalist account of the *value* of aesthetic value. Ross, Beardsley, and Stecker all share a dispositionalist account of the descriptive definition of aesthetic value and an instrumentalist account of the value of aesthetic value. In contrast, on a dispositionalist account of *value*, the power to produce aesthetic experience is not merely instrumentally valuable but intrinsically valuable. The power has intrinsic value, in addition to what it can produce. Budd's view aligns more closely with a dispositionalist account of the value of aesthetic value, rather than an instrumentalist one.

Stecker, however, provides a nice argument against the dispositionalist account of value in support of instrumentalism that bolsters the case for Ross's and the other instrumentalists' position: milk is conducive to certain intrinsic values that follow from health, but this by no means provides any support for a claim that milk has intrinsic value (Stecker 1997b, 57). Likewise, artworks are conducive to certain intrinsically valuable experiences, but we cannot conclude from this that they have intrinsic value. Stecker makes the appealing point that instrumental value is not a clear source of intrinsic value, strengthening the case for instrumentalism over dispositionalism.[5]

But we can in turn press an objection against the instrumentalist. Some people may find ugly what others find beautiful—the same object, that is, may have power

---

[5] Other philosophers have argued compellingly that instrumental value can indeed be a source of intrinsic value. Shelly Kagan points to the pen that Lincoln used to sign the emancipation proclamation (Kagan 1998).

to induce both positive and negative aesthetic experience. Ross acknowledges this point, as any instrumentalist must (Ross 1930, 129). While disagreement is a feature of matters of taste, it would be a more appealing account if it could attribute beauty more stably than it appears to—after all, Ross insists that his view of beauty is partly objective, as we saw above. What, exactly, is the best way to construe the power to induce aesthetic experience? Induce it in whom, under what circumstances, and how often? If it's enough simply that an object is beautiful if there is some possible world in which some person responds to an object with aesthetic experience, then it seems that virtually every object will be beautiful, and by the same token, virtually every object will also be ugly.

Now, this may not be such a deep concern—it isn't that difficult to suppose that the same object can be both beautiful and ugly—but it has a further impact on whether the object has positive or negative value. The very same object may have positive instrumental value, in virtue of the positive value of the aesthetic experience that it induces, as well as negative instrumental value, since it is equally capable of inducing an aesthetic experience of negative value. Having a power to produce good and a power to produce bad make the object both positively and negatively valuable.

But this too may not be a deep concern. We are, after all, talking about *instrumental* value. Many things have both positive and negative instrumental values. A fire extinguisher can be instrumentally positively valuable when it is used to extinguish a harmful fire, and it can be instrumentally negatively valuable if it is used as a murder weapon.

Reflecting on the instrumental effects of various things leads one to question just what instrumental value is, however, and why it matters. If it is the power to cause some effect that has intrinsic value, then virtually everything has instrumental value since virtually everything can be put to some good use. Yet the same is of course true of instrumental negative value. Virtually everything can be put to some ill use. As a result, the significance of anointing something as instrumentally valuable seems unilluminating. It does not reveal much of anything significant about a thing's nature, but merely makes a claim about a causal role it might play, which is a feature of virtually everything else in the universe.

Understood this way, to say that beauty is merely of instrumental value is to truly deflate its axiological significance—it is no more important for value than anything else might be. Ross's position, understood this way, is, as a result, somewhat radical in contrast to the philosophically traditional attitudes towards aesthetic value, especially Moore, who includes beauty and its enjoyment among the highest goods.

Dispositionalism about the value of aesthetic value is more seriously under threat by the observation that the same object can be both beautiful and ugly. If an object can have the power to induce both positive aesthetic experience and negative experience, the dispositionalist must say that the object has both positive and negative value.

If we also hold the view that aesthetic value has *intrinsic value*, this means the object is both intrinsically good and intrinsically bad. One might think that's perfectly fine, if something is good and bad in different respects. But the possibility is open that the same object will be both good and bad in the same respect—i.e., the very same feature could have both the power to produce aesthetic positive experience in some and aesthetic negative experience in others. This becomes even worse if we hold that it is analytic that something being intrinsically good (with respect to R) entails it is not intrinsically neutral and not intrinsically bad (with respect to R). If that is true, the dispositionalist account of aesthetic value generates a contradiction.

But a dispositionalist about value can say more. There are grounds on which a dispositionalist may say that a power is good rather than bad. One plausible option is a matter of robustness of the disposition. If most nearby worlds where the power to produce good is manifested are in contrast to a scant minority of worlds where the power to produce bad is manifested, the dispositionalist might with more confidence claim the power is for good rather than bad. This puts the dispositionalist on steadier footing to continue the argument that the disposition to produce good is itself intrinsically good.

Another alternative is proposed by Robert Audi, who proposes *inherent* value as the value that objects such as works of art may have that is a matter of their "power to yield intrinsic value in an experience that is appropriately responsive" to their intrinsic properties (Audi 2023, 242; cf. Frankena 1963, 66). Audi restricts intrinsic value to experiences, and so the innovation of inherent value allows for a distinct kind of value in the world apart from experience. Inherent value is grounded in the intrinsic properties of the object and its power not simply to *cause* intrinsically valuable experience, but to be a "constituent in such an experience" (Audi 2023, 243, emphasis original).[6] This view is similar to Malcolm Budd's account of aesthetic value discussed earlier: works have the power to be constituents of intrinsically valuable experiences, and therefore have intrinsic value themselves. Put this way, we can see that such a view needs a few more steps in order to avoid the fallacy of division. Audi's proposal does this by locating the value in the power itself, and the properties of the object that ground this power.

Now, this dispute about dispositionalism about value appears to be neither here nor there for Ross, since he is not a dispositionalist about the *value* of beauty. But since he is a dispositionalist about the definition of the property of beauty, Ross's account would benefit from greater detail regarding the relevant disposition in such a way that either attributes beauty in a meaningful way, or, alternatively, embraces the radical position that virtually every object is both beautiful and ugly.

---

[6] Stecker too holds that artworks have inherent value, although in his view, inherent value is better understood as "a species of instrumental value" (Stecker 1997a, 258).

Moreover, he should have something to say about instrumental value if the same object can produce both intrinsic good and intrinsic bad, or, again, he could alternatively embrace the radical position that instrumental value, and hence beauty, is axiologically insignificant. Appealing to robustness of disposition, or establishing some other feature to distinguish beauty from ugliness when an object may have the power to cause both. would help support Ross on his account of beauty.

II Artistic Value

An important philosophical development is the possibility of a distinction between aesthetic value and *artistic value*. Indeed, Budd, discussed above, is in fact explicitly discussing not aesthetic value but artistic value. However, as an account of artistic value, an instrumentalist account is less plausible.

Artistic value is the value that a work of art has *qua* work—it is present in greater or lesser degrees in greater and lesser works and indeed is what constitutes the difference between a great work of art and a lesser one. Monet's *Nymphées* are great works of art, which is to say they have great artistic value. In contrast, Thomas Kinkade's *Make a Wish Cottage* is a work of art but not a great one, which is to say it has less artistic value (or so I assume). What properties ground artistic value is a substantive matter we can put aside here, but typically they include formal properties, such as shapes and colours, and also contextual and historical properties, such as when the work was made, by whom, and in what art-historical context. Thus, even if a child's drawing has very similar formal properties to a Cy Twombly, the Twombly has many contextual properties that ground its great artistic value.

Beauty may or may not be an element in artistic value. The *Nymphées* are certainly beautiful, and their beauty contributes to their artistic value, but it is less clear that Twombly's *Fifty Days at Iliam* (1978) is beautiful, and, rather, to some extent its artistic value is enhanced by aggression which borders on the ugly. Moreover, whereas beauty and other kinds of aesthetic value can be found in other objects beyond works of art, such as nature, artistic value is only to be found in created art objects (construed broadly).[7]

A dispositionalist account of artistic value is far less plausible than a dispositionalist account of aesthetic value. Recall Ross's instrumentalist view of aesthetic value is that beauty is entirely a matter of the disposition to induce aesthetic experience. So long as something has the power to produce that experience, it has beauty. The dispositional property is instantiated by the object, but its content is fully a matter of the reaction that it has the power to produce.[8] Ross rejects

---

[7] To be sure, the relationship between artistic and aesthetic value is far from uncontroversial, e.g. (Lopes 2011).

[8] One might think that there is something necessarily incoherent about this: isn't the fragility of the vase grounded in the various structural properties of the vase? Yet Ross's comments suggest that it

that there is any sense in which aesthetic enjoyment is *merited* or fitting. One might think that if an object is beautiful, then it merits aesthetic enjoyment, and if you yourself don't enjoy it, you, then, in some sense, ought to. But Ross explicitly rejects this, saying, rather, that "no one can judge an object to be very beautiful or very ugly except on the strength of a vivid feeling towards it" (Ross 1930, 131). In contrast, artistic value is less plausibly construed purely dispositionally. That the Twombly has artistic value is not, it seems, simply a matter of it being disposed to cause people to judge it does, or to have some experience. Rather, the properties of artistic value, it is more accurate to say, are properties of the work, and ground the fact that appreciation is merited. Although it may indeed be conducive to a response of a certain kind, artistic value is not plausibly response-dependent. Now, of course this point is *pace* Budd, discussed above, who would not be troubled by this observation since he argues for this very view. My complaint here is that such views are subject to the point I am now raising, namely, that they get the direction of explanation wrong: that works have artistic value is what explains why they merit admiration and aesthetic enjoyment, and not the other way around.

Moreover, it is also implausible that the value of artistic value is located solely in this response of appreciation, rather than in the object. The artistic value of the Twombly is not plausibly simply a matter of the response of appreciation that one might fittingly take towards it. Rather, it is the work of art that's valuable, which explains why the attitude of appreciation is merited. It is not implausible that the merited response of appreciation is also itself intrinsically valuable, and not implausible that the value of this appreciative response could be a matter of the value of pleasure and knowledge (more on this later). But the point here is that it isn't as appealing to locate the value *solely* in the response and not at all in the work. So Ross's account of aesthetic value and the value of aesthetic experience is not plausibly extended to the artistic value of works or its appreciation.

Ross does, however, have more to say about artistic value. In *Foundations of Ethics*, Ross draws a distinction between aesthetic experience on the one hand and artistic creation on the other. He re-emphasizes his view that aesthetic experience is pleasure, and so good only insofar as pleasure is good. He further elaborates in contrast that artistic creation is a mental activity, which, "like knowledge, appears to me to be good not only in the sense that we like it, but in the sense that it is an admirable activity of the human spirit; and it owes its goodness to its own intrinsic character" (Ross 1939, 270). He continues:

The characteristics that are the base or foundation of artistic excellence have not been worked out, and probably cannot be worked out, with anything like the

---

is only the fact that it is capable of producing a reaction that makes it beautiful. Ross is what we might call a particularist about beauty—there are no common properties of objects that ground it (Ross, 1930, 132).

precision with which the conditions of scientific excellence have been worked out by logic. Yet in a vague way we have some knowledge of the intrinsic features of good artistic work—vividness and breadth of imagination, vigour of execution, economy in the use of means, simplicity of plan. We think there is something admirable in these things, and it is for this reason that we honour the great artist. We think there is displayed in great art an activity of the human spirit which is admirable for its own sake, just as virtuous actions or the triumphs of the scientific mind are. (Ross 1939, 270–1)

Ross here is putting forwards the view that artistic activity has intrinsic value. He puts it in the same class as virtuous activity and knowledge, both of which are intrinsic goods on his view, and he is claiming it is the proper object of the attitude of admiration, as virtue and the other intrinsic goods are. In this section in *Foundations of Ethics*, Ross is developing an aspect of his view that divides intrinsic goods into those that are worthy objects of satisfaction but not admiration, and those that are worthy objects of admiration. The latter are discontinuously more valuable than the former, and pleasure comprises the category of goods that are merely worthy objects of satisfaction (specifically others' pleasure, whereas one's own is not valuable in this way, according to Ross). Since artistic activity is the proper object of admiration, and not simply the proper object of satisfaction, it is a relatively high intrinsic good.

Interestingly, it appears that Ross is appealing to a quasi-perfectionist rationale to establish the value of knowledge and artistic activity. The "admirable activity of the human spirit" as an explanation for the intrinsic value of knowledge and artistic activity is a distinctively perfectionist claim, perfectionism being the view that the exercise and development of characteristic human features is intrinsically good (e.g. Hurka 1993; Bradford 2016). Ross appears to deepen his explanation for value by appealing to "activity of the human spirit" as a ground for value. He appears to do this also in *The Right and the Good* at the end of the chapter "What Things are Good?" where he says this: "while this list of goods has been arrived at on its own merits, by reflection on what we really think to be good, it perhaps derives some support from the fact that it harmonizes with a widely accepted classification of the elements in the life of the soul" (Ross 1930, 140).

He increasingly appeals to this rationale in *Foundations of Ethics*. In his arguments against subjectivism,[9] Ross says this:

It seems to me, then, that knowledge, or perhaps we should rather say the activity of the mind which leads to knowledge, is good, *not* in the sense that human nature likes having it (although in fact most men do like having it), but in the sense that

---

[9] Specifically against (Campbell 1935).

it is an admirable activity of the human spirit; that this activity owes its excellence not to our liking it, but to its being conducted according to its own proper principles, i.e. according to the principles discovered by logic; and that different instances of this activity are good in proportion as they are conducted according to these principles. (Ross 1939, 270)

However, looking closely, the idea may not be purely perfectionist. These activities owe their excellence "to ... being conducted according to ... proper principles," that is, it appears that Ross is saying that it is formal features of the activities of the mind such as knowledge and artistic creation that make them good, to wit, their being in accord with certain principles, rather than the fact of their being part of human nature. The latter is the distinctive claim of perfectionism.[10]

Nevertheless, Ross's quasi-perfectionist justification allows him to expand his axiology in a principled and appealing way to value artistic activity directly. It is valuable in the same way that knowledge is valuable and for the same reasons: it is "an activity of the human spirit which is admirable for its own sake" (Ross 1939, 270-1). This acknowledgement affords the Rossian account additional resources to deepen the value of aesthetic experience, which I will turn to in the next section.

But what about art *objects*? Ross denies that artworks themselves have any intrinsic value by locating all relevant value in aesthetic experience and artistic activity. As we have seen, Ross's stated view in *The Right and the Good* rejects that attitudes towards works of art can be merited (Ross 1930, 131). His view commits him to holding that artworks themselves are merely instrumentally valuable, and, moreover, the value they may produce is derivative, being a matter of the two intrinsic goods of pleasure and knowledge. The expansion of axiology in *Foundations of Ethics* includes artistic activity as a worthy object of admiration, but still Ross does not go so far as to say that it is art *objects* that are worthy of admiration, rather it is the *activity* involved in their production. Hence his view regarding the value of artworks themselves remains instrumentalist. Presumably one might say that the works themselves have a symbolic value, as a manifestation of or as evidence of the process of artistic creation. But Ross appears to locate the value in the activity of artistic creation rather than the work itself, and the work itself is of primarily instrumental value insofar as it induces aesthetic experience.

That Ross rejects that attitudes of appreciation towards artworks are merited is a drawback of the view. His commitment to instrumentalism leaves him vulnerable to objections. First, the view is subject to the direction of explanation objection I raised earlier, namely, that it is most natural to hold that artworks have value, which is why they merit admiration and aesthetic enjoyment, and not the other way around.

---

[10] Nevertheless, formal features of activities can still be part of the perfectionist explanation of value, as exemplified in (Hurka 1993).

Additionally, any strict instrumentalist about aesthetic or artistic value is committed to the position that there is in fact nothing of value in the Louvre, say, or any art museum. There are, of course, many things of instrumental value. And perhaps this gives a good enough explanation for why it's important to guard it so heavily, since the same is true of a bank vault, after all. But the strict instrumentalist must also agree that the sum total of value in the world, as it were, plummets by a great deal when the visitors leave and the museum is closed at night. And insofar as we have reason to promote the good, we have reason to, say, have people stay up all night admiring the artworks, so as to maintain the level of value in the world from art. Now, this way of putting things may sound somewhat un-Rossian, but Ross does not deny that there is reason to bring about intrinsic good; quite the contrary, he holds that there is, and in fact that is the rationale behind the duty of beneficence.

Because the value of, e.g., Picasso's *Guernica* is strictly instrumental, Ross and any instrumentalist must say that the only reason the loss of the Picasso is a tragedy is on account of the possible loss of aesthetic enjoyment from looking at it. We could exactly make up for the destruction of the *Guernica* by having contemporary artists create new works that produced just as much enjoyment. The loss of *Guernica* would be in no way other than amount different from the loss of a donut, which could be replaced with an equally tasty fresh one tomorrow. But this position is at odds with the deeply intuitive thought that, even if new art could replenish the total value in the world, the destruction of *Guernica* would nevertheless remain a loss. Attributing intrinsic value to the works themselves (as Moore does, or is often read as doing) has the often-overlooked advantage of avoiding this objection.[11] Indeed, the Moorean position on beauty being intrinsically good even in the absence of appreciation is much maligned and mocked, but it has the upper hand in explaining why there is no reason to pay extra to the museum nightwatch to look at and appreciate the art during their shifts, and why replicas or replacements wouldn't be the same.

On a view where intrinsic good-making properties reside in the art object itself, we can capture the very natural thought that artworks are merited objects of appreciation, and they ought to be preserved and protected for their own sakes, and not merely for the sake of the enjoyment that we may happen to take in them. Ross's view does not have these features.

In this section I have assessed the extent to which Ross's account of aesthetic value is a good one. What we saw is that while it has some attractive features and some companions in the contemporary literature, it has drawbacks as well. Nevertheless, Ross's expanded axiology in *Foundations of Ethics* values artistic

---

[11] Although not entirely, since one can still object to a view such as Moore's that the value of the artworks is, in some sense, replaceable. See Bradford (2024).

activity directly, which paves the way to a richer account of the value of aesthetic experience, which I will turn to now.

III Ross on Aesthetic Experience

Aesthetic experience, according to Ross, has intrinsic value. Aesthetic experience on Ross's view is a matter of pleasure and knowledge: "Aesthetic enjoyment … seems to be a blend of pleasure with insight into the nature of the object that inspires it" (Ross 1930, 141). Now, at first this seems like a rather paltry account of aesthetic experience—great works can induce the full range of emotions and thoughts, pain, sorrow, elation, fear, and move us to tears. Pleasure and knowledge are a tiny fraction of what might characterize aesthetic experience. But Ross is not giving an account of what aesthetic experience *is* but of what makes it *valuable*. So understood, the view is slightly more plausible, although one might nevertheless be inclined to think that aesthetic experience is *sui generis* and a distinct underivative good (as Moore seems to hold).

But Ross's analysis of the value of aesthetic experience is more plausible than it might first appear. If a work induced *nothing* but fear, say, one might *not* be so inclined to hold that experiencing this work had much of any value. It is aesthetic *enjoyment* that is of value according to Ross, not just any response or experience. Ross's account that it is *pleasure* as well as knowledge that are the sources of value in an aesthetic encounter is a helpful specification. A work must not *only* inspire fear, but also do so in a way that is enjoyable.

But one then might wonder how Ross can distinguish between, say, the titillation of a haunted house and genuine aesthetic experience of, say, being moved and horrified by *The Bacchae* of Euripides. Again, it's not an account of the nature of aesthetic experience, but an account of its value. The haunted house experience might be valuable for the same reasons the experience of tragedy is, i.e., it is enjoyable (at least for some)—and so difference of perhaps only degree rather than kind.[12]

We can draw from Kendall Walton's theory of aesthetic value to bolster the plausibility of Ross's account. Walton's theory of aesthetic value proposes that aesthetic experience is characterized by a second-order experience of pleasure as one appreciates the first-order experiences, emotions, etc. that the work has induced. It is this enjoyment of the work's effects that is characteristic of enjoyment of works of art. "After listening to a late Beethoven string quartet or reading *War and Peace* or watching a performance of *King Lear* I exclaim, 'That was wonderful!

---

[12] Moreover, contemporary aesthetic thought would likely acknowledge that the experience of the haunted house is indeed an aesthetic one. See e.g. (Carroll 1990) for the pathbreaking discussion of the aesthetics of horror.

Marvelous!'... if I merely felt pleasure or enjoyment as a result of my experience with it, I would not be appreciating it" (Walton 1993, 504). Even if a work is so tragic as to inspire one to feel nothing but sorrow at first, marvelling at the power of the work to have such a moving effect that induces pure sorrow is what characterizes appreciation of the work and is, also, according to Walton, a source of the value of so doing. Every instance of aesthetic experience is characterized by a specific kind of pleasure, the second-order pleasure of having been moved by a work.

Thus, if we have a Rossian account of what things are good, we can draw from a view such as Walton's to agree that *all* aesthetic enjoyment is good insofar as it involves pleasure. Even seemingly unpleasant aesthetic experiences involve pleasure in the form of second-order pleasure, according to this view. Ross further adds that knowledge is a component of aesthetic experience, and this too harmonizes with Walton's account since it seems natural to suppose that the second-order "how marvellous" experience is partly induced by (at least some) knowledge of the work and the fact that it has had a certain effect. Ross himself does not appear to consider the notion that aesthetic experience involves second-order pleasure, but such a view is nevertheless compatible with his, and affords some advantages.

A key difference between Ross and Walton, however, is that Walton's account is specifically regarding aesthetic appreciation of *works of art*, whereas it is less clear that Ross's view of aesthetic experience is specifically for works of art or can be experienced in response to *any* instance of beauty, including natural beauty.

Another difference, presumably, is also that Ross only counts *beauty* as the relevant property for inducing aesthetic experience, at least as far as the discussion in *The Right and the Good* goes. One might think that it is not beauty that we respond to when being moved by *The Bacchae*, but of course tragedy.

Supplemented with Walton's insight of the second-order appreciation that characterizes aesthetic appreciation, Ross's view gains advantages. As noted above, there would be nothing valuable in reading or watching a performance of *The Bacchae* if it made one feel *nothing but* sorrow, but the fact that the experience is mixed with if not characterized by *pleasure*—the "how marvellous!" moment—makes it a more appealing source of value. As a result, the combination of a view like Ross's with Walton's is mutually strengthening. Walton's view allows for a wide range of aesthetic properties beyond beauty to be enjoyed aesthetically, yet maintains that pleasure is the common thread that runs through all such experiences. Pleasure's value, then, is what (or at least part of what) explains why such experiences are valuable. The two positions are compatible and add to the others' appeal.

Further, Ross can say even more about the value of aesthetic experience. It is not merely valuable *qua* pleasure, but also valuable insofar as it includes knowledge (Ross 1930, 141). Drawing more from what Ross says about the value of knowledge, we can deepen his view of the value of aesthetic experience. In *Foundations of Ethics*, Ross characterizes the value of pleasure as a lesser intrinsic good, because it is merely the fitting object of satisfaction but not of admiration. Knowledge, in contrast, as well as virtuous action and artistic activity, are fitting objections of admiration and therefore superior goods.

To elaborate on Ross's view of knowledge, Ross holds that knowledge is intrinsically good, which suggests that, say, *your* knowledge of someone else's scientific achievement is intrinsically good, in addition to the scientific achievement itself, and is worthy of admiration: "knowledge, or perhaps we should rather say the activity of the mind which leads to knowledge, is good ... in the sense that it is an admirable activity of the human spirit" (Ross 1939, 270). Yet your appreciation of someone else's artistic activity is merely valuable as pleasure, a lesser intrinsic good that is not worthy of admiration, or so it seems Ross is saying.

But given what Ross says about the value of knowledge, we can extend his view to say more about the value of aesthetic experience. Consider knowledge once again. Simply knowing that, say, the theory of general relativity is considered accurate may not be knowledge worthy of admiration, but *understanding* general relativity is. Even if you yourself did not discover it, it is nevertheless a cognitive achievement—an "activity of the human spirit"—to come to know it. It is indeed fitting to admire people who have a great knowledge of this sort. Similarly, there is a difference between simply *enjoying* an artwork, on the one hand, and having a rich appreciation of and critical engagement with the artist's work. It is, in a way not dissimilar from knowledge, a cognitive achievement to fully engage with and come to understand and appreciate artworks. Indeed, it is Ross's affirmed view that aesthetic enjoyment is in fact comprised of both pleasure and knowledge (Ross 1930, 141). So this rationale for Ross's view of the value of knowledge can also be extended to the value of aesthetic experience. Instances of aesthetic experience that involve the cognitive achievements of understanding and critical engagement can have intrinsic value worthy of admiration, according to Ross, in spite of what he says.

Just as it is fitting to admire people who have a rich understanding of, say, physics, it is also fitting to admire people who have a rich understanding of art. Both involve the kind of cognitive activity that Ross considers to be an admirable activity of the human spirit, and, accordingly, they merit not simply an attitude of satisfaction but one of admiration. Aesthetic experience is not just a matter of pleasure, by Ross's own lights, but also involves precisely this kind of knowledge. As a result, aesthetic experience, at least in certain instances, is an intrinsic good of the best kind, as knowledge is—to wit, an intrinsic good that is a manifestation of the human spirit and therefore worthy of admiration.

Moreover, Ross also acknowledges artistic creation as an intrinsic good. Beyond the passage I quoted above, Ross does not furnish us with more detail about the nature of artistic creation, but it is clear from his discussion that he regards it as intrinsically valuable for similar reasons as virtuous activity or scientific discovery by way of his quasi-perfectionist rationale—all are manifestations of distinctive aspects of human nature at its finest. Such endeavours of the "human spirit" are worthy of admiration, indicating that they are intrinsically good.

Additionally, we are now closer to supporting the claim that works of art themselves merit admiration. Insofar as a work of art is a manifestation of artistic creation, it is fitting to admire art, just as it is fitting to admire a scientific discovery. Now, I doubt that Ross would go so far as to endorse that objects have intrinsic value, but we can see how the door is open for a view such as his.

There are further questions regarding the relationships between artistic creation, artistic value, and aesthetic value. It's natural to think there is some connection, but Ross himself does not give us many clues as to his thoughts on these relationships, since his focus is largely on intrinsic value. Artistic creation and its admiration are intrinsically good, as is the enjoyment of aesthetic value, i.e., aesthetic experience. But we might very well wonder what artistic creation has to do with aesthetic value. Not all artworks are characterized by beauty, which is Ross's sole acknowledged aesthetic property. Nevertheless, since Ross does not regard beauty as having central significance for value, but rather aesthetic *experience*, the question we should be asking is what is the relationship between artistic creation and *aesthetic experience*?. And indeed we have already answered this question from Ross's point of view and developed it: aesthetic experience can be augmented in intrinsic value when or to the extent that it involves knowledge, in particular the knowledge and appreciation of the artistic activity that is manifested in the work.

So, then, Ross's view of aesthetic value is that beauty is the power to induce aesthetic experience. Aesthetic experience is intrinsically valuable because it is comprised of two underivative intrinsic goods, namely pleasure and knowledge. We have enriched his account by drawing from the expansion of his axiology in *Foundations of Ethics* to see a path towards holding the view that aesthetic experience is among the highest goods such as knowledge. This puts his stance on the value of aesthetic experience closer to that of Moore. However, he remains distinctive in holding a strict instrumentalist account of the value of artworks and beauty.

Ross's view also differs from and improves upon Moore's view in an important way. Moore only considers beauty and aesthetic experience to have intrinsic value, but does not, so far as I'm aware, hold that artistic creation is intrinsically good. Not only does Ross's account have this advantage, but also Ross's quasi-perfectionist stance generates an appealing justification for its value.

No doubt there is far more to say about the various strengths and weaknesses of Ross's thoughts on aesthetic value, but this comprises a first look. It's my hope that this exploration of Ross's views on aesthetic value enriches our understanding of the breadth of Ross's ideas and shows him to have an original take on aesthetic value that was not well represented at the time he was working. In spite of what he says in *The Right and the Good*, his view on the value of aesthetic experience can be seen as closer to Moore's than one might have originally thought, and even improves upon it. This expansion of Ross's axiology is thanks in part to his quasi-perfectionist basis for value. There is more to explore, to be sure, and I'm not suggesting that Ross's view of aesthetic value is the best or the most accurate, but, rather, putting it forwards to deepen our understanding both of the space of possible views within aesthetics and within Ross's thought.[13]

Works Cited

Audi, Robert. *Of Moral Conduct: A Theory of Obligation, Reasons, and Value.* Cambridge: Cambridge University Press, 2023.
Beardsley, Monroe. *Aesthetics: Problems in the Philosophy of Criticism*, second edition. Indianapolis: Hackett, 1981 [1958].
Bradford, Gwen. Perfectionism. *The Routledge Handbook of Philosophy of Well-Being*, Guy Fletcher, ed. London: Routledge (2016): 124–34.
Bradford, Gwen. Irreplaceable Value. *Oxford Studies in Metaethics, vol. 19.* Russ Shafer-Landau, ed. Oxford University Press (2024): 152–73.
Bell, Clive. *Art.* New York: Stokes, 1914.
Budd, Malcolm. *Values of Art.* London: Penguin, 1995.
Campbell, C. A. Moral and Non-Moral Values: A Study of the First Principles of Axiology. *Mind* vol. xliv, no. 175 (1935): 273–99.
Carroll, Noël. *The Philosophy of Horror or Paradoxes of the Heart.* New York: Routledge, 1990.
Frankena, William. *Ethics.* Englewood Cliffs: Prentice-Hall, 1966.
Hurka, Thomas. *Perfectionism.* Oxford: Oxford University Press, 1993.
Kagan, Shelly. Rethinking Intrinsic Value. *The Journal of Ethics* vol. 2 (1998): 227–97.
Lopes, Dominic McIver. The Myth of (Non-Aesthetic) Artistic Value. *The Philosophical Quarterly* vol. 61, no. 244 (2011): 518–36.
Moore, G. E. *Principia Ethica*, revised edition, Thomas Baldwin, ed. Cambridge University Press, 1993 [1903].
Ross, W. D. *The Right and the Good.* Oxford: Clarendon Press, 1930.
Ross, W. D. *Foundations of Ethics.* Oxford: Clarendon Press, 1939.
Stecker, Robert. *Artworks.* University Park: The Pennsylvania State University Press, 1997a.
Stecker, Robert. Two Conceptions of Artistic Value. *Iyyun: The Jerusalem Philosophical Quarterly* (1997b): 51–62.
Stecker, Robert. *Intersections of Value: Art, Nature, and the Everyday.* Oxford: Oxford University Press, 2019.
Stecker, Robert. Notes on Aesthetic Value. *The Journal of Aesthetics and Art Criticism* vol. 81 (2023): 103–4.
Walton, Kendall. How Marvelous! Toward a Theory of Aesthetic Value. *The Journal of Aesthetics and Art Criticism* vol. 51, no. 3 (1993): 499–510.

---

[13] Many thanks to Robert Audi, Amanda Lopatin, David Philips, and Robert Stecker for wonderfully helpful comments. Thank you also to the National Humanities Center for truly exceptional support during the summer residency in which much of this paper was written, and to Rice University for supporting the residency.

13
On the Value of Intellectual and Aesthetic Activity: A Reply to Ross

L. Nandi Theunissen

I Introduction: The Chief Controversy

In a suggestive aside in *The Right and the Good*, W. D. Ross tells us that he agrees with Meinong that there are 'unpersonal goods' in the sense that there are goods which are not essentially *for* a subject at all, though they are *in* a subject*. Ross tells us: "This is exactly the position I wish to establish" (2002, 104). The passage foregrounds a central distinction, and with it a foundational question about the nature of value. Is value *personal* in the sense that what is of value is of *value for someone*, or is it *impersonal* in the sense that what is of value, while it pertains to a subject, is of *value simpliciter*? Ross was a staunch proponent of the view that value is impersonal. I am a proponent of the view that value is personal. This essay asks which of us is right. Or if that is too grandiose a question to settle here, it seeks to clarify the terms of the debate and why it matters. Since I have proverbial skin in the game, I will articulate a personal theory of value in terms I find plausible. And since I am personally exercised by a dispute that may appear scholastic to outsiders, I will endeavor to make clear what turns on it for me.[1]

The controversy concerns the nature of *non-instrumental* value. You could say that the dispute is about the character of 'intrinsic value', though that term would need to be understood in such a way that a personal conception of intrinsic value is not a contradiction in terms.[2] The controversy belongs to axiology—a term Ross

---

* Many thanks to Robert Audi for comments on a draft of this chapter. I am grateful to Robert and David Phillips, both, above all for their patience. I am grateful to Sofia Berinstein, Eric Brown, Taylor Coles, Rajiv Hurhangee, Jason Kay, Richard Kraut, and Gabe Vasquez-Peterson for helpful discussion.

[1] Like any set of technical terms in philosophy, the meaning of 'impersonal' and 'personal' value is up for grabs. I am treating the terms as synonymous with *good simpliciter* and *good for* respectively. Raz (2004) also uses the terms in broadly this way. This usage contrasts with that of Ronnow-Rasmussen (2011), and Nagel (1986) for whom the distinction is the evaluative analogue of agent-netural and agent-relative reasons. More on terminology below.

[2] For Ross, 'intrinsic value' is simply a synonym for impersonal value, and where I describe Ross's view, I use it in that way. For the personal theorist (as I understand her), the concept of intrinsic value is the concept of what is non-instrumentally good for a subject. In my view, this is the notion of intrinsic value that is of central importance in ethics. Compare Kagan (1998).

L. Nandi Theunissen, *On the Value of Intellectual and Aesthetic Activity: A Reply to Ross* In: *The Moral Philosophy of W. D. Ross*. Edited by: Robert Audi and David Phillips, Oxford University Press. © Oxford University Press 2025. DOI: 10.1093/9780198914839.003.0013

himself uses for the metaphysical part of ethics that is a theory of value (2002, 103)—and crosscuts questions in metaethics. There are anti-realist conceptions of impersonal value, and realist conceptions of personal value.[3] Indeed, one of Ross's chief aims is to liberate impersonal value from the form of metaphysical realism to which it had been consigned by G. E. Moore in the latter's remarks about the impersonal value of a beautiful world that has not and could not be seen and appreciated by anyone.[4] Against Moore's stance here, Ross takes the view that impersonal value is a quality of states of mind, so that it always involves a subject.[5]

Detaching questions about the nature of value from issues of realism and anti-realism can make the dispute between personal and impersonal theorists seem less pressing or its stakes less clear, and I will come back to this. Moreover, the detachment is hard to effect in practice since complete views tend to involve commitments along both dimensions. Ross most often addresses the personal theorist in the figure of the 'subjectivist'—a figure who takes value to be, or to be dependent on, "motive-affective-life," that is, on states such as approval, instinct, and desire.[6] This is not the figure I am concerned to rescue. Unlike Korsgaard's (1997, Ch. 1) critical discussion of Ross, I am not targeting Ross's realism. In fact, I favor a realist account of personal value (Theunissen 2023a), and my characterization of a personal theory of value will implicitly reflect this commitment. I look past those of Ross's objections that are designed to combat forms of 'subjectivism' and confine my attention to the arguments that succeed in making contact with the guiding question of whether value is personal or impersonal.

The chief controversy is over the metaphysical structure of non-instrumental value, and it is a univocal dispute. It is possible to think that some non-instrumental values are personal and others impersonal, but all parties to this dispute are making claims about the nature of non-instrumental value as such. This abstract question

---

[3] Ross shows awareness of the distinction between axiology and metaethics. For example, see his remarks about an 'ontological' conception of personal (or in the terms he uses there 'relational') value (2002, 79–80). The distinction between axiology and metaethics is drawn by Rabinowicz and Ronnow-Rasmussen, who give the example of a preferentialist conception of impersonal value (2000, 38). Railton (1986, 174) provides classic discussion of a relational (or 'personal' in the language I am using here) realist conception of value. For a recent defense of this style of proposal, see Theunissen (2023 a).

[4] Moore (1988, 83–4). As Gwen Bradford pointed out to me, and Tom Hurka with her, even in *Principia Ethica* Moore's commitment to the view that objects isolated from conscious appreciation nevertheless have value is somewhat tentative, as Moore tells us he is inclined to agree with Sidgwick that "[the] mere existence of what is beautiful has value, so small as to be negligible, in comparison with that which attaches to the consciousness of beauty" (1988, 189). Furthermore, by the time he writes *Ethics*, Moore takes the view that "nothing can be an intrinsic good unless it contains both some feeling and also some other form of consciousness" (1965, 129). On the development of Moore's view, see Korsgaard (2013), 3 fn. 5. For Ross's remarks on Moore's thought experiment, see (2002), 130–1.

[5] See for example (2002), 79, 86.

[6] Ross takes the term 'motive-affective-life' from Professor Perry (Ross 2002, 85), his primary interlocutor in the opening sequence of the central chapter on goodness in *The Right and the Good* (2002, 75–104). To take value to depend on motive-affective states is not yet to endorse anti-realism, as the example of Railton (1986) shows. That Ross's arguments betray a preoccupation with subjectivism in particular is plausibly due to the rise of emotivism and its kin. The intellectual context here is aptly discussed by Foot (2001, Ch. 1). For a less editorial treatment, see Darwall, Gibbard, and Railton (1992).

is brought to bear on particular kinds of evaluative phenomena, and the phenomena arguably lend the dispute its liveliness and point. In this context, the battle is over forms of value that are properly thought 'admirable' or 'commendable', or, put otherwise, forms of value that involve excellence or exemplariness.[7] In the broadly Moorean tradition to which Ross belongs and (I think) improves upon, these forms of value are taken to pose a challenge to the view that good is good for.[8] Ross's inventory of basic intrinsic goods—which is to say, the irreducible components out of which all other, non-basic impersonal goods are comprised—is knowledge, virtuous disposition, and cosmic justice.[9] He regards aesthetic experience as likewise impersonally valuable even as it is a complex intrinsic good that consists of pleasurable insight into an appropriately constituted object. Contemporary theorists of the Moorean-Rossian persuasion similarly foreground the value of worthwhile artworks, natural beauty, and intellectual accomplishments.[10] These values are marshaled as hard cases for the personal value theorist, so a lot turns on whether she can give a plausible account of them. I will focus on this kind of case, prioritizing the aesthetic and intellectual examples.[11]

But I begin with the general debate between the personal and impersonal value theorist, taking special pains to clarify what the *personal* dimension of a personal theory of value precisely is, or, put otherwise, how value is essentially *for* a subject. In this I respond to a challenge from Ross but also from contemporary theorists working broadly in Ross's tradition (Section I).[12] With the conceptual questions so clarified, I offer a personal account of aesthetic and intellectual values, exploiting resources within Ross's own discussion of beauty from *The Right and the Good* (Section II). Next, I respond to Ross's signature line of objection to the view proposed, viz., that whatever is admirable or commendable is so only if and because it is impersonally good (Section III). The response is that what makes works admirable (when they are) is that they have features that are apt to be engaged in excellent activities that are constitutively beneficial for their participants. I conclude by stating a key point of difference between impersonal and personal theories of value: a cosmic versus a human perspective on the good (Section IV).

A note on terminology. The key distinction that interests me is the distinction between *good simpliciter* and *good for*. I have followed Ross in using the language of 'impersonal' and 'personal' value to express this distinction and to formulate the chief controversy. It must be said that Ross more often invokes the language

---

[7] The terms 'admirable' and 'commendable' are from Ross (2000).
[8] In the Kantian tradition, the battleground is rather the value of persons. I discuss the dispute between personal and impersonal theorists of the value of humanity in Theunissen (2018; 2020; 2023b).
[9] I make the charitable gesture of dropping well-grounded opinion on Ross's behalf: it was not a good idea. See Stratton Lake (2000, xli) for discussion.
[10] So it is with Nagel (1976; 1986; 1991); Wolf (2010); Raz (2004); and Regan (2004).
[11] I leave aside the case of virtuous disposition because I have discussed it elsewhere. See Theunissen (2023b). Cosmic justice is a story for another day (but I make a start in Section 4).
[12] Chiefly Hurka (2021) and Regan (2004).

of 'non-relational' and 'relational' value, and this is the more common idiom in contemporary discussions too. This second set of terms can be used, and is used by Ross, to express more than one distinction, but on a common usage it also reflects the distinction between *good simpliciter* and *good for*. While there are reasons for putting the distinction in this way, I have come to think that the language of 'relationality' and 'non-relationality' has its limits.[13] The terminology finds point when predicated of objects (works of art or scholarship for example), but it is not suited to express the value bearing status of activities, as I will explain. I begin with the language of 'non-relational' and 'relational' value but eventually cede it to 'impersonal' and 'personal' value for reasons I make clear.

II The *For* in *Good For*

Is value a quality, or is it a relation? Ross presents this as the chief controversy in value theory, and you could say that the controversy is very much alive today. Ross's engagement with relational theories of value has a restive quality. His opposition to the view is unyielding, and yet he comes back to address one and then another style of relational proposal.[14] Ross works hard to bring his relational opponent into focus. And he rather admirably gives voice to the fear that his objections may rest on confusion—as if his opponent has slipped out the back door.[15] It is in *The Foundations of Ethics* that Ross meets the figure whom I regard as the classic relational opponent. This relational theorist takes *good* to be *good for* a subject.[16] In what follows, I outline the key commitments of the view that good is good for, before describing the central points of difference from Ross's view that good is not *for* a subject but a quality *in* or *of* a subject.

Non-relational theorists are apt to express confusion about what the concept of being good for a subject precisely is. Is it the concept of what is good from a

---

[13] Thanks to Robert Audi for discussion.
[14] The discussion fills much of the central chapter on goodness in *The Right and the Good* ("The Nature of Goodness"). Ross engages closely with particular lines of argument from figures who have not survived for posterity, and it must be admitted that this lends the discussion a tedious quality.
[15] Ross (2002), 85.
[16] Ross's interlocutor for this sequence is one Professor Campbell (cf. 1939, 262–71) whose views are not widely remembered. It is striking that, as a scholar and translator of ancient philosophy, Ross does not take Socrates, Plato, or Aristotle as interlocutors instead. For discussion of the ancients as proponents of the view that good is good for see Kraut (2007); Kraut (2011); and Vogt (2017). Some may see Ross's deep engagement with Kant as a fetter to his appreciation for ancient conceptions of value, perhaps adapting Anscombe's remarks about teeth not coming together in a proper bite (1959). Others may be inclined to draw the conclusion that the ancients are not relational theorists of the relevant kind. For remarks along these lines, see Hurka (2021, 808–9). Contemporary proponents of the view that good is good for variously include Thomson (1997); Korsgaard (2013); Finlay (2014, Ch. 2); and Theunissen (2020); Theunissen (2023a); Theunissen (2023b); Theunissen (forthcoming). In characterizing the position, I will draw on the version of the proposal that I find most plausible. For influential discussion of the notion of good for, see Railton (1986); and Rosati (2008).

subject's point of view? Is it the concept of what the subject (but not others) has reason to do? Is it the concept of a subject's possessing a simply good thing? It is none of these things.[17] Nor do we get far by attending to sundry uses of 'good for' in ordinary language which tend to be trivial at best ("this is good for making cheesecake") and degenerate at worst ("this is good for white supremacy").[18] Insofar as good for is a central concept in ethics, it is a technical concept, and in my view it is the concept of *benefit*. So the slogan "good is good for" means good *is* benefit. The concept of benefit relates an *object*, which is to say, a bearer of value, to a *subject*, which is to say, a beneficiary. 'Benefit' makes reference to a subject analytic in the same way that adjectives (in Ross's examples) like 'coveted', 'boresome', 'tiresome', and 'hopeful' do.[19] The object is supposed to be related to the subject in such a way that it is *non-instrumentally* beneficial for them. Let's consider these terms—object, subject, and non-instrumental benefit—in more detail.

Start with the notion of an *object*. Unlike Ross, the relational theorist does not restrict the bearer of (non-instrumental) value to facts or states. Rather, she allows that *objects* can be bearers of non-instrumental value: a work of art, a work of scholarship (the abstract entity, whatever it is, but equally, the physical copy on the bookshelf), a tree, a person, and so on.[20] This is to say that it is not the existence of the work of art that is good, or the state of affairs in which a person exists, but the painting itself, the person themselves. Now non-instrumentally valuable objects can figure in more complex evaluative configurations. A work of art may be non-instrumentally valuable insofar as it is an ineliminable constituent of the valuable activity of engaging with it. Or so I will argue in Section II. The point for now is that dry goods and animate beings may be bearers of value for the relational theorist, and so may activities or forms of engagement. (That the relational theorist emphasizes *activities* over *states* will become important.)

Now consider the *subject*. Insofar as the claim that good is benefit is a general thesis about the nature of value, it takes the beneficiary to be some subject or other. Hence, good is good for *someone*. There is no good that is not relative to some subject. Good is relative to a subject in the sense that the constitution and capacities of different kinds of subject condition the value that arises in connection with

---

[17] These readings have been canvassed by Moore (1903); Hurka (1987); and Regan (2004). The misreadings have been corrected by Raz (2004); Kraut (2007; 2011); and Rosati (2008).

[18] The cheesecake example is drawn from Thomson's (1997) much discussed treatment. For the white supremacy example, see Theunissen (2023a). Finlay (2014) gives central place to ordinary uses of 'good for' in his account of the semantics of good, but I think better data for linguistic analysis would be the concepts of benefit, flourishing, happiness, virtue, excellence, and their kin.

[19] It is striking that Ross does not consider 'benefit' (advantage, well-being, welfare, or happiness) as a cognate of 'good'. For his argument that good is unlike 'hopeful', 'coveted', etc., see Ross (2002, 88–9). While the relational theorist holds that good *is* benefit, she need not make the further claim that 'good' *means* 'benefit'.

[20] In this respect, the view shares points of emphasis with Anderson (1993); Scanlon (1998); and Raz (2001). On the issue of value-bearers it has more in common with 'Kantian' than Moorean axiology. On this distinction, see Bradley (2006).

them. Hence talk of what is good for fish, and what is good for human beings.[21] For obvious reasons, the discipline of ethics takes particular interest in the good for human beings.[22] That is, ethics centrally investigates what is good in the sense that it is beneficial for people. It seeks to identify the things that are good, better, or best for us.[23] Ross asks pertinent questions about the concept *human being* as it figures in the account. Are we making claims about how human beings have historically been, or statistically are? Do the claims purport to have universal scope? Ross rightly sets these candidates aside as implausible. Ross's relational opponent appeals to a notion of human nature (2002, 265), and Ross is right to notice that this is in some sense a normative notion. I would put this by saying that the relational theorist makes a *generic* claim about goodness as it pertains to how human beings *characteristically and typically* are, a claim that anticipates and allows for differences among us.[24] Insofar as the relational theorist is concerned with what is *best* for human beings, she is making a claim about what is best for us given how we characteristically or typically are (again, admitting variation among us).[25]

Now consider the concept of an object (understood capaciously now to include activities) as *non-instrumentally good for* a subject (taking the subject to be a person henceforth). Start with an example. The activity of reading Kant's works in all their details (this is an example from Joseph Raz, and one imagines that Ross would approve of it) may be good for a reader in at least two ways.[26] The activity could benefit the reader insofar as it allows her to impress her friends with her learnedness and erudition. In that case, the activity of reading Kant facilitates a further state in which friends think well of the reader (supposing the friends care about such things, think of our reader at all, and so on). Perhaps this "thinking well" has beneficial effects, in turn. This is so far to speak of the reading as *instrumentally* good for the reader. But the activity of reading Kant could also benefit our reader in and of itself, which is to say, independently of some separate reward that may be hoped to result from it. In reading, the reader contemplates the works of a great mind. Colloquially, we put this by saying that the activity of reading is by itself enriching or edifying for our reader—independently of its standing to

---

[21] Aristotle, NE VI.7, 1141a22–8. This passage is discussed by Vogt (2017, 92).

[22] This is of course not to deny that the relational theorist is also concerned with the good for other animals and forms of life. But it is to say that she is concerned with those questions from the point of view of how we human agents should take the flourishing of other life forms to be practically relevant in *our* thoughts, feelings, and actions. See Vogt (2017, Ch. 4). I return to this point in Section IV.

[23] And this is true of Ross's relational opponent (Prof. Campbell): he is self-consciously offering a theory of goodness as it pertains to or affects human beings, and he is interested in the things that are not merely good but best for us.

[24] See Thompson (2008). That Ross is in need of the concept of generics is particularly clear in his discussion of relational theorists in *The Right and the Good* (see esp. 82–4), where he struggles with the question of whether we are talking about this man, that man, the majority of mankind, etc.

[25] I cannot here take up the important question of how to think about the relationship between the good for human beings and the good for a particular person at particular times. For discussion of this issue, and further references, see Theunissen (2023a).

[26] Raz (1986, 200–1).

impress friends with quips and such. Now we are considering the reading as *non-instrumentally* good for the reader.

The non-relational theorist is poised to raise an objection here. The good for theorist has said that reading Kant can be non-instrumentally good for the reader. The non-relational theorist will 'good-simpliciterize' her 'good for' by redescribing the example as follows: the state of affairs in which the reader contemplates Kant's works is simply good.[27] Taken this way, the bearer of value is a complex or relational state. It is a state that includes a reader whose state of mind corresponds to Kant's works.[28] In describing the case this way, the non-relational theorist is not subscribing to the view that non-relational value has non-relational grounds, or, put more familiarly, that intrinsic value necessarily depends on intrinsic properties.[29] The grounds of goodness are held to be relational, and once they are admitted, the non-relational theorist will urge that there is no *further* role for relationality in a theory of value. For they maintain that goodness *itself*, that is, the value that supervenes on relational grounds, is perfectly non-relational.[30]

Now it is true that relational theorists make a point of saying that relational value "depends on" the nature of the object, the subject, and their interaction. This is a statement about the grounds of value, and the non-relational theorist is right that it does not bring out the 'relationality' of the resulting value that is supposed to be in question. But before we turn to *that* issue, it should be said that the good for theorist's point about dependence is also *worth* making, for it brings out a genuine difference between the views. It is a self-conscious part of the good for theorist's proposal that the peculiarities of subjects condition the values that arise in connection with them, and this is simply not a point of emphasis for Ross. Recall that Ross restricts the presence of value to the mental. As he puts it: "while I do not think it [i.e goodness] is essentially for minds, I think it is essentially a quality of states of mind" (2002, 86).[31] It is tempting to think that when Ross speaks of 'minds' he is implicitly countenancing *human* minds, for the items on his list of basic intrinsic goods are often cited as objective components of the human good. And true enough, there are moments in *Foundations* where Ross refers to the items on his list as *human* goods (1939, 270). It may be tempting to pick up on these remarks in such a way as to take Ross's subject matter to be the human good.[32] But this is not the official doctrine. The official doctrine is that basic value attaches to the stuff in the universe which we can identify as 'mental'. Ross does not take a fine-grained interest in the nature of the minds whose mental states have value. He does

---

[27] I am grateful to Taylor Coles for suggesting the idiom of 'good simpliciterizing good for'.
[28] For the formulation in terms of 'correspondence' see Hurka (2021), 812.
[29] This is one of Ross's innovations over Moore. For discussion, see Hurka (2021), 812.
[30] The argument is made by Hurka (2021).
[31] For discussion of Ross's exclusion of plants as subjects for which things can be good and bad, see Kraut (2007), 88 and *ff*.
[32] Compare the particular form of perfectionism defended by Hurka (1993).

draw a distinction between 'sentient animals' and 'moral beings'. For example, his position in *The Right and the Good* is that the pleasure of sentient animals is always good, while the pleasure of 'moral beings' is good only on the condition that it is deserved (making the pleasure of moral beings, in his terminology, a prima facie good) (2002, 137–8). But unlike the relational value theorist, Ross does not make anything of the idea that the constitution and capacities of different kinds of subject have a bearing on the value that arises in connection with them. That is, unlike the relational value theorist, who insists on the point, it is not part of his proposal that investigation of the nature of goodness requires an understanding of the peculiar natures and psychologies of the subjects whose mental states are supposed to have value.[33] This is a telling difference (about which, more later).

For now, go back to the non-relational theorist's claim that once relational grounds are admitted, it is hard to see what the supervening evaluative *relation* is supposed to be. This is a fine question, indeed challenge, and I think it brings out the limits of the language of relationality—as I will now explain. Classically, the view that good is benefit is the view that whatever is deemed 'good' by definition *does good*, so that good is the *cause* of doing well.[34] Now it is customary for contemporary value theorists to conceive of *instrumental* value causally. What is instrumentally valuable does good in the sense that it causes some separate value-bearing state to come into being. Instrumental value involves a *relation* to this extent: it involves a *causal* relation between a bearer of value and something else of value. As we have seen, however, the chief controversy is about *non-instrumental* value. So the question is how the concept of *non-instrumental* good for a person could involve a *relation*.

Some have proposed that the value of what is non-instrumentally good *is* a function of effects (so that the relation *is* causal), only the effects in question are what a bearer of non-instrumental value does taken alone. Recall our reader of Kant. We said that reading Kant's works can be instrumentally good for the reader by allowing her to impress her friends with her learnedness. But we also said that reading Kant could be non-instrumentally good for our reader, and on the model we are now considering, that may be to say that the reading causes the reader to learn something, or understand something, about Kant. Taken that way, the distinction between instrumental and non-instrumental value is a distinction between two kinds of effect. Instrumental values are of value because they give rise to

---

[33] I am here in agreement with Kraut (2007), 88 and *ff*. For compatible remarks about Ross's unintegrated discussion (2002, 140) of elements of the human soul—cognition, conation, and volition—see Kraut (2007, 91).

[34] It is a conception of the good that is associated with Socrates. Socrates marshals claims to the effect that wisdom is the only good, which is to say, the only cause of doing well. It is not part of this proposal that doing well is *itself* something good. Insofar as the concept of instrumental value is the concept of that which is the cause of something good, it would not be right to say that wisdom is instrumentally valuable on this way of thinking. I have learned from discussion and correspondence with Eric Brown, and from his manuscript "Glaucon, Socrates, and Plato on Goods."

valuable effects given the cooperation of other contributory causes, whereas non-instrumental values give rise to valuable effects that follow from them directly.[35]

This is a possible view. But (among other things) it naturally invites the objection we are considering. Why not simply say that the state of having understanding (of Kant's works) is simply good? If the value of reading is a function of what it does, then it is natural to conceive of the produced effect as the more ultimate bearer of value, and possible to conceive of this as a simply good state. I have come to think that the difficulty here lies in a conception of value as a power to *produce a change*, as if the reading is of value insofar as it produces a state of understanding. Now it could do that—reading Kant could allow the reader to find out something of which she was formerly ignorant, and to incorporate the finding into an essay she is writing. But then the value is not interestingly different from instrumental value. If we are looking for a sense in which the reading is non-instrumentally good for the reader, then this is not the right description. We should rather say that the non-instrumental value is *the achieved activity*, in the present case, *of reading Kant comprehendingly*. The reader who can do this, the reader who has acquired the skills that are needed to engage in this activity (who can read, who has some exposure to philosophy, who can sit still, who can think her way into a framework that may or may not feel foreign, who has a spirit of patience and charity, etc.) has the ability to do it, but this ability is not a power to produce a change but to be in the more fully realized condition of engaging in the activity of reading Kant's works comprehendingly.[36]

To mark this difference in the description, I propose to give up the language of 'relationality' in favor of the language of value as 'personal'. I will say that the activity of reading Kant with understanding is *personally* good in the sense that the activity of reading with understanding is itself (i.e., constitutively) good *for* the one who does it. Now the question arises again. "How does saying that something is good for someone on a certain basis differ from saying that it's simply good on the very same basis?"[37] To see the difference, consider the following statements:

PERSONAL: The activity of reading Kant's works comprehendingly is constitutively good for the reader.
IMPERSONAL: The state in which the reader has comprehension of Kant's works is simply good.

---

[35] This is essentially Nick White's (1984) proposal for how to interpret the division of instrumental and final goods in *Republic* bk. II. It is Brown's view (ms) that it is wrong-headed to attribute this division to Socrates.

[36] Without adopting the whole framework, this is to lean into Aristotle's distinctions between *dunamis, kinesis*, and *energeia*. Thanks to Eric Brown for discussion of Aristotle's reactions to the Socratic view of good as the cause of doing well. But see Note 40 below for the ongoing relevance of ideas of difference-making.

[37] Again, the questions are put by Hurka (2021, 813).

According to IMPERSONAL *what is good* is the state affairs in which a reader has comprehension or knowledge of Kant's works. *What it is for that state to be good* is for it to possess the simple property of goodness. One way to get at the *simplicity* of the goodness is to say that while the state that is good involves a subject, goodness itself is fully *impersonal*. A rational spectator can survey a state of affairs in which that subject has knowledge of Kant and approve, i.e., think that it is a good thing occurring there (see Ross, 2002, 137). Value includes a subject's state of mind as a constituent, but the value is no more *for* the subject than it is *for* the rational spectator or anything else.[38] While goodness attaches to mind-stuff, goodness itself is, as some have said, "just there."[39]

According to PERSONAL, *what is good* is the activity of reading Kant comprehendingly. *What it is for the activity to be good* is for it to exercise the reader's capacity for reading comprehendingly. This may be offered as part of a general view on which exercising our characteristic powers is the schematic explanation for whatever is non-instrumentally good for us.[40] Roger Crisp makes the nice point that while any theory of value must distinguish between *what is good* and *what it is for that thing to be good* (in Crisp's terms, between enumeration and explanation in a theory of value), the distinction itself may be hard to draw in practice because it is possible to cite the same thing in both cases. An enumeration may be intended to be explanatory, and an explanatory theory may be expressed as an enumeration (2006).[41] This is the case with PERSONAL. *What is good* is an activity that essentially involves understanding, thinking, contemplating, etc. At the same time, *what it is for the activity to be good* is for it to engage powers of understanding, thinking, contemplation, etc. The good-making feature of reading Kant *is* the exercise of the reader's capacities to understand, think, etc. According to IMPERSONAL, by contrast, the state of having understanding is *what is good*, but it is not *what it is* to be so.

The emphasis on *activity* rather than *states* makes the personal character of value obvious.[42] (And that value is taken to be personal is the reason the good for theorist interprets the distinction between *the good* and *good* as a distinction between *what is good for someone* and *what it is for something to be good for someone*.) Reading Kant with understanding, listening to a piece of music attentively—these activities find their point for the person doing them. This is because the person

---

[38] Here is Regan (2004), 221: we could as well say that the value "is 'for' the sunset, or the theorem, or the cantata, as insist that the value is 'for' the subject."

[39] Regan (2004), 221.

[40] Insofar as exercising one's capacities serves to maintain, develop, hone, and at the limit perfect, those capacities, then its propensity to do these things features in an account of what makes exercising those capacities valuable. Engaging in an activity in ways that are appropriate is what it is to be benefited by it. And by engaging, one improves, or at least keeps up, one's ability to do so. In that case we reintroduce productive ideas. And it is in this spirit that we may say that value is a difference-maker.

[41] This point is importantly missed by Regan (2004).

[42] This is a point of emphasis for Raz (2004), though the explanation offered here is different.

is being active, using her powers and her agency. The one who is exercising her muscles is the one who is made healthy thereby, and the one who is exercising her psychological and rational abilities is the one who is benefited thereby. So the personal theorist says: the value of the exercise is not "just there" to be approved by a rational spectator; it is of value *for* the person doing it. Doesn't the Rossian point arise again, namely, that the case can be redescribed as *the state in which a person exercises her psychological and rational powers is simply good*? As we will see, this is the position that Ross is inclined to take in *Foundations*, where he shifts the emphasis from mental *states* to *activities* as the bearers of value. I think the shift marks an improvement in his view. But the position is different from that of the personal theorist. The good for theorist's view is that exercising powers is not merely the thing that counts as 'a good', it is *what it is* for it to be so, whereas her opponent thinks that it is a thing that counts as 'a good' but is not *what it is* for it to be so.

I submit that impersonal theorists are apt to miss the 'for' in 'good for' because they insist on a false distinction between the evaluative and the empirical (or the normative and the descriptive). They urge that insofar as 'good for' is used descriptively, as it is in talk of what is good for someone's health, it is used "purely naturalistically" and carries no, not even pro tanto, normative significance.[43] I reject this assumption. The concept of benefit, like the concept of health, is *both* empirical *and* evaluative.[44] To point out that something is 'unhealthy' is not to point to some merely natural fact that is without normative implications. Being unhealthy is a way of being harmful, and what is harmful for someone should be given up (perhaps not ultimately). The concept of health is closely related to the concept of *need*, and the fact that someone needs something without which things will go badly for them is quite relevant to their deliberations. Matters are no different with the concept of benefit. On the explanation that I favor, what explains why something benefits someone is that it properly exercises their natural capacities. That benefit is a function of natural capacity does not mean that it lacks practical significance on its own.

There are questions about the scope of the practical significance. The burning question for many is whether *this* person's reading Kant comprehendingly can be practically relevant for *others* on a personal account.[45] Elsewhere I argue that it can be, indeed *is* (Theunissen 2020, Ch. 5; Theunissen 2023b), so I do not take the question here.[46] But a related question does arise. What sense do good for theorists give to iterated claims such as: "it is good that it is good for you"? My view is that

---

[43] The argument is made by both Hurka (2021) and Regan (2004).
[44] Anscombe's (1959) discussion of Hume on is and ought is most relevant in this connection. Naturally there is more to say about these questions than I have space for here.
[45] This question is emphasized by Regan (2004).
[46] Rosati (2008) argues that for what is beneficial to be of agent-neutral significance it must be beneficial for a being who has non-relational value. I contest that argument in Theunissen (2018); (2020); and (2023).

the proposition expressed by this statement is that the fact that something is good for a person is reason-giving. In Section IV I will make the point that it is importantly reason-giving for other *human agents*, rather than, as in Ross, for a rational spectator abstractly considered. But I postpone this discussion for now.

III A Personal Account of Aesthetic and Intellectual Values

I have sought to clarify the difference between personal and impersonal conceptions of value in general. On the personal conception of value outlined above, *activities* are of value *for* the people who engage in them by exercising their capacities to engage appropriately. The discussion has so far concerned the nature of value. The task before us is to put this abstract discussion to work in thinking more determinately about particular values.

I used reading Kant comprehendingly as an extended example to illustrate what is distinctive about a personal conception of value. But it must be said that it is a contentious example for the personal value theorist. It belongs to a class of what, following Nagel, I will call 'perfectionist values', which is to say, values that involve excellence or exemplariness (Nagel 1979, 129–30). Typical examples of perfectionist value are intellectual and aesthetic accomplishments, and they are thought to pose a challenge for the theory of value that I favor. The challenge is that the values we properly find commendable or admirable (and Ross will certainly so regard the state of having knowledge of Kant's works) are commendable or admirable insofar as and *because* they are good simpliciter. I will turn to this objection, and offer a reply, in Section III. But to get there, I first need say more about how a personal theorist conceives of perfectionist values in particular. I will focus on the aesthetic case, but what I say is intended to apply, *mutatis mutandis*, to the intellectual one.

Strikingly, Ross himself lights the way forward for the personal value theorist. In a particularly rewarding sequence of *The Right and the Good*, Ross offers a theory of the aesthetic case—or in his terms, of 'beauty'—that someone of my persuasion finds much to agree with.[47] Ross presents his account of beauty as a mixed or intermediate 'objectivist'-'subjectivist' account and offers his endorsement. Since Ross is offering a theory of aesthetic *objects*—of the property that makes beautiful objects beautiful—it is fitting to describe Ross's theory of beauty as 'relational'. Ross thinks that beauty and goodness are crucially disanalogous, so that while beauty admits of a relational account, goodness does not. What I propose to do now is reconstruct the key elements of Ross's relational theory of beauty. Then I will offer some amendments to his view so that it takes the shape I am prepared to endorse.

---

[47] Ross (2002), 120–31. Ross's discussion anticipates the 'sensible subjectivism' of Wiggins (1998).

To repeat, I am working through Ross's account of beauty because I am looking for an adequate personal account of perfectionist value of which the aesthetic is a paradigm case.

As Ross is wrestling with the question of what the property of beauty is, he identifies twin pitfalls in existing approaches. Either beauty is thought to be solely a property of subjects ('pure subjectivism'), or it is thought to be solely a property of objects ('pure objectivism'). Ross seeks to correct for these joint excesses. Beauty involves *both* subjects *and* objects, and in making this case, Ross offers several desiderata for a theory of beauty. Let me reconstruct and give labels to these desiderata (a)–(f):

(a) *Object-directedness*: in judging that something is beautiful, one is focused on an object and its qualities, and one ascribes an attribute to it.
(b) *Stability*: if something is beautiful, it is so prior to judgments that it is so, and independently of whether it is currently being seen and appreciated.
(c) *Normativity*: judgments about beauty can be correct or incorrect, or more or less well supported.
(d) *Subject-involving*: beauty necessarily makes reference to subjects.
(e) *Relationality*: beauty necessarily involves subjects being affected by objects in a particular way.
(f) *Variation*: people are constituted differently so that while aesthetic judgments are normative, there is also justified variation in taste.

I think Ross is right to offer these as desiderata for a plausible theory of beauty, and I will simply assert that a theory of beauty should meet (a)–(f). Theories of beauty differ according to how they propose to meet them. Let's consider Ross's own set of proposals.

Start with (a) *object-directedness*. Ross proposes that beauty is a consequential attribute, and that it depends more particularly on the intrinsic nature of its bearer.[48] Ross proposes that beauty is a consequential attribute, and that it depends more particularly on the intrinsic nature of its bearer. So judgments of beauty are *object-directed* in the sense that we ascribe beauty to an object in virtue of its constitutive features. Judgments of beauty are object-directed in the further sense that beauty itself is the *power* an object has, in virtue of its constitutive features, to affect subjects in a particular way. Ross tends to spell out 'the power' not in terms of a *disposition* to affect subjects, nor in terms of a *fitness* to affect subjects, but in terms of the *possibility* of affecting subjects. And Ross expresses the idea that beauty has (b) *stability* in these terms. So long as there is the possibility of affecting a subject, an object is beautiful though no one has been or is now being affected by it. And

---

[48] It was Ross who introduced the now pervasive talk of 'consequential' or 'resultant' qualities: properties that depend on more basic constitutive features. Ross (2002), 79 *ff*.

this is Ross's response to Moore's thought experiment about whether a beautiful world is of value in a world without actual or possible valuers.[49] Ross's response is that the beautiful world is of value only on the condition of the possibility of affecting subjects.

Object-directedness and stability together imply (c) *normativity*: when two people make incompatible aesthetic judgments, one of them is wrong. Judgments of beauty are supported, or not, by claims about the features in virtue of which they are beautiful. And an object either has or does not have the power to affect subjects in the relevant way. People can be wrong about whether the object has this power because their judgments are not sufficiently object-directed (they have not appreciated its qualities). But they can also be wrong because they are not situated or constituted so as to be affected in the relevant way.[50] Ross expresses openness to the possibility that there is no-fault (f) *variation* in judgments of beauty owing to the fact that sense organs themselves may vary, so that while aesthetic judgments are normative, there is scope for incompatible judgments.[51] The same object can be both beautiful for some and not-beautiful for others and, to this extent, we need to reform our ordinary understanding of beauty which, he thinks, does not countenance variation.[52] In fact, Ross suggests that ordinary ideas about beauty need to be doubly reformed because we usually take beauty to be "entirely resident in the object" (2002, 128, n. 1). He is suggesting, by contrast, that beauty necessarily makes reference to how a mind is affected (*relationality*), and that there is scope for some admissible variation in judgments since there is variability in the constitution of minds (*variation*).

For Ross, that beauty is (d) *subject-involving* is seen by the fact that beauty is 'sensuous'—"inseparably bound up with colors and sounds" (2002, 126)—and by the fact that accounts of sensuous or perceptible qualities plausibly make reference to sensing or perceiving subjects. Beauty is (e) *relational* in the sense that beauty is the power an object has to engender the experience of aesthetic enjoyment in a subject, where aesthetic enjoyment is the pleasure taken in insight about a relevantly constituted object (2002, 141). Beauty is accordingly *relationally* valuable for Ross. The object that has the property of being beautiful is valuable insofar as it can produce these valuable kinds of experience, and so its value is straightforwardly *instrumental*. On the other hand—and now the view takes an expected

---

[49] Ross (2002), 130.
[50] Ross's stance here is well captured by Hume's familiar refrain about "the flutter and hurry of thought" that attends first impressions, and the need to correct for this. See Hume (1985, 238).
[51] And these are familiar moves in discussions of how we can countenance normative standards for aesthetic judgment together with admissible variation. They are moves spelled out at greater length by Hume (1985) and the sensible subjectivists like Wiggins (1998) who adapted him.
[52] This is the one moment where Ross shows appreciation for a point that relational theorists insist on, namely, that the same object can be both good and bad without contradiction. For the relational theorist, an object can be both good and bad in the sense that it is good for *s* and bad for *p*. For discussion of this point, see Kraut (2007, 70). For moments where Ross denies that an object can be both good and bad, see (2002).

turn—the *experience* that beautiful objects can give rise to is *non-relationally* valuable: the state in which someone takes well-founded pleasure in an appropriately constituted object is good simpliciter. Even as its value is non-relational it is not basic, however, for its value is a composite of pleasure and knowledge which are *basically* intrinsically good.[53]

As I anticipated, I find much to like in Ross's view. I also have some quarrels, and I will air these now, making amendments that are designed to address them. In doing so I am working my way to a theory of aesthetic value that I find plausible and ready to face the objections to a personal account of perfectionist values in Section III.

Ross has offered a theory of beauty—of the property that makes beautiful objects beautiful. And as we have seen, Ross takes beauty to be the power an object has to engender aesthetic experience in a suitably placed subject. My first reforming gesture is to treat 'beauty' as a name for the property that makes aesthetically valuable objects aesthetically valuable. That is, my first move is to treat 'beautiful object' as synonymous with 'aesthetically valuable object'. The move fits Ross inasmuch as he is not saying that beautiful objects are beautiful because they stand to produce experiences-as-of-the-beautiful, but more generically, because they stand to produce experiences that are aesthetically valuable.[54] So henceforth, I will speak not of 'beauty' but of 'aesthetic value'.

Next, consider that it is an important part of Ross's proposal that judgments of aesthetic value are *object-directed* in the sense that we ascribe aesthetic value to an object in virtue of its constitutive features, and we will be in a position to see the importance of this point in Section III. What I want to draw attention to now is that Ross has judgments of aesthetic value be object-directed in the further sense that aesthetic value itself is the *power* an object has (in virtue of its constitutive features) to affect subjects in a particular way, where this power is thought to consist in the *possibility* an object has of doing so. Invocation of possibility has venerable precedent,[55] and it is familiar in contemporary discussions. Think of claims to the effect that there would be no value in the Frick Collection if all sentient life were destroyed.[56] The thought is that aesthetic value is in some way dependent on the possibility of subjects to appreciate them or be affected by them—however this is spelled out.[57] I will not join Ross and others in putting the point in terms of

---

[53] I am here setting aside the complexities that are introduced by Ross's change of mind about the status of the value of pleasure in *The Foundations of Ethics*.

[54] Moreover, treating 'beauty' and 'aesthetic value' as synonymous is a common move in philosophical aesthetics.

[55] We find this talk of 'possibility' in Sidgwick: "no-one would think it made sense to aim at the production of beauty in external nature apart from any possible human experience of it." Sidgwick (1907), Bk. 1, Ch. 9, Sec. 4. Sidgwick is Moore's interlocutor in the latter's reflections on the value of the uninhabited beautiful world which Ross is implicitly referring to when this notion comes up (Ross 2002, 130).

[56] Nagel (1986), 153.

[57] See Raz (2004), 274; and Wolf (2010), 56, for comparable claims.

possibility.[58] I would rather spell out the power in terms of *suitability* or *aptness*. That is, I would rather say that an object is aesthetically valuable insofar as it is *apt* to bear the relevant relation to subjects. This does not require that subjects actually or possibly exist for there to be aesthetically valuable objects. So it takes discussion of the *existence* of subjects, which Moore brought to the foreground, to be beside the point.

Now consider the *relation* that is supposed by Ross to obtain between objects and subjects. For Ross the relation is *causal*. An object is aesthetically valuable insofar as it can *cause* pleasant experiences in a subject. To this extent, Ross's view is that aesthetically valuable objects—the sunset, the artwork itself, etc.—are *instrumentally* valuable. I join with those who have long complained that this style of proposal makes the value of artworks *fungible*, as if the aim is to have pleasurable experiences, experiences that can just as well be caused in some other way.[59] If we see the value of aesthetic objects as a function of their *aptitude* or *fitness* for certain kinds of valuable experience (and I will withhold assent from the antecedent as formulated in a moment), then I would rather say that the artworks are not apt to *cause* but to be *constituents* of the relevant experience. Their value is *relational* to this extent: the objects are apt to be part of a characteristic kind of experience that is a bearer of non-instrumental value. Given my emphasis on activities and forms of engagement in Section I, it may come as no surprise that I will qualify the antecedent by saying that the primary bearer of value is not the *experience* but the *activity* of engaging with the object. This is an activity in which one participates in a practice of reflection, interpretation, and exploration of a suitably constituted object, and does so successfully insofar as one's reflections are insightful, one's interpretations generative, one's responses apt, and so on.[60] These activities are typically accompanied by positive states of experience, such as pleasure, but the value of the activities need not be taken to consist in pleasure or any other occurrent mental state.

Here is my final reform, a reform that will by now come as no surprise. The value of the activity of engaging with aesthetic objects is *personal* rather than, as Ross thinks, *impersonal*. (Since we have to do with activities as the bearer of value, I shift into this vocabulary.) The activity in which a person engages with an aesthetic object appropriately is *good for* them (given, at least, that they have

---

[58] For what is the sense of 'possibility' that is meant to be in question? Non-zero possibility looks too weak for a view that takes aesthetic value to be essentially tied to responsive subjects. Thanks to Gwen Bradford for this point. On the other hand, the notion of 'live possibility' to which appeal is made in this context looks too imprecise. On the notion of 'live possibility', see Raz (2004, 290). Discussion with Gwen and a conversation with Wlodek Rabinowicz at a conference in York, 2018, were helpful in thinking through my stance on possibility.

[59] For this complaint, see for example Raz (1986), 201. For a more recent discussion, see Shelley (2009).

[60] Here I join with Nguyen (2020) in foregrounding engagement rather than experience. I develop this position at greater length in Theunissen (forthcoming).

actualized their capacity to engage). On the view I favor, it exercises (and also develops, hones, maintains, and at the limit perfects) imaginative, emotional, and cognitive capacities it is constitutively beneficial for a person to exercise. The value of the object—that is, the artwork—is a function of its fitness to be engaged in this beneficial way.[61]

I have used Ross's own discussion of beauty and its value to lay the building blocks for a personal theory of aesthetic value, and I mean the account to extend, mutatis mutandis, to intellectual values, where both are species of perfectionist goods. While I find much to agree with in Ross's discussion, I have offered amendments to his view, some minor and some far-reaching. In the end, I have in a crucial respect read Ross against himself because while he offers a relational theory of beautiful objects, he offers a non-relational theory of the aesthetic experiences they give rise to, and I am resisting this. The task now is to consider how the view fares in response to a signature line of objection from Ross, an objection from the attitude of admiration.

IV Must the Values We Admire Be *Simply Good*?

What I am calling Ross's signature line of objection is one he puts to various kinds of relational theory of value (where 'relational' is being used in a very broad sense). In *Foundations*, his immediate interlocutor is the relational theorist who defines good as that which it is fitting to admire, and this is part of Ross's extended engagement with the view he finds in Brentano.[62] Ross's basic point against Brentano is that the attitude of admiration cannot *define* good because it *presupposes* good (simpliciter). But the objection also finds purchase with respect to the view that is in contention here, viz., that good is good for. It finds purchase as a claim about what the attitude of admiration shows about its object, namely, that it is good simpliciter. To the extent that perfectionist values are admirable or commendable, the argument advances the case that a personal theory of value cannot do justice to this class of values.[63] I consider the argument in what immediately follows, making replies that exploit features of the personal theory of intellectual and aesthetic values developed in Section II.

Sometimes Ross marshals the argument from admiration as a piece of self-evidence. We admire intellectual and aesthetic values, and our admiration reveals that the values in question are good simpliciter. For "it is self-evident that the only ground on which a thing is worthy of admiration is that it is good in itself" (2000,

---

[61] There are complexities here about differences between bad, good, and excellent intellectual and aesthetic works that I cannot enter into here. I discuss these complexities in Theunissen (forthcoming).
[62] See Ross (2000), 278–83.
[63] I consider additional such objections in Theunissen (forthcoming).

279). It must be said that appeals to self-evidence have not on the whole aged well, courting resistance of a familiar kind. ("What is self-evident to this quaint Englishman, is not self-evident to me!") People naturally hunt around for exceptions. For example, we admire skills of various kinds: this person's facility with baking, that person's ability to pitch the ball. The value of these skills is a function of what they do or bring about (the delicious soufflé, the batter striking out), and given Ross's definition of intrinsic value as what is of value independently of its consequences, that means they are not intrinsically valuable (good simpliciter). But it *is* fitting to admire them![64]

At other times, Ross simply claims that good simpliciter is plausibly the object of the attitude of admiration. Of things we find admirable, Ross says: "We think of its goodness as what we admire in it, and as something it would have even if no one admired it, something that it has in itself."[65] This is what I now look into. As we saw in Section II, personal value theorists do not shy away from treating *objects* as bearers of value. In the context of aesthetic and intellectual values, they are happy to say that the *artwork* or *work of scholarship* is admirable—*The Critique of Pure Reason* (considered as an abstract object), Schiele's *Self-Portrait with Chinese Lantern Plant* (considered as a concrete particular), or whatever. Of course, the personal value theorist denies that the works are admirable *because* they are good simpliciter. Instead, the way is prepared for her to take the content of the evaluative attitude to be more particular features of the object. For example, it is the work's systematicity, rigor, and depth, or its use of flatness and distortion. It is these more particular features that absorb one's attention in one's reflections, interpretations, and responses. (Think back to *object-directedness*: in judging that something is aesthetically or intellectually valuable, one is focused on an object and its qualities.) In this, the personal value theorist shares something with the buckpasser who, like her, denies that simple goodness features in the content of valuing attitudes. She disagrees with the buckpasser, however, in offering an evaluative explanation of why the features make the object valuable: the features make the object suitable for being engaged in the excellent activity of interpreting, responding, and reflecting on the object—an activity that is constitutively beneficial for its participants. (This is the personal theorist's way of capturing *relationality*: the value of aesthetic and intellectual objects involves subjects being affected in a particular way.) It is more particular features that figure in disagreements about a work's value, and that are cited as (at least among the) reasons for finding a work worthwhile or not. (Think back to *normativity*: judgments about aesthetic and intellectual values can be correct or incorrect, or more or less well supported.) For the personal value theorist,

---

[64] For the definition of intrinsic value as what is of value independently of its consequences, see Ross (2002). The baseball example was suggested to me by Taylor Coles.

[65] Ross (2000), 89. Ross makes this as a point about admirable actions, but I am leaving a discussion of virtuous action to one side (see Note 11).

more particular features make the object such that it is *apt* to be engaged with well and finely by people, and this aptitude is a feature the object has independently of (actual or possible) episodes of admiration. (Think back to *stability*: if something is aesthetically or intellectually valuable, it is so prior to judgments that it is so, and independently of whether it is currently being seen and appreciated.)

The notion of good simpliciter does not feature in the personal value theorist's account of the ground of the admirability of admirable aesthetic and intellectual works. What makes these works admirable (when they are) is that they have features that are apt to be engaged in excellent activities that are constitutively beneficial for their participants. On this style of proposal—it is recognizably perfectionist—what picks out the activities as 'excellent' is that the capacities involved are higher capacities of human beings. There are different ways to spell out the 'higher' here. Perhaps the capacities are higher because they are more difficult to develop and exercise successfully. Perhaps they are what other (lower) capacities serve.[66] But as the explanation stands to be developed, these higher capacities are better (or best) for people to exercise. Exercising these capacities makes a difference, perhaps all the difference, to a person's life.

I have offered a line of response to Ross's argument from admiration. Let me now say something by way of comparison between this proposal and Ross's own. As we will see, his view changes in interesting ways over time. But start with Ross's view about the object of admiration in *The Right and the Good*. Where we have to do with intellectual and aesthetic values, Ross treats the object of admiration as the *state* of having knowledge (of Kant's works), or the aesthetic *experience* (of Schiele's self-portrait) which constitutively involves knowledge or insight about its object. This state is good simpliciter. As we saw in Section II, the works themselves are *instrumentally* valuable: valuable insofar as they cause these valuable experiences. Ross will have to deny that it is proper to admire *the works* to this extent (for admiration is a supposed mark of good simpliciter). The entailment strikes me as highly implausible because quite out of step with our evaluative practices: we admire the works. Together with concerns about fungibility, I think it gives reason to reject the instrumental account of the value of the works.

Ross's position in *Foundations* marks a shift—and I would say an improvement—in several respects. Speaking of artworks, Ross now says:

> We have some appreciation of the intrinsic features of good artistic work: vividness and breadth of imagination, vigour of execution, economy in the use of means, simplicity of plan. We think there is something admirable in these things, and it is for this reason that we honor the great artist.[67]

---

[66] For a defense of the traditional Aristotelian line, see Nagel (1980).
[67] Ross (2000), 270.

Here Ross appears to be prepared to say that the *works* are what we admire. And he makes a point that is in keeping with his view that value is a consequential property, citing the features in virtue of which the work is admirable, and accordingly on his view, good simpliciter. He makes the further point that what is admirable redounds positively on the creator, so that we have respect for Kant insofar as he wrote the *Critique*. Now the astute reader may wonder whether Ross's considered view is that *objects* rather than *states* may be bearers of non-instrumental value. And in a way the answer is *yes*. For consider what Ross goes on to say:

> We think there is displayed in great art an activity of human spirit which is admirable for its own sake, just as virtuous actions or the triumphs of the scientific mind are.[68]

There is an emphasis on *activity* here that strikes me as precisely right. But before we turn to Ross's stance on activity, note the relation the *object* is supposed to bear to it. The artwork is of value insofar as it *displays* the admirable activity of the artist. This is some kind of relational proposal about the value of the artwork, but it is *not* instrumental.[69] And this is an improvement.

Now consider Ross's claim that the primary object of admiration is the fine activity of the human spirit evinced by the great thinker or artist and captured (displayed) in their creation. On this picture, the activity is not essentially a form of *poesis*—an activity that involves making something that is apt to be engaged finely by others, and whose value depends on its fitness to do so. This is a striking point of difference from the personal theory of perfectionist values that I have countenanced in this chapter.[70] Another point of difference is that the value of the activity of the creator is not good for them, or good for the audience who stands to engage with the work they create, it is simply good. Good is indefinable for Ross, but as we have seen, he offers the heuristic of the stance of the rational spectator who alights upon the activity (or more likely evidence of it in the form of the work) and approves of the presence of simple goodness there. Earlier I made the point that an emphasis on activity over states favors a personal theory of value. The one who is exercising her muscles is the one who is made healthy thereby, and the one who is making use of her psychological and rational abilities is the one who is benefited thereby. I regard Ross's considered position on activity as the primary bearer of intellectual and aesthetic value as an improvement, but also a concession, to this extent.

---

[68] Ross (2000), 270.
[69] By way of analogy, consider Langton's (2007) example of the relationship between wedding rings and marriage.
[70] I say something about this question in Theunissen (2023c).

Let me offer some diagnosis of what appears to speak in favor of Ross's *impersonal* conception of the value of artistic activity. The artist's or intellectual's feat is not of purely *individual* import—not merely of significance to the artist herself. The feat redounds positively on her to be sure (so we may say, for example, that she has some form of excellence). But it also sets a *standard* for the rest of us (a standard that is subject to disagreement, variation, and refinement in ways that are familiar, at least, since Hume). Standards are in a perfectly intelligible sense *public* or *general* or *shared*. And this may push one to an invocation of simple goodness. The personal theorist has a different way of capturing the sense in which perfectionist values set standards. The capacities exercised by the great artist are *human* capacities: capacities of a subject with a mind like ours. The excellent expression of human capacities is normative for individuals with those capacities, albeit normative in ways that admit of range (think back to *variation:* people are constituted differently so that while judgments of aesthetic and intellectual excellence are normative, there is also justified variation in taste.) Hence the personal value theorist's focus, in the first place, not on the good for *individuals*, but on the good for *human beings*.

I have been discussing Ross's claim that the values we properly and characteristically admire, such as intellectual and aesthetic ones, are admirable only if and because they are good simpliciter. I canvassed an alternative explanation that makes no such appeal. I suggested that it is an explanation that better fits a picture on which *activity* is the primary bearer of value, and on which we are self-consciously offering a theory of the *human* good.

V A Cosmic Versus a Human Perspective on the Good

I close with some reflections on the figure of Ross's rational spectator. As we have seen, Ross's project is to search for basic intrinsic goods. These are the irreducible components out of which all other, non-basic intrinsic goods are comprised. When making judgments about what is basically good, Ross tells us that we are to take "the most commanding point of view that can be taken with regard to the value of the things in the universe" (2002, 102). What is revealed from this impartial, contemplative standpoint on the whole of existence is said to be self-evidently good, so that what is basically intrinsically good is knowable a priori. Ross does not here enlarge on his conception of a priori knowledge, and naturally, it raises many questions. But the point here is that it is not a self-conscious part of Ross's proposal that what is identified as good "in the universe" is identified as such by human cognizers and agents.

One would be forgiven for thinking that a human perspective is implicitly assumed by Ross given his inventory of basic intrinsic goods: virtuous disposition, pleasure in proportion to virtue, and knowledge. For the items on the list appear to be things human beings are inclined to find good. To make the point vivid, we can imagine kinds of agent, Homeric gods let's say, for whom courage, in Ross's oft-used example of virtue, is not regarded as good because the gods are sufficiently powerful and independent that there is no need for bravery. So similarly, we can countenance forms of divine intelligence, Aristotle's God let's say, for whom what passes for knowledge on earth, not to mention well-grounded opinion, are notably underperforming values (if they are possible values at all). From either perspective, we should anticipate uproarious reactions to the suggestion that the paltry goods of mortal beings are the things that shine out in the universe as notably good. But the idea that ethics is undertaken from a human perspective is not an official part of Ross's view.[71]

By contrast, the personal value theorist approaches ethics from a *human* perspective. This is in no way to deny that she is concerned with the good for other animals and forms of life. But it is to say that she is concerned with those questions from the point of view of how we human agents should take the flourishing of other life forms to be practically relevant in our thoughts, feelings, and actions. This introduces a related but distinct dimension along which the personal theorist insists on relativization. The first is the one that has been centrally at issue in this essay: the idea that good is relative in the sense that good is good for a subject, for example, human beings—call this Rgoodfor. The second is that there is a perspective from which questions about the good are being raised and examined, and for the personal value theorist, this is importantly a human perspective—call this Rperspective.[72] For creatures like us, with our characteristic cognitive, affective, and volitional make-up, the world is a certain way and has a certain practical significance. There are naturally differences and disagreements among us, but these are of a different order from the differences between us and the perspectives of other animals, gods, or God. This commitment departs decisively from traditions (however otherwise dissimilar) in which moral philosophy takes the standpoint of pure practical reason (as in Kant), or the standpoint of the universe (as in Sidgwick). It rejects the idea that there is a supra-human or cosmic standard by which conduct can be assessed as rational or irrational, and objects, motives, and individuals good and bad. Instead, ethics is addressed to and is normative for beings like us. According to human beings, there are truths about what is good

---

[71] Moreover, Ross shows himself unmoved by the 'relational' (his term here) value theorist's observation that when we make determinations about intrinsic goods, we have a tendency to forget that the goods we pick out as good are seen by us as so, and imagine that they are good in virtue of their intrinsic nature alone (2000, 264–5).

[72] That ethics is investigated from the perspective of human beings is a methodological commitment that is variously spelled out. Vogt (2017), Ch. 4, discusses the origins of this commitment in Protagoras, and my discussion is much indebted to hers. Where Vogt sees the perspective of human beings as the epistemic side of the relation *being good for*, I treat it as a distinct dimension along which a theory involves relativization (one that is neutral on the question of whether good is good for). Thompson (2012) articulates this methodological commitment against Kant's stance on metaphysics of morals, and Williams (1995), Ch. 13, against Sidgwick's invocation of the standpoint of the universe.

for human beings, just as there are truths about what is good for some particular species of plant or animal, and these make certain kinds of claim on our understanding and practice.

References

Anscombe, G. E. M. (1958). "Modern Moral Philosophy." *Philosophy*, 33(124), 1–19.
Crisp, Roger. (2006). "Hedonism Reconsidered." *Philosophy and Phenomenological Research* 73(3), 619–45.
Darwall, Stephen, Allan Gibbard, and Peter Railton. (1992). "Toward Fin de Siecle Ethics: Some Trends." *Philosophical Review* 101(1), 115–89.
Finlay, S. (2014). *Confusion of Tongues: A Theory of Normative Language*. New York, US: Oxford University Press.
Foot, Philippa. (2001). *Natural Goodness*. Oxford: Oxford University Press.
Hume, D. (1985). Of the Standard of Taste. In Eugene F. Miller (ed.), *Essays: Moral, Political and Literary* (revised ed. 226–49). Indianapolis, US: Liberty Classics.
Hurka, T. (1993). *Perfectionism*. New York, US: Oxford University Press.
Hurka, T. (2021). "Against 'Good for'/'Well-Being', for 'Simply Good.'" *Philosophical Quarterly*, 71(4), 803–22. https://doi.org/10.1093/pq/pqaa078
Kagan, S. (1998). "Rethinking Intrinsic Value." *The Journal of Ethics*, 2(4), 277–97. https://doi.org/10.1023/a:1009782403793
Korsgaard Christine. 1996. *The Sources of Normativity*. Cambridge: Cambridge University Press.
Korsgaard, C. M. (2013). "The Relational Nature of the Good." *Oxford Studies in Metaethics*, 8, 1–26.
Kraut, R. (2007). *What is Good and Why: The Ethics of Well-Being*. Cambridge, Mass.: Harvard University Press.
Kraut, R. (2011). *Against Absolute Goodness*. New York, US: Oxford University Press.
Langton, R. (2007). "Objective and Unconditioned Value," *Philosophical Review* 116 (2), 157–85
Moore, G. E. (1988). *Principia Ethica* (T. Baldwin, ed.). New York, US: Prometheus Books.
Nagel, T. (1979). The Fragmentation of Value, in *Mortal Questions* (pp. 128–40). New York, US: Cambridge University Press.
Nagel, T. (1980). Aristotle on Eudaimonia. In Amélie Oksenberg Rorty (ed.), *Essays on Aristotle's Ethics* (7–14). University of California Press.
Nagel, T. (1986). *The View from Nowhere*. New York, US: Oxford University Press.
Nagel, T. (1991). *Equality and Partiality* (L. P. Pojman and R. Westmoreland, eds.). New York, US: Oxford University Press.
Nguyen, C. T. (2019). "Autonomy and Aesthetic Engagement." *Mind*, 129(516), 1127–56. https://doi.org/10.1093/mind/fzz054
Railton, P. (1986). "Moral Realism." *Philosophical Review*, 95(2), 163–207. https://doi.org/10.2307/2185589
Raz, J. (1986). *The Morality of Freedom*. Oxford, GB: Oxford University Press.
Raz, J. (2004). "The Role of Well-Being." *Philosophical Perspectives*, 18(1), 269–94. https://doi.org/10.1111/j.1520-8583.2004.00029.x
Regan, D. H. (2004). Why Am I My Brother's Keeper? In R. J. Wallace, S. Scheffler, and M. Smith (eds.), *Reason and Value: Themes from the Philosophy of Joseph Raz* (202–30). Oxford, GB: Clarendon Press.
Rosati, C. S. (2006). Personal Good. In T. Horgan and M. Timmons (eds.), *Metaethics After Moore* (107–32). Oxford, GB: Oxford University Press.
Rosati, C. S. (2008). "Objectivism and Relational Good." *Social Philosophy and Policy*, 25(1), 314–49. https://doi.org/10.1017/s0265052508080126

Ross, W. D. (2002). *The Right and the Good* (P. Stratton-Lake, ed.). Oxford: Oxford University Press.

Ross, W. D. (2000). *Foundations of Ethics*, The Gifford Lectures delivered in the University of Aberdeen, 1956–6, Oxford: Oxford University Press.

Shelley, J. (2010). "Against Value Empiricism in Aesthetics." *Australasian Journal of Philosophy*, 88(4), 707–20. https://doi.org/10.1080/00048400903207104

Theunissen, L. N. (2018). "Must We Be Just Plain Good? On Regress Arguments for the Value of Humanity." *Ethics*, 128(2), 346–72. https://doi.org/10.1086/694273

Theunissen, L. N. (2020). *The Value of Humanity*. Oxford University Press.

Theunissen, L. N. (2023a). Realism About the Good for Human Beings, in *The Oxford Handbook of Moral Realism*, Oxford: Oxford University Press.

Theunissen, L. N. (2023b). Explaining the Value of Human Beings, in *Rethinking the Value of Humanity*, Oxford: Oxford University Press.

Theunissen, L. N. (2023c). "Activity, Consciousness and Well-Being." *Analysis*, 83(1), 134–46, https://doi.org/10.1093/analys/anac081

Theunissen, L. N. (forthcoming). "Against the Fundamentality of GOOD." *Journal of Philosophy*.

Thomson, J. (1997). The Right and the Good. *Journal of Philosophy*, 94(6), 273–98.

Vogt, K. M. (2017). *Desiring the Good: Ancient Proposals and Contemporary Theory*. New York, US: Oxford University Press.

Wiggins, D. (1998). A Sensible Subjectivism. In *Needs, Values, Truth: Essays in the Philosophy of Value* (3rd ed., 185–215). Oxford, GB: Clarendon Press.

Wolf, S. (2010). "Good-for-Nothings." *Proceedings and Addresses of the American Philosophical Association*, 85(2), 47–64.

14
Heterarchy and Hierarchy in Ross's Theories of the Right and the Good

Anthony Skelton

William David Ross defends pluralism about both the right and the good.[1] His development and defence of pluralism about the right has received sustained attention. Of particular interest has been Ross's view that the non-derivative requirements of morality are prima facie duties rather than absolute duties and that his pluralistic deontology is superior to its utilitarian and deontological competitors.[2]

Interest in Ross's brand of deontology is partly due to its relative novelty. A. C. Ewing opined that "Sir David Ross, I think, made one of the most important discoveries of the century in moral philosophy in recognizing the fundamental character of these prima facie duties" of beneficence, non-maleficence, promise-keeping, and so on (Ewing 1959, 126). There is, of course, no doubt that Ross's development and clarification of the notion of a prima facie duty is a major accomplishment.[3]

---

[1] Abbreviations of works by Ross take the following form: RG = W. D. Ross, *The Right and the Good* (Oxford: Oxford University Press, 1930); FE = *Foundations of Ethics* (Oxford: Oxford University Press, 1939); KT = *Kant's Ethical Theory* (Oxford: Oxford University Press, 1954).

[2] For discussion, see, for example, Ewing (1959), Ch. 4; Hooker (1996), 531–52; McNaughton (1996), 433–47; Stratton-Lake (1997), 751–8; Hurka (2014), 72–8 and Ch. 8; Phillips (2019), Ch. 2.

[3] Following Ewing, many think that Ross's novelty lies in the fact that he was the first to recognize the notion of a prima facie duty. This is a plausible claim given that the view seems not to have been considered in any clear or consistent way by critics or proponents of non-utilitarian views before Ross wrote. Ross revived the views of Joseph Butler and Richard Price. Both Price and Butler defended non-utilitarian approaches to morality. Ross's view is closest to Price's. Some suggest that Price developed the idea of prima facie duties before Ross. But this is not entirely clear from reading Price. Price notes that various heads of virtue (e.g. the duties of justice, gratitude, veracity, and beneficence) might in some cases not be coincident with each other and so "interfere" with each other(Price 1948 [1787], 166). He says that in some instances of such interference "any appearance or possibility of greater good may *suspend* their [rival duties] influence" (Price 1948 [1787], 152; emphasis added). He also remarks that when the benefit of some act to the public good is considerable this consideration "may set aside every obligation" which might compete with it (including the obligations of justice and promise-keeping) (Price 1948 [1787], 153). This is different from what Ross said about his prima facie duties. They are not set aside or suspended or cancelled (as Price says elsewhere [Price 1948 {1787}, 167]) in cases where they point to different courses of action than the one thought right all things considered. On the contrary they continue to remain in force so that, for example, even if you justifiably break a promise, you have a duty to do something to "make up somehow" to the promisee for breaking the promise (RG 28). Price does not clearly say anything like this. Price may not quite have had the idea of prima facie duties, but Ross's colleague H. A. Prichard did. Ross self-consciously developed his view based on Prichard's thoughts (Hurka 2014, 70) in a way that avoided some of the excessive dogmatism that characterizes Prichard's work. Prichard had suggested in lectures he gave in the 1920s that what

---

Anthony Skelton, *Heterarchy and Hierarchy in Ross's Theories of the Right and the Good* In: *The Moral Philosophy of W. D. Ross*. Edited by: Robert Audi and David Phillips, Oxford University Press. © Oxford University Press 2025. DOI: 10.1093/9780198914839.003.0014

However, Ross clarified and gave expression to not only a distinct view of the right. In *The Right and the Good*, Ross argued for a unique form of value pluralism, according to which there are four non-instrumental goods—virtue, knowledge, justice (desert),[4] and pleasure (RG 134–41)—and for the claim that they may be ranked in order of importance, with virtue being the most important of the goods (RG 144–54). He clarified, refined, and modified the view in important ways in *Foundations of Ethics*, where he argues (again) that there are four non-instrumental goods—virtue, intellectual and artistic activities, others' (innocent) pleasure, and justice (desert)—with virtue and intellectual and artistic activities being the most important of the goods (FE 252–89).

In developing his value theory, Ross made important contributions to our theoretical thinking about the value of knowledge, the nature and value of virtue and virtuous motives, and the value of pleasure. Despite this, much less attention has been paid to Ross's value theory than to his theory of prima facie duties. The lesser attention paid to Ross's value pluralism is likely due to the fact that unlike the theory of prima facie duties, value pluralism was already a common and well-developed position when Ross was writing. It was held, for example, by Ross's ideal utilitarian foes G. E. Moore and Hastings Rashdall (Moore 1903; Rashdall 1924). And even those who disagree with value pluralism grant that it is the common-sense view. Despite endorsing hedonism, Sidgwick, for example, suggests that according to adherents of common-sense thinking or "cultivated persons ... knowledge, art, etc.—not to speak of Virtue—are ends independently of the pleasure derived from them" (Sidgwick 1981 [1907], 401).

This chapter focuses on Ross's value theory. It focuses specifically on Ross's view that any amount of the non-instrumental value of virtue outweighs any amount of the non-instrumental value of pleasure or avoidance of pain (RG 150, 152–3; FE 275, 283). The chapter raises two challenges to the status that Ross accords the

---

in common-sense thinking is referred to as a conflict of duties ought to be understood as a conflict between rival claims.

> [W]hat is called a conflict of duties is really a conflict of claims on us to act in different ways, arising out of various circumstances of the whole situation in which we are placed. Further we find no difficulty whatever in allowing that what we call claims on us may differ in degree, or that where there are two claims on us so differing, the act which there is the greatest claim on us to do is duty. (Prichard 2002, 79)

Although Ross may not have been entirely novel in introducing the notion of a prima facie duty, he did clarify and elevate the view into a serious rival to existing moral views and his influence in this respect has been palpable. What he emphasized in his theory of prima facie duties is the view's sensitivity to the nuances of the situations in which we find ourselves and its ability to accommodate a range of morally relevant factors in ways superior to how its rivals attempt to do so.

[4] Ross says that although the word justice covers many things, he uses the word to denote only "a distribution of happiness between other people in proportion to merit" (RG 26; also 58, 138; FE 286, 319).

value of virtue relative to the value of pleasure (pain). First, it argues that Ross fails to provide a good argument for thinking that virtue is always better than pleasure and that it is in any case implausible to think that any amount of virtue (or avoidance of vice) is better than the avoidance of any amount of pain or suffering. Second, it argues that the inflexibility of Ross's value theory exhibited in his claim about the relative value of virtue produces tension with and mars the attractive non-hierarchical (or heterarchical) structure of his theory of rightness or prima facie duties.

I Ross's Heterarchical Theory of the Right

In *The Right and the Good* and his other works in ethics, Ross settles on the view that there are five basic prima facie duties (RG 24–7):

1. A duty of *fidelity*, that is, a duty to keep our promises (which includes the duty not to lie) (RG 21; FE 76–77; KT 21).
2. A duty of *reparation*, that is, a duty to correct a previous wrong or injury we have inflicted on others (RG 21; FE 76; KT 21).
3. A duty of *gratitude*, that is, a duty to return services to those from whom we have in the past accepted benefits (RG 21; FE 76; KT 21).
4. A duty of *beneficence*, that is, a duty to maximize general good (RG 25–6, 39; FE 67, 99, 130, 252, 257, 271, 313; KT 21).
5. A duty of *non-maleficence*, that is, a duty not to harm or injure others (RG 21–2, 26; FE 75, 130n1, 272).

Each of these basic duties points to a moral consideration that is always directly, fundamentally relevant to determining what we ought, morally, in the end to do or to what Ross calls our actual moral duty or duty proper (RG 20, 28). The fact that by failing to show up to a faculty meeting I would break a promise to be there is a basic moral consideration that counts against not showing up. The fact that by failing to show up to the meeting I would be able to provide vital succour to some accident victims counts, morally, against attending the meeting. Figuring out what to do in part involves attending to all the morally relevant considerations present in a situation and their relative weight in that situation (RG 20, 41–2; KT 33–4). One's duty proper is, of the acts open to one, the act with the greatest balance of prima facie rightness over prima facie wrongness (RG 41; FE 85). Suppose that my two options are either to attend the faculty meeting or attend to the accident victims. We might think that my duty proper would be to help the accident victims, since that act contains of the two acts a greater balance of prima facie rightness over prima facie wrongness. In this case, the duty of beneficence weighs more heavily than the duty of fidelity.[5]

Apart from painting an attractive portrait of moral deliberation and decision-making, perhaps one of the most desirable features of Ross's view is its heterarchical structure. He maintains that some prima facie duties "normally" come before others and that some are initially more stringent than others, e.g., "normally" the duty of fidelity comes before the duty to promote as much good as we can (RG 19) and the duty of non-maleficence is more "stringent" than the duty of beneficence (RG 21; also 22; FE 75, 130n1). We should not, Ross says, break a promise or tell a lie to gain a bit more surplus good than we otherwise might produce by keeping a promise or not telling a lie (RG 35, 38; FE 77). And it is not permissible to harm one person to prevent two other people from being harmed (RG 22; FE 75). In some cases, then, the duties of fidelity and non-maleficence outweigh the duty of beneficence.

However, there are cases in which we are justified in breaking a promise or in saying what is untrue or in harming someone, namely, when doing do so produces a sufficiently large quantity of surplus good or prevents a sufficiently large quantity of harm (RG 18, 35, 61, 64; FE 75, 77, 313). So, there are cases in which the duty of beneficence outweighs the duties of fidelity and non-maleficence. Ross does not talk about cases involving the duty of reparation or the duty of gratitude, but it seems clear that he would hold that there are cases in which each would outweigh other prima facie duties and cases in which they would themselves be outweighed by other prima facie duties.

Ross's basic, distinctive, and plausible idea is that there exists a plurality of prima facie duties (or non-derivatively, fundamentally relevant moral considerations), each "definitely arising from certain features of the moral situation" and each of which is "capable of being overruled by other prima facie duties" (KT 32). The moral considerations are drawn on and weighed against each other in figuring out what we ought in the end to do. Ross thinks the main features of his view are key to it avoiding some of the defects he finds in his competitor's views and to capturing in an attractive way the complexities of moral decision-making. He thinks his view avoids the defects of utilitarianism, on the one hand, which ignores the (basic) moral significance of the relations in which we stand to one another beyond that of being beneficiaries of each other's actions (RG 19, 22; FE 76–7), and (Kantian) absolutism, on the other hand, which deals poorly with the complexities of moral life, including and especially moral dilemmas (FE 189, 312–13).

---

[5] Ross thinks that while we can be certain that we have the five prima facie duties he defends, we can only ever have probable opinion or fallible judgement about duty proper (RG 28–32, 33, 41–2; FE 189). For doubts about Ross's claim that we can only ever have probable opinion about duty proper, see Price 1931, 344 and Hurka 2014, 125.

II Ross's Hierarchical Theory of Value

In *The Right and the Good* and in *Foundations of Ethics* Ross argues for value pluralism. In the former work, he argues that virtue, knowledge, justice (desert), and pleasure are non-instrumentally valuable, and in the latter work he argues that virtue, intellectual and artistic activities, others' (innocent) pleasure, and justice (desert) are non-instrumentally valuable. In both works, he adopts a rigid hierarchy among the values. In *The Right and the Good*, he maintains that virtue is infinitely superior to (bare) knowledge, pleasure, and justice; in *Foundations of Ethics*, he argues that virtue and intellectual and artistic activities always outrank all the other goods.

In developing his theory of prima facie duties, Ross tries to accommodate the attractive elements of his rivals while avoiding their defects. He rejected ideal and other forms of utilitarianism, but he did not ignore their attractions. His theory of prima facie duties includes a strong commitment to beneficence. He says, for example, that

> if we are ever under no special obligation such as that of fidelity to a promisee or of gratitude to a benefactor, we ought to do what will produce most good. (RG 39; also FE 130, 252)

Ross rejected absolutist forms of deontology, but he retained the attractive idea behind deontology that there are constraints on what it is permissible to in the service of maximizing the good. He says, for example, that

> Kant overshot the mark when he tried to vindicate for such rules [tell the truth, injure no man] absolute authority admitting of no exception; but he would have been right if he had confined himself to insisting that any act which violates such a rule must be viewed with suspicion until it can justify itself by appeal to some other rule of the same type. (FE 313)[6]

As noted, Ross's value theory has a hierarchical structure. This stands in stark contrast to the (attractive) heterarchical structure of his theory of the right. The hierarchical structure is nowhere clearer than in his treatment of the value of pleasure, where his value theory shares aspects in common with the rigid views of rightness he rejects in developing his theory of prima facie duties. Ross considered the main monistic rival to his value theory—that is, hedonism—to be a dead end (RG 99; FE 65); accordingly, he did not consider it worthy of refutation. But by contrast with his engagement with utilitarianism, Ross did not, it seems, attempt to give expression to the hedonist's intuitions about the value of pleasure or (more importantly)

---

[6] Ross did not defend what are not called agent-centred options permitting agents to do less than the best (Hurka 2014, 179–80). This leaves his view exposed to the complaint that it is too demanding, especially as regards the duty of beneficence.

the evil of pain in his value theory. In both *The Right and the Good* and *Foundations of Ethics*, Ross maintains that any amount of the non-instrumental value of virtue outweighs any amount of the non-instrumental value of pleasure or avoidance of pain (RG 150, 152–3; FE 275, 283).[7]

In *The Right and the Good*, he says that in relation to other non-instrumental values, virtue is the greatest good, "infinitely" better than pleasure, (bare) knowledge, and justice (desert) (RG 151, 152, 152–3). He holds that

> With regard to pleasure and virtue, it seems to me much more likely to be the truth that *no* amount of pleasure is equal to any amount of virtue, that in fact virtue belongs to a higher order of value, beginning at a point higher on the scale of value than that which pleasure ever reaches. (RG 150; emphasis in original)

While the two goods are comparable, they are not commensurable. As many have pointed out, the claim that virtue is infinitely superior to pleasure seems implausibly strong (Price 1931, 354; Hurka 2014, 226; Phillips 2019, 120). A small sacrifice of virtue seems to be more than compensated for by a very large gain in surplus pleasure. And, even stronger still, a small sacrifice in virtue seems to be more than compensated for by the prevention of a large quantity of surplus pain. For Ross's point to go through he would need strong arguments for it. It is to Ross's arguments that we will now turn.

III Ross on the Superiority of Virtue to Pleasure

Ross gave two arguments for the claim that virtue is always better than pleasure. But neither is persuasive. The first argument is this:

> P1. If the acquisition of pleasure for oneself "rarely, if ever, presents itself as a duty … while the attainment of moral goodness habitually presents itself as a duty," then virtue has "infinite superiority" over pleasure, "a superiority such that no gain in pleasure can make up for a loss in virtue" (RG 151).

---

[7] Ross says little about the nature of pleasure (pain) or the quality in virtue of which pleasures (pains) count as pleasures (pains). He describes pleasures as "feelings" and as possessing in common the quality of "pleasantness" (RG 132, 137, 145). He nowhere seems to offer an analysis of pleasantness, suggesting that he accepts internalism about pleasure (pain) on which all pleasures (pains) share a homogenous positive (negative) feeling tone in common (Hurka 2014, 194–5). (For detailed discussion of the distinction between internalism and externalism about pleasure (pain), see Sumner (1996), 87–92. Ross says more about the nature of virtue. For Ross, only motives or desires seem to qualify as virtuous (RG 132–3, 135, 156–7, FE 290ff.). He sometimes suggests that character may be virtuous (RG 155), but his considered view seems to be that a character is virtuous because of the interests or desires composing it (FE 293). Actions are virtuous when they spring from certain kinds of motives, including the desire to do the right thing and the desire to produce something good (e.g., knowledge) (RG 160). The intrinsic value that an action may possess is, Ross says, something it "owes [only] to the nature of its motive" (RG 133; also 160). It is possible, on Ross's view, that "a morally good action need not be the doing of a right act" (RG 156).

P2. The acquisition of pleasure for oneself "rarely, if ever, presents itself as a duty... while the attainment of moral goodness habitually presents itself as a duty."

C. Therefore, virtue has "infinite superiority" over pleasure, "a superiority such that no gain in pleasure can make up for a loss in virtue" (RG 151).

This is a strange argument for Ross to offer. Earlier in *The Right and the Good* he had wondered whether we have a duty to promote our own pleasure (RG 24). It is, he says, "a very stubborn fact, that in our ordinary consciousness we are not aware of a duty to get pleasure for ourselves" (RG 25–6). Although he flirted with the idea that we might not have such a duty, he eventually convinced himself that we do have such a duty. If our own pleasure is an objective good, as Ross thought, then, he argued, "we can think of the getting it as a duty" (RG 26). It seems, then, that Ross himself raises doubts about the plausibility of his argument.

This is just as well. Neither of Ross's arguments for doubting that we have a duty to promote our own pleasure are any good. He says that doubts about a duty to promote one's own pleasure arise from two "facts" (RG 24). The first fact is that

> [t]he thought of an act as our duty is one that presupposes a certain amount of reflection about the act; and for that reason does not normally arise in connexion with acts towards which we are already impelled by another strong impulse. (RG 24)

Ross seems committed to the idea that we ought to maximize the items possessing non-instrumental value (RG 24, 25, 39; FE 257, 313). The reason Ross provides for thinking that we lack a duty to promote our own pleasure seems not to impugn a view on which the duty is to maximize pleasure or happiness, temporally neutrally construed. Trying to do this requires a fair amount of reflection, since figuring out what will promote one's own happiness in the long run is no simple or straightforward task, as many have emphasized, including Kant and Sidgwick.

The second fact is that

> since the performance of most of our duties involves the giving up of some pleasure that we desire, the doing of duty and the getting of pleasure for ourselves come by a natural association of ideas to be thought of as incompatible things. (RG 25)

Again, this cannot explain why the duty to maximize one's own pleasure or happiness (as an objective good) is not a duty. For such a duty would involve giving up or forgoing some smaller present pleasures for the purpose of gaining some greater (possibly quite distant) future pleasures. One might have to forgo certain pleasures now (relaxing) in favour of the future benefits (physical fitness). This seems to follow from the idea Sidgwick expresses, that "equal and impartial concern for all parts of one's conscious life is perhaps the most prominent element in the common notion of the *rational*—as opposed to the merely *impulsive*—pursuit of pleasure" (Sidgwick 1981 [1907], 124n1).

But even if we are persuaded by P2 (as Ross was in FE [273–9])[8], we still might doubt the move from the claim that we have no duty to promote our own pleasure to the claim that virtue is infinitely superior to pleasure. Ross never properly explains how lacking a duty to promote our own pleasure supports the claim that virtue is infinitely superior to pleasure. One might think that we ought not to promote our own pleasure at the expense of our duty and still hold that virtue is not infinitely more valuable than pleasure.

Ross's P2 seems to involve the idea that we lack a duty to avoid or prevent our own pain. He seems at times to be of the view that we have no duty to avoid or prevent our own pain. This is clearest in how he describes the duty of non-maleficence:

if there are things that are bad in themselves we ought, prima facie, not to bring them *upon others*; and on this fact rests the duty of non-maleficence. (RG 26; emphasis added)

the primary duty here is the duty *not to harm others*. (RG 22; emphasis added)

The duty of non-maleficence may be

summed up under the title of '*not injuring others*'. (RG 21; emphasis added)

In *Foundations of Ethics*, when he describes his position that we lack a duty to promote our own pleasure, he says,

we are never conscious of a duty to get pleasure *or avoid pain to ourselves*. (FE 277; emphasis added)

While it might seem plausible to think that we have no duty to promote our own pleasure, it is not plausible to think that we lack a duty to prevent our own pain or (more plausibly still) our own suffering or ill-being. Failure to prevent our own (at least serious) suffering seems blameworthy because prima facie wrong (cf. FE 277). If we think we have a duty to avoid our own pain or suffering, it is not clear that Ross can claim that virtue is infinitely better than the other goods (bads). It is

---

[8] For effective criticism of Ross's *Foundations* argument for the thesis that we do not have a duty to promote our own pleasure, see Shaver (2014), 303–20, at 309–13.

highly plausible that it is better to give up or forgo some virtue to prevent or eliminate a large amount of suffering or pain for ourselves.

In his discussion of the duty of non-maleficence, Ross frequently remarks that duties not to harm and to prevent harm are more important than the duty to promote pleasure (RG 22; FE 75, 130n1, 275, 287). He does not see that this might suggest that a unit of pain or suffering is a greater evil than an equivalent unit of pleasure or enjoyment is a good, as Moore had maintained (Moore 1903, 212).

Ross is not much moved by Moore's work on value theory. He seems to endorse Moore's most important innovation in value theory, his principle of organic unities, which says that the value of a whole is not necessarily equal to the sum of the values of its parts (RG 69-73.; FE 185-6; KT 11). The value, for instance, of the whole comprising pleasure taken in the contemplation of beauty is not equal to the value of the sum of the values that the pleasure and the contemplation of the beauty possess when each is considered separately. The value of the whole might be much higher. On Moore's view, neither has much value when considered alone (Moore 1903, 27-30, 93, 184).

But Ross ignores other aspects of Moore's value theory, including Moore's views on the value of pleasure and pain. Sidgwick said that by "the greatest amount of happiness" he means

> the greatest possible *surplus* of pleasure over pain, the pain being conceived as balanced against an equal amount of pleasure, so that the two contrasted amounts annihilate each other for purposes of ethical calculation. (Sidgwick 1981 [1907]: 413; emphasis added)

The assumption here is that if you have one unit of pain and one unit of pleasure, the pain is as disvaluable as the pleasure is valuable. That is, it is not true that the badness of one unit of pain is more evil than the goodness of an equal unit of pleasure is good. Pain and pleasure are to be treated symmetrically. It is possible that Ross felt that pain and pleasure had to be treated symmetrically, too, so that if you accept that one's own pleasure is not good, then you must concede that one's own pain is not bad.

Moore disagreed with Sidgwick. In *Principia Ethica*, Moore maintained that while pain by itself is a great non-instrumental evil, pleasure is by itself not a great good, though it has "some slight intrinsic value" (Moore 1903, 212).[9] In short, he says

> pain (if we understand by this expression, the consciousness of pain) appears to be a far worse evil than pleasure is a good. (Moore 1903, 212)

---

[9] Moore later came to doubt that pleasure possessed intrinsic value. See his (1907-8), 446-451, at 450. Moore did not say there whether he thought pain lacked intrinsic disvalue.

Moore thus rejected Sidgwick's symmetry claim and argued that pain is a worse evil than pleasure is a good. He held that pain is a unique evil as it is the only one of his great evils (including loving the bad and hating the good) that is not a very complex organic unity (Moore 1903, 212).

Moore, or someone agreeing with him, might, then, agree with Ross's claim that we have no or no strong duty to acquire our own pleasure because it is a small good or not a good at all, but deny that we have no duty to avoid our own pain since it is a great evil. If pain is a great evil, he might contend, then while virtue might always outweigh pleasure, it might not always outweigh pain, our own or others. The point might be magnified by the idea that it is not pain that matters but suffering or serious ill-being. Imagine you could either prevent some small amount of virtue in your already reasonably virtuous self or you could prevent some significant suffering or ill-being of your own. Suppose at the cost of a very slight deterioration in your character produced by lying, you could convince someone to give up some surplus medicine that you need to prevent a serious illness. It seems not implausible to choose to prevent the suffering and that you have a duty to so choose.

The second argument Ross relies on for the thesis that virtue is always better than pleasure is as follows:

P1. If pleasure and virtue are commensurable with each other, then we would be bound to hold that if some pleasure taken in some act of cruelty was sufficiently intense, "it would be possible that such a pleasure ... should be good on the whole" (RG 151; also FE 274).

P2. It is not the case that it would be possible that such a pleasure should be good on the whole.

C2. Therefore, it is not the case that pleasure and virtue are commensurable with each other.

The most plausible reply to this argument is to deny P2 and claim that not all vicious pleasures are bad on the whole. One might argue that there are cases in which vicious pleasure does seem good on the whole. This might happen when one finds enjoyable humour in the minor misfortunes of another,[10] or when one experiences a bit of *schadenfreude* in someone's relatively minor failure. It is hard to deny that at least in some cases such experiences are good on the whole. True, it might be a bit naughty to enjoy another's minor misfortune or failure, but the enjoyment seems in some cases sufficient to outweigh the naughtiness.

---

[10] For this point, see Hurka (2001), 149–50.

Of course, Ross would not want to grant that pleasure in the major misfortunes of others or in (say) torturing others would be on the whole good.[11] To block this, he could endorse another different potential difference between pain and pleasure. He might claim that each unit of intensity of pain has the same value, so that if pain A is twice as painful as pain B, then pain A is twice as evil as pain B but deny that the same is true of each unit of intensity of pleasure. He might, that is, argue that it is not true that each unit of intensity of pleasure has the same value; A might be twice as pleasurable as B, though A is not twice as valuable as B. Each additional unit of intensity of pleasure, he might suggest, has a smaller quantity of value, with the value decreasing with each unit until the value reaches zero. This makes it possible to prevent having to say that if the pleasure taken in a major misfortune of another is intense enough the state is good on the whole. On the proposed view, it would take a lot of pleasure in someone's major misfortunes or suffering to outweigh both the pain and the vice involved in enjoying it,[12] especially if the upper bound on how valuable pleasure can be is not very high.

In any case, Ross will have a more plausible conception of the ideal life if he rejects the view that the value of virtue (and of knowledge that is the actualization of a desire for it) always outweighs the value of pleasure.[13] He addresses the objection that if "virtue and knowledge are much better things than pleasure," then the best or ideal life will be rather "ascetic" in practice (RG 152). The concern seems to be that if knowledge and virtue are always better—or infinitely better—than pleasure, the best life will be devoted primarily (if not exclusively) to the former goods and consequently end up bereft of pleasure. There is always going to be more value in knowledge and virtue so that one should always put more weight on them than on pleasure or the prevention of suffering. But, Ross seems to think, a life without pleasure would not be ideal or best. This seems right: a life lacking in pleasure or rich in suffering would not be good seemingly no matter how much virtue and knowledge it included.

Ross says he has two reasons for thinking that his theory of value will not "in practice" be as "ascetic" as it might initially appear, and that the life devoted to virtue and knowledge (when it is the "actualization of a desire for knowledge" [RG 151]) may well include a sufficient quantity of pleasure. First, he argues that in promoting virtue and knowledge both for ourselves and for others "we shall inevitably produce much pleasant consciousness" (RG 152). This claim rests on the alleged empirical fact that the promotion of knowledge and virtue are among the "surest sources of happiness" for those who possess them. Second, he says that each of us will be more efficient at producing knowledge and virtue if we are left free at

---

[11] The point in this paragraph is taken from Hurka 2001, 150–1.
[12] Ross thinks it is vicious to want or will another's pain (RG 154, 163; FE 298).
[13] Ross says that knowledge that is to "some extent an actualization of a desire for knowledge ... has *moral* worth, [and] is of the nature of virtue" (RG 151-2). He seems to reject this view in FE where he maintains that only virtue is morally good (FE 290).

various intervals to "give ourselves up to enjoying ourselves and helping others to enjoy themselves" (RG 152).

For those wishing for a more secure place for pleasure in the "best life," as Ross puts it, these replies will not be persuasive. In reply to his first reason, one might agree with Ross that knowledge and virtue are among the "surest sources" of happiness but question whether the pursuit of knowledge and virtue are the surest sources of *surplus* pleasure. It is obvious that the acquisition of knowledge and the development of virtue in oneself and others involves the exertion of effort and lots of disappointment and frustration (including and especially acquisition of the kind of virtue [desires] and knowledge [certainty] Ross thinks most valuable). Ross does not talk about the pain involved in pursuing knowledge and virtue for oneself and others and so he does clearly establish that the pursuit of knowledge and virtue are the surest sources of (a *sufficient* quantity of) surplus happiness.

It is not clear that Ross is entitled to offer this argument to deflect this worry about his value theory in any case. Before arguing that virtue is infinitely more valuable than pleasure, he gives two arguments for thinking that in general "pleasure is definitely inferior in value to virtue and knowledge" (RG 149). One involves rejecting hedonist views in part on the grounds that they cannot reliably support the values of knowledge and virtue. The problem is that one might produce more surplus good by "indulgence of cruelty, the light-hearted adoption of ill-grounded opinions, and enjoyment of the ugly" (RG 150). The hedonist might, of course, reply that such a state could not, in our world, be one in which there was "maximum happiness" (RG 150).

Ross says in response that

> But that, if true, is simply a consequence of the laws of the world we live in, and does not absolve them from facing the problem, what if the laws of nature *were* such as to make such a life the most pleasant possible? (RG 150; emphasis in original)

But an opponent of Ross's view that knowledge and virtue are the surest sources of pleasure might make a similar reply to his attempt to deflect the charge of asceticism. They might say, true, the connection between knowledge and virtue and pleasure may be a consequence of the laws of nature of the world we live in, but what if the laws of nature were different and the life high in virtue and knowledge lacked pleasure or the former values were not the surest sources of the latter value? If the laws of nature were different and virtue and knowledge were not the surest sources of pleasure, Ross's reply would not deflect the concern that his view will in practice imply a form of aestheticism. In this case, it may be necessary to grant that Ross's view may avoid aestheticism only by granting that pleasure is not only comparable to but commensurable with virtue and knowledge.

If this objection to Ross's first reply to the charge of asceticism holds, Ross might concede it and rely on his second reason for thinking that the implications of his value theory will not in practice be ascetic as it may at first appear. But Ross's second reason for thinking his value theory is not susceptible to the charge of asceticism fares no better than his first.

The reply to the second reason is that Ross's claim gives the wrong explanation for the value or importance of pleasure to the ideal life. First, it is far from clear that the reason for thinking that a good life includes pleasure or happiness is that its pursuit or possession will make us in the end more efficient or effective at pursuing the other, higher goods. It seems much more plausible that there is a place in the ideal or good life for pleasure regardless of its impact on efficiency for promoting knowledge and virtue. Just as, for Ross, it is not true that "[t]o make a promise is not merely to adapt an ingenious device for promoting the general well-being" (RG 38), it is not true that pursing pleasure (or avoiding pain) is merely to adapt an ingenious device for promoting virtue and knowledge.

Second, Ross seems again to be susceptible to the worry he has about hedonism. The concern with his second reply is that it might be true that in this world our pursuit of pleasure and enjoyment makes us more efficient and reliable generators of knowledge and virtue, but that may be true only of our world as we know it. What if this was false? It seems implausible that we would have no reason in this case to "give ourselves up to enjoying and helping others to enjoy themselves" (RG 152).

Third, even if Ross is right about the connection between pleasure and efficiency, he has not shown in any meaningful way that the amount of pleasure that is required for efficiency is the right or plausible amount of pleasure that we think belongs in the good life.

Fourth, Ross says that it is only permissible to pursue pleasure when it does not "interfere with the production of virtue" (RG 151). If the intervals in which we give ourselves over to pleasure come at the expense of pursing knowledge or virtue (which, surely, they will), then he must have to hold that there are cases in which (in practice) it is permissible to pursue pleasure at the expense of virtue or knowledge. This seems like the right view, but in *practice* and in *theory*.

Finally, in his value theory he seems to be thinking only of the ideal life for adults. He does not seem to be thinking of the ideal or good life for children. One might think it especially perverse that for children it is permissible to pursue or acquire pleasure only when it makes them more efficient (now or in the future) at promoting virtue and knowledge. This seems to ignore the fact that things like play or enjoyment have independent value for children.

To avoid the problems that he encounters in defending the claim that virtue is infinitely better than pleasure (or the avoidance of pain), Ross should adopt in his value theory the heterarchical structure that he adopts in his theory of prima facie duties. In this case, his value theory would hold that each of the non-instrumental values matters, but there are cases or contexts in which they may be outweighed by another value or combination of values. He must, it seems, agree that virtue and pleasure are both comparable and capable of some kind of (at least rough) commensurability.

IV The Unhappy Marriage Between Ross's Heterarchical Theory of Rightness and his Hierarchical Theory of Value

Above it was suggested that one of the most attractive features of Ross's theory of prima facie duties is its heterarchical structure. Ross thinks that there is a plurality of prima facie duties and that for each prima facie duty, though it points to a moral consideration that matters directly, fundamentally to what we ought in the final analysis to do, there will be some moral situation in which it is outweighed by one or more of the other prima facie duties.

Ross clearly thinks that his opposition to rigid hierarchies in his theory of prima facie duties is one of its main selling features. This is especially clear in his criticism of Kant's absolutism, which, he thinks, "unduly simplifies the moral life" by ignoring the fact that "in many situations there is more than one claim upon our action, that these claims often conflict, and … it becomes a matter of individual and fallible judgment to say which claim is in the circumstances the overriding one" (FE 189; also 312–13; KT 33–4). However, as we shall see, the concern is that in defending a rigidly hierarchical value theory he ends up coming into conflict with and undermining this highly attractive feature of his theory of rightness.

In *Foundations of Ethics*, Ross argues that both virtue and intellectual and artistic activity are good in the same sense.[14] Both are worthy objects of admiration (FE 283). An individual is admirable for being virtuous or artistic or intelligent. The values of virtue and intellectual and artistic activity are, Ross says, intrinsically valuable or good in the "proper" sense of the word (FE 283). These goods are distinguished from pleasure and justice (desert) which are objects worthy of satisfaction or objects that it is right to take satisfaction in (FE 283) but not worthy objects of admiration. Neither pleasure nor justice is intrinsically valuable; rather, they are non-instrumentally valuable, that is, worth having for their own sake, but not due to their "intrinsic nature" (FE 283).

---

[14] Ross characterizes intellectual activity as the "activity of the mind which leads to knowledge" that is good in the sense that "it is an admirable activity of the human spirit" that owes its excellence to "being conducted according to … the principles discovered by logic" (FE 270; also 283). Artistic activity is also an admirable activity of the human spirit which owes its excellence, Ross says (tentatively), to "the vividness and breadth of imagination, vigour of execution, economy in the use of means, simplicity of plan" (FE 270).

Ross suggests that this helps him secure the point that virtue is infinitely superior to pleasure.

> The natural moral consciousness finds it very hard to believe that any amount of pleasure can thus outweigh a given good activity in goodness; and the recognition of two senses of goodness has vindicated the natural moral consciousness. (FE 283–4)

It is not clear how this distinction in goodness can secure the claim that no amount of pleasure can outweigh a given amount of virtue. As David Phillips rightly asks, "why should the fact that virtue and knowledge are good in one sense and pleasure good in another mean that, when we are deciding what we ought to produce or aim at, virtue turns out to be a greater good than pleasure?" (Phillips 2019, 129)

But there is a more pressing issue here for Ross. He seems not to notice that this value hierarchy is in tension with and mars the attractive heterarchical structure of his theory of rightness or prima facie duties. He says immediately following his claim that his distinction between objects worthy of admiration and objects worthy of satisfaction secures the claim that virtue is infinitely superior to pleasure that one is (because of this distinction and its alleged implications) "still free" to

> believe that the prima facie duty of producing what is intrinsically good always takes precedence over the prima facie duty of producing pleasure for others. (FE 284)[15]

Ross therefore introduces a hierarchy within his duty of beneficence. The duty to promote virtue and intellectual and artistic activity is prior to and always trumps the duty to promote pleasure or to prevent pain. This is antithetical to the attractive heterarchical structure of his theory of rightness in which, as we saw, each of the duties is "capable of being overruled by other prima facie duties." Ross suggests that both Kant and the utilitarians rely on views about the moral status of lying that "shut" their "eyes to the detail of" moral situations, and that deprive them "of data for a true judgment" about what to do in a particular situation (KT 33–4). Kant says never lie and the utilitarians say in general it is justified to lie to those posing

---

[15] Ross does not make this claim explicitly in *The Right and the Good*. However, he does argue that both virtue and knowledge (actualized by a desire for it) outrank pleasure and justice (RG 152–3). He says virtue outranks pleasure and justice (RG 152, 153–4) but not knowledge (actualized by a desire for it) (RG 153). Virtue and knowledge (actualized by a desire for it) seem, then, to be of the same axiological status. So it seems that knowledge in this sense might in some cases outrank virtue. But if virtue and knowledge are of the same status, and virtue is always superior to justice and pleasure, then knowledge (actualized by desire for it) must be too. This suggests that in the context of beneficence the duty to promote virtue and knowledge always takes precedence over the duty to promote pleasure and justice.

a significant threat. One cannot help but think that Ross's hierarchy in the duty of beneficence is guilty of a similar charge.

Imagine that I am a philanthropist with an opportunity to befriend some high-profile, very wealthy individuals. Imagine that by making friends with these individuals I will be able to convince them to devote a sizable portion of their personal wealth to effective charities and that this will prevent a great deal of suffering for the least well-off denizens of the world. Unfortunately, by befriending these individuals I will cause a slight deterioration in my (now quite virtuous) character. It is not obvious that it would be wrong to befriend the wealthy individuals given the size of the benefit, although Ross's view suggests otherwise. Ross's hierarchy in the duty of beneficence seems to blind him to certain features of such moral situations (the suffering prevented), depriving him of the data to make a true judgement about it.

In claiming that the duty to promote virtue and intellectual activities always takes precedence over the duty to promote pleasure or (one assumes) to prevent pain or suffering (FE 287), Ross seems forced to admit that there is a hierarchy within the duty of beneficence and that there would, it seems, be no case in which the duty to promote pleasure (or prevent pain) outweighs the duty to promote virtue. This is (again) in direct conflict with the attractive feature of his theory of prima facie duties. A view like this seems no different than views like Kant's, which, Ross says, "over-simplifies the moral life" by insisting, for example, that it is never permissible to tell a lie (KT 33–4).

After Ross says that the duty to promote virtue and intellectual and artistic activity comes before the duty to promote pleasure, he says that the goods of intellectual and artistic activity and virtue are comparable in terms of their goodness, since they are good in the same sense. He goes on to say that it will be an open question, then,

> whether in any given situation it is rather our duty to promote some good moral activity [virtue], or some good intellectual activity, in ourselves or others; and in deciding which we ought to do we have to rely on our very fallible apprehension of the degrees of goodness belonging to each. (FE 284)

Ross admits that in some cases, then, it may be permissible to promote one's own or others' intellectual or artistic activity at the expense of one's own or others' virtue. Imagine that I am a very proficient scientist who works on and desires to know about courtship behaviour in fruit flies and that if I continue with my research, I will gain a significant amount of knowledge about it. However, this research will involve killing a lot of flies and this will, in turn, somewhat coarsen my character, leading to a deterioration in it. On Ross's view, it seems that provided that the value of the intellectual activity is on balance greater than the loss of virtue, it is, other things equal, right to promote the intellectual activity. Or imagine I am the father of a budding artist and I see that if I encourage my child she will develop artistic talents to a high degree. Imagine, further, that this will lead her to develop a sense of entitlement and so make her less virtuous. Again, provided that the good of artistic activity outweighs the disvalue of the deterioration of character, Ross says it is our duty to promote the artistic activity.

Balancing the duty of beneficence when the goods of virtue and artistic and intellectual activity are at play mirrors the manner in which Ross balances the duties of promise-keeping and beneficence in his heterarchical theory of prima facie duties. Suppose we agree with Ross in the verdicts about the above cases. One might think it a bit implausible that while one is permitted to sacrifice virtue to promote certain intellectual and artistic activities, one is not permitted to sacrifice virtue to prevent suffering or pain or to promote a surfeit of pleasure. Putting this aside, the main worry is that this structure exposes Ross (again) to the charge that his theory (like Kant's) shuts our eyes to the details of the moral situation. In the above case of the father, the structure of Ross's theory seems to blind the father to the moral relevance of any pain or suffering his daughter's character might impose on others (her friends and fellow classmates), since presumably the duty to promote artistic activity always takes precedence over the duty to promote pleasure or prevent pain and suffering.

The concerns about Ross's hierarchical value theory may not end here. Ross is clear that in some cases the duties of promise-keeping and non-maleficence can outweigh the duty of beneficence and that in some cases the duty of beneficence can outweigh the duties of promise-keeping and non-maleficence. It is no longer clear, given that he says that the promotion of virtue and intellectual and aesthetic activities always takes precedence over the promotion of pleasure (or the prevention of pain), that this is still an option for him.

Ross says that you ought to keep your promises unless keeping the promise is "likely to do much more harm than good" (FE 77; also RG 35). He seems to hold, then, that the duty of promise-keeping can *sometimes* outweigh the duty of beneficence. This suggests that the duty of promise-keeping is in the same category as the duty to promote virtue and intellectual activity, that is, the category including the element of the duty of beneficence that *always* takes precedence over the duty to promote pleasure and avoid pain (the other element of the duty of beneficence). It might be strange to hold that while the duty to promote pleasure and avoid pain could never outweigh the duty to promote virtue and intellectual and artistic activities, the former duty could outweigh the duty to keep your promises, a duty which, Ross says explicitly, has the stringency sufficient to outweigh the duty to promote virtue and intellectual and artistic activity in some cases. This might suggest that no matter how much pain or pleasure is at stake we ought always to keep our promises. This seems not only false but completely contrary to the original spirit of the heterarchical structure of Ross's theory of rightness, and it puts his view (again) in the same (dubious) category as Kant's (at least on Ross's reckoning).

Of course, the duty of promise-keeping could be demoted so that the duty to promote pleasure and avoid pain sometimes outweighs it and vice versa. But in this case, the duty of promise-keeping falls into the category of those duties that are always outweighed by the duty to promote virtue, in which case the duty to promote virtue would always outweigh the duty to keep your promises. This (again) seems to conflict with the attractive heterarchical structure of Ross's theory of rightness and it seems just plain false. Suppose I have promised to help you enhance your virtue. On my way to discharge my duty I see that I can enhance a slight bit more virtue in someone else to whom I have made no promise. Let's assume the other consequences of the two acts are of equal value. Ross is highly likely to reject that it is permissible to break the promise to promote more virtue on the grounds that to break the promise would involve treating a promise rather too lightly (RG 35), though his own value theory implies this when married to his theory of rightness.

In reply, Ross might argue that the reason the duty to promote virtue and intellectual and artistic activity always comes before the duty to promote pleasure or to prevent pain is that this is necessary to preserving the intuition that it is never permissible to promote vicious pleasures. There is no similar reason for maintaining that the duty to keep one's promises comes before the duty to promote pleasure or to prevent pain. This might leave Ross free to say the duty to keep promises can both outweigh the duty to promote virtue and intellectual and artistic activity and in some cases be outweighed by the duty to promote pleasure and to prevent pain. But, as we have seen above, it is not always true that we have no reason to promote vicious pleasures. This is not a good reason to give absolute priority to the duty to promote virtue and intellectual and artistic activity over the duty to promote pleasure and to avoid pain. In any case, Ross can avoid concerns of the kind raised above in a generally more attractive way, namely, by dropping the claim that virtue is always better than pleasure and the avoidance of pain, which, as we have seen, has some, quite counter-intuitive implications of its own.

There seems, then, to be several potentially very unattractive implications of the hierarchy among values in Ross's value theory. The hierarchy among values has undesirable implications for Ross's heterarchical theory of rightness, marring and conflicting with the structure that made it attractive in the first place and that arguably gave it advantage over its utilitarian and deontological competitors. Ross should adopt a heterarchical structure in both his theory of rightness and his theory of value. With this structure in place in both cases Ross can avoid falling prey in his theory of value to some of the worries that he poses for the rivals to his theory of prima facie duties, though whether this will be defensible in the final analysis remains to be seen.

V Conclusion

Ross defends both a pluralistic theory of value and a pluralistic theory of rightness. His theory of rightness has a plausible and attractive heterarchical structure. His theory of value has by contrast a hierarchical structure. This comes out very clearly in Ross's claim that any amount of the non-instrumental value of virtue outweighs any amount of the non-instrumental value of pleasure or avoidance of pain. The chapter raised two challenges to the status that Ross accords virtue relative to pleasure (pain). First, it argued that Ross failed to provide a good argument for thinking that virtue is always better than pleasure and that it is in any case implausible to think that any amount of virtue (or avoidance of vice) is better than the avoidance of any amount of pain or suffering. Second, it argued that the inflexibility of Ross's value theory exhibited in his claim about the relative value of virtue produces tension with and mars the attractive or heterarchical structure of his theory of prima facie duties. Ross would have developed a more plausible version of value pluralism had it included the attractive heterarchical structural that was core to his highly plausible and influential theory of prima facie duties.[16]

References

Ewing, A. C. *Second Thoughts in Moral Philosophy* (New York: Macmillan, 1959).
Hooker, Brad. 'Ross-Style Pluralism Versus Rule-Consequentialism', *Mind* 105 (1996): 531–52.
Hurka, Thomas. *Virtue, Vice, and Value* (Oxford: Oxford University Press, 2001).
Hurka, Thomas. *British Ethical Theorists from Sidgwick to Ewing* (Oxford: Oxford University Press, 2014).
McNaughton, David. 'An Unconnected Heap of Duties?', *Philosophical Quarterly* 46 (1996): 433–47.
Moore, G. E. *Principia Ethica* (Cambridge: Cambridge University Press, 1903).
Moore, G. E. 'Review of Hastings Rashdall, *The Theory of Good and Evil*', *Hibbert Journal* 6 (1907-8): 446–51.
Phillips, David. *Rossian Ethics: W. D. Ross and Contemporary Moral Theory* (Oxford: Oxford University Press, 2019).
Price, H. H. 'Critical Notice of W. D. Ross, *The Right and the Good*', *Mind* 40 (1931): 341–54.
Price, Richard. *A Review of the Principal Questions in Morals*, D. D. Raphael (ed.), (Oxford: Oxford University Press, 1948 [1787]).
Prichard, H. A. 'A Conflict of Duties', in Jim MacAdam (ed.), *Moral Writings: H. A. Prichard*, 77–83. (Oxford: Oxford University Press, 2002).
Rashdall, Hastings. *The Theory of Good and Evil*, volumes I and II, second edition (Oxford: Oxford University Press, 1924).
Ross, W. D. *The Right and the Good* (Oxford: Oxford University Press, 1930).
Ross, W. D. *Foundations of Ethics* (Oxford: Oxford University Press, 1939).
Ross, W. D. *Kant's Ethical Theory: A Commentary on the* Grundlegung zur Metaphysik der Sitten (Oxford: Oxford University Press, 1954).
Shaver, Robert. 'Ross on Self and Others', *Utilitas* 26 (2014): 303–20.
Sidgwick, Henry. *The Methods of Ethics*, seventh edition (Indianapolis, IN: Hackett, 1981 [1907]).
Stratton-Lake, Philip. 'Can Hooker's Rule-Consequentialist Principle Justify Ross's Prima Facie Duties?', *Mind* 106 (1997): 751–58.
Sumner, L. Wayne. *Welfare, Happiness, and Ethics* (Oxford: Oxford University Press, 1996).

---

[16] The author wishes to thank Robert Audi and David Phillips for extremely helpful comments on previous drafts of this chapter.

Index

For the benefit of digital users, indexed terms that span two pages (e.g., 52–53) may, on occasion, appear on only one of those pages.

apprehension 13–14, 95–96, 152, 199, 265
a priori 24, 53, 74–75, 157–58
  see also prima facie duty; priority
Aristotle 1–10, 32, 44–47, 172, 179–80, 182, 195–200, 234n.36
  and orthos logos 195, 196, 203
  see also virtue; priority
attribute
  parti-resultant 9–10, 118
  toti-resultant 9–10, 27–29, 33–34, 118
Audi, Robert 1–10, 13–36, 39, 50n.30, 118, 123–24, 203n.57, 215
axioms 9–10, 22–23, 26, 28–29, 30n.18, 95, 108–15, 214–16
  and axiological organicity 27
  categorical imperative as 19n.9, 25
  egoistic 101
  putative 111–13
  utilitarian 101, 110–11
  of value and duty 13, 15

beauty 9–10, 105, 209–25, 227–28, 237–42, 258
beneficence 3, 7–10, 13, 29–33, 73–76, 155, 252–53, 264–66
  definition as prima facie duty 19–20
  as imperfect duty 155–56
  and maximization 29–31
  and self-improvement 76–83
  vs. non-maleficence 264–66
  see also duty; non-maleficence
Berker, Selim 161
Bradford, Gwen 9–10, 28n.16, 209–25, 227n.3, 241n.58
Broad, C. D. 98
  review of *Foundations of Ethics* 1, 4–5
  review of *The Right and the Good* 1

certainty 14–15, 20–35, 112–14, 261
  epistemic 13
  psychological 20
Chan, Bowen 169–88
conflicts of duty 33–36, 43–46 *see also* duty
consequentialism 17, 25, 58, 94–99, 113–15, 238–39, 245

critique by Ross 1–3, 5
and outcome-based ethics 32–33
  see also deontology; beneficence
constitutive means 28, 35, 228, 234, 238–39, 240–44
contextualism 118–24
  and emotions 128
  and technology 125
contractualism 54–55, 165
contributory causes 5–6, 106–8, 115, 228–29
convictions 13–14 *see also* intuitions
Crisp, Roger 7, 37–51, 73, 80
Cullity, Garrett 52–72, 154

Dancy, Jonathan 25n.13, 123–24
deontology 37–38, 58, 96–99, 250
  absolutist 1–2, 98, 101
  and egoism 106, 115
  Kantian vii, 5, 8–10, 120, 189–92
  language 195–96
  moderate 1–5, 98, 114
  pluralistic 4, 73–83, 87–88, 250
  see also pluralism; virtue
derivation 25, 53–58, 62–67, 70
desert 27, 84–85, 87, 104, 105, 109, 169, 171, 176, 197–98, 251, 254 *see also* justice
desire 171
  de dicto and de re 171, 175
  intrinsic 26–27, 31, 79, 105, 178–79, 197–98, 263
disagreement *see* rational disagreement
dispositionalism 7, 28, 209, 212–17
dogmatism 17, 22–25, 35–36, 101, 112, 113
dualism 95, 101–2
  Parfitian 100–1, 103–4
  of practical reason 100, 106
duty (*also* obligation) 13–51
  actual 19–20, 39, 138–41, 199
  all things considered 20
  conflicts of 33, 43, 45–46
  consequential 17–19 *see also* consequentialism
  final 16–20, 33, 74
  gradation of vii–viii, 15–16

duty (*also* obligation) (*cont.*)
  imperfect 155–56
  non-derivative 7–8, 210–11, 250
  perfect 19n.9, 32, 199
  pro tanto 5–6n.4, 15–18, 118n.3, 135
    see also prima facie duty
  see also residues
duty proper (*also* overall duty) 2–3, 19–22, 38–39, 98, 101–2, 118–22, 173–74

egoism 101–3, 107, 115, 141–42, 203
  objection of 202–3n.56
  rational 100
emotions
  affective phenomenology of 128
  cognitive theory of 117–18, 127, 132
  doxastic 127–29, 132
  evidential value of 7–8
  moral 129–32
epistemology
  Non-naturalist framework 33–34
  see also intuitionism; moral epistemology; reasoning
Ewing, A.C. 37, 41, 44, 93–95, 106, 250
excellence 217–19, 227–28, 237, 246, 263n.14
excuses 21

fairness 84–87, 161–63
fidelity 3, 8–9, 19, 30, 56–57, 142, 144–45, 252–53
fittingness (*also* worthiness *and* aptness) 61–62, 161n.6

goodness (*also* good)
  attributive vs. predicative 26
  contributory 5–6, 106–8, 115
  definition 59, 242
  good for 26, 76–83, 97, 173, 226–49
  inherent 215
  instrumental 26, 28 *see also* instrumentalism
  intrinsic 8–9, 26–29, 105, 197–98, 200–1, 216–25, 227–28, 246–47
  moral 30, 58, 169, 172–73, 184, 197–98, 255–56
  relational 59, 226–49
  see also value
gratitude 3, 8–9, 18, 27
grounding 7–9, 18–19, 25, 28–29, 33–36, 39, 44n.24, 66, 135–48, 164, 174, 232–33
  core deontic 136, 145, 150–52
  see also resultancy

Harman, Gilbert 34n.24
hedonism 104, 105, 251, 254–55, 262
  anti- 3–4

heterarchy 252–53, 263–67
hierarchy 19, 30–32, 254–55, 263–67
Hooker, Brad 7, 73–89
Horton, Joe 47–50
Huemer, Michael 14n.2, 135
Hume, David 21–22, 34, 127, 236n.44, 239n.50
Hurka, Thomas 6, 38n.6, 93, 96–97, 169–88, 189, 193n.18

inference 4, 13–14, 23–24, 108, 127–28
  deductive 21–22
  rules of 22, 23n.10
instrumentalism 209–25 *see also* goodness; value
intuition 7–9, 13–14
  cognitive 117–18, 126–28, 132
  as data of ethics 14, 199–200
  doxastic 14, 117n.1, 127
  non-doxastic 117–18, 127
  and seemings 14
intuitionism 4, 13, 23
  epistemological 4, 14–15
  generic 14–15
  non-cognitivist 15n.3
  and phenomenology 7–8, 119–20, 127
  philosophical 108–15
  Rossian 13–14
  see also Nagel, Thomas; Parfit, Derek; Scanlon, T.M.; Thomson, Judith
intuitionists vii, 14, 23–24, 32, 117–18, 126–28, 145
  dogmatic 113
  Rossian 136–37
intuitiveness 7–8, 14, 20, 108, 140
Irwin, Terence E. 1n.2

justice 9–10, 16–17, 23–24, 29–30, 43, 45, 82–87, 95–96, 109–11, 197–98, 251, 254, 263 *see also* desert
justification 14–18, 21, 22–25, 52, 202–3

Kagan, Shelly 5–6n.4, 135, 213n.5
Kant, Immanuel
  Kantian ethics 1, 189–90
  Metaphysics of Morals 42n.22, 155–56, 226–28
  see also deontology
Kaspar, David 7–8, 135–53
knowledge *see* certainty

merit 29–30, 64–65, 82, 83, 216–17, 219, 251n.4
  see also desert
metaphysics 13, 18n.6, 28
  moral 102, 135–53, 155–56

Moore, G.E. 3–8, 120–21, 210
  on beauty 210, 214
  Principia Ethica (1903) 1
  and value theory 26–27, 30, 220
moral deliberation 2–3
moral disagreement 24–25, 42–43
moral epistemology vii, 13–15, 23–24, 35, 73, 117, 130–32, 135
moral worth 47, 182–85, 197n.37

Nagel, Thomas 5, 73–75, 226, 237
  see also intuitionism
naturalism
  moral 34–35
  non- 4, 33–35, 136n.2
non-injury 16–17, 19, 32
  see also non-maleficence
non-maleficence 3, 19, 38–39, 77, 86, 99–100, 149, 253, 257–58, 266
  see also beneficence and non-injury
normative theory 1, 4–6, 19, 93–116

obligation see also duty
  theory of 5–6, 9–10, 21, 26, 30n.18
O'Neill, Onora 42n.22
outweighing 38–39, 74, 75, 102, 150n.13, 175–79, 183–87, 255–68
overriding 15–16, 19–20, 39n.7, 40–41, 44, 118, 138, 140–41, 148

Parfit, Derek 34n.24, 100–1, 103–4, 106, 107
  see also intuitionism
particularism 25, 35–36, 123–24, 191n.12, 217–18
perfectionism 209, 218–19, 223–24, 237, 240, 244–46
permissibility 29, 30–31, 47–50, 78–82, 87–88, 154–66, 254, 266–67
  defined in relation to duty 7–8
  see also obligation
Phillips, David 1–10, 93–116, 175, 264
pleasure 26–31, 79, 105, 169–88, 193, 197–98, 239–40, 250–68
  vicious 259, 267
pluralism 3–4, 7–8, 28–32, 250
  deontological 73–83, 87–88
  Rossian 52–55, 61–70, 87–88, 95–104, 119, 169
  value 251, 254, 267–68
Price, Richard 15n.4, 37, 41–44, 46, 50, 114, 250–51n.3
Prichard, H.A. 1–2n.3, 15n.3, 15n.4, 20–21, 23
prima facie duty 1–9, 13–16, 19–22
  a priori 13–17

  basic 16–17
  principles of 3, 16–17, 52–53, 62–63, 109
  conditional 15–17, 37–41, 118, 141, 176
  see also duty
priority 9–10, 19, 74–75, 154, 157–58 see also a priori
  Aristotelian 172–73
  lexical 3–4
promise 1–3, 7–9, 15–17, 19–22, 31–32, 37–41, 56–57, 135–53, 198n.40, 199, 250–54, 262
  binding 73–75, 96
  -keeping 27, 78, 82–83, 139–40, 144, 148, 177–78, 266–67
  see also fidelity; obligation
properties 18n.6, 25, 33–35, 46–47, 59, 136, 141–43, 146–47, 169–76, 212–17
  and moral scale 148–49, 151
  natural 33, 137, 139–40
  normative 110, 122

Railton, Peter 226–27
rational disagreement 13, 23, 24, 25
rational egoism 100
rational impartialism 100
rationality 25, 130–31
realism 34, 226–27
  mathematical 22–25, 34
  metaphysical 226–27
  moral 34, 122
reason 15–19, 93–116, 127–28, 256, 267
reasonableness 103, 165, 180–82
reasoning 131, 199–200
  moral 127–28
reasons
  explanatory 135–53
  moral 7, 17–19, 42, 52–53, 78, 123–24, 136–37, 159–60
  pro tanto (*also* prima facie reasons): 39n.10, 135, 137n.3
  Rossian definition of moral reasons 203
reflective equilibrium 33, 112
regress 14
reparation 3, 8–9, 77–78, 82–83
residues 2–3, 75
resultancy (*also* grounding) 33–36
right-making 54–55
rightness 2, 4, 8–10, 21, 33n.21, 35, 41n.15, 42n.22, 52–72, 138–39, 141, 151–52, 180–81, 203, 263–68
rights 40, 76–87
Roeser, Sabine 7–8, 117–34
Ross, W.D.
  Foundations of Ethics 1, 4–5, 13, 20–21, 79
  in historical context 5–6

Scanlon, T. M. 157n.1, 165
  see also contractualism; intuitionism
self-evidence 13–17, 22–25, 95–104, 108–15, 199
self-improvement 6, 29, 30–32, 78, 144, 198
Sidgwick, Henry 4–8, 13
  The Methods of Ethics (1874) 1
Skelton, Anthony 9–10, 30n.18, 189n.1, 250–68
skepticism 20–23, 122, 132
Sophocles
  Oedipus Rex 24–25
Stratton-Lake, Philip 7–8, 18n.6, 24n.12, 160–61
stringency 19, 32–33, 143–51, 253, 266
subsumption 53, 56–58, 60, 70, 155
supererogation 30–31, 48, 49–50, 79, 154–55
Szutta, Artur 8–9, 189–205
Szutta, Natasza 8–9, 189–205

tendency 34, 41–44, 118
  moral laws of 69
Theunissen, L. Nandi 9–10, 226–49
Thomson, Judith Jarvis 154–59, 230n.18
  see also intuitionism
Timmons, Mark 88

unities 3, 105, 258
utilitarianism 3, 7–8, 30, 77–78, 101, 105, 141–43, 250–51, 253, 264–65
  hedonistic 120–21, 254–55
  ideal 3, 17, 24, 99, 120–21

value
  aesthetic 209–25, 240–41
  inherent 215
  instrumental 9–10, 28, 209–16
  intellectual 237–44
  intrinsic, 9–10, 13–36
  moral 9–10, 179–88
  non-instrumental 26, 28, 192, 226–37, 241, 245, 251–52, 255, 267–68
  perfectionist 209, 218–19, 237, 240, 242, 245–46
  personal 226–29, 243–44, 247–48
  relational 29, 31, 226n.1, 228–29, 232–33
  Ross's theory of 26–29, 254–55, 260, 263–68
veracity 16–20, 114
vice 8–9, 44–45, 169–88
  definition 169–70
  see also virtue
vicious circle objection 202
virtue 8–9, 18, 27, 169–88, 254–68
  ethics of 189–205
  moral 28, 87, 195
  see also Aristotle; vice
virtue ethics vii
  see also virtue

World War II 4–5
wrongness 2, 21, 34, 40, 52–56, 68, 146, 252–53

Zagzebski, Linda 128–30, 132, 199–200